Beiträge zum Islamischen Recht IV

Leipziger Beiträge zur Orientforschung

Herausgegeben von Hans-Georg Ebert
Begründet von Günter Barthel

Band 15

PETER LANG
Frankfurt am Main · Berlin · Bern · Bruxelles · New York · Oxford · Wien

Silvia Tellenbach
Thoralf Hanstein
(Hrsg.)

Beiträge zum Islamischen Recht IV

PETER LANG
Europäischer Verlag der Wissenschaften

Bibliografische Information Der Deutschen Bibliothek
Die Deutsche Bibliothek verzeichnet diese Publikation in der Deutschen Nationalbibliografie; detaillierte bibliografische Daten sind im Internet über <http://dnb.ddb.de> abrufbar.

ISSN 0942-2323
ISBN 3-631-52990-2

www.peterlang.de

VORWORT

Die Jahrestagung 2003 der Gesellschaft für arabisches und islamisches Recht (GAIR) e.V. fand am 10./11. Oktober in Freiburg/Breisgau statt. Die dabei gehaltenen Vorträge bilden wiederum das Kernstück der „Beiträge zum islamischen Recht IV", dem 15 Band der Leipziger Beiträge zur Orientforschung. Wenn das bewährte Herausgebergespann Ebert/Hanstein teilweise gewechselt hat, so hängt das damit zusammen, dass die GAIR e.V. beschlossen hat, dass das jeweils für die Organisation der Tagung verantwortliche Vorstandsmitglied künftig auch den Tagungsband (mit)herausgibt.

Auch die Freiburger Tagung war traditionsgemäß in zwei Schwerpunkte gegliedert, einem themenbezogenen, islamisches Strafrecht, und einem länderbezogenen, Iran. Die Reihenfolge der Beiträge im Buch orientiert sich an der der Vorträge auf der Jahrestagung. Der Beitrag von R. Peters behandelt das Strafrecht in einem Land, das eher als islamisches Randgebiet gilt, aber durch die Wiedereinführung des islamischen Strafrechts in einer sehr konservativen Form und durch die Fälle seiner Praktizierung in den letzten Jahren weltweit viel Aufsehen erregt hat, nämlich Nigeria. B. Johansen setzt sich mit Prozessen wegen Apostasie in verschiedenen muslimischen Ländern auseinander und arbeitet heraus, wie der Begriff der Apostasie nicht mehr als subjektive Glaubenseinstellung, sondern als Werturteil über andere Lehrmeinungen aufgefasst und als Mittel des politischen Kampfes benutzt worden ist. S. Tellenbach hinterfragt die tatsächliche Anwendung islamischer Strafen in der Islamischen Republik Iran und schlägt damit schon den Bogen zu dem länderbezogenen Thema Iran. N. Yassari stellt die neuesten Entwicklungen im iranischen Familienrecht dar und schildert den Alltag vor einem iranischen Gericht. H. Thoms befasst sich mit dem selten behandelten, aber in der Praxis durchaus wichtigen Erbrecht der offiziell anerkannten nichtmuslimischen Minderheiten. K. Bälz beschreibt wichtige Rechtsfragen, die den Praktiker interessieren, der im deutsch-iranischen Wirtschaftsverkehr tätig ist, und stellt fest, dass die vorhandenen Schwierigkeiten nicht etwa auf islamisches Recht zurückzuführen sind. H. Rezaei gibt zum Abschluss einen Ausblick auf die Möglichkeiten, welche die Internetnutzung für eine freie Diskussion über Fragen des islamischen Rechts und für seine Entwicklung bietet.

Die Tagungsbände der Gesellschaft waren darüber hinaus immer für andere wichtige Beiträge offen, soweit sie einen Band nicht umfangmäßig sprengten. Dieses Mal konnte eine sehr gelungene Magisterarbeit von H. Denker – wenn auch in gekürzter Form – aufgenommen werden. Sie behandelt die *ḫul'*-Scheidung in Ägypten nach dem Gesetz Nr. 1/2000, wo durch den Verzicht auf die Zustimmung des Ehemannes eine bedeutsame Rechtsfortbildung zugunsten der scheidungswilligen Frau realisiert wurde.

Die Beiträge widerspiegeln die Meinung der einzelnen Autoren; nicht die der Herausgeber. Bei der Transliteration wurde auf die in den bisherigen Bänden geübte Praxis zurückgegriffen.

Gedankt sei allen, die am Zustandekommen dieses Buches beteiligt waren, zunächst natürlich den Autoren männlichen und nicht zu vergessen weiblichen Geschlechts, die sich ihre „Weisheit entreißen" (Brecht) ließen, sowie den Mitarbeiterinnen des Peter Lang Verlags Frau Dr. K. Timme und Frau Dr. Cl. Frank, die den Band verlegerisch betreut haben. Die Herausgeber hoffen auf geneigte Leser, die auch über die immer besser bestückte Homepage der GAIR e.V. (www.gair.de) weiterhin der Reihe die Treue halten. Wie bei den Beiträgen zum Islamischen Recht III wird pünktlich zur Drucklegung dieses Bandes auf der Homepage der GAIR eine Seite unter dem Menüpunkt "Publikationen" freigeschaltet, auf der alle in den einzelnen Beiträgen erwähnte Internetseiten mit direkter Verlinkung gelistet werden.

Freiburg/Leipzig im Mai 2004 Die Herausgeber

INHALTSVERZEICHNIS

THE REINTRODUCTION OF SHARIA CRIMINAL LAW IN NIGERIA: NEW CHALLENGES FOR THE MUSLIMS OF THE NORTH

Professor Dr. Ruud Peters, Amsterdam

1. Introduction

The introduction of shari'a criminal law in most states of Northern Nigeria has been received with mixed feelings: jubilation and high expectations on the part of large sections of the Muslim population of the North and reserved feelings and even fears on the part of the Christian Nigerians. In addition, concerns have been expressed at the international level. An important cause of these fears was, and still is, the question of whether the newly introduced shari'a penal codes are consonant with the Nigerian constitutional order and, especially, whether they comply with the human rights standards of the Nigerian constitution and international conventions to which Nigeria is a signatory. In this article, I will precisely discuss this topic.

2. The introduction of shari'a criminal Law[1]

On 27 January 2000, Zamfara, one of the Northern states of the Nigerian federation, enacted the first Shari'a Penal Code in Northern Nigeria, having first established Shari'a courts to apply the code. Like in the United Sates, the states of the Federal Republic of Nigeria have the power to enact legislation in the domain of criminal law. The example of Zamfara was followed in May by Niger State, where the government, like that in Zamfara, fully supported the re-Islamisation of the legal system. Other Northern states, prompted by popular pressure, followed suit. In Katsina and Sokoto, Shari'a criminal sentences were pronounced and executed (in one case a sentence of amputation of the right hand was carried out) even before a Shari'a Penal Codes came into force, on the strength of Shari'a Courts Laws stipulating that the Shari'a courts must apply the provisions of the Koran and hadîth and those found in the traditional authoritative Malikite works of law. By the beginning of 2004, twelve Northern states have introduced Shari'a criminal law by setting up Shari'a courts with jurisdiction in criminal matters and promulgating Shari'a Penal Codes.[2] These

---

1 For a more detailed survey of the re-introduction of Sharia criminal law in Northern Nigeria, see *Peters, R.*, Islamic criminal law in Nigeria. Ibadan: Spectrum Books, 2003, viii, 87 pp.

2 Bauchi, Borno, Gombe, Jigawa, Kaduna, Kano, Katsina, Kebbi, Niger, Sokoto, and Yobe. The Shari'a Penal Codes of most of these states follow the example of the Zamfara codes

codes include the Malikite law of *hudûd,* homicide and wounding, and under the heading of *ta`zîr*, most offences mentioned in the 1959 Penal Code for Northern Nigeria that was in force until then and is still effective for non-Muslims. All codes follow Malikite doctrine but there are some differences on points of detail. The Shar'ia Penal Codes apply only to Muslims (or to non-Muslims who desire to be tried under these codes and present a written document of consent to the court). Non-Muslim citizens are tried by Magistrate Courts under the 1959 Penal Code.

The swift success of the Islamisation movement in Northern Nigeria was due to powerful popular pressure. It is remarkable that Northern Nigeria is the only region where Islamic criminal law has been put into force by means of legislation passed by elected parliaments. Except in Zamfara and Niger State, the state governments were not enthusiastic about Islamisation of the legal system but were forced to enact it under popular pressure. The general clamour for Islamic criminal law was due to more factors than just religious zeal. The most prominent one was that many believed that Islamic criminal law would be the answer to widespread criminality and government corruption. Further, it was a protest against federal politics. Since the end of military dictatorship in 1997, the centre of gravity of Nigerian politics had moved to the mainly non-Muslim South. The Islamisation movement was a reaction against this: a challenge to federal politics and an attempt to reassert Muslim political power. There was also the idea that imposing Islamic norms on public life, by banning drinking and closing bars and by putting an end to prostitution, would secure God's help in making the Nigerian Muslims stronger. Finally, like in most other countries where Islamic criminal law has been introduced, it was a conscious reassertion of cultural roots against Western political and cultural dominance.

An important effect of the Islamisation of criminal law is that the codes are not regarded as exhaustive. Acts not mentioned in the codes may also be punishable offences, if they are so under classical Islamic criminal law. Most of the new codes contain the following provision:

> Any act or omission which is not specifically mentioned in this Shari'ah Penal Code but is otherwise declared to be an offence under the Qur'an, Sunnah and *Ijtihad* of the Malikite School of Islamic thought shall be an offence under this code and such act or omission shall be punishable:
> (a) With imprisonment for a term which may extend to 5 years, or
> (b) With caning which may extend to 50 lashes, or

---

with minor changes. Whereas Kano State has enacted an independent Shari'a Penal Code, Niger State has contented itself with adding a few amendments to the 1959 Penal Code for Northern Nigeria.

(c) With fine which may extend to N5,000.00 or with any two of the above punishments.[3]

Some codes contain provisions about the applicability of the Islamic rules of evidence. That most codes are silent on this point, although it is an essential part of the laws of fixed penalties and retaliation, must be attributed to a conscious omission by the various legislators. They must have been aware of the fact that according to the federal constitution of Nigeria legislation in the field of evidence is a federal matter. By now it has become clear that the Shari'a courts follow the Malikite doctrine with regard to evidence. This means for instance that unlawful intercourse can be proven by extramarital pregnancy, if there is no confession nor four eyewitnesses to the act. Two women (Safiyyatu Hussaini in Sokoto State and Amina Lawal in Katsina State) were sentenced in 2002 by lower Shari'a courts to be stoned to death for unlawful sexual intercourse, on the strength of pregnancy without being married. Both sentences, however, were quashed on appeal. This was partly for technical reasons: they were charged of having had unlawful sexual relations at a time that the Shari'a Penal Code in their states had not yet been promulgated. But more importantly, both Shari'a Courts of Appeal ruled that pregnancy of an unmarried woman is, in and by itself, not sufficient evidence of unlawful sexual intercourse, in view of the Malikite doctrine that the maximum period of gestation is five years.[4]

In some codes certain offences are equated with theft and can also be punished by amputation. Most Penal Codes make the kidnapping of a child under seven (or before puberty in some codes) punishable by amputation. The Zamfara Penal Code (Art 259) has a clause imposing amputation as the penalty for forgery of documents if the value they represent is more than the *nisâb*. The Kano Penal Code has made embezzlement of public funds or of funds of a bank or company by officials and employees an offence punishable by amputation (Art 134B). For these provisions there is some support of less authoritative Malikite opinions who regard amputation as a lawful penalty for these offences, however not as a fixed punishment (*hadd*) but as a discretionary punishment (*ta`zîr*). These provisions may result in more frequent enforcement of amputation, since, for these offences, the strict conditions for awarding the fixed penalty for theft, a critical constituent of this part of the law, do not seem to apply here.

---

3 Zamfara Shari'a Penal Code, Section 92. Other Penal Codes contain a similar section.

4 For a detailed discussion of the Safiyyatu Hussaini case, see *Peters, R.*, "The re-Islamization of criminal law in Northern Nigeria and the judiciary: the Safiyyatu Hussaini case," in: Dispensing justice in Islamic courts, ed. M.K. Masud, R. Peters, and D. Powers, Studies in Islamic Law and Society (Leiden: Brill, forthcoming).

The law of homicide and wounding follows closely the classical doctrine. Some codes specify that the killer can be sentenced to be executed in the same way as he killed his victim. As in Malikite law, assassination (*qatl ghila*, defined as "the act of luring a person to a secluded place and killing him" (Zamfara Shari'a Penal Code Art 50; Kano Shari'a Penal Code, 50) is a capital offence for which the position of the prosecutors is irrelevant. A striking omission in the Northern Nigerian Shari'a Penal codes is that they are silent on the requirement of equivalence in value between victim and killer or attacker. It is to be expected that on this points Malikite doctrine is applicable.

Several cases of judicial amputation have been reported. Appeals were not lodged, either because the convicts were put under pressure by their social environment with the argument that they would not be good Muslims if they would oppose the sentence, or because of their convictions that undergoing the punishment in this life would ease the sufferings in the Hereafter. In passing a sentence of retaliation for manslaughter, the *qadi* may order that the perpetrator is to be executed in the same way as he has killed his victim. At least one such sentence has been pronounced.[5] A few sentences of retaliation for wounding have been pronounced. On 26 May 2001 Ahmed Tijani was sentenced in Malunfashi, Katsina, to have his right eye removed after blinding a man in an assault. The victim was given the choice between demanding 'an eye for an eye' and 50 camels. In a bizarre case, a 45 year old man was sentenced in January 2003 by the Upper Shari'a Court in Bauchi to have his right leg removed from the knee (without anaesthesia or painkillers, as the court directed) for having done the same to his wife, whom he had accused of overexposing herself to a doctor when she took an injection. I have no information on whether these sentences have actually been carried out.

The enforcement of the new Shari'a Penal Codes is sometimes problematical due to the structure of the Nigerian federation. The police is a federal institution and police personnel often work outside the region of the origin, which means that in Muslim states there are also many non-Muslim policemen. They are not overzealous in tracing specific Shari'a offences. Indeed, there have been reports about police stations in the North that began to function as beer parlours after the prohibition of drinking alcohol was enforced. This lax attitude on the part of the police resulted in vigilantism: Muslims, discontent with the level of enforcement of Islamic criminal law, would form what they called *hisba* groups and start patrolling urban neighbourhoods, attacking places where they suspected that alcohol was served or prostitutes were plying their trade. To

---

5 Zamfara Penal Code, Section 240. In November 2001, a Katsina Shari'a Court sentenced Sani Yakubu Rodi to be stabbed to death in the same way as he had killed his victims. At this moment I do not know whether the sentenced has been carried out.

counter this phenomenon, some states established official *hisba* organisation that would operate in close co-operation with the police.

The reintroduction of Islamic criminal law in the North is surrounded by political and legal complications. It will remain a bone of contention between the Muslim North and the rest of Nigeria. One of the major legal problems is that the Shari'a Penal Codes are on several scores at variance with the Nigerian federal constitution. The first controversy is on whether the introduction of these laws can be reconciled with the secular character of the Nigerian state. Article 10 of the Constitution reads: 'The Government of the Federation or of a State shall not adopt any religion as State religion.' The issue, however, is not as clear as it *prima facie* would seem to be, since the Shari'a has for a long time been accepted as a part of the legal systems of the Northern states in the domain of family, private and commercial law. There is no doubt, however, about the unconstitutionality of the implicit introduction of the Malikite law of evidence: The Constitution stipulates that legislation on evidence is a prerogative of the federal legislature. Finally the Shari'a Penal Codes are in conflict with several human rights guaranteed in the federal constitution. We will return to this issue in the following section, dealing with Islamic criminal law and human rights. So far no sentences pronounced under the Shari'a Penal Codes, have been tested against the constitution by the Federal Supreme Court. Since it is expected that the court will find many of the provisions of these Shari'a Penal Codes unconstitutional, there are widespread fears that such a decision might fuel the antagonism between the North and the South to the point of even endangering the existence of the federation.

3. Conflicts between the shari'a penal codes and the constitution

Here we shall discuss the potential areas of conflict between the provisions of the Shari'a penal codes and the constitutions. I want to stress, however, that the exact definition and purport of human rights provisions are in many cases subject to cultural interpretations. This means that their contents are not for 100% fixed and are, within limits, subject to negotiation. Defining them would be the task of the national judiciary, and, more specifically, the Supreme Federal Court.

3.1. Torture or cruel, degrading or inhuman punishment

Torture or cruel, degrading or inhuman punishment is outlawed by both the Constitution and the Convention against Torture and other Cruel, Degrading or Inhuman Punishment or Treatment, 1989 (CAT). They lay down that no person shall be subjected to torture or to inhuman or degrading punishments and that states shall take measures to prevent public servants from committing acts of torture or administering such punishment.[6]

Here we have one of the most conspicuous domains of conflict between the new Penal Codes and human rights principles. Few jurists would deny that amputation of limbs and retaliation for grievous hurt such as blinding or the pulling out of teeth are indeed a form of torture. The same is true in regard to death by stoning and crucifixion (at least if the latter punishment is taken to mean that the convict will be killed after having been crucified) and to the execution for manslaughter carried out in the same way as perpetrator killed his victim.

3.2. Violation of the basic rights of children

In classical Islamic law, majority begins with puberty. The criterion is a purely physical one: it is established by physical signs such as menstruation and the growth of breasts (women) and the appearance of hair under the armpits and ejaculation (men). The classical doctrine is adopted by the new shari'a penal codes. This means that children in their very early teens can be punished with mutilating *hadd* punishments, and with retaliation for wounding and homicide,[7] which violates the Convention on the Rights of the Child (1989) (CRC). That this is not an academic question is shown by a decision passed on 5 July 2001 sentencing a fifteen year old boy to amputation for theft in Birnin Kebbi, the capital of Kebbi state.

Both the Zamfara and the Kano Penal Codes, following the 1959 Penal Code, explicitly recognise that parents, guardians, schoolmasters and masters are entitled to physically discipline their children, wards, pupils and servants, as long as such castigation does not amount to grievous hurt and is not unreasonable in kind or degree.[8] This seems to justify quite severe physical injury, since the upper limit (grievous hurt) is defined as emasculation, permanent deprivation of one of the senses, deprivation or destruction of a member or joint, permanent disfigurement of the head and face, fracture or dislocation of a bone or tooth or injuries that endanger life or cause severe bodily pain or render the sufferer unable to pursue his ordinary pursuits (Kano Penal Code, Section 159; Zamfara Penal Code, Section 216).

---

6 Constitution, Section 34; CAT, Art. 1 (1) and 16 (1).

7 Zamfara Penal Code, Section 47, 63(1), 71; Kano Penal Code, Section 47, 62A.

8 Zamfara Penal Code, S.76; Kano Penal Code, Section 76.

3.3. The principle of legality, i.e. that no act can be punished unless it has been made a punishable offence by enacted law

Section 36 (12) of the Constitution stipulates that "a person shall not be convicted of a criminal offence unless that offence is defined and the penalty therefore is prescribed in a written law." In violation of the constitutional provision, all Shari'a Penal Codes (with the exception of the Kano Penal Code) contain a section making punishable any act or omission that is an offence under the Shari'a even if not mentioned in the Penal Code itself.[9]

3.4. Equality before the law

One of the most prominent principles in human rights discourse is that all persons are equal before the law and entitled to the same legal protection. This principle is embodied in Section 42 of the Constitution. The same principle is expressed in international human rights instruments.[10] Here we will examine whether the Shari'a Penal Codes violate the principle of equality with regard to gender and religion.

In the new Penal Codes there are only a few provisions that discriminate on the basis of gender. As in the 1959 Penal Code,[11] the new Penal Codes allow the physical correction of a wife by her husband (Zamfara Penal Code, Section 76 (d)) and stipulate that, because of implied consent, a man is not capable of raping his wife in the sense of the law. The Niger Penal Code, Section 68 (A)(3)(b) is the only one stipulating that in the requirement for proving the offence of unlawful sexual intercourse (*zinâ)*, the testimony of men is of greater value than that of women. On the other hand, men are placed in a disadvantageous position in the Kano Penal Code (Section 125), where the punishment for *zinâ* committed by unmarried men is caning as well as imprisonment for one year, whereas unmarried women are only to be punished by caning. On the whole, there is little gender bias in the texts of the new Penal Codes. However, where the codes are silent, the courts apply classical Malikite doctrine, which at a number of issues is discriminatory. The most prominent form of gender discrimination is the application by lower Shari'a courts, unwarranted by the Shari'a Penal Codes, of the classical Malikite doctrine that

---

[9] Zamfara Penal Code, Section 92; Jigawa Penal Code, 92; Bauchi Penal Code, Section 95; Yobe Penal Code, Section 92; Kebbi Penal Code, Section 93.

[10] Art. 14 and 26 International Convention for Civil and Political Rights (ICCPR): "All persons shall be equal before the courts and tribunals." "All persons are equal before the law and are entitled without any discrimination to the equal protection of the law."

[11] Section 55 (1) (d), subject to the condition that such correction was lawful under customary law of the spouses.

extramarital pregnancy constitutes proof of unlawful intercourse. However, now that two Shari'a Courts of Appeal have reversed trial court sentences of stoning based of extramarital pregnancy, it seems that this is not anymore admitted as proof.[12] Another form of discrimination on the ground of gender, is the difference in the amount of bloodmoney for men and women in cases of homicide and hurt. The codes only specify the blood price of a Muslim male, implying that the lives of women and non-Muslims have a different monetary value.

With regard to religion, it is clear that Muslims and non-Muslims are treated differently. However, I have not found instances of discrimination against non-Muslims, since the Shari'a Penal Codes apply only to Muslims. In fact, this also violates the principle of equality, but then to the advantage of non-Muslims. For example, the punishment for certain forms of theft, amputation for Muslims and imprisonment for Christians, is patently in conflict with this principle. However, since the 1959 Penal Code also distinguished between Muslims and Christians with regard to certain offences (e.g. drinking alcohol), it would seem that such distinctions are accepted and not regarded as an essential violation of the equality principle.

3.5. Violations of the freedom of religion

One of the most significant conflicts between the Shari'a and internationally recognised human rights principles is the Shari'a provision that Muslims cannot change their religion and that, if they do, they face a death sentence. Apostasy (*ridda*) also entails the loss of civil rights, such as the right to be married (the marriage of an apostate is dissolved immediately) and the right to hold property. However, none of the new Penal Codes has included apostasy as a punishable offence, no doubt because the conflict with Section 38 of the Constitution, which explicitly mentions the freedom to change one's religion, was too glaring. This does not necessarily mean that apostasy cannot be punished under these laws. The Zamfara Penal Code, as we have seen, stipulates in Section 92 that acts and omissions that are punishable offences under the Shari'a, may be punished even in the absence of a provision in the Penal Code. It is plausible that those who drafted the law had apostasy in mind. However, as yet no cases of prosecution for apostasy have been reported.

Since Christians are not governed by the new Shari'a Penal Codes, they cannot be said to suffer from religious oppression. However, the new codes contain

---

12 See *Peters, R.*, "The re-Islamization of criminal law in Northern Nigeria and the judiciary."

some provisions which may affect the practice of traditional religions and magical practices. Section 406 (d) of the Zamfara Penal Code reads:

> Whoever presides at or is present at or takes part in the worship or invocation of any juju which has been declared unlawful under the provisions of Section 405 will be punished with death;

The previous Section 405, to which it refers, makes the worship or invocation of juju unlawful and explains that "juju" includes the worship or invocation of any subject or being other than Allah. This forms part of Sections 405 to 409 (see Appendix Five), dealing with magical practices and witchcraft. The 1959 Penal Code contained an almost identical section, but with much lighter punishments. The explanation of Section 405, which extends the meaning of juju to the "worship or invocation of any subject or being other than Allah", and the fact that this has been made a capital offence render the provisions dangerous, since they could be used against all religious practices that are deemed un-Islamic. The exact purport of the section is not clear. Since the code only addresses Muslims, the provision seems to refer to persons who regard themselves as Muslims but nevertheless participate in the practices mentioned in these sections.

4. The challenge

4.1. Legislative reform

This tension between the Federation and the Muslim states of the North regarding the constitutionality of the shari'a penal codes poses new challenges, especially to the Muslims of Nigeria. If the Northern states with their Muslim majorities want to stay in the Federation there must be compliance with the constitution, assuming that there is no majority to be found within the federation to drastically change it and to revoke the human rights conventions. The Northern states, then, must make clear that shari'a criminal law does not necessarily constitute a problem in this respect. On the other hand, the South must realise that once shari'a law has been introduced, it is very difficult to abolish it. Any Muslim politician who would announce that he intends to do so, commits political suicide and looses his legitimacy. This means that the only option is reformulating shari'a codes. For a number of practical reasons, it is to be recommended that this be carried out as a common effort of all states that have introduced shari'a criminal law. Then, ultimately, there will be one Shari'a Penal Code operative in all these states, as was the case with the Penal Code (1959) for Northern Nigeria.

Now, what are the options for reformulating the Shari'a Penal Codes that are now in force? The first one is relatively simple: Drafting a shari'a penal code with the provision that the *hadd* penalties will not be applied until all citizens are free of want. This is not a totally novel notion with regard to the enforcement of *hadd* penalties. It was proposed for the first time, to the best of my knowledge, by the Egyptian Muslim Brothers in the 1940s and 1950s.[13] Application of the *hadd* punishment for theft, they argued, can only be enforced after the state has taken care that all citizens are free from want by providing sufficient food, clothing and shelter. It is based essentially on the *hadîth al-maja`a* (famine), i.e. a report that the Caliph `Umar once, during a year of famine, suspended the enforcement of the *hadd* penalty for theft, because under such circumstances theft is excusable. The argument can be extended to the punishment for highway robbery (*hiraba, qat` al-tarîq)* and even to illegal sexual intercourse (*zinâ*), in view of the material burdens that must be assumed in order to be able to conclude a marriage (residence, cost of wedding, bridal price, etc.).

Other options are a complete overhaul of the penal codes. Often proposals to do so are met with the reply that these codes contain God's law and that God's law cannot be changed. However, this argument does not cut ice. The Shari'a Penal Codes that have been introduced so far are codifications of the Malikite school of jurisprudence complemented with a great many provisions taken from the Penal Code of 1959 that was in force until then. This, however, cannot be regarded as the only legal doctrine of the shari'a, since as we all know, there are several schools of legal interpretation (*madhâhib*). Therefore, these Shari'a Penal Codes of the Northern States give an incorrect impression of what the shari'a really is, since they are based on a selection of several options offered by the various schools of jurisprudence.

Moreover, the shari'a is not a static body of rules, laid down once and for all by the jurists of the early centuries of Islam. Most authoritative Muslim scholars would nowadays agree that the obligation of *taqlîd* (i.e. following the authoritative opinions of a School of Jurisprudence, without testing the arguments for such opinions) is now obsolete. However, *taqlîd* of the Malikite opinions is exactly what those who drafted the Nigerian Shari'a Penal codes, have done. A view generally shared by a great number (and maybe a majority) of present-day Muslim scholars is that the shari'a is a legal system suitable for all times and places. Some of its principles are fixed and unchangeable but the details can be adapted. Since society changes, this requires a continuous dialogue with the revealed sources of the shari'a, i.e. the Koran and the Sunna,

---

[13] See *Mitchell, R.P.*, The Society of the Muslim brothers, (London: Oxford University Press, 1969) 240-1, quoting Hasan al-Banna', Sayyid Qutb, and `Abd al-Qadir `Awda.

by means of *ijtihâd*. This is a collective duty (*fard kifâya*) for the Muslim community.

If one regards this new *ijtihâd* as a too daring, it is possible to reformulate the codes by remaining within the orbit of the opinions accepted by the various schools of jurisprudence. This is the way in which in most Muslim countries nowadays family law and the law of succession have been reformed. The codes of personal status that have been enacted in the overwhelming majority of Muslim countries, have selected those opinions that were deemed to be most in consonance with modern circumstances. Thus, in countries where the Hanafite doctrine was applied by the courts, the law codes have introduced parts of the Malikite law in order to expand the possibilities for wives to obtain a divorce, whereas some Malikite countries have adopted the Hanafite doctrine that legally capable women always must give their consent to marriage, even if they marry for the first time. In some cases these codes have introduced new interpretations based on *ijtihâd*. Thus we find that in Egypt, since the year 2000, women can claim a divorce on the strength of *khul`*, even against their husbands' will. What this demonstrates is that it is regarded as perfectly acceptable in the world of Islam, to make creative use of the variety of opinions and even to use ijtihâd, taking the notion of the common good (*maslaha*) as a guideline in order to reach socially desirable solutions.

Many codes of personal status that have been enacted in the Islamic world have introduced minimum ages for concluding a marriage, although this was not known in the classical doctrine. This reform was inspired by the idea of *maslaha*, since large parts of the population regarded child marriages as socially undesirable. A similar step could be taken in the Shari'a Penal Codes: restricting criminal responsibility for *hadd* offences and homicide and wounding to those older than eighteen years, which would then make these codes more in agreement with the International Convention on the Rights of the Child.

That enforcement of shari'a penal law under the present circumstances does not just mean the slavish following of the texts of medieval Islamic jurists is gradually accepted even in countries where shari'a criminal has been codified, such as Iran and Pakistan. I will give a few examples to show that the scope for discussion is much larger that is usually thought.

One of the issues that have been widely discussed is the question of whether the penalty of stoning is really a *hadd* punishment. The problem is that it is not mentioned in the Koran. Koran 24:2 reads:

> Men and women who have unlawful intercourse, scourge ye each one of them (with) a hundred stripes. And let not pity for the twain withhold you from obedience to Allah, if ye believe in Allah and the Last Day. And let a party of believers witness their punishment. (K. 24:2)

When Libya introduced shari'a criminal codes in the early 1970s, unlawful sexual intercourse was not made punishable by stoning with the argument that stoning to death is not mentioned in the Koran. In the same vein, the Pakistani Federal Shariat Court ruled that the law imposing stoning as a punishment for unlawful intercourse was inoperative, as it was repugnant to the injunctions of Islam. The Pakistani Constitution lays down that laws are inoperative if they are repugnant to the injunctions of Islam. Unfortunately the decision was revoked when the President of the Republic interfered and replaced a number of judges in the court with more conservative ones. However, in spite of this, the punishment of stoning has never been enforced in Pakistan.

Even in Iran, which is regarded as one of the most conservative Islamic countries, such debates take place. Lately, a discussion about stoning was initiated and on 29 December 2002, the head of the judiciary ordered the courts not to pronounce sentences of stoning. This seems to have been the result of a campaign launched by a number female MPs and fatwas pronounced by leading ayatollahs. Another issue that was discussed there was whether the differentiation in the bloodprice between men, women and non-Muslims is justified. As a result a draft bill has been introduced removing the difference in blood price between Muslims and Christians.

These examples show that even in countries that are regarded as conservative in applying the shari'a, debates take place on the assumption that the exact contents of the shari'a have to be determined according to the circumstances of time and place.

4.2. The role of the judiciary

One of the most serious problems that accompanied the introduction of the sharia penal codes in Nigeria was the fact that the judiciary was not yet sufficiently equipped to enforce these laws. And this was the more serious because the new penal codes contained many gaps that had to be filled through case law. It is striking that in both the Safiyyatu Hussaini case and in the Amina Lawal case the sentences of the trial courts were quashed mainly on technical and procedural grounds. This, I am afraid, is indicative for the state of knowledge of shari'a criminal law and procedure among the lower court alkalis. A number of elementary rules are expressed in the following hadîth:

> A Muslim man came to the Prophet when he was in the mosque and shouted to him: "O Messenger of God, I have had illegal sexual relations." The Prophet then turned away from him. But the man moved in order to face him and said: "O Messenger of God, I have had illegal sexual relations." Again the Prophet turned away, until he had repeated it four times. After he had testified against

> himself four times, the Prophet called at him: Are you perhaps a bit insane? The man answered no. Then he asked: Have you ever been married. The man answered yes. Then the Prophet said: take him away and stone him.

From the sentences I have just mentioned, it appears that these lower court alkalis, did not even follow this basic rule stating that the court, before sentencing, must actively ascertain whether there are any legal defences and should not leave that to the defendant.

Legislative reform then cannot be successful unless the judges that must apply the laws have been better trained in the new codes and, even more importantly, in the spirit of Shari'a criminal law. There are so many hadîths expressing reluctance of the Prophet Mohammed and the Well Guided Caliphs in applying *hadd* penalties. The best known is the saying: "Ward off the fixed punishments on the strength of *shubha* as much as you can.' (*udru'u al-hudûd bi-l-shubuhât ma istata`tum*). [14] In order to fully implement this principle, Northern Nigeria might follow the example of Pakistan. Here, sentences for *hadd* offences and sentences of retaliation must be confirmed by the Federal Shariat Court. Since this court very strictly applies the law of *hadd* and retaliation, no sentences of amputation, stoning, mutilation for wounding and crucifixion have ever been carried out. This is a very important step, since the Federal Court does not hear the case by way of appeal, conditional on whether the defendant has lodged an appeal, but as a legal obligation without which such sentences cannot be executed. A similar institution in Northern Nigeria would be beneficial. It could remedy the shortcomings of the lower courts and secure a more correct application of the law.

5. Conclusions

I will briefly summarise my findings with regard to the possible solutions for the conflicts between the present Shari'a Penal Codes and the human rights guaranteed by the federal constitution. What I wanted to show is that the present stalemate can be overcome and that the claim of some Northern Muslims that the present Shari'a Penal Codes are identical with Gods law and, therefore, cannot be changed is incorrect and can be refuted if we take a look at the Muslim world at large and especially at such countries as have recently reintroduced shari'a legislation.

My point of departure is, as many Islamic scholars have asserted, that the shari'a is a flexible and adaptable doctrine of law. It is a collective duty of Muslim

---

[14] *Ibn Hajr al-`Asqalani*, Bulugh al-maram min adillat al-ahkam, (Cairo: Dar al-Kitab al-`Arabi, n.d.), no. 1044.

scholars of every age to exercise *ijtihâd* and search for new interpretations, taking into account the specific circumstances of their period and thus develop a viable legal system that can applied in their time. This idea is contrary to what the legislators of the Northern states have done when they codified Shari'a penal law. For they went back to the classical Malikite doctrine, which they thus slavishly adopted, without taking into account the requirements of this age and place, and, especially, the position of the Northern states in the Nigerian federation.
In trying to reformulate Shari'a criminal law and achieve a greater compliance with human rights standards without abandoning the principle of application of the shari'a, three strategies might be followed:

1. Drafting a shari'a penal code with the provision that the *hadd* penalties will only be applied when all citizens are free of want
2. Drafting a penal code incorporating only the very few immutable and unambiguous source texts and further elaborated through ijtihâd.
3. Drafting a shari'a penal code on the basis of the doctrines of the four (or five, if we include the Imami Shiites) schools of jurisprudence, selecting those provisions that are most in consonance with the modern times and in case of need, supplemented by provisions based on ijtihâd.

But whichever of these strategies will be chosen, a prerequisite is a better training of the judges of the lower courts, who sometimes are overzealous in enforcing shari'a punishments but lack the knowledge required for adjudicating in matters of *hudûd* and retaliation. In an Egyptian theft case tried in 1862, a lower qadi had sentenced two defendants to amputation of the right hand. The sentence was quashed by the High Court, which reprimanded the qadi and the mufti who confirmed the decision, saying that

> they ought to have been very cautious with regard to this kind of judgement and only have ventured to pronounce it after having reached complete certainty, for in this type of cases a sentence of amputation must not be pronounced like they did, by [only] dipping the fingertips in the sea of Abu Hanifa's jurisprudence.[15]

After nearly a century and a half, this warning has lost nothing of its aptness.

---

15 See *Peters, R.*, "Islamic and secular criminal law in 19th century Egypt: the role and function of the qadi." Islamic Law and Society, 4 (1997), pp. 70-90.

ZWISCHEN VERFASSUNG, KODIFIZIERTEM RECHT UND ŠARĪ'A: DIE APOSTASIE IN GESETZGEBUNG UND RECHTSPRECHUNG EINIGER ARABISCHER STAATEN

Professor Dr. Baber Johansen, Paris

I. Kodifiziertes Recht und Apostasieprozesse in der arabischen Welt

Seit den 80er Jahren mehren sich die Fälle, in denen die Gerichte arabischer Länder angerufen werden, um Interpretationen des islamischen Rechts, der islamischen Offenbarung und der arabischen und islamischen Geschichte durch arabische und muslimische Intellektuelle als Apostasie zu charakterisieren und ihre Verbreitung durch Wort und Schrift zu verbieten. Diese Verfahren sind einzuordnen in den umfassenden Prozess, in dem seit dem Beginn des 20. Jahrhunderts, verstärkt aber in dessen zweiter Hälfte, das Interpretationsprivileg der Religionsgelehrten in Bezug auf Recht und Religion des Islam von muslimischen Intellektuellen in Frage gestellt wird. Dieser Prozess hat seine Ursprünge in der Periode der *tanẓīmāt* (1839-1876). Er ist vom Ende des 19. Jahrhunderts an eng verknüpft mit der Einordnung des islamischen Rechts in die vom staatlichen Gesetzgeber erlassenen Gesetzesbücher der arabischen Länder, d.h. mit der Geschichte der Kodifikation des Rechts in den arabischen Staaten.[1] Er ist aber ebenso abhängig vom Verständnis legitimer Normativität, das eine in modernen Universitäten und Hochschulen ausgebildete Elite arabischer Intellektueller entwickelt und in den Medien zur öffentlichen Diskussion stellt. Die Konflikte, die in solchen Ansätzen zum Tragen kommen, sollen durch die Anrufung der Gerichte entschieden werden.

---

1 Zur Geschichte der Kodifikation der Arabischen Staaten siehe: *Liebesny, H. J.*, The Law of the Near and Middle East. Readings, Cases, and Materials. Albany: State University of New York Press, 1975; *Borrmans, M.*, Statut Personnel et Famille au Maghreb de 1940 à nos jours. Paris et La Haye: Mouton, 1977; *Chehata, C.*, Droit musulman. Applications au Proche Orient. Paris: Dalloz, 1970; *Botiveau, B.*, Loi islamique et droit dans les sociétés arabes. Paris et Aix-en-Provence: Karthala et IREMAM, 1993; *Krüger, H.*, Überblick über das Zivilrecht der Staaten des ägyptischen Rechtskreises. in: Recht van de Islam (14) 1997, S. 67-131; *Brown, N. J.*, The rule of law in the Arab world. Courts in Egypt and the Gulf. Cambridge: Cambridge University Press, 1997; *Charfi, M.*, L'influence de la Religion dans le droit international privé des pays musulmans. Recueil des Cours 203 [Collected Courses of the Hague Academy of International Law] (1987-III); *Deprez, J.*, Droit International Privé et conflit des civilisations Aspects méthodologiques. Recueil des Cours 211 (1988-IV).

Die Funktion, die den Apostasie-Urteilen für die Freiheit wissenschaftlicher Forschung, für die Freiheit öffentlicher Meinungsäußerung und für die Religionsfreiheit zukommt, will ich anhand von drei Verfahren zu klären versuchen, die in den 80er und 90er Jahren des 20. Jahrhunderts im Sudan, im Jemen und in Ägypten vor Gericht verhandelt wurden.

Diese drei Fälle beenden eine lange historische Periode, die von der zweiten Hälfte des 19. Jahrhunderts bis in die 60er Jahre des 20. Jahrhunderts reicht[2]. Aus dieser Zeit sind mir Gerichtsurteile, die Intellektuelle wegen ihrer Interpretation des Islam zu Apostaten erklären, nicht bekannt. Die 70er Jahre des 20. Jahrhunderts markieren in dieser Frage eine Zäsur: Zensur - in den meisten arabischen Staaten als Verwaltungsakt von den Behörden vorgenommen - wird - zumindest in einigen Staaten, wie Ägypten, dem Jemen und dem Sudan - auf die Gerichte verlagert und als Urteil über die religiösen Qualitäten der Autoren und ihrer Werke formuliert. Das gilt allerdings bisher nur von Veröffentlichungen muslimischer Intellektueller, die beanspruchen für die Interpretation der Offenbarung und der juristischen und ethischen Normen des *fiqh* durch ihre wissenschaftliche Ausbildung und ihre Fähigkeit zur Reflexion legitimiert zu sein.

II. Die "Kodifizierung der šarī'a" und die "Prinzipien der islamischen šarī'a"

Die Zäsur der 70er Jahre resultiert aus einem veränderten Verständnis von der Rolle des islamischen Rechts für die Gesetzgebung, die Verfassung und die Rechtsprechung der arabischen Staaten. Die Krise des Nasserismus wächst sich Anfang der 70er Jahre zu einer Krise des Modells des säkularen arabischen Staats aus. Die arabischen Staaten suchen in dieser Zeit nach einem Kompromiss mit den oppositionellen islamischen Bewegungen. Als Feld für die Formulierung eines Kompromisses bieten sich in erster Linie Recht und Verfassung an. Für den Sudan unter Numairi und Ägypten unter Sadat ist das offensichtlich. Mit Einschränkungen gilt das auch für die Arabische Republik Jemen. Diese hat zwar von 1962-1970 kein eigenständiges säkulares Recht ausgebildet, aber die Verfassung von 1970 - ebenso wie die Provisorische Verfassung von 1974 und die Gründung des Büro für religiöse Rechtsgutachten und Gesetzgebung im Jahre 1979 - haben der Republik als Form des

---

2 *Peters, R. u. de Vries, G. J. J.*, "Apostasy in Islam", *Die Welt des Islams*, XVII, 1-4 (1977), S. 2-25.

Kompromisses mit den ehemals royalistischen Kräften gedient und den Einfluss religiöser Gelehrter auf diese wichtige Institution verstärkt[3].

In Ägypten und dem Sudan geht es vor allem darum, das bestehende Recht einerseits zu erhalten und andererseits das islamische Recht nicht nur, wie das seit dem Ende des 19. Jahrhunderts zur Regel geworden ist, im Bereich des Familien-, Ehe und Erbrechts zu kantonieren, sondern ihm Einfluss auf die Gesetzgebung in allen Bereichen zu sichern. Dieser Anspruch wird in zwei verschiedenen Strategien verfolgt. Die eine verlangt "die Kodifizierung der *šarīʿa*" (*taqnīn al-šarīʿa*), d.h. die Transformation der Normen des *fiqh* und der *šarīʿa* in Gesetze und die Vereinbarkeit aller staatlichen Gesetze mit diesen Normen. Diese Strategie ist in Ägypten vor allem in den 1982 vom ägyptischen Parlament verabschiedeten islamisierten Straf- und Zivilgesetzbuch wirksam geworden, Gesetzesbüchern, die im übrigen der Präsident der Republik nie verkündet hat[4]. Im Sudan verkörpert sich in den 80er Jahren die Forderung nach der Kodifizierung der *šarīʿa* in der Liste der "islamischen Gesetze" Numayris vom September 1983, die vorrangig einer Verschärfung des Strafrechts und der damit einhergehenden Veränderung des Prozess- und Beweisrechts dienten. Nach dem Sturz Numayris ist die Aufhebung dieser Gesetze vom September 1983 durch den Militärputsch vom 30. Juni 1989 verhindert worden[5]. Auch in der Arabischen Republik Jemen sieht der Artikel 152 der Verfassung von 1970 die "*Kodifizierung der šarīʿa*" vor[6]. Die zweite Strategie verfolgt das Ziel, die "*Prinzipien der šarīʿa*" zur wichtigsten Quelle der staatlichen Gesetzgebung zu erheben und so alle Bereiche der Gesetzgebung diesen Prinzipien zu unterstellen. Diese Strategie nährt seit langem die Debatte über die möglichen theoretischen Grundlagen einer Reform des islamischen Rechts. Viele Verfassungen der ostarabischen Länder erklären "*die Prinzipien der šarīʿa*" zu einer Quelle der Verfassung. Der Artikel 2 der ägyptischen Verfassung von

---

3 *Amin, S. H.*, Law and Justice in Contemporary Yemen: People's Democratic Republic of Yemen and Yemen Arab Republic, Glasgow: Royston Limited, 1987, S. 28-29, 48-59, 85.

4 *Botiveau*, sociétés arabes, op. cit., S. 271-302, insbesondere 282-283.

5 Zu den Gesetzen vom September 1983 siehe: *Zein, I. M.*, Religion, Legality, and the State: 1983 Sudanese Penal Code, Ph.Diss. thesis, Temple University, August 1989; *Köndgen, O.*, Das islamisierte Strafrecht des Sudan. Von seiner Einführung 1983 bis Juli 1992, Hamburg: Deutsches Orient-Institut, 1992; *Layish, A. u. Warburg, G. R.*, The Reinstatement of Islamic Law in Sudan under Numayrî, Leiden: Brill, 2002. Zum Militärputsch von 1989 und seiner Funktion für die Erhaltung der Septembergesetze siehe: *Layish u. Warburg*, Sudan under Numayrî, op. cit., S. 79, 300-301; *Köndgen*, Strafrecht des Sudan, op. cit., S. 72-73. Zum *taqnīn al-šarīʿa* in der Theorie Turabis siehe: *Layish and Warburg*, Sudan under Numayrî, op. cit., S. 85, 87, 94-95.

6 *Amin*, Contemporary Yemen, op. cit., S. 52.

1971, in der veränderten Fassung von 1980, erhebt diese Prinzipien zur Hauptquelle der Gesetzgebung. Als konstitutionelles Konzept findet sich die Berufung auf die Prinzipien der *šarīʿa* in den Schriften der sudanesischen *Anṣār*[7]. Auch der Artikel 153 der jemenitischen Verfassung von 1970 sieht "die Prinzipien der islamischen *šarīʿa*" als Quelle des Rechts in allen Bereichen vor, in denen das Gesetz schweigt[8].

Es liegt auf der Hand, dass unter diesen Bedingungen Konflikte zwischen unterschiedlichen Interpretationen der Prinzipien der *šarīʿa* für die Gesetzgebung und die Verfassungsauslegung eine praktische Bedeutung gewinnen, die ihnen nicht zukam, solange das islamische Recht im Bereich des Personalstatuts kantoniert war. Für die religiösen Institutionen und die islamistischen Bewegungen dient die Forderung nach der "Kodifizierung der *šarīʿa*" häufig dazu, säkulare Interpretationen des Rechts, der Verfassung, der Human- und Sozialwissenschaften, insbesondere der Geschichtswissenschaft abzuwehren und alle Ideen, die sich nicht in die normativen Ordnungen der Vergangenheit integrieren lassen, als unislamisch und daher illegitim zu denunzieren. Umgekehrt können muslimische Intellektuelle in den "Prinzipien der islamischen *šarīʿa*" die Rechtfertigung für eine rationale Analyse des religiösen Erbes, eine auf ihr basierende Kompetenz aller Muslime zur Interpretation ihrer Religion, für eine Konzeption von Religion, Recht und Staat finden, die Gleichheit und Freiheit aller Bürger bei der Schaffung neuer Formen von Gesellschafts-, Rechts- und Staatsordnung garantiert. Eine systematische Trennung zwischen beiden Ansätzen ist sicher nicht tragfähig. Die Übergänge bleiben fließend. Man kann aber doch davon ausgehen, dass im Rahmen des ersten Ansatzes der *šarīʿa*-Begriff so konzipiert ist, dass darunter nicht nur die normativen Texte der Offenbarung (Koran, *sunna*, consensus der Gemeinde) fallen, sondern auch die von den muslimischen Juristen über Jahrhunderte ausgearbeiteten Bestimmungen des klassischen *fiqh*, des Systems ethischer und juristischer Normen, das seit dem 9. Jahrhundert die religiöse Normenproduktion dominiert. Das Konzept der "Prinzipien der *šarīʿa*" impliziert dagegen, dass aus den Texten der Offenbarung deren Prinzipien ableitbar sind. Diese Ableitung setzt immer einen Prozess der Interpretation voraus. Es handelt sich also bei den "Prinzipien der *šarīʿa*" um eine wichtige Kompromissformel, die einerseits die Interpretationskompetenz der Muslime und andererseits die Bindung des Rechts an die Prinzipien der *šarīʿa* voraussetzt. Die Apostasie-Prozesse, über die ich heute reden werde, betreffen vor allem Konflikte über die

---

7 Zu den *Anṣār* siehe *Layish u. Warburg*, Sudan under Numayrî, op. cit., S. 18-19.

8 *Amin*, Contemporary Yemen, op. cit., S. 52.

Kompetenz muslimischer Intellektueller, die Prinzipien, Normen und Grundlagen der *šarīʿa* zu interpretieren.

III. Die klassische Apostasie-Doktrin des *fiqh*

Bevor ich die einzelnen Fälle vorstelle, einige Worte über die klassische *fiqh*-Doktrin zur Apostasie. Der Sachverhalt, der als Apostasie erfasst werden kann, ist in den Quellen nirgends klar definiert. Rudolf Peters hat ihm in seinem bekannten Aufsatz zur "Apostasy in Islam" eine zusammenfassende Präzisierung gegeben, die für meine Darstellung nützlich ist[9]. Ein Muslim, der erklärt, dass er nicht mehr an den Islam glaube und nicht an seinen axiomatischen Glaubensvorstellungen festhalte, ist ein Apostat. Das gleiche gilt für den Muslim, der sich einer anderen Religionsgemeinschaft anschließt. In beiden Fällen geht es um die vom Handelnden selbst bestimmte und gewählte religiöse Identität. Selbst- und Fremddarstellung stimmen also bis zu einem gewissen Grade überein. Das ist nicht notwendig der Fall in der dritten Form der Apostasie, den "Worten des Unglaubens" (*kalimāt al-kufr*). Für diese gibt es weder erschöpfende Listen noch übergreifende Regeln (*qawā'id*). Vom 13. Jahrhundert an hat die juristische Diskussion der Apostasie einen fast ausschließlich kasuistischen Charakter.

Dieser kasuistische Charakter der Apostasie-Diskussion erklärt den Dissens zwischen den Schulen des *fiqh*. Der juristische Status des Apostaten und die juristischen Folgen der Apostasie sind zwischen den Schulen und auch innerhalb der Schulen umstritten. Der *fiqh* ist ein Juristenrecht, in dem ständig mehr Rechtsmeinungen produziert werden, als in die Schuldoktrinen integriert werden können. Zu Einzelfragen gibt es daher sehr häufig einen Dissens nicht nur zwischen den Doktrinen verschiedener Schulen, sondern auch innerhalb der einzelnen Schulen. Bezogen auf den Apostaten und die Apostasie hat dieser Dissens vor allem Auswirkungen auf die Eigentumsrechte der Apostaten und ihrer Erben einerseits[10], auf das Prozess- und Beweisrecht andererseits. Das Prozess- und Beweisrecht der Apostasie ist sehr wenig ausgebildet, verglichen mit dem Prozess- und Beweisrecht anderer Delikte. Eine ausführliche Diskussion, die sich auf unterschiedliche Positionen bezieht, findet sich, wenn

---

9 *Peters u. Vries*, "Apostasy", op. cit., S. 2-4.

10 Siehe dazu mein "The Law's subject: believer or proprietor? The case of the apostate in Muslim Law" (Beitrag zum Seminar von Patricia Crone at the School of Historical Studies, Institute for Advanced Study, Princeton, in 2002).

ich richtig sehe, nur bei den Hanbaliten[11]. In allen Schulen ist es aber einem Muslim, der von glaubwürdigen Zeugen der Apostasie angeklagt wird, praktisch unmöglich, sich zu verteidigen. Er kann nur Formeln benutzen, die dazu dienen, die Apostasie zu widerrufen und ihn so einerseits der Apostasie schuldig zeigen und ihn andererseits vor der Bestrafung als Apostaten schützen. Widerruft er nicht, so wird er - in der Doktrin der meisten Schulen - zum Widerruf aufgefordert, und falls er nicht rechtzeitig widerruft, getötet. Der Apostat kann weder sich selbst noch andere verheiraten, und er kann auch seine bestehende Ehe nicht aufrechterhalten[12]. Ich gehe auf den Dissens über die Apostasiefähigkeit von Minderjährigen ebenso wenig ein wie auf das Verhältnis zwischen Religion und Filiation, weil diese Rechtswirkungen der Apostasie für mein heutiges Thema nicht relevant sind.

Wichtig bleibt aber bis ins 20. Jahrhundert die sowohl von den Hanbaliten[13] als auch von den Hanafiten vertretene These, dass - gleich ob man dem Apostaten verzeiht oder ihn hinrichtet - die Entscheidung darüber, ob er tatsächlich gegen Religion und Glauben verstoßen habe, nicht in dieser Welt, sondern von Gott im Jenseits gefällt werde. Die Hanafiten ziehen daraus den Schluss, dass der Apostat nicht wegen mangelnden Glaubens bestraft wird, weil eine solche Bestrafung allein Gott zustehe, sondern wegen der politischen Konsequenzen, die aus dem Abfall von der Religion folgen. Ich zitiere Saraḫsī, den bedeutendsten hanafitischen Autor Transoxaniens im 11. Jahrhundert:

> "Der Religionswechsel ebenso wie der ursprüngliche Unglaube gehören zu den abscheulichsten Verbrechen; aber sie betreffen das Verhältnis zwischen Gott und seinem Diener und ihre Vergeltung ist vertagt bis zum jenseitigen Gerichtsort (*dār al-ǧazā'*). Was in dieser niedrigen Welt vorgezogen wird, das sind Maßnahmen der politischen Zweckmäßigkeit (*siyāsāt*), die das Gesetz legalisiert hat, um Interessen der Gottesdiener zu schützen [...] Dadurch, dass er auf seinem Unglauben insistiert, erklärt der Apostat den Muslimen den Krieg. Man tötet ihn deswegen, um seine Kriegführung abzuwehren."[14]

---

11 *Ibn Qudāma, M. al-Dīn*, Al-Muġnī, Beirut: Dār al-kutub al-ʿilmiyya, o.D., Bd. X, S. 98-102.

12 *Peters u. Vries*, "Apostasy", op. cit., S. 5-6; Johansen, "The law's subject", op. cit.

13 *Ibn Qudāma*, Al-Muġnī, op. cit., Bd. X, S. 80.

14 *Muḥammad ibn Abī Sahl al-Saraḫsī*, Al-Mabsūṭ, Beirut: dār al-maʿrifa, o.D., Bd. X, S. 110.

Sein Unglaube, so führt Saraḫsī weiter aus, ist nur die Ursache (*sabab*), die zur *ratio legis* (*'illa*) der Todesstrafe führt. Die *ratio legis* selbst ist die politische Wirkung der Apostasie, der durch sie ausgelöste Krieg gegen die Muslime. Aus diesem Grunde kann eine Frau nicht wegen Apostasie zum Tode verurteilt werden, weil sie nicht fähig ist, gegen die Muslime Krieg zu führen[15].

Es sind also die politischen Konsequenzen der Apostasie, die bestraft werden, nicht der Abfall vom Glauben. Diese Tradition determiniert in allen drei hier vorzustellenden Verfahren die Form der Auseinandersetzung mit den Angeklagten.

IV. Apostasie-Urteile der 80er und 90er Jahre im Sudan, im Jemen und in Ägypten

Muḥammad Maḥmūd Ṭāhā, ein sudanesischer Ingenieur, Gründer der religiös-politischen Assoziation der *Republikanischen Brüder*, wird am 8. Januar 1985 nach zweitägiger Haftdauer in einer zweistündigen Verhandlung in erster Instanz zum Tode verurteilt. Anlass war ein Flugblatt, in dem die *Republikanischen Brüder* sich unter Berufung auf ihr Verständnis des Islam gegen Numayris Septembergesetze von 1983 wandten. Das erstinstanzliche Gericht stützt sich auf die Paragraphen 96 (Absätze ṭā' und kāf) und 105 des STGB von 1983 und auf den Paragraphen 20a des sudanesischen Staatssicherheitsgesetzes von 1983. Beide Abschnitte des Paragraphen 96 StGB betreffen die Verbreitungen von Nachrichten, Schriften, Kassetten oder Radiosendungen, die zur illegalen Opposition gegen die Regierung aufrufen. Der Paragraph 105 enthält ein striktes Verbot aller Formen nicht legalisierter organisierter Opposition gegen die Regierung, inklusive der Verbreitung von Schriftstücken, die dazu anhalten, solche Opposition zu entfalten[16]. Die Einleitung zum Paragraphen 96 bedroht die in den Absätzen ṭā' und kāf benannten Verhaltensweisen mit dem Tod. Ich zitiere:

> "Jedermann, [der die folgenden Taten begeht] wird betrachtet als habe er das Verbrechen des Verfassungsbruchs und des Aufrufs zum Krieg gegen den Staat vollendet und wird mit der Todesstrafe oder lebenslänglichem Gefängnis oder Gefängnis von kürzerer Dauer

---

15 ibidem.

16 *Layish u. Warburg*, Sudan under Numayrī, op.cit., S. 55-60, 177-180; *Zein*, Sudanese Penal Code, op. cit., S. 288-297; *Köndgen*, Strafrecht des Sudan, op. cit., S. 55-58.

> bestraft. Dabei ist es zulässig, sein gesamtes Vermögen zu beschlagnahmen."[17]

Es folgt eine lange Liste von mit diesen Strafen bedrohten Taten, unter ihnen die in den Absätzen ṭā' und kāf aufgeführten Tatbestände. Im Verfahren vor der ersten Instanz klagt die Staatsanwaltschaft Ṭāhā unter Berufung auf den Paragraphen 96 StGB an, d.h. unter dem Vorwurf des **Kriegs gegen den Staat**. Es ist der Justizminister, der der Anklage den Verweis auf den Paragraphen 458, 3 StGB hinzufügt. Dieser 3. Abschnitt des Paragraphen 458 enthält die folgende Bestimmung: "Das Fehlen eines [diesbezüglichen] Textes in diesem Gesetz hindert nicht daran, eine gesetzliche *ḥadd*-Strafe zu exekutieren."[18] Mit anderen Worten, die *šarīʿa* nimmt, wie Layish und Warburg zu Recht betonen[19], den Platz eines Naturrechts ein, das immer dann in Kraft ist, wenn das Gesetz schweigt. Diese Rechtsquellenlehre war im Zivilrecht bereits durch den Paragraphen 4 des sudanesischen Zivilgesetzbuchs von 1971verkündet worden. Sie wird in den 80er Jahren auch für das Strafrecht verbindlich.[20]

Als Resultat dieser ministeriellen Intervention fallen Anklage, Urteil und Urteilsbegründung des Gerichts erster Instanz weitgehend auseinander. Olaf Köndgen fasst den Vorgang in den folgenden Worten zusammen:

> "In erster Instanz war von einer Anklage wegen Apostasie nur implizit die Regel gewesen; in der Urteilsbegründung wurden dann aber die religiösen Überzeugungen der Republikanischen Brüder zur Begründung herangezogen, nicht jedoch die Delikte gegen den Staat, die ja *de iure* der eigentliche Grund für die Anklage sein sollten."[21]

---

17 *Qānūn al-ʿuqūbāt li-sanat 1983* (*amr muʾaqqat raqam 30 li-sanat 1983*), [art.] 96.

18 Eine *ḥadd*-Strafe ist nach der Doktrin des klassischen *fiqh* eine vom Gesetz in Form und Ausmaß festgelegte Strafe, die nicht als Rechtsanspruch eines menschlichen Individuums, sondern ganz oder überwiegend als Rechtsanspruch Gottes (*ḥaqq allāh*) verhängt wird. Die klassischen Juristen machen keinen Hehl daraus, dass Gott hier für "die Interessen der Allgemeinheit" steht (*li-maṣāliḥ al-ʿāmma*), also als Symbol eines öffentlichen Rechtsanspruchs. Siehe dazu mein "Eigentum, Familie und Obrigkeit im hanafitischen Strafrecht. Das Verhältnis der privaten Rechte zu den Forderungen der Allgemeinheit in hanafitischen Rechtskommentaren", *Die Welt des Islams*, XIX, 1-4, S. 1-73, insbesondere S.38.

19 *Layish u. Warburg*, Sudan under Numayrî, op. cit., S. 277.

20 op. cit., S. 74.

21 *Köndgen*, Strafrecht des Sudan, op. cit., S. 56.

Im Berufungsverfahren lautet die Anklage sowohl auf Apostasie als auch auf Verbrechen gegen den Staat. Dem Gericht geht es nicht um das religiöse Selbstverständnis Ṭāhās, die Frage, ob er sich als Muslim oder Nicht-Muslim sieht, welche Gründe ihn zu seinen Erklärungen bewegen. Es untersucht vielmehr seine Schriften und Veröffentlichungen und deren Abweichen von den normativen Konzepten, die das Gericht für Grundlagen des Islam hält. Das Gericht qualifiziert die Veröffentlichungen des sudanesischen Reformers als Tatbestände der Apostasie, weil Ṭāhā die Gleichstellung von Männern und Frauen im islamischen Erbrecht ebenso fordert wie die rechtliche Gleichheit für Muslime und Nicht-Muslime und weil er der Meinung ist, dass die religiöse Pflichtenlehre des Islam, die die Juristen des *fiqh* aufgebaut haben, für den Muslim des zwanzigsten Jahrhunderts nicht notwendig verbindlich sei.[22] Layish und Warburg fassen die Urteilsbegründung des Berufungsgerichts wie folgt zusammen: Das Berufungsgericht

> "... analyzed Ṭāhā's teachings on questions such as prayer, the alms tax, *jihād*, and matters of personal status and succession, status of women, as well as on ontological questions such as free choice and predestination, and incarnation (*tajsīd*). It concluded that Ṭāhā had become an apostate (*murtadd*) in thought and deed, and that his teachings called for the destruction of the entire basis of the Islamic religion[...] hence, the court viewed the publications and ideological platform of the Republican Brothers as heretical acts equivalent to apostasy and the creation of a "new religion."[23]

Am 18. Januar 1985 wird Ṭāhā aufgrund dieses Urteils hingerichtet.

Die Zweideutigkeit eines Verfahrens, das den sudanesischen Reformer wegen **Kriegs gegen den Staat** und wegen **Apostasie** gleichzeitig verurteilt, unterstreicht den politischen Charakter des Urteils. Das Gericht legt die zulässigen Glaubensformen auf ihre vergangenen Interpretationen fest und trennt sie von den Glaubensüberzeugungen des Angeklagten. Insofern diese von jenen abweichen, und damit den islamischen Charakter der Rechts- und Religionspolitik Numayris in Frage stellen, werden sie zu Vergehen gegen Religion und Staat.

---

22 *Layish u. Warburg*, Sudan under Numayrî, op. cit., S. 58; *Köndgen*, Strafrecht des Sudan, op. cit., S. 55.

23 *Layish u. Warburg*, Sudan under Numayrî, op. cit., S. 178-179.

Nur wenige Tage nach der Hinrichtung Ṭāhās wird am 22. Januar 1985, in Sanaa der erste Apostasieprozess der Arabischen Republik Jemen eingeleitet. Angeklagt wird der Soziologieprofessor Ḥamūd al-ʿAwdī von vier *ḥisba*-Zeugen, d.h. Personen, die keinerlei privates Interesse mit dem Fall verbinden,[24] und die beanspruchen, sich nach der religiösen Maxime zu richten, dass man das Gute gebieten und das Böse verbieten müsse. Das klassische islamische Recht kennt weder einen Staatsanwalt noch erkennt es Privatpersonen, die von Rechtsverletzungen Dritter nicht persönlich betroffen sind, im Bereich des öffentlichen Rechts eine Klagebefugnis gegen diese Dritten zu. Privatpersonen, die ein Gerichtsverfahren gegen solche Dritte einleiten wollen, erscheinen daher nicht als Kläger, sondern als *ḥisba*-Zeugen. De facto nehmen sie aber die Funktion von Klägern wahr, weil der Richter aufgrund ihrer Aussagen ein Verfahren gegen die benannten Dritten einleiten kann. Sie unterscheiden sich von Klägern dadurch, dass ihnen aus dem Urteil des Richters keine Ansprüche gegen den Angeklagten entstehen.[25]

Die *ḥisba*-Zeugen klagen den Ḥamūd al-ʿAwdī der Apostasie, des Unglaubens, der Ketzerei und des Kommunismus an. Sie stützen sich für diese Anklage nicht auf die Kenntnis der Person des Angeklagten, sondern auf seine Bücher und Veröffentlichungen[26]. Der Betroffene interpretiert ihre Aktion als Teil einer umfassenden Säuberung der Universität von linken Professoren und Studenten. Er flieht deshalb noch am Tage der Klageerhebung zuerst in den Süden des Landes und von dort aus nach Damaskus[27]. Der Prozess wird in seiner Abwesenheit gegen ihn geführt.

Wie im sudanesischen Fall ist die Prozessgeschichte komplex. Das erste Dokument der Anklage besteht aus dem Schreiben der vier *ḥisba*-Zeugen an den

---

24 *Ḥamūd al-ʿAwdī*, Al-tuhma wa l-difāʿ min maḥkamat al-ṣamt ilā maḥkamat al-tārīḫ (1985-1986), 2. Aufl., Beirut, 1989, S. 10-21.

25 In den "Rechtsansprüchen Gottes" (*ḥuqūq allāh*) ist eine Klageerhebung nicht möglich: *Abū Bakr ibn Masʿūd al-Kāsānī*, Kitāb badāʾiʿ al-ṣanāʾiʿ fī tartīb al-šarāʾiʿ, Beirut, o.D. Bd. VI, S. 277; *Ibn ʿĀbidīn*, Radd al-muḥtār ʿalā al-durr al-muḫtār, Kairo, o.D. [1307 H.], Bd. III, S. 439. Daher gilt das Zeugnis in diesem Bereich als eine um Gottes willen erbrachte Leistung im öffentlichen Interesse (*ḥisba*), siehe *Kāsānī*, badāʾiʿ, op. cit., Bd. VI, S. 282; *ʿAlī ibn Abī Bakr al-Marġīnānī*, Al-Hidāya šarḥ bidāyat al-mubtadiʾ, abgedruckt im Kommentar des *Muḥammad ibn ʿAbd al-Wāḥid al-Sīwāsī Ibn al-Humām*, Fatḥ al-qadīr (ed. ʿAbd al-Razzāq Ġālib al-Mahdī), Beirut: dār al-kutub al-ʿilmiyya, 1995, Bd. VII, S. 340-341; *Ibn ʿĀbidīn*, Radd al-muḥtār, op. cit., Bd. III, S. 438-439. Zum Konzept der "Rechtsansprüche Gottes", siehe *Johansen, B.*, "Eigentum, Familie und Obrigkeit, op. cit. S. 38-46.

26 *ʿAwdī*, Al-tuhma, op. cit., S. 10.

27 op. cit., S. 20.

Staatsanwalt[28]. Auf dessen Grundlage erstellt die Staatsanwaltschaft eine Zitatensammlungen aus den Büchern des Professors, die ihr ausreicht, diesen wegen Apostasie, Unglaube und Kommunismus anzuklagen[29]. Auf diese Klageschrift antwortet der Angeklagte in mehreren Schriftstücken. Im Urteil von 1986 wird auf diese Anklageschrift nicht mehr direkt Bezug genommen. Die Urteilsbegründung der Richter zitiert sie nur in der Form, in der die Verteidigung ihre Argumente gegen einen Teil dieser Vorwürfe vorträgt[30]. Die Richter selbst orientieren sich nur an wenigen der ursprünglichen Klagepunkte und ergänzen diese durch Argumente, die in den Dokumenten der Staatsanwaltschaft und der *ḥisba*-Zeugen nicht enthalten waren. Das Urteil, das als Datum nur das Jahr, nicht aber Tag und Monat angibt, gliedert sich in vier Punkte: es sieht erstens die Beschlagnahme der Bücher des Autors vor, zweitens seine Entlassung aus den Diensten der Universität von Sanaa und ein Unterrichtsverbot für ihn in allen jemenitischen Regionen. Es verlangt drittens die Einsetzung einer Kommission von führenden Religionsgelehrten durch den Obersten Justizrat, der die Aufgabe zufallen solle, die falschen Lehren des Soziologieprofessors zu widerlegen. Der vierte Abschnitt des Urteils fordert den Obersten Justizrat auf, den Angeklagten zum öffentlichen Widerruf seiner falschen Aussagen zu bewegen und zur Aufzählung aller von ihm begangenen Fehler, die das Urteil gegen ihn notwendig gemacht hätten. All dies solle geschehen, ohne den geringsten Druck auf den Angeklagten auszuüben. Sollte der Angeklagte allerdings trotzdem auf seinen Irrlehren bestehen nachdem man ihm eine Frist gesetzt und mit ihm diskutiert und ihm erklärt habe, worauf das Urteil beruhe, dann müsse an ihm das von Gott festgesetzte Todesurteil als *ḥadd*-Strafe vollzogen werden.[31]

Mir fehlt die Dokumentation, um auf den politischen Hintergrund des Prozesses einzugehen. Aus den Dokumenten der Anklage, der *ḥisba*-Zeugen, des angeklagten Professors und aus der Verteidigungsschrift ebenso wie aus der Urteilsbegründung und dem Urteil lassen sich aber Teile des Konflikts rekonstruieren. Es geht um die Auseinandersetzung zwischen einer religiösen und einer säkularen Deutung der jemenitischen Nationalgeschichte. Die *ḥisba*-Zeugen und die Staatsanwaltschaft klagen den Soziologieprofessor der Apostasie an, weil er davon spricht, dass die jemenitische Landwirtschaft vor dem Islam ein Geschenk und ein Produkt der Menschen sei, das diese

---

28 op. cit., S. 134.

29 op. cit., S. 138-141.

30 *Ḥamūd al-ʿAwdī,* Al-Milaff al-ṯānī muttaham bi l-kufr yabḥaṯ ʿan maḥkama (*1987-1988*), o. D., o.O., S. 21-28.

31 op. cit., p. 31.

geschaffen hätten (*ḫalq al-insān*)[32]. Dass er führende Stammesvertreter des 7. Jahrhunderts von der Anklage der Apostasie freispricht, trägt ihm den Vorwurf ein, diese Qualität mit ihnen zu teilen[33]. Die Tatsache, dass er politische Gründe anführt, die dazu beigetragen hätten, dass die jüdische, christliche aber auch die islamische Religion von den Jemeniten akzeptiert worden sei, wird ihm angekreidet als Beleidigung des jemenitischen Volks in seiner religiösen Würde[34]. Das Gericht widmet eine ganze Seite seiner Urteilsbegründung dem Versuch - unter Nutzung jemenitischer Poesie und regionaler Gelehrtentradition des 12. Jahrhunderts - den Nachweis zu führen, dass der im Koran erwähnte *Ḏū al-qarnayn*, der in der klassischen islamischen Tradition und in der modernen Forschung eher als eine Alexander-Repräsentation gilt, ein Jemenit gewesen sei und als jemenitischer Weltbeherrscher nicht unfromm oder a-religiös gewesen sein könne[35]. Die Tatsache, dass Ḥamūd al-ʿAwdī ismailitische Dynastien des 11. und 12. Jahrhunderts ausführlicher würdigt als zaiditische, trägt ihm den Vorwurf der Ketzerei ein[36]. Seine Bücher dienen der Anklage und den Richtern dazu, Belegstellen für eine Geschichtsschreibung zu finden, die dem religiösen Charakter der Nationalgeschichte des jemenitischen Volks nicht zureichend Rechnung trage und den Autor so als Feind des Islam ausweise.

Diese Argumentation überschneidet sich mit einer zweiten, die ihm vorwirft, Aussagen zur Geschichte zu machen, die dem Koran und der *Sunna*, d.h. der normativen Praxis des Propheten widersprechen. Wenn, so sagt das Gericht, der Angeklagte behaupte, die Jemeniten hätten den Islam benutzt, um ihre politischen Konflikte einzudämmen, dann behaupte er ja, die Jemeniten seien vom religiösen Denken des Propheten nicht überzeugt gewesen: "Das widerspricht der Realität und straft die Geschichte und den Koran gleichzeitig Lügen"[37]. Gott und sein Gesandter hätten die Jemeniten ja gelobt und das hätten sie nicht getan, wenn diese unaufrichtig oder Heuchler in ihrer Religion gewesen wären. Es ist, schließt das Gericht, "als wenn der Autor nicht wüsste, dass was im Koran steht Wahrheit ist, die keinerlei Diskussion erlaubt"[38]. Dieser Strang der Argumentation dient dazu, ihm Unglauben in Bezug auf Koran und Sunna und damit Apostasie vorzuwerfen. An diesen Strang der Argumentation knüpft sich der Vorwurf, der Autor behandle Offenbarungsaussagen als Mythen und

---

32 *ʿAwdī*, Al-tuhma, op. cit., S. 138.
33 op. cit., S. 17, 73.
34 *ʿAwdī*, Al-Milaff, op. cit., S. 27.
35 op. cit., S. 29-30.
36 *ʿAwdī*, Al-tuhma, op. cit., S. 17.
37 *ʿAwdī*, Al-Milaff, op. cit., S. 29.
38 op. cit., S. 28.

strafe damit die islamische Offenbarung Lügen[39]. Darauf antwortet der Soziologe mit einer ausführlichen Darstellung seines Mythosbegriffs.

Ein dritter Strang betrifft ʿAwdīs Vorstellungen von den kulturellen Entwicklungshindernissen im Jemen, unter denen er die Polygynie, die Verstümmelungsstrafen, die Sklaverei und die Auspeitschung derjenigen, die illegale sexuelle Beziehungen haben, benennt. Das Gericht zählt diese Stellungnahme zu den "höchst bedauerlichen Dingen" (*ašyāʾ mubkiyya*), auf die es im Detail nicht eingehen könne.[40]

Es ist offensichtlich, dass es sich in diesem Verfahren um einen Konflikt zwischen unterschiedlichen Konzeptionen von historischen Analysen und Methoden handelt, in dem es darum geht, ob die Autorität der Offenbarung auch für die wissenschaftliche Forschung und Lehre und die Veröffentlichung von deren Resultaten gilt. Dieser Konflikt soll durch ein Todesurteil, dem der Angeklagte nur durch den Widerruf seiner veröffentlichten Meinungen entgehen kann, die Beschlagnahme seiner Bücher und Veröffentlichungen und ein Verbot für Professor ʿAwdī, im Jemen zu lehren, zu Lasten des Wissenschaftlers entschieden werden. Die Einsetzung einer gelehrten Kommission soll die für dieses Urteil notwendige Legitimation liefern.

Der Oberste Gerichtshof des Jemen hat in seiner Sitzung vom 7. Mai 1992 das von der ersten Instanz am 2. Februar 1986 ausgesprochene Apostasie-Urteil gegen Professor Ḥamūd al-ʿAwdī mit der folgenden knappen Begründung aufgehoben:

> "Nach Prüfung des Urteils und des in der Akte des Falls enthaltenen Anfechtungen und Expertisen hat die Kammer für militärische und strafrechtliche Fragen den Angeklagten von der Anklage der Apostasie freigesprochen. Der Angeklagte hat sich von Beginn an in seinen Aussagen bei der Staatsanwaltschaft von der Apostasie distanziert und erklärt, dass er am Islam festhalte und auf ihn stolz sei."[41]

---

[39] *ʿAwdī*, Al-tuhma, op. cit., S. 32-33.

[40] *ʿAwdī*, Al-Milaff, op. cit., S. 30.

[41] *Mallat, C.*, "Three recent decisions of the Yemeni Supreme Court", *Islamic Law and Society*, vol. 2 n°1 (March 1995), pp. 71-91, see in particular pp. 75, 87-90; the Arabic text of the judgment p. 90, an English translation p. 75.

Professor ʿAwdī ist in den Jemen zurückgekehrt und lehrt wieder an der Universität Sanaa.

Der Fall des Naṣr Ḥāmid Abū Zayd, Professor für Islamwissenschaft und arabische Literatur an der Universität Kairo, ist von mehreren Kollegen, insbesondere von Kilian Bälz, ausführlich behandelt worden[42]. Ich stütze mich in meinen Ausführungen, vor allem was die prozessrechtliche Seite angeht, auf diese Arbeiten. Im Gegensatz zum Sudan und dem Jemen hat die Apostasie in Ägypten keine strafrechtlichen Konsequenzen. Die Geltung der hanafitischen Doktrin als Rechtsquelle, die bei Gesetzeslücken zu nutzen ist, ist durch das Gesetz N° 78/1931 auf das Familien-, Ehe und Erbrecht beschränkt[43]. Die seit 1929 angekündigte Gesetzgebung zur Apostasie ist nie eingeführt worden, was den Richtern einen weiten Spielraum bei der Ausfüllung dieser Gesetzeslücke gibt, den sie bis in die 90er Jahre mit Zurückhaltung genutzt haben. Nach der Abschaffung der religiösen Gerichte und der Übertragung ihrer Kompetenzen auf die Zivilgerichtsbarkeit im Jahre 1955 ist die Entscheidung darüber, was Apostasie in letzter Instanz ist, in die Hände des Kassationsgerichtshofs gegeben, der bis in die 90er Jahre Apostasie-Verfahren wegen neuer Interpretation von Recht und Religion des Islam nicht zugelassen hat. Zum ersten Mal qualifiziert das Kassationsgericht im Verfahren gegen Professor Abū Zayd die Re-Interpretation der islamischen Offenbarung und des islamischen Rechts durch einen muslimischen Intellektuellen als Apostasie.[44]

Wie im Fall des jemenitischen Soziologieprofessors, so sind es auch im Fall von Professor Abū Zayd *ḥisba*-Zeugen, die im Jahre 1993 den Prozess einleiten. Es handelt sich um eine Gruppe von Rechtsanwälten, die Abū Zayd zum Apostaten erklären und vom Gericht die Auflösung der Ehe des Professors mit seiner muslimischen Frau verlangen. Das angerufene Gericht weigert sich am 27. Januar 1994, den Fall anzunehmen, weil das ägyptische Recht die Institution der *ḥisba*-Zeugen nicht kenne. Die Rechtsanwälte gehen in die Berufung, und am 14. Juni 1995 erklärt das Berufungsgericht Kairo den Professor zum Apostaten

---

42 *Bälz, K.*, "Submitting Faith to Judicial Scrutiny through the Family Trial: The Abû Zayd Case", *Die Welt des Islams*, XXXVII,2 (1997), S. 134-155.

43 *Marsūm bi–qānūn raqam 78 li–sanat 1931 muštamil ʿalā lāʾiḥat tartīb al–maḥākim al–šarʿiyya wa l–iğrāʾāt al–mutaʿalliqa bihā, mādda 280, Al–Waqāʾiʿ al–miṣriyya, n° 53 "ġayr ʿādiyy"*, 20. Mai 1931, hier zitiert aus *M. Raššād ʿAbd al–Wahhāb u. Ḥilmī ʿAbd al-Aẓīm Ḥasan (Hrsg.)*, Al–Aḥwāl al–šaḫṣiyya li l–muslimīn ṭibqan liʾaḥdaṯ al–taʿdīlāt, Kairo, 1984, S. 52. Siehe dazu auch *Menhofer, B.*, Religiöses Recht und internationales Privatrecht dargestellt am Beispiel Ägypten, Heidelberg: C. Winter, 1995, S. 59 und ibid. S. 56-57 zur Entwicklung der Zuständigkeit der *šarīʿa*-Gerichte.

44 *Bälz*, The Abû Zayd Case, op. cit., S. 140, 143-145.

und befiehlt, seine Ehe zu trennen. Der Kassationsgerichtshof bestätigt diese Entscheidung am 5. August 1996. Das Ehepaar verlässt Ägypten im selben Jahr. Professor Abū Zayd lehrt seither an der Universität Leiden. Die Ausführung des Urteils wird - aufgrund der Reaktion des Gesetzgebers – suspendiert.[45]

Das Argument, mit dem das angerufene Gericht die Klage abwies, war offensichtlich nicht tragfähig. Zwar war die vor 1955 genutzte gesetzliche Grundlage für das Ablegen von *ḥisba*-Zeugnissen anlässlich der Vereinheitlichung der ägyptischen Justiz im Jahre 1955 entfallen[46], aber der Kassationsgerichtshof hatte schon am 30. März 1966 entschieden, dass der Paragraph 6 des Gesetzes 462/1955 in Vereinigung mit dem Paragraphen 280 des Gesetzes 78/1931 eine ausreichende Grundlage für die Zulassung von *ḥisba*-Zeugen biete. Er verlange ja, dass die Richter beim Vorliegen von Gesetzeslücken auf die herrschende Doktrin der hanafitischen Schule als Gesetzesquelle zurückgreifen. Allerdings beschränkt der Kassationsgerichtshof die Anwendung dieser Regel auf Fälle, in denen sich Muslime fremden Religionsgemeinschaften anschließen oder muslimische Frauen nicht-muslimische Männer ehelichen. Diese Entscheidung des Kassationsgerichts vom 30. März 1966 schafft die prozessrechtlichen Bedingungen für Apostasie-Prozesse[47]. Zehn Jahre später hat der Vorläufer des 1979 gegründeten Höchsten Verfassungsgerichts Ägyptens (*al-maḥkama al-dustūriyya al-ʿulyā*), das 1969 ins Leben gerufene und bis 1979 wirkende Höchste Gericht (*al-maḥkama al-ʿulyā*)[48], in einem Urteil vom Juli 1976 den Paragraphen 280 des Gesetzes n° 78/1931 als verfassungsgemäß bestätigt und damit die verfassungsrechtliche Grundlage für die Anwendung dieses Paragraphen in Apostasieprozessen geschaffen. Unter Berufung auf dieses Urteil verwirft das Kassationsgericht die Argumente, die Abū Zayd und seine Ehefrau gegen den konstitutionellen Charakter dieses Paragraphen in ihrem Kassationsbegehren vorbringen.[49]

---

[45] op. cit., S. 135-136.

[46] Das Gesetz 462/1955 hatte die Bestimmungen der Paragraphen 88, 89 und 110 des Gesetzes 78/1931 annulliert. Die Akzeptanz von *ḥisba*-Zeugen hatte sich bis 1955 auf diese Paragraphen gestützt. Zur Annullierung siehe *ʿAbd al-Wahhāb u. ʿAbd al-ʿAẓīm Ḥasan*, Al-Aḥwāl al-šaḫṣiyya, op. cit., S. 47 und 49.

[47] *Bälz*, The Abû Zayd Case, op. cit., S. 140; idem, "Eheauflösung aufgrund von Apostasie durch Popularklage: der Fall Abū Zayd", IPRax, 1996.

[48] *Brown*, The rule of law, op. cit., S. 91-92, 94-95, 102.

[49] Klage N° 10, Jahr 5 der Verfassungsjustiz, veröffentlicht im *Bulletin officiel* (*ǧarīda rasmiyya*) am 29.7. 1976. Der Urteilstext im Bulletin officiel war mir nicht zugänglich. Ich stütze meine Aussagen über den Inhalt des Urteils auf den Text des Urteils des Kassationsgerichts vom 5. August 1996 gegen die Kassationsbegehren des Ehepaars Abû Zayd und der Staatsanwaltschaft (Kassationsgericht, Zivil-, Handels- und

In der ersten Hälfte der 90er Jahre leiten *ḥisba*-Zeugen in Kairo eine wahre Flut von Verfahren gegen Intellektuelle, Künstler und Gelehrte ein, deren Bücher und Bilder als Beweis ihrer Apostasie angesehen werden. Unterschiedliche Schätzungen sprechen für diese Zeit von 80 bis 200 vor den Gerichten anhängiger Apostasie-Verfahren. Das Verfahren gegen Abū Zayd ist das am besten dokumentierte. Das Berufungsgericht Kairo, das den Professor verurteilt, sieht die Schwierigkeit, das verfassungsmäßig geschützte Recht auf Religionsfreiheit mit einem Apostasie-Verfahren gegen Intellektuelle zu vereinbaren. Es löst diese Schwierigkeit, indem es Apostasie als ein objektives und materielles Faktum behandelt und es vom Glauben des Betroffenen trennt. Nur Apostasie sei der Überprüfung durch ein Gericht zugänglich, nicht der Glaube. Ich zitiere das Gericht:

> "Apostasie ist ein Angriff auf die islamische Ordnung [...] und ihre wichtigsten Grundlagen durch sichtbare, materielle Handlungen. Im positiven Recht kommen der Angriff auf die Staatsordnung oder der Hochverrat ihr nahe. Die Bestrafung des Angriffs auf den Islam durch Apostasie widerspricht nicht der Freiheit im persönlichen Leben. Die Freiheit des Glaubens verlangt, dass die Person gläubig ist in Wort und Tat und dass sie in ihrem Angriff auf das Glaubenssystem einer zuverlässigen Logik folge. Aber ein Angriff auf den Islam resultiert immer aus einer Korruption des Denkens oder aus der Tatsache, dass der Angreifende seinen materiellen, sexuellen oder anderen weltlichen Begierden folgt. In dieser Weise Krieg zu führen, heißt nicht für die Glaubensfreiheit kämpfen. Und gegen dergleichen Krieg zu führen ist nicht ein Kampf gegen die Glaubensfreiheit, sondern eher ein Schutz des Glaubens gegen diese frivolen und korrupten Ideen."[50]

Hätte Abū Zaid, so führt das Gericht aus, seine Gedanken für sich behalten, so wäre er nicht wegen Apostasie verurteilt worden. Sie aber in die Universitätslehre einzuführen und sie zu drucken, setzt ihn der Bestrafung durch das Gericht aus. Wie im Fall von Muḥammad Maḥmud Ṭāhā und Ḥamūd al-ʿAwdī handelt es sich also um einen Prozess gegen Bücher und Veröffentlichungen. Abū Zayd wird in dem gesamten Verfahren nicht einmal gehört. Wie im Fall des jemenitischen Professors, so wird auch im Fall des Abū Zayd eine Zitatensammlung erstellt, die dann mit den Anschauungen des

---

Personalstatuskammer zu den Kassationsanträgen n°s 475, 478 und 481 des Jahres 65 [der Kassationsgerichtsbarkeit] in Personalstatusangelegenheiten, S. 7-9).

50 Urteil des Berufungsgerichts Kairo vom 14. Juni 1995 in Sachen Berufungsklage (Personalstatut) N° 287 des Jahres 111 [der Gerichtsbarkeit Kairo], S. 5-6.

Gerichts von den notwendigen Glaubenssätzen des Islam verglichen wird. Aus diesem Vergleich ergibt sich die Apostasie des Professors.[51]

Abū Zayd interpretiert die koranischen Verse über Gottes Thron, Gottes Königtum, *ǧinn*, Teufel und magische Praktiken als metaphorische und mythische Aussagen. Das Gericht sieht das als Beweis für seinen Abfall vom Glauben an. Abū Zayd vertritt die Meinung, dass jede neue Generation von Muslimen das Recht habe, den Koran im Lichte ihrer eigenen historischen Erfahrung neu zu interpretieren. Er folgt dem gleichen Ansatz, wenn er ausführt, dass die koranischen Normen als Indikatoren der Richtung verstanden werden müssen, die Gott den Gläubigen zeigen will. Das Recht der Frauen, von ihren Ehemännern und Verwandten zu erben, sei vom Koran in Abwendung von vorherigen arabischen Praktiken verkündet worden. Diese Abwendung konsequent fortzusetzen bedeute, dass heute die Muslime auf die Gleichheit von Männern und Frauen im Erbrecht und in anderen Bereichen hinarbeiten müssten. Er wendet die gleiche Interpretation auf die Aussagen des Koran zur Sklaverei an: der Koran habe die Situation der Sklaven verbessert, also sei es Aufgabe der Muslime, auf diesem Wege fortzufahren und die Sklaverei ganz abzuschaffen. Alle diese Forderungen erscheinen sowohl dem Berufungsgericht Kairo als auch dem Kassationsgerichtshof als Formen des Abfalls vom Glauben. Beide Gerichte verlangen striktes Festhalten am wörtlichen Verständnis der koranischen Verse; sie betonen, dass Gott im Koran immer schon die besten Lösungen festgelegt habe und dass daher Abū Zayds Behauptung, man könne bessere Regeln finden, nicht mit dem Islam vereinbar seien. Für den Kassationsgerichtshof hat der Koran einen objektiven und essentiellen Sinn (*mafhūm mawḍūʿī*), der sich nie ändert. Jeder Versuch, das zu leugnen, sei Unglaube. Diesen Sinn zu verteidigen ist Aufgabe des Gerichts. Deswegen muss es nicht den Glauben von Individuen untersuchen, sondern die Verbreitung falscher und zerstörerischer Ideen verhindern. Es muss daher Bücher und Kunstwerke verbieten, um die Öffentlichkeit vor den Folgen von Apostasie zu schützen. Die Religionsfreiheit deckt also nicht die Interpretation der Offenbarung und ihrer Normen im Lichte moderner Theorien oder veränderter gesellschaftlicher Verhältnisse. Kilian Bälz hat zu Recht betont, dass diese Argumentation die Religionsfreiheit auf das *forum internum* der Individuen reduziere, ihr aber keinen öffentlichen Raum zuweise und keine gesellschaftliche Wirksamkeit gestatte.[52]

---

[51] Zu den weiteren Ausführungen zum Fall Abû Zayd siehe *Johansen, B.*, "Apostasy as objective and depersonalized fact: two recent Egyptian Court Judgments", in *Social Research*, vol. 70, n°3 (fall 2003), S. 687-710.

[52] *Bälz*, The Abû Zayd Case, op. cit., S. 150.

Die prozedurale Zulassung von *ḥisba*-Zeugnissen im Verein mit der Doktrin des Kassationsgerichtshofs vom objektiven, essentiellen und unveränderlichen Sinn des Islam und den Aktivitäten islamistischer Aktivisten bei der Zusammenstellung von *ḥisba*-Dossiers missliebiger Intellektueller hätte eine ständige Vergrößerung der Zahl von Apostasie-Verfahren und ein Ende der öffentlichen Diskussion über neue Interpretationen des Islam erwarten lassen. Der Gesetzgeber hat aber durch seine Intervention neue Bedingungen für solche Debatten geschaffen. Im Januar 1996 hat das Parlament ein Gesetz (3/1996) erlassen, das dem Staatsanwalt die Kontrolle über die Zulassung von *ḥisba*-Zeugnissen gibt. Wichtiger ist das Gesetz (81/1996) vom Mai 1996 das allen Personen verbietet, Fälle vor Gericht zu bringen, an denen sie kein unmittelbares persönliches Interesse nachweisen können und das so das Prozess- und Beweisrecht nachhaltig ändert. Das Gesetz kam zu spät, um Abū Zayd zu helfen. Der Kassationsgerichtshof hat es in seiner Entscheidung nicht berücksichtigt. Aber auf der Grundlage dieses Gesetzes hat im September 1996 ein Kairiner Gericht beschlossen, die Exekution des vom Berufungsgericht Kairo gesprochenen und vom Kassationsgericht bestätigten Urteils zu suspendieren, weil keiner der *ḥisba*-Zeugen, die den Prozess eingeleitet hatten, ein persönliches Interesse an der Ausführung des Urteils nachweisen könne. Für öffentliche Debatten über die Interpretation des Islam ist damit wieder etwas mehr Raum geschaffen worden als nach den Urteilen des Berufungsgerichts und des Kassationsgerichts gegen Abū Zayd zu erwarten war.

V. Schlussbetrachtungen

Apostasie und Angriff auf den Staat erscheinen durchgehend in den drei hier vorgestellten Prozessen als ein von den Gerichten konstruiertes einheitliches Delikt. Diese Denkform hat eine lange Tradition: sie versteht die politische Obrigkeit als Schutz und Garantie der Religion und die Religion als wichtigste Legitimierung der politischen Ordnung. Sie setzt daher eine Einheit von Staat und Religion voraus, die sich weder mit der Religionsfreiheit noch mit der Meinungsfreiheit verträgt. Um sie mit der Religionsfreiheit kompatibel zu machen, müssen die ägyptischen Gerichte eine private Glaubens- von einer öffentlichen Apostasiesphäre trennen und die Glaubensfreiheit auf die erste beschränken.

In keinem der drei hier vorgestellten Apostasiefälle gab es ein Gesetz, das Regelungen für Apostasieprozesse enthielt. Im Sudan und in Ägypten mussten die Richter sich auf die *šarīʿa* als eine Form des Naturrechts beziehen, die beim Schweigen des Gesetzgebers dessen Platz einnimmt. Im Sudan war dem Richter zwar das Recht beim Schweigen des Gesetzes *ḥadd*-Strafen zu verhängen, im § 458, Abs. 3 StGB ausdrücklich gegeben, aber kein Gesetz regelte Prozessrecht und materielles Recht der Apostasie. In Ägypten formulierte der Kassationsgerichtshof die Regel, dass die Richter davon auszugehen hätten, dass der Gesetzgeber nicht wichtige *šarīʿa*-Normen aufgeben wolle[53]. Im Jemen konnte die Staatsanwaltschaft sich auf einen vorliegenden Entwurf zu einem StGB berufen.[54]

Damit stellt sich die Frage nach dem Verhältnis von *šarīʿa* und positivem Recht in den drei hier untersuchten Staaten. Ist die *šarīʿa* nur anzuwendendes Recht, wo das positive Recht schweigt? Oder ist das positive Recht nur Recht, wo es mit der *šarīʿa* kompatibel ist? Diese letztere Lösung schlagen die sudanesischen Interpretationsregeln[55] des *Judgments Act* von 1983 vor[56]. Auch der ägyptische SCC formuliert diese Position im Blick auf die unveränderlichen Normen der *šarīʿa*, lässt aber dem Gesetzgeber und dem Verfassungsrichter freie Hand in den Bereichen veränderbarer Normen[57]. Es ist offensichtlich, dass schon der erste Ansatz den Richtern einen erheblichen Spielraum für Rechtsetzung lässt. Wo der zweite Ansatz generalisiert wird, wie im Sudan, macht der Richter dem Gesetzgeber praktisch den Rang streitig: eine Folge, die in Ägypten der SCC durch sein Urteil im Azhar-Prozess vermieden hat, ein Urteil, das in die gleiche Periode fällt, wie die hier vorgestellten sudanesischen und jemenitischen Apostasie-Prozesse.

Das Verhältnis von Richter und Gesetzgeber hängt davon ab, wie man die *šarīʿa* begreift: als ein System von Normen, das jeder Richter sofort anwenden kann, und das ihm erlaubt, die Rechtmäßigkeit der Gesetze festzustellen? Das wäre eine Möglichkeit, die sich aus dem zweiten Ansatz ergeben könnte. Die Azhar hat in ihrem Musterprozess von 1978 den Artikel 2 der ägyptischen Verfassung so auslegen wollen. Der SCC hat dem nicht zugestimmt, sondern die Interpretation der *šarīʿa* im Lichte des Artikels 2 der Verf. ausdrücklich nur dem Gesetzgeber und dem Verfassungsgericht vorbehalten. Nur im Bereich der unveränderlichen Normen sieht er Gesetzgeber und Verfassungsgericht als reine Vollzugsorgane. Ansonsten seien die Gesetze gültig, auch wenn sie den

---

53 Urteil des Kassationsgerichtshofs vom 5. August 1996, S. 9.

54 *ʿAwdī*, Al-Milaff, op. cit., S. 19.

55 *Layish u. Warburg*, Sudan under Numayrī, op. cit., S. 101-104.

56 op. cit., S. 77-78.

57 *Johansen, B.*, "The relationship between the constitution, the *sharī'a* and the *fiqh* in the adjudication of Egypt's Supreme Constitutional Court", Vortrag gehalten am Max-Planck-Institut für ausländisches öffentliches Recht und Völkerrecht in Heidelberg, am 20.2.2004.

veränderlichen Regeln der šarīʿa widersprächen. Der Gesetzgeber hat daher die Möglichkeit, verändernd zu intervenieren und der Verfassungsgerichtshof hat in einer Reihe wichtiger Urteile solchen verändernden Interventionen zugestimmt[58]. Es ist von grundlegender Bedeutung für den Unterschied zwischen den drei hier behandelten Ländern, dass Ägypten die Apostasie nur im Bereich des Erbrechts und des Eherechts, aber nicht im Strafrecht kennt. Das positive Recht in Verbindung mit der ständigen Rechtsprechung des Ägyptischen Verfassungsgerichts zum Artikel 2 der Verfassung, die die Gesetzgebung vor 1980 nicht für verfassungswidrig erklärt, wenn sie mit den Prinzipien der *šarīʿa* nicht vereinbar ist, setzt hier also der Versuchung, intellektuelle und religiöse Konflikte unter Berufung auf eine Lücke im Strafgesetzbuch durch Todesurteile zu entscheiden nicht zu übersteigende Grenzen. Der Versuch des ägyptischen Parlaments im Jahre 1982, diese Grenzen zu überschreiten, ist am Widerstand des Präsidenten gescheitert[59]. Diese Ausgangsposition hat wesentlich dazu beigetragen, dass der Gesetzgeber im Jahre 1996 durch die Intervention in der Frage der Klageberechtigung der *ḥisba*-Zeugen die Apostasieklagen als politisches Instrument weitgehend wirkungslos machen konnte.

Im Sudan hat zwar das Höchste Gericht 1986 das Urteil gegen Ṭāhā aufgehoben und der Gesetzgeber hat im gleichen Jahr in den *Judgments Act* von 1983 einen Paragraphen eingefügt, der bestimmt, dass Interpretationen des Islam künftig nicht mehr als Apostasie verurteilt werden dürfen[60]. Im Paragraphen 126 des neuen Strafgesetzbuchs von 1991, der die Apostasie-Strafe regelt, ist eine solche Ausnahme nicht explizit enthalten. Der Paragraph liegt mir leider nur auf Englisch vor. Er enthält im ersten Abschnitt die folgende Tatbestandsdefinition:

> "There shall be deemed to commit the offence of apostasy, every Muslim who propagates for the renunciation of the creed of Islam or publicly declares his renouncement thereof by an express statement or conclusive act."[61]

---

58 *Johansen, B.*, "Supra-Legislative Norms and Constitutional Courts: the case of France and Egypt", in: Eugene Cotran and Adel Omar Sherif, *The Role of the Judiciary in the Protection of Human Rights,* London-The Hague-Boston: Kluwer Law International, 1997, S. 347-376, siehe insbesondere S. 370-372.

59 S.o. Fn. 4.

60 *Layish u. Warburg*, Sudan under Numayrî, op. cit., S. 179.

61 Den Text dieses Paragraphen hat mir freundlicherweise Dr. Silvia Tellenbach zugänglich gemacht.

Auch das jemenitische StGB von 1994 enthält jetzt im Artikel 259 einen Paragraphen, der die Apostasie definiert und ihre Rechtswirkung festlegt. Dort heißt es:

> "Jeder, der von der Religion des Islam abfällt, wird mit dem Tode bestraft, nachdem man ihn vorher dreimal aufgefordert hat, zu widerrufen und ihm eine Frist von dreißig Tagen gesetzt hat. Als Apostasie gelten vorsätzlich vorgenommene öffentliche Aussagen oder Taten oder das Beharren auf solchen Aussagen und Taten, die mit den grundlegenden Normen des Islam und seinen essentiellen Bestandteilen (*arkān*) unvereinbar sind. Wenn Vorsatz oder Beharren nicht festgestellt werden und der Verbrecher seine tätige Reue erklärt, so wird er nicht bestraft."[62]

Im Sudan und im Jemen ist die Todesstrafe für Apostasie heute also nicht mehr eine Norm, die aus der Sunna und den juristischen Lehrmeinungen des *fiqh* abzuleiten ist, sondern Teil des vom Gesetzgeber kodifizierten Strafrechts. Das heißt nicht notwendig Minderung des Einflusses der *šarīʿa*-Normen, aber es schränkt den Handlungsspielraum der Richter gegenüber dem Gesetzgeber ein. Es ist also zu verstehen als ein Schritt zur Realisierung jenes Programms, das der führende Theoretiker der sudanesischen *Muslim-Brüder*, Hasan al-Turabi, mit der Formel umschrieben hat, dass der "revolutionäre *iǧtihād* " der modernen muslimischen Juristen und Politiker der Einführung des *šarīʿa-Staats* zu dienen habe. Im *šarīʿa-Staat* sei die *šarīʿa* vom Gesetzgeber in kodifiziertes Recht überführt. Damit würden die Vielfalt unkontrollierter Meinungen, die Konflikte zwischen verschiedenen Doktrinen und die gefährlichen Neuerungen, die notwendig mit einem Juristenrecht verbunden seien, durch die staatliche Gesetzgebung unter Führung eines Präsidenten oder Imams unter Mitwirkung der Juristen gebannt. Eine einheitliche Doktrin muslimischer Normativität, die für alle gleichermaßen verbindlich sei, könne so effektiv das intellektuelle und soziale Leben kontrollieren und leiten[63]. Die Todesstrafe für Apostasie scheint ein wichtiger Bestandteil dieses Programms zu werden.

---

62 *Al–ǧarīda al–rasmiyya* n° 19/1994, Teil 3, S. 1-118: *qarār ǧumhūrī bi l–qānūn raqam 12 li–sanat 1994 bi–šaʾn al–ǧarāʾim wa l–ʿuqūbāt, mādda 259.*

63 *Layish u. Warburg*, Sudan under Numayrî, op. cit., S. 85-87.

ZUR STRAFRECHTSPFLEGE
IN DER ISLAMISCHEN REPUBLIK IRAN*

Dr. Silvia Tellenbach, Freiburg

An dem Tag, an dem ich den endgültigen Titel für diesen Vortrag festzulegen hatte, war die Meldung durch die Nachrichten gekommen, dass der iranische Präsident Khatami mit seinem Rücktritt gedroht habe. Es waren überdies die Tage um den Jahrestag der Studentenunruhen von 1999, und die Atmosphäre war gespannt. So schien es auch mir geraten, für diesen Vortrag einen Titel zu wählen, der alle Optionen offen ließ, wenn nötig auf aktuelle Geschehnisse einzugehen. Darum bin ich Ihnen heute als erstes schuldig, vorab etwas genauer zu sagen, um was es im heutigen Vortrag gehen wird. Ich werde auf das Strafensystem im Islam eingehen, einige Anmerkungen zu dem machen, was im real existierenden Islam in der Islamischen Republik Iran daraus geworden ist, und ferner die Strafgerichtsbarkeit für Jugendliche behandeln.

Todesstrafe, Steinigung, Verstümmelungs- und Auspeitschungsstrafen werden immer wieder genannt, wenn internationale Organisationen und Menschenrechtsorganisationen im Zusammenhang mit der Menschenrechtswidrigkeit grausamer Strafen von islamischen Strafen sprechen. Unbemerkt bleibt, dass die wohl grausamste aller im islamischen Strafrecht vorgesehenen Strafen ungenannt bleibt, nämlich die Kreuzigung. Die Kreuzigung ist noch heute im iranischen Strafgesetzbuch ausdrücklich vorgesehen und zwar im Falle des Kampfes gegen Gott und des Verderbenstiftens auf Erden. Das iranische Strafgesetzbuch beschreibt sogar genau, wie sie zu vollstrecken ist (Art. 195): der Verurteilte ist lebend ans Kreuz zu binden und zwar so, dass er nicht schon durch die Art des Bindens stirbt. Dann hat er drei Tage dort hängen zu bleiben. Stirbt er im Lauf dieser drei Tage, so darf man ihn abnehmen; ist er am Ende der drei Tage noch am Leben, so wird ihm das Leben geschenkt. Und doch haben diese Organisationen bis zu einem gewissen Maße recht, wenn sie die Kreuzigung nicht nennen. Es ist nämlich in den nunmehr fast 25 Jahren des Bestehens der Islamischen Republik Iran noch kein einziger Fall einer Anwendung bekannt geworden. Bei einer Strafe, die zu dem Kernbereich der von Gott gegebenen und damit nicht abschaffbaren *ḥadd*-Delikte gehören, fragt man sich, wie es dazu kommt, denn die einschlägigen Straftatbestände an sich, Art. 193-196, werden in der Islamischen Republik Iran sehr wohl und nicht einmal selten angewendet. Für Iran findet sich die Lösung darin, dass das Strafgesetzbuch eine Minderheitsmeinung bei den Schiiten aufgegriffen hat, die

* Die Vortragsform wurde beibehalten, der Text leicht überarbeitet und um Anmerkungen ergänzt.

bei den Sunniten nur von der malekitischen Rechtsschule geteilt wird. Diese gibt zwar dem Richter vier Tatmodalitäten und vier mögliche Strafen an die Hand, Hinrichtung, Kreuzigung, Abhacken von Hand und Fuß und Verbannung, überlässt es aber dem Richter, welche Strafe er für welche Tatmodalität verhängt. Das bedeutet, dass der iranische Richter die Kreuzigung umgehen kann und das auch tut. Aber auch die anderen Staaten mit islamischen Strafgesetzen, in denen die Kreuzigung vorgesehen ist, Sudan[1] und Jemen,[2] sowie Saudiarabien, wo das islamische Strafrecht nicht kodifiziert ist, wenden sie extrem selten an. Über viele Jahre hinweg lassen sich im Sudan zwei Kreuzigungen im Jahr 1990 nachweisen,[3] in Saudiarabien ebenfalls ein Fall 1990 und ein Fall im Jahr 2000. Dabei ist noch festzuhalten, dass in diesen Ländern die Kreuzigung *nach* der Hinrichtung stattfindet, also im Gegensatz zu der Regelung, die in Iran vorgesehen ist, nicht eine Tötungsart, sondern das entwürdigende Zurschaustellen eines Toten ist. - Andere Staaten, die islamisches Strafrecht wieder eingeführt haben, haben von der Aufnahme der Kreuzigungsstrafe ins Gesetz von vornherein stillschweigend abgesehen, nicht nur Libyen, das hier sowieso einen Sonderfall darstellt, sondern auch Pakistan und Mauretanien. Man redet darüber nicht, man lässt sie einfach unter den Tisch fallen. Ein Kollege hat vor langen Jahren und in ganz anderen Zusammenhängen einen Aufsatz über das Schweigen des Gesetzgebers als Mittel der Rechtsfortbildung geschrieben.[4] Man könnte sich beinahe fragen, unter welchen Umständen es letztlich auch hier zu einer Rechtsfortbildung durch Schweigen kommen könnte.

Noch in einem anderen Bereich sind grausame Strafen auch in Staaten, welche die Geltung des islamischen Strafrechts postulieren, ausgestorben. Fügt jemand einem anderen vorsätzlich eine Körperverletzung zu, so ist an sich das Opfer berechtigt, dem Täter eine gleichartige Körperverletzung zuzufügen, also ihm gegebenenfalls die Hand abhacken zu lassen, ihn zu blenden oder ähnliches. Aber wo man in der islamischen Welt hinsieht, gibt es zwar Fälle, wo eine

---

1 Art. 64 StGB v. 1983, Art. 168 StGB v. 1991.

2 Art. 307 StGB v. 1994.

3 *Köndgen, O.*, Das islamisierte Strafrecht des Sudan – Von seiner Einführung 1983 bis Juli 1992, Hamburg 1992, 77, und *amnesty international*, Jahresbericht 1991, 417. Amnesty international, Jahresbericht 1985, 122, berichtet überdies von einer Verurteilung zu Kreuzigung, die nicht vollstreckt werden konnte, da die „entsprechenden Vorrichtungen nicht zur Verfügung standen."

4 *Dilger, K.*, Das Schweigen des Gesetzgebers als Mittel der Rechtsfortbildung im Bereich des islamischen Rechts, in: Die islamische Welt zwischen Mittelalter und Neuzeit – Festschrift für Hans Robert Roemer zum 65. Geburtstag, Hrsg. Ulrich Haarmann/Peter Bachmann, Beirut 1979, 81-93.

Opfersippe darauf besteht, den Mörder des eigenen Familienmitglieds hinrichten zu lassen, fast nirgends aber finden wir noch Fälle, dass das Opfer einer Körperverletzung dem Täter ein Gleiches zufügt. Aus Saudiarabien wird aus den letzten Jahren ein Fall einer Blendung berichtet, ferner ein Fall, bei welchem dem Täter, der dem Opfer zwei Zähne eingeschlagen hatte, zwei Zähne gezogen wurden – durch einen Zahnarzt.[5] Als vor einigen Jahren in Iran tatsächlich ein Opfer darauf bestand, den Täter, der ihm das Augenlicht geraubt hatte, gleichfalls blenden zu lassen, fand er im ganzen Land keinen Augenarzt, der bereit gewesen wäre, diese Strafe zu vollstrecken.

Steinigungen waren wegen der hohen Beweisanforderungen zwar immer selten, kamen aber in den Staaten mit islamischem Strafrecht noch vor, auch in der Islamischen Republik Iran. Aber wenn Iran im Rahmen des EU-Iran-Menschenrechtsdialogs Ende 2002 offiziell versprochen hat, von Steinigungsstrafen abzusehen und das Oberhaupt der Justiz eine Direktive an die Richterschaft erteilt haben soll, in derartigen Fällen Gefängnisstrafen und sonstige Strafen zu verhängen,[6] so fragt man sich dennoch, wie sich eine solche Zusage mit dem islamischen Recht verträgt, selbst wenn Stimmen mehr Gewicht gewinnen sollten, die darauf verweisen, dass ja die Steinigung wegen Ehebruchs keineswegs im Koran unabänderlich festgelegt ist.[7] – Kommt ein Ehebruch vor Gericht und sind alle Beweisanforderungen – Geständnis, Zeugenaussagen oder – nicht unumstritten – das Wissen des Richters – erfüllt, so hat der Richter keine andere Wahl und muss zur Steinigung verurteilen. Es bleibt hier systemgerecht eigentlich nur ein einziger Weg, den die iranische Strafprozessordnung von 1999 schon eingeschlagen hat, nämlich eine Einschränkung der Zulässigkeit, in derartigen Sachen überhaupt zu ermitteln.[8] Diese könnte noch stärker werden, auf gesetzlichem Wege oder auch über eine Interpretation der Rechtsprechung. Dass es zu einer Änderung des Strafgesetzbuchs kommt, wie es die weiblichen Abgeordneten des iranischen Parlaments in einem gemeinsamen Gesetzesvorschlag erreichen wollen,[9] dürfte kaum durchsetzbar sein.

Hervorgehoben werden muss hier aber, dass es im Bereich des Ehebruchs oder auch nur des Verdachts in diese Richtung Vorfälle gibt, die in der Praxis ein weitaus größeres Gewicht haben als die Steinigungsstrafen für Ehebruch, so

---

5 Amnesty international, Jahresbericht 2001, 478 und Jahresbericht 2003, 488.

6 Vgl. dazu http://www.state.gov/g/drl/rls/hrrpt/2002/18276.htm, abgerufen am 4.10.2003.

7 Vgl. dazu näher EI (2), s.v."zinā"(R. Peters).

8 Vgl. gesetzliche Erläuterung zu Art. 43 StPO: Ermittlungen in Sittlichkeitsdelikten sind verboten, außer wenn diese in flagranti geschehen oder ein Privatkläger vorhanden ist. Im letzteren Fall werden sie durch den Richter geführt.

9 Vgl. dazu http://www.state.gov/g/drl/rls/hrrpt/2002/18276.htm, abgerufen am 4.10.2003.

aufsehenerregend die einzelnen Fälle auch sein mögen. Die Strafrechtsreform von 1996 fügte eine Vorschrift wieder ins Gesetz ein, die in ähnlicher Form bereits in der Schahzeit bestanden hatte, aber mit den Gesetzen von 1982/1983 verschwunden war. Art. 630 StGB besagt nämlich, dass ein Mann, der seine Frau beim Ehebruch ertappt, sie und ihren Geliebten straffrei töten bzw. verletzen kann.[10] Wird die Frau vergewaltigt, so darf er den Vergewaltiger töten. Zynisch gesprochen macht diese Vorschrift eigentlich die Ehebruchsvorschrift des islamischen Rechts überflüssig. Und noch etwas muss in diesem Zusammenhang bedacht werden. Besonders bei den arabischen Minderheiten im Südwesten Irans kommt es nicht selten zu Ehrenmorden an Frauen, die in irgendeiner Weise die Ehre ihrer Familie verletzt haben. Sie müssen dabei keineswegs einen Ehebruch begangen haben, jegliches tatsächliche oder auch nur vermeintliche Verhalten, das den Moralkodex im Umgang mit dem anderen Geschlecht verletzt, kann dem zugrunde liegen, mit der Folge, dass die eigene Familie die Tochter oder Schwester tötet – Vorgänge, die nur selten in den Bereich der staatlichen Gerichtsbarkeit kommen, die man aber ebenso wenig wie ähnliche Geschehnisse in Jordanien[11] oder in der Türkei[12] ohne Weiteres, wie es bei uns häufig geschieht, auf das Konto des Islams schreiben kann.

Die Todesstrafe wird in Iran vergleichsweise häufig verhängt, aber auch vollstreckt. In den Statistiken von amnesty international gehört Iran zu den Staaten, die zusammen mit China, Saudiarabien und USA in der Spitzengruppe lagen, was die Häufigkeit angeht.[13] Der ehemalige Sonderbeauftragte der UNO für die Menschenrechtssituation in Iran nannte in seinem Bericht die Zahl von etwa 200 Hinrichtungen im Jahr 2000, deren Vollstreckung bekannt geworden ist,[14] von mindestens 113 wird für das Jahr 2002 ausgegangen,[15] aber man wird

---

10 Vgl. dazu eingehend *Hāšimī, 'Abd al-Ǧabbār*, Qatl dar maqām-i difā' az nāmūs, Magisterarbeit an der Teheran-Universität 1378.

11 *Tellenbach, S.*, Ehrenmorde an Frauen in der arabischen Welt – Anmerkungen zu Jordanien und anderen Ländern, wuquf 13 (2003), 74-89.

12 *Tellenbach, S.*, Zur Ehre im türkischen Strafrecht, in: Akten des 27. Deutschen Orientalistentages (Bonn 28.September bis 2. Oktober 1998): Norm und Abweichung, Hrsg. Stefan Wild und Hartmut Schild, Würzburg, 2001, 473-479.

13 Laut amnesty international erfolgten 90% der amnesty bekannt gewordenen Hinrichtungen 2001 in diesen vier Ländern. Für 2002 sollen 81% der amnesty bekannt gewordenen Hinrichtungen in China, Iran und den USA stattgefunden haben. http://www2.amnesty.de/internet/ai-theme.nsf/db2320ec1f478ab641256737002 (abgerufen am 24.3.2004).

14 Report on the situation of human rights in the Islamic Republic of Iran, prepared by the Special Representative of the Commission on Human Rights, Mr. Maurice Danby Copithorne, pursuant to Commission resolution 200/28, E/CN.4/2001/39, 16 January 2001.

hier noch mit einer erheblichen Dunkelziffer rechnen müssen. Bis Herbst 2003 war grundsätzlich eine Hinrichtung durch Erhängen im Morgengrauen im Gefängnis vorgesehen, und nur mit ausdrücklicher richterlicher Anordnung war eine andere Form zugelassen.[16] Dennoch wurde sie häufig öffentlich vollstreckt, Schätzungen sprechen von ca. zwei Dritteln aller Hinrichtungen,[17] und es werden immer wieder Medienberichte, ja auch Bilder davon veröffentlicht, auch wenn das Bild einer Frau im Tschador am Galgen ein Extremfall ist.[18] Eine neue Verordnung lässt in erster Linie den Richter über die Hinrichtungsart entscheiden.[19]- Das iranische Strafgesetzbuch, aber auch weitere Gesetze, enthalten eine große Anzahl von Delikten, die mit der Todesstrafe bedroht sind, vor allem im Rauschgiftbereich,[20] Verderbenstiften auf Erden und Kampf gegen Gott (Art. 183ff StGB), Beleidigung des Propheten (Art. 513 StGB) und andere mehr. Bei dem Tatbestand aber, der in westlichen Strafgesetzen als der schwerste gilt, bei der vorsätzlichen Tötung eines Menschen, liegt die Sache komplizierter. Die Opfersippe kann zwar die Hinrichtung des Täters verlangen, kann aber auch darauf verzichten und ein Blutgeld fordern oder selbst darauf verzichten. Verzichtet die Opfersippe aber auf die Vergeltungsstrafe und begnügt sich mit dem Blutgeld, so kann das staatliche Gericht den Täter bestrafen, wenn die Tat die öffentliche Ordnung oder Schutz und Sicherheit der Gesellschaft tangiert oder die Gefahr besteht, dass der Täter oder ein anderer eine entsprechende Tat wiederholt (Art. 612). Aber diese Strafe nun besteht keineswegs aus der Todesstrafe, sondern aus einer Gefängnisstrafe von drei bis zu zehn Jahren, einer Strafe also, die nach unseren Maßstäben für eine vorsätzliche Tötung sehr milde ist. - Der Widerstand gegen jegliche Diskussion über die Abschaffung der Todesstrafe mag mit dadurch verstärkt werden, dass der Islam den Tod durch die Todesstrafe als ein durch Gott bestimmtes Ende des Lebens ansieht wie andere Arten des Sterbens auch. Das schließt aber nicht aus, dass die Todesstrafe als Strafe für einzelne Delikte durch andere Strafen ersetzt wird.

---

15 Amnesty international Jahresbericht 2003, 255.

16 Art. 10, 13, Ā'innāma-yi naḥwa-yi iğrā-yi aḥkām-i iʾdām, rağm, ṣalb, qaṭʾ yā naqṣ-i ʾuḍw-i mauḍūʾ-i tabṣira-yi yak-i mādda-yi 28 qānūn-i taškīl-i dādgāhhā-yi kaifarī-yi yak wa-du v. 15.2.1370.

17 Vgl. http://www.state.gov/g/drl/rls/hrrpt/2002/18276.htm, abgerufen am 4.10.2003.

18 http://www.peacelink.nu/KVINNER/iran_woman_execution_2001, abgerufen am 24.3.2004.

19 Ā'innāma-yi naḥwa-yi iğrā-yi aḥkām -i qiṣāṣ, rağm, qatl, ṣalb, iʾdām wa-šallāq v. 5. 7. 1382.

20 Art. 2, 4- 6, 8, 9 und 11 Qānūn-i mubāraza bā muḫaddirāt v. 3.8.1367 i.d.F. v. 17.8.1376.

Die letzte Strafe, die sich im islamischen Kernstrafrecht findet, ist die Auspeitschung, nämlich als Strafe für einen Geschlechtsverkehr außerhalb einer Ehe – der mit Steinigung bedrohte Ehebruch ist also modern gesprochen kein Grundtatbestand, sondern eine Qualifikation des Grundtatbestands außerehelicher Geschlechtsverkehr –, für die Verleumdung des Inhalts, einen außerehelichen Geschlechtsverkehr begangen zu haben, und schließlich die Strafe für das Weintrinken. Darüber hinaus wurde aber nach der Islamischen Revolution noch bei einer ganzen Reihe weiterer Tatbestände die Auspeitschungsstrafe eingeführt. Dabei ist zu bedenken, dass diese Strafe ja durchaus nicht nur einen islamischen Hintergrund hat. Sie war auch anderwärts üblich und in Europa beim Militär bis weit ins 19. Jahrhundert hinein gängig. In Iran wurde sie erst im 20. Jahrhundert abgeschafft,[21] lag also durchaus nicht so weit in mittelalterlichen Zeiten zurück, wie man sich das bei uns bisweilen fälschlicherweise vorstellt. In den Augen ihrer Befürworter hat die Auspeitschung insbesondere gegenüber der Gefängnisstrafe viele Vorteile: Sie kostet den Staat kein Geld für Strafvollzugseinrichtungen, sie belässt den Täter in seinem Lebenskreis, er behält seine Arbeitsmöglichkeit und kann seine Familie weiter ernähren. Dennoch ist auffallend, dass die Strafrechtsänderungen von 1996 die Auspeitschungsstrafe, die im *ta'zīr*-Gesetz von 1983 aufgenommen worden war, in zahlreichen Tatbeständen wieder gestrichen oder ihr zumindest Freiheitsstrafe und Geldstrafe als wahlweise Strafmöglichkeit zur Seite gestellt hat.[22] Außerdem erlaubt Art. 22 StGB bei *ta'zīr*-Strafen und abhaltenden[23] Strafen in einem weiten Ausmaß die Umwandlung der gesetzlich vorgesehenen Strafen in andere Strafen, sobald der Richter Milderungsgründe sieht und andere Strafen für geeigneter hält. Der Richter hat also heute weite Möglichkeiten, der Auspeitschungsstrafe aus dem Wege zu gehen. Amnesty international spricht in seinem Bericht 2003 von mindestens 84 Auspeitschungen im Jahr 2002, weist aber darauf hin, dass die tatsächliche Zahl noch weit höher liegen könnte.[24] Dennoch ist die Zahl der Auspeitschungen im

---

21 Qānūn-i laġw-i muǧāzāt-i šallāq v. 6. Tīr 1344 (=27.6.1965).

22 *Tellenbach, S.*, Neues zum iranischen Strafrecht, ZAR 18 (1998), 38-42.

23 Die abhaltenden Strafen (muǧāzāt-i bāzdāranda) wurden 1991 noch als weiterer Straftyp neben *ḥadd-*, *qiṣāṣ-* und *ta'zīr*-Strafen in das iranische Strafgesetzbuch aufgenommen. In Art. 17 StGB sind sie folgendermaßen beschrieben: Die abhaltende Strafe ist eine Züchtigung bzw. Strafe, die von der Obrigkeit zur Wahrung der Ordnung unter Berücksichtigung des Interesses der Gesellschaft für Verstöße gegen staatliche Bestimmungen und Vorschriften festgelegt wird, wie z.B. Gefängnisstrafen, Geldstrafe, Betriebsschließung, Entzug von Erlaubnissen und Aberkennung von bürgerlichen Ehrenrechten, Verbot oder Verpflichtung, sich an einem bzw. mehreren Orten aufzuhalten, und dergleichen.

24 Amnesty international Jahresbericht 2003, Frankfurt 2003, 255.

Verhältnis zu den Anfangsjahren der Islamischen Republik deutlich zurückgegangen.

Die zahlenmäßig wichtigsten Strafen sind auch heute noch in der Islamischen Republik Iran die Freiheitsstrafen und die Geldstrafen. Nicht umsonst hat ein weit verbreitetes iranisches Lehrbuch über Vermögensdelikte nicht etwa eine abgehackte Hand, sondern das berühmte Bild von van Gogh „Rundgang der Häftlinge im Gefängnishof“ als Deckelbild.[25] Freiheitsstrafen sind in Gefängnissen zu verbüßen, die in offenen, halboffenen und geschlossenen Vollzug unterteilt sind.[26] Ein Bericht des schon genannten UNO-Sonderbeauftragten Copithorne von 1996 schildert die Zustände in dem bekannten Evin-Gefängnis als nicht menschenrechtswidrig.[27] Ob das für alle Gefängnisse gilt oder auf einige Vorzeigegefängnisse beschränkt ist, sei hier dahin gestellt. Heute lässt sich jedenfalls feststellen, dass die Gefängnisse seit einigen Jahren völlig überfüllt sind; man rechnet mit ca. 180.000 Gefangenen bei ca. 65.000 Haftplätzen,[28] sie haben also fast das Dreifache an Häftlingen, das sie nach den ausgelegten Kapazitäten fassen könnten.

Etwa 70% aller Häftlinge sollen im Zusammenhang mit Drogendelikten einsitzen.[29] An zweiter Stelle liegen Scheckfälschungsdelikte, was auf die wirtschaftlichen Probleme des Landes hinweist. Alle anderen Delikte stellen zusammen nur noch eine Minderheit von Häftlingen. Ein Bericht der Working Group on Arbitrary Detention der Vereinten Nationen über einen Besuch in iranischen Gefängnissen 2003 moniert u.a., dass die Länge der verhängten Haftzeiten nicht nur von Gericht zu Gericht recht unterschiedlich sei und diese

---

25 *Ṣādiqī, Ḥusain Mīr Muḥammad*, Ǧarā'im ʾ alaih-i amwāl wa-mālikīyat, Teheran 1376.

26 Ā'in-nāma-yi iǧrā'ī-yi sāzamān-i zandānhā wa-iqdāmāt-i ta'mīnī-o-tarbiyatī-yi kišwar dar iǧrā-yi madda-yi 9 qānūn-i tabdīl-i šūrā-yi sarparastī-yi zandānhā wa-iqdāmāt-i ta'mīnī-o-tarbiyatī-yi kišwar ba- sāzamān-i zandānhā wa-iqdāmāt-i ta'mīnī-o-tarbiyatī-yi kišwar v. 6.11.1364 i.d.F. v. 26.4.1380. In den halboffenen oder offenen Vollzug werden Verurteilte eingewiesen, die Fahrlässigkeitstaten oder leichte Vorsatztaten begangen haben oder die zwar schwerere Taten begangen haben, aber bereits einen Teil ihrer Strafe im geschlossenen Vollzug verbüßt haben.

27 Report on the situation of human rights in the Islamic Republic of Iran, prepared by the Special Representative of the Commission on Human Rights, Mr. Maurice Copithorne (Canada), pursuant to Commission resolution 1995/68 of 8 March 1995 and Economic and Social Council decision 1995/279 of 25 July 1995, E/CN.4/1996/59, 21 March 1996.

28 So die Angaben von Penal Reform International, vgl. http://www.penalreform.org/english/region_middle%20.htm, abgerufen am 27.2. 2004.

29 Penal Reform International a.a.O.

vor allem oft in keinem Verhältnis zur Schwere der Straftat stünden.[30] - Da es keine Höchstdauer bei der Untersuchungshaft gibt, kann es sein, dass auch Untersuchungshäftlinge jahrelang im Gefängnis sitzen. Auch Verhandlungen zwischen einem Täter und einer Opfersippe, ob wegen einer Tötung eine Hinrichtung erfolgen oder ein Blutgeld gezahlt werden soll, können sich lange hinziehen. Mir ist der Fall eines Mannes unvergesslich, den ich in einem iranischen Gefängnis erlebte, der bereits neun Jahre einsaß, weil die Verhandlungen mit der Opfersippe noch immer nicht zu einem Ergebnis geführt hatten.

Eine Freiheitsstrafe kann, wie im Übrigen auch eine Geldstrafe bei *ta'zīr*-Strafen und abhaltenden Strafen, für zwei bis fünf Jahre zur Bewährung ausgesetzt werden, wenn der Verurteilte noch nicht mit einer *ḥadd*- oder *qiṣāṣ*-Strafe, einer Freiheitsstrafe von über einem Jahr oder einer Geldstrafe von über zwei Millionen Rial rechtskräftig vorbestraft ist, noch nicht wegen mindestens zwei vorsätzlichen Straftaten, unabhängig vom Strafmaß verurteilt wurde und das Gericht unter Würdigung aller Umstände der Tat und der Persönlichkeit und Lebensführung des Täters eine Verbüßung der Strafe ganz oder teilweise nicht für angemessen hält (Art. 25 StGB). Ausgeschlossen von dieser Möglichkeit sind Verurteilungen wegen der meisten Rauschgiftdelikte, wegen Unterschlagung, Bestechung, Betrugs, Dokumentenfälschung und Gebrauchs gefälschter Dokumente, Veruntreuung, Diebstahls, der unter die *ta'zīr*-Delikte fällt, oder Menschenraubs, ferner wegen Beihilfe zu *ḥadd*-Delikten (Art. 30). Die Strafaussetzung zur Bewährung kann mit Weisungen verbunden werden, z.B. sich in klinische Behandlung zu begeben, eine bestimmte Tätigkeit oder Arbeit zu meiden oder umgekehrt eine Ausbildung aufzunehmen (Art. 29)

Hat ein erstmalig Verurteilter die Hälfte der im Urteil vorgesehenen Strafe verbüßt, so kann er bedingt entlassen werden, wenn er sich während der Strafverbüßung gut geführt hat, erwarten lässt, dass er nicht wieder straffällig wird und einen Schaden entweder schon wieder gut gemacht hat oder zumindest mit Zustimmung des Staatsanwalts einen Zahlungsplan aufgestellt hat (Art. 38 StGB). Das Gericht setzt eine Frist zwischen einem und fünf Jahren fest; hat sich der Verurteilte in dieser Zeit straffrei geführt, so ist die Reststrafe erledigt.

Schließlich bestehen bei *ta'zīr*-Strafen und abhaltenden Strafen die Möglichkeit von Begnadigung und Amnestie. Verurteilte und ihre Angehörigen können einen

---

30 Civil and Political Rights, Including the Question of Torture and Detention – Report of the Working Group on Arbitrary Detention. Addendum: Visit to the Islamic Republic of Iran (15-27 February 2003), (E/CN.4/2004/3/Add.2 27 June 2003), Nr. 58.

entsprechenden Antrag bei der Kommission für Amnestie und Begnadigung der Provinz stellen, die ihn nach Bearbeitung an eine zentrale Kommission weiterleitet, die ihn ihrerseits über das Oberhaupt der Justiz dem religiösen Führer zur Entscheidung zuleitet; Amnestien werden zu einer großen Anzahl religiöser Festtage gewährt, z.B. zum Ende des Ramadan, zum Opferfest, zum Geburtstag des Propheten Muhammad, zum Geburtstag Alis und Hosseins, aber auch zum Jahrestag der Islamischen Revolution und zur Gründung der Republik.[31] Bei Amnestien und Begnadigungen sind u.a. gesellschaftliche und politische Bedürfnisse und Interessen, aber auch die Besserung des Verurteilten, sein Vorleben, seine Situation und die Situation seiner Familie maßgebliche Gesichtspunkte. Insbesondere sind bei einer Amnestie Personen zu berücksichtigen, die wegen der Unfähigkeit, eine Geldstrafe zu zahlen, ins Gefängnis gekommen sind. Ausgeschlossen sind Amnestie und Begnadigung bei Spionage, Bestechlichkeit, Vergewaltigung, Geiselnahme, bewaffnetem Diebstahl und dort, wo es um menschliche Interessen geht, insbesondere bei vorsätzlicher Tötung.[32]

Bei den Vermögensstrafen sind zwei Grundtypen zu unterscheiden, einmal das Blutgeld für Tötungs- und Körperverletzungsdelikte und zum anderen Geldstrafen für alle nichtreligiösen Delikte. Für das Blutgeld gibt es zwar gewisse Vorgaben, z.B. dass das Blutgeld für einen Nichtmuslim[33] oder für eine Frau nur die Hälfte des Blutgelds für einen Mann beträgt. Letztlich ist es jedoch zwischen den Parteien in hohem Maße verhandelbar, und das mag heute die Einführung einer ganz neuen Konfliktlösungsstrategie, nämlich der Mediation erleichtern. Sie trifft in Iran derzeit auf großes Interesse. Art. 189 des Gesetzes über das 3. Programm zur wirtschaftlichen, gesellschaftlichen und kulturellen Entwicklung der Islamischen Republik Iran schuf im Jahr 1381 die gesetzliche Grundlage für die Einsetzung zahlreicher Konfliktlösungsräte (*šūrāhā-yi ḥall-i*

---

[31] Art. 8 Ā'in-nāma-yi kumīsyūn-i ʾafw- wa-baḫšūdagī v. 19.3.1373.

[32] Art. 9 Ā'in-nāma-yi kumīsyūn-i ʾafw- wa-baḫšūdagī v. 19.3.1373.

[33] Eine Gerichtsentscheidung von 2002 erkannte zwar einen gleichen Blutgeldanspruch für Muslime und Nichtmuslime an (vgl. *Goldouzian, I.*, L'arrêt récent de la cour d'appel iranienne modifiant la jurisprudence discriminatoire entre les musulmans et les minorités religieuses à propos de l'indemnisation de la victime dans l'infractions contre l'intégrité corporelle, Revue pénitentiaire et de droit penal 2003, 256ff.) und der einzige jüdische Abgeordnete im iranischen Parlament brachte im August 2002 einen Gesetzesentwurf ein, das Blutgeld für Muslime und Nichtmuslime gleichzustellen. Dieser Antrag dürfte jedoch spätestens beim Wächterrat scheitern. Vgl. dazu Human Rights Watch World Report 2003, http://www.hrw.org/wr2k3/mideast3.html, abgerufen am 10.7.2003.

iḫtilāf) [34] Dahinter steckt die Einführung der Mediation für den Bereich der Bagatellstrafen. Das ist gewissermaßen als Probelauf gedacht, mit der Überlegung, den Bereich der Straftaten, die auf diesem Wege gelöst werden sollen, auszuweiten. Die bisherigen Erfahrungen scheinen befriedigend zu sein. Jedenfalls ist bereits ein umfassendes Gesetz über Mediation in Arbeit. Die Überlegung ist, dass es bereits eine erhebliche Entlastung der Justiz bedeuten würde, wenn man auch nur 20% der Verfahren auf diese Weise erledigen könnte.

Geldstrafen greifen nur dort, wo auch Geld vorhanden ist, und das ist in einem Land, in dem viele Bürger in einer wirtschaftlich prekären Situation leben, häufig zu wenig der Fall, als dass Geldstrafen eine erhebliche Wirkung entfalten könnten. Moderne Formen von Strafen, die z.B. in Richtung community service gehen, fehlen bisher, wobei freilich im Einzelnen zu prüfen wäre, welche Arbeitsleistungen bei den wirtschaftlichen und gesellschaftlichen Umständen sinnvollerweise verhängt werden können.

Ein weiterer Weg zu Strafmilderungen ist dem Richter durch den Art. 22 StGB eröffnet. Dieser schafft für den Richter bei allen *ta'zīr*-Strafen und abhaltenden Strafen die Möglichkeit, bei Vorliegen mildernder Umstände Strafen herabzusetzen oder in andere geeigneter erscheinende Strafen umzuwandeln, die der Lage des Angeklagten angemessener sind. Zwar sind im Gesetz eine Reihe solcher Milderungsgründe aufgezählt und die Anwendung im Urteil auch zu begründen, aber ein Strafmilderungsgrund, der z.B. aus „besonderen Umständen in der Person oder dem Vorleben des Angeklagten" resultiert, kann ja sehr weit interpretiert werden. Man kann ruhig überspitzt formulieren, wenn das Gericht eine bestimmte hohe Strafe nicht verhängen will, dann findet es eben den dazu passenden Strafmilderungsgrund. Dass die Gerichte das so handhaben, wird vielleicht bei einem Delikt deutlich, an das man gerade im Zusammenhang mit Strafmilderungsgründen nicht sofort denkt, nämlich Rauschgiftdelikte. Die Rauschgiftdelikte sind in Iran außerordentlich häufig, man rechnete nach offiziellen Quellen im September 2002, dass 3% einer Bevölkerung von fast 70 Millionen rauschgiftsüchtig seien oder Rauschgift konsumierten, also ca. zwei Millionen und das mit steigender Tendenz.[35] Das ist eine Folge der Nachbarschaft zu Afghanistan, dem seit Jahren größten Rauschgiftproduzenten

---

34 *Abbāsī, M.*, Ufuqhā-yi nuwin-i ʾadālat-tarmīmī - Miyānǧīgirī-yi kaifarī, Teheran 1382, 306,

35 http://www.ind.homeoffice.gov.uk/default.asp?/Pageld=525, Nr. 6.202. Vgl. zur Drogenproblematik in Iran auch den Bericht des Sonderbeauftragten Copithorne vom 16. Januar 2001, Nr. 128-134.

der Welt, das Iran mit Rauschgift überschwemmt. Daher hat Iran eine außerordentlich harte Rauschgiftgesetzgebung; bereits der Besitz von wenigen Gramm Heroin, aber auch relativ mäßigen Mengen von Opium ist mit der Todesstrafe bedroht.[36] Wenn alle die Rauschgifthändler, deren Rauschgiftbesitz diese Mengen überschreiten, tatsächlich zum Tode verurteilt und hingerichtet würden, dann müsste die Zahl der Hinrichtungen in Iran noch weit höher liegen, als es tatsächlich der Fall ist.

Im Folgenden sei noch auf ein Problem mit einem Rechtsgebiet eingegangen werden, das in der Islamischen Republik Iran bisher recht unbefriedigend gelöst ist, nämlich die Jugendstrafrechtspflege. In der Schahzeit gab es eine Jugendgerichtsbarkeit; die Jugendlichen wurden mit 18 Jahren voll strafmündig, nachdem sie ab zwölf Jahren eingeschränkt strafrechtlich verantwortlich waren und ab sechs bis zu zwölf Jahren gegen sie Erziehungsmaßnahmen verhängt werden konnten.[37] Nach der Islamischen Revolution wurde das alles abgeschafft. Das ğa'faritisch islamische Recht knüpfte für die Strafmündigkeit an die physische Reife an (Art. 49 StGB), und diese wurde bei Jungen mit 15 Jahren, bei Mädchen dagegen schon mit neun Jahren angesetzt, und zwar nach Mondjahren, die bekanntlich zehn Tage kürzer sind als Sonnenjahre. Das wurde geltendes Recht in der Islamischen Republik Iran, die damit nicht nur ein extrem frühes Alter für die volle Strafmündigkeit hat, sondern zudem wohl auch als einziges Land ein unterschiedliches Strafmündigkeitsalter für Mädchen und Jungen, das noch dazu so weit auseinander liegt. Überdies gibt es auch nicht mehr ein stufenweises Hineinwachsen in die Strafmündigkeit, wie es international üblich ist.[38] Noch das Gesetz über die Bildung der Gerichte I und II und der Senate des Obersten Gerichtshofs von 1368/1989 erwähnt Jugendgerichte nicht, wenn dann auch tatsächlich im Wege der Geschäftsverteilung eine Kammer des Teheraner Gerichts II Jugendstrafsachen behandelte und als Jugendstrafkammer bezeichnet wurde. Art. 8 der Durchführungsverordnung zum Gesetz über die Bildung von Allgemeinen und Revolutionsgerichten von 1373/1994 erwähnte erstmals wieder Jugendliche, indem vorgesehen wurde, dass bei einem Gericht bestimmten Richtern bzw. Kammern bestimmte Aufgabengebiete wie Kinder besonders zugewiesen werden könnten. Erst die Strafprozessordnung von 1378/1999 enthält dann wieder einen Abschnitt Jugendgerichtsbarkeit (Art. 219 ff. Strafprozessordnung), der vor allem vorsieht, dass nicht nur Kinder, sondern Jugendliche bis

---

36 Vgl. oben S. 49.

37 Vgl. Qānūn-i marbūṭ ba taškīl-i dādgāh-i aṭfāl-i bizihkār v. 10.9.1338.

38 Vgl. *Nadjafi*, *Ali-Hossein*, Les Mineurs Délinquants en Droit Iranien, Revue Pénitentiaire 2003, Nr. 1, 209-217(212).

zu 18 Jahren (Art. 220 Erl.1) von einer Jugendkammer abzuurteilen sind,[39] die nach bestimmte Verfahrensgrundsätzen vorzugehen hat. Diese beziehen sich vornehmlich darauf, dass die gesetzlichen Vertreter des Kindes bzw. Jugendlichen beigezogen werden (Art. 220), die Ermittlungshandlungen sorgsamer und schonender geführt werden (Art. 221ff) und die Verhandlung nichtöffentlich ist (Art. 225), ja sogar, wenn es das Interesse des Kindes/Jugendlichen erfordert, teilweise oder in Sonderfällen sogar ganz in seiner Abwesenheit geführt werden können (Art. 226f). Was die Sanktionen betrifft, so sieht Art. 49 StGB vor, dass Kinder, die eine Straftat begangen haben, unter der Aufsicht des Gerichts einem Vormund oder notwendigenfalls einem Heim zur Besserung und Erziehung von Kindern zu übergeben sind. Aus dem Satz „Wenn für die Erziehung eines Kindes, das eine Straftat begangen hat, eine körperliche Ermahnung notwendig ist, so hat diese maßvoll und interessengemäß (*ba mīzān wa-maṣlaḥat*) zu erfolgen“[40] ergibt sich, dass das Gericht z.B. auch eine Prügelstrafe verhängen kann. Nirgends äußert sich das Gesetz aber zu etwaigen reduzierten Strafen oder zu andersartigen speziellen Sanktionen für Jugendliche. Der wichtigste gesetzliche Ansatzpunkt, den der Richter hier nutzen kann, ist wiederum Art. 22 StGB, wo er das jugendliche Alter eines Täters als eine „besondere Situation“ (Nr. 5) geltend machen kann, die es ermöglicht, Strafen zu mildern. Hilfreich ist auch, dass der Richter ein Gutachten über den psychologischen Zustand des Jugendlichen und sein soziales Umfeld einholen kann, was ihm gegebenenfalls die Begründung einer anderen als der primär im Gesetz vorgesehenen Strafe erleichtert.[41] Iranische Richter ziehen in diesem Zusammenhang zunehmend Art. 17 heran, der die abhaltenden Strafen definiert. Dass hier die einzelnen Strafen nur beispielhaft aufgeführt werden, machen sie sich zunutze, um im Gesetz nicht ausdrücklich vorgesehene, für Jugendliche geeignete Strafen als abhaltende Strafen zu verhängen, treffen hierbei aber nicht immer auf die Zustimmung der Richter in der nächsten Instanz, die darin einen Verstoß gegen das Gesetzlichkeitsprinzip sehen.[42]

Iran hat das UN-Abkommen zum Schutze von Kindern unterschrieben, wenn auch mit dem Schari‘a-Vorbehalt.[43] Das würde aber nicht hindern, dass in einem

---

39 In den meisten Gerichtsbezirken sind diese Kammern mittlerweile gebildet, *Nadjafi* a.a.O. 214.

40 *Nadjafi* weist a.a.O. 213 daraufhin, dass diese Bestimmung sehr problematisch ist, weil sie weder angibt, was genau unter körperlicher Ermahnung zu verstehen ist und dadurch gegen den Bestimmtheitsgrundsatz verstößt, noch erklärt, wessen Interesse dabei zu berücksichtigen ist (des Jugendlichen? Seiner Eltern? Des Tatopfers? Der Gesellschaft?)

41 Siehe auch *Nadjafi*, a.a.O. 215.

42 *Nadjafi* a.a.O. 216.

43 http://www.unhchr.ch/html/menu2/6/treaties/status-crc.htm, abgerufen am 4.10.2003.

weiten Bereich der iranischen Gesetzgebung und Rechtsprechung ein differenziertes Jugendstrafrecht, vor allem mit höheren Altersgrenzen, entwickelt würde. Das ist umso wichtiger, als die iranische Bevölkerung eine sehr junge Bevölkerung ist – von den ca. 66 Millionen Iranern wurden über 30 Millionen erst nach der Islamischen Revolution geboren. Eine Reform der Jugendgerichtsbarkeit würde daher auch für einen weit größeren Anteil der Bevölkerung Bedeutung haben, als etwa das Jugendstrafrecht in einem mitteleuropäischen Staat. Derzeit hat der Oberste Rat der Justiz, der auch für die Ausarbeitung von Gesetzesentwürfen zuständig ist, den Entwurf eines Jugendgerichtsgesetzes erarbeitet und dem Parlament zugeleitet, und es ist hochinteressant, wie dieser Entwurf jetzt versucht, die unabänderlichen Vorschriften der Schari'a in einer Weise in einen Zusammenhang mit Vorschriften einzubetten, dass sie einem modernen Jugendstrafrecht nicht im Wege stehen. Zunächst nennt sich der Text „Entwurf eines Gesetzes über eine Gerichtsbarkeit bei Kindern und Jugendlichen". Diese Nebeneinanderstellung hält er den ganzen Text konsequent durch, und lässt dadurch manchmal offen, ob es um Kinder oder um Jugendliche geht. Dann erklärt er ganz brav und linientreu – schließlich soll er ja den Wächterrat passieren – Kinder seien nicht strafrechtlich verantwortlich und ein Kind (*ṭifl*) sei eine Person, die die Grenze der Mündigkeit (*bulūġ*) noch nicht erreicht hätte. Damit haben wir wieder den Verweis auf das schiitische Konzept der Strafmündigkeit bei Mädchen mit neun und bei Knaben ab 15 Jahren. Dann sieht das Gesetz vor, dass alle Verfahren gegen Kinder und Jugendliche ab neun bis zu 18 Jahren vor Jugendgerichten zu führen sind, die aus einem Richter und zwei beratenden Beisitzern bestehen sollen, wobei ausdrücklich auch Frauen Beisitzer sein können. Es gibt dann eine Reihe von Verfahrensbesonderheiten für Jugendliche, die ihren Schutz betreffen, z.B. was Verteidiger oder Öffentlichkeit des Verfahrens angeht. Schließlich folgen die Strafvorschriften. Hier wird in Altersgruppen von 9-12, von über 12 bis 15 und von über 15 bis zu 18 Jahren abgestuft. Die Jüngsten von 9-12 werden ihren Erziehungsberechtigten übergeben, die zu bestimmten Maßnahmen verpflichtet werden, bei der zweiten Gruppe wird neben Erziehungsmaßnahmen schon ein Tadel des Richters, aber bei schwereren Delikten auch schon die Möglichkeit einer Einweisung in eine Besserungseinrichtung (Jugendgefängnis) bis zu einem Jahr vorgesehen, bei den 15-18jährigen werden die Strafen noch schärfer; hier sind nach Schwere des Delikts bis zu 8 Jahren Jugendstrafe möglich.

Aber noch steht im Raum, dass ja nach der Schari'a ein Mädchen mit neun und ein Junge mit 15 Jahren strafmündig ist, das ist zumindest für die religiösrechtlich festgelegten *ḥadd*-Delikte und *qiṣāṣ*-Delikte noch nicht aus der Welt. Und was sieht der Entwurf vor? Er erklärt, dass bei Vorliegen dieser

Delikte besonders geklärt werden *muss*, ob das Kind tatsächlich schon die sexuelle und geistige Reife erreicht hat, und zwar ist diese Klärung durch ein ärztliches Gutachten oder jedes andere geeignete Mittel zu treffen. Der Richter könnte also drei Nachbarn vorladen, die erklären, dass der jugendliche Angeklagte zwar schon 16 Jahre alt sei, aber von Reife könne bei ihm noch keine Rede sein. Damit wäre der Richter des Problems enthoben. Er könnte erklären, dass er die Überzeugung gewonnen habe, dass Jugendliche noch nicht die Reife im Sinne des Gesetzes besitze, und dann wäre er in der Lage, die geringeren und flexibleren *ta'zīr*- Strafen und abhaltenden Strafen anzuwenden. Dieser Weg wird wohl auch heute schon häufig versucht, aber erst durch eine Festlegung in einem Gesetz in der geschilderten Form würde er einen wirklichen Durchbruch bedeuten.

DAS IRANISCHE FAMILIENRECHT UND SEINE ANWENDUNG IM TEHERANER FAMILIENGERICHT [1]

Dr. Nadjma Yassari, LL.M., Hamburg

1. Einführung

Mit der Verleihung des Friedensnobelpreises an die iranische Rechtsanwältin Šīrīn ᶜEbādī und der Würdigung ihres Einsatzes für die Rechte der Kinder und Frauen im Iran rückt das iranische Rechtssystem, insbesondere das Familien- und Erbrecht in das Rampenlicht der Öffentlichkeit. Und somit fällt Licht auf ein Rechtsgebiet, das die Widersprüche der iranischen Gesellschaft zwischen patriarchalischem Gewohnheitsrecht, islamischem Recht und den Ansprüchen des modernen Lebens eindrucksvoll widerspiegelt. Iranische Mädchen sind mit Vollendung ihres neunten Lebensjahres strafmündig, mit dreizehn Jahren ehemündig, aber erst mit Vollendung des fünfzehnten Lebensjahres aktiv wahlberechtigt. Jungen können mit Vollendung des fünfzehnten Lebensjahres heiraten und eine Familie gründen, sind aber erst mit vollendetem achtzehnten Lebensjahr voll geschäftsfähig. Ehefrauen haben ein Recht auf Auszahlung ihrer Brautgabe und bei Nichtbeachtung ihrer Rechte die Möglichkeit ihre Ehemänner ins Gefängnis zu schicken. Daneben können die Ehemänner den ehelichen Wohnort bestimmen und ihren Ehefrauen die Ausübung einer Erwerbstätigkeit oder eines Berufes untersagen, wenn diese Arbeit den Interessen der Familie oder der gesellschaftlichen Stellung der Frau nicht entspricht.
Im Folgenden möchte ich einen Überblick über das iranische Familienrecht und die wichtigsten Kodifikationen, Entwicklungen und Reformen geben. Dabei werde ich insbesondere auf die gesetzlichen Änderungen und die Reformbestrebungen in den letzten zehn Jahren eingehen. Am Ende des Vortrages möchte ich von meinen Erfahrungen am Teheraner Familiengericht berichten.

2. Privatrechtsgeschichte

Der Beginn der modernen iranischen Privatrechtsgeschichte ist Mitte der 20er Jahren des letzten Jahrhunderts mit der Thronbesteigung des Kosakenoffiziers Reżā Ḫān als Reżā Šāh Pahlavī im Jahre 1925 und der Kodifikation eines iranischen Zivilgesetzbuches in den Jahren 1928 und 1935 anzusetzen. Die Pahlavīs herrschten von 1925-1979. Die Zeit von 1925-1941 unter Reżā Šāh kann als Phase der Kodifikationen bezeichnet werden und die Zeit von 1941-

[1] Die Vortragsform wurde beibehalten.

1979 unter Moḥammad Reżā Šāh als die Phase der Expansion und Konsolidierung.
Die Pahlavī-Ära war im politischem Bereich von Despotismus und Absolutismus gekennzeichnet, in rechtlicher Hinsicht jedoch war sie eine sehr progressive Periode. Es ist die Zeit einer energischen und rücksichtslosen rechtlichen Modernisierung.[2] Unter Reżā Šāh beginnt eine intensive Phase der Rezeption fremden, insbesondere französischen Rechts.

2.1. Die Phase der Kodifikationen 1925-1941 unter Reżā Šāh

Reżā Šāh verfolgte vor allem zwei Ziele: die Bildung einer starken Zentralmacht, um den Iran zu modernisieren und zu kontrollieren, und die Zurückdrängung der Geistlichkeit aus Politik und Machtpositionen.[3]

2.1.1. Die gesetzlichen Maßnahmen dieser Zeit

Die gesetzgeberischen Aktivitäten, die in diese Zeit fallen, stehen ganz im Zeichen dieser Ziele. 1927 wird ein Gesetz zur Ordnung der Gerichtsbarkeit und der Gerichte erlassen. Im gleichen Jahr beruft Reżā Šāh eine Kommission bestehend aus in Europa ausgebildeten iranischen Juristen und islamischen Theologen ein, die ein iranisches Zivilgesetzbuch (ZGB) entwerfen sollen.[4] Es wird 1928 und 1935 in zwei Phasen verabschiedet.[5] Das ZGB ist das Ergebnis weitreichender rechtsvergleichender Arbeit, wobei das französische Model des Code Napoléon in Aufbau und Struktur als Vorbild diente. Es besteht aus 1335 Artikeln. Die Regelungen zum Familien- und Erbrecht beruhen weitgehend auf dem islamisch-schiitischen Recht.
1931 wurden staatliche Nachnamen eingeführt. Dieses Gesetz ebnete den Weg zur Einführung eines Grundbuchregisters im gleichen Jahr.[6] 1931 war auch ein wichtiges Jahr für die Familienrechtsgesetzgebung. Das Gesetz über die Eheschließung[7] (Ehegesetz) führte die obligatorische Erfassung und Eintragung aller Angelegenheiten des Personalstatuts, wie Eheschließungen und

---

2 Siehe zur iranischen Privatrechtsgeschichte: *Owsia, P.*, Formation of Contract, a Comparative Study under English, French, Islamic and Iranian law. London 1994, S. 25-40.

3 *Young, T.*, The problem of Westernization in Modern Iran. In: The Middle East Journal, Januar 1948, S. 54 (47-59).

4 Siehe *Amir-Soleimani, A.*, La formation et les effets des contrats en droit iranien. Teheran 1936, S. 2-11.

5 Qānūn-e madanī, das iranische Zivilgesetzbuch vom 17. Februar und 12. März 1935 sowie vom 17., 19., 20. April 1935 in der geltenden Fassung (im weiteren ZGB).

6 Qānūn-e s̱abt-e asnād va amvāl von 1931.

7 Qānūn-e rāğeᶜ be ezdevāğ vom 15. August 1931.

Scheidungen ein. Zwar konnten die Geistlichen weiterhin gültig Ehen schließen, ihre staatliche Anerkennung erlangte die Ehe aber erst mit ihrer Eintragung bei neu gegründeten staatlichen Eheschließungs- und Scheidungsbüros. Um der Einhaltung dieser Vorschrift Nachdruck zu verleihen, verfügte das Ehegesetz eine ein- bis sechsmonatige Freiheitsstrafe für denjenigen, der eine Ehe oder eine Scheidung nicht eintragen ließ.[8]

Als Begleiterscheinung seines Bestrebens, die iranische Gesellschaft zu modernisieren und der Zeit anzupassen, verbot Reżā Šāh 1936 gegen den heftigen Widerstand der Geistlichen die Verschleierung der Frau.[9] Aus der Erfahrung meiner Familie war die Generation meiner Großmutter die erste städtische Generation von Frauen, die sich nicht mehr verschleiert hat. In ländlichen Gebieten ist das Tragen des *ḥeğābs*, der islamischen Kopfbedeckung, seit jeher Tradition gewesen und diese Tradition hat sich durch die politischen Veränderungen nicht geändert. 1941 wird dieses Verbot durch Moḥammad Reżā Šāh auf Druck konservativer Kreise wieder aufgehoben, und es bleibt den Frauen bis 1980 freigestellt, wie sie sich in der Öffentlichkeit zeigen wollen.

2.1.2. Das Familienrecht im ZGB

Das Familienrecht, wie es im iranischen ZGB kodifiziert wurde, umfasst das Personenrecht, das Eherecht, d.h. die Eheschließung und die Eheauflösung (Scheidung und Annullierung der Ehe) einschließlich der Folgen wie Unterhalt und Vermögensaufteilung, das Kindschaftsrecht (einschließlich des Sorgerechts und der Abstammung) und schließlich das Vormundschaftsrecht. Weitere Bestimmungen zum Familienrecht finden sich im Gesetz zum Schutze der Familie 1975 (FSG 1975) und weiteren Nebengesetzen.[10]

2.1.3. Das System des iranisch-islamischen Familienrechts

Dem iranischen Familienrecht liegt das klassische Konzept der Familie zugrunde: Es unterliegt der Idee einer Rollenverteilung, die ein Gleichgewicht der Rechten und Pflichten der jeweiligen Parteien herstellen soll. Dies führt zu unterschiedlichen Rechten und Pflichten bei den Beteiligten eines Familienverhältnisses, und es spiegelt eine gesellschaftliche Werteordnung wider, in der der Ehemann und Vater der pater familias mit allen Rechten und Pflichten insbesondere im Außenverhältnis ist und die Ehefrau vor allem in ihrer Stellung als Mutter insbesondere im Innenverhältnis wirken soll. Dieses System

---

8 Art. 1 II EheG.

9 *Massé, H.*, Le dévoilement des Iraniennes. In: Revue des Études Islamiques, Cahiers 1935, S. 411-418.

10 Siehe *Mansūr, Ğ.*, Qavānīn va moqarrarāt-e marbūt be ẖānevāde (Gesetze und Vorschriften des Familienrechts). Teheran 2003.

hat auch seinen Niederschlag in den gesetzlichen Regelungen des ZGBs gefunden. Im Folgenden soll anhand der Regelungen zum Ehe- Sorge- und Scheidungsrecht dieses System veranschaulicht werden.

2.1.3.1. Das Eherecht

Gemäß Art. 1062 ZGB ist die Ehe ist ein zivilrechtlicher Vertrag, der durch die Willenseinigung der Verlobten zustanden kommt und ein Verhältnis begründet bei dem Mann und Frau einander zu gutem Betragen verpflichtet sind. Sie müssen sich bei der Festigung der Grundlagen der Familie und bei der Erziehung der Kinder unterstützen.[11] Dabei unterscheidet das ZGB unterschiedliche Rollen für Mann und Frau und d.h. auch unterschiedliche Rechte und Pflichten bei Ehemann und Ehefrau.

2.1.3.1.1. Die Rechte und Pflichten des Ehemannes

Die vornehmliche Pflicht des Ehemannes gegenüber seiner Ehefrau und den gemeinsamen Kindern ist die Unterhaltspflicht[12]: sie beinhaltet die Ernährung, die Wohnung, die Wohnungsausstattung und die Bekleidung. Dieser Anspruch ist unabhängig von der Bedürftigkeit der Ehefrau oder von der Tatsache, dass sie von dritter Seite Zuwendungen erhält. Der Anspruch orientiert sich an der gesellschaftlichen Stellung der Frau.[13] Zum Anspruch kann auch die Bereitstellung von Dienstpersonal gehören, sofern die Ehefrau auch im Hause ihres Vaters über Personal verfügte, oder wenn sie aufgrund von Krankheit oder Schwäche einer Hilfe bedarf.[14]

Diese vermögensrechtliche Pflicht macht den Ehemann im Gegenzug zum Haushaltsvorstand.[15] Aus dieser Position ergibt sich, dass der Ehemann den Wohnsitz der Familie bestimmen kann[16] und der Ehefrau die Ausübung einer Erwerbstätigkeit oder eines Berufes untersagen kann, wenn diese Arbeit den Interessen der Familie oder der gesellschaftlichen Stellung der Frau nicht entspricht.[17]

Die Rolle als Haushaltsvorstand führt insgesamt dazu, dass der Ehemann in Streitigkeit bezüglich des gemeinsamen Lebens das letzte Wort hat, vorausgesetzt seine Entscheidungen sind nicht bar jeder Vernunft.[18]

---

[11] Art. 1103, 1104 ZGB.
[12] Art. 1106 ZGB.
[13] *Ṣafā'ī, S.Ḥ., Emāmī, A.*, Ḥoqūq-e ẖānevāde. Teheran 2002, Bd. 1, S. 151.
[14] Art. 1107 ZGB.
[15] Art. 1105 ZGB.
[16] Art. 1004, 1114 ZGB.
[17] Art. 1117 ZGB.
[18] *Ṣafā'ī, S.Ḥ., Emāmī, A.*, Ḥoqūq-e ẖānevāde. Bd. 1, S. 138.

2.1.3.1.2. Die Rechte und Pflichten der Ehefrau

Die Ehefrau hat zunächst finanzielle Ansprüche gegen ihren Ehemann. So hat sie mit Eheschließung ein Recht auf ihre Brautgabe.[19] Obwohl sie einen Anspruch auf Unterhalt hat, ist sie weder ihrem Mann noch ihren Kindern gegenüber zu Unterhalt verpflichtet. Sie ist Eigentümerin ihres eigenen Vermögens und kann ohne Mitwirkung ihres Ehemannes frei darüber verfügen.[20] Der gesetzliche Güterstand ist der der Gütertrennung. Sie muss sich aber ihrem Ehemann, sofern dieser seinen ehelichen Pflichten nachkommt, fügen, d.h. zum Beispiel die von ihm bezeichnete Wohnung beziehen.[21]

Es ist wichtig festzuhalten, dass die meisten gesetzlichen Normen, sofern sie nicht das Wesen der Ehe berühren, dispositiv sind, und in den Eheverträgen anders lautende Regelungen möglich sind. Hier herrscht weitgehend das Prinzip der Vertragsfreiheit.

2.1.3.2. Das Sorgerecht[22]

Das ZGB unterscheidet im Bereich des Sorgerechts zwischen der Personensorge im engeren Sinne, *negahdārī* oder *ḥeżānat*,[23] und der Vermögenssorge oder der väterlichen Gewalt, *velāyat*. Das ZGB enthält keine ausdrückliche Definition der Begriffe *negahdārī* oder *ḥeżānat* und *velāyat*.

Mit *velāyat* wird das Recht bezeichnet, das das Gesetz dem Vater und dem Großvater väterlicherseits für die Verwaltung des Vermögens und der finanziellen Angelegenheiten des Kindes einräumt. Dieses Recht entsteht mit der Geburt des Kindes und bedeutet eine Handlungsmacht über das Vermögen des Kindes und die Autorität, zum Wohle des Kindes Rechtshandlungen zu setzen.[24] Der *valī* ist der gesetzliche Vertreter des Kindes[25] und zur Wahrnehmung der vermögensrechtlichen Interessen des Kindes verpflichtet. Die *velāyat* obliegt allein dem Vater oder dem Großvater (väterlicherseits), niemals jedoch der Mutter.[26]

Unter *negahdārī* oder *ḥeżānat* versteht man die Erziehung und Pflege des Kindes, die Aufsicht über das Kind, die Ordnung seiner gesellschaftlichen

---

[19] Art. 1078-1101 ZGB. Zur Brautgabe im iranischen Recht siehe *Yassari, N.*, Die Brautgabe nach iranischem Recht. In: StAZ (Das Standesamt) 7/2003, S. 198-201.

[20] Art. 1118 ZGB.

[21] *Ṣafā'ī, S.Ḥ., Emāmī, A.*, Ḥoqūq-e ẖānevāde. Bd. 1, S. 139.

[22] Das iranische Kindschaftsrecht ist geregelt in den Art. 1168-1194 ZGB.

[23] Das ZGB benutzt den persischen Begriff *negahdārī* und den arabischen Begriff *ḥeżānat* als Synonyme.

[24] *Kātūzīān, N.*, Ḥoqūq-e madanī. Teheran 1999, Bd. 2, S. 202. *Ṣafā'ī, S.Ḥ., Emāmī, A.*, Ḥoqūq-e ẖānevāde. Bd. 2, S. 162.

[25] Art. 1183 ZGB.

[26] Art. 1194, 1180 und 1181 ZGB.

Verhältnisse und die Regelung und Berücksichtigung seines Umgangs mit seinen nahen Verwandten.[27] Die Personensorge beinhaltet den körperlichen Schutz und die geistige und moralische Pflege.[28]

Im Bereich der Personensorge im engeren Sinne finden wir dieses System der Rollenverteilung wieder. Zunächst gilt grundsätzlich, dass Vater und Mutter gemeinsam zur *negahdārī*, also Sorge und Erziehung berechtigt und verpflichtet sind.[29] Das ZGB sieht jedoch eine Prioritätsregelung vor, die von der Idee ausgeht, dass Mutter und Vater in verschiedenen Altersstufen des Kindes besser geeignet sind, für es zu sorgen.

Gemäß Art. 1169 ZGB steht die Priorität zunächst der Mutter zu, und zwar bis zum vollendeten siebenten Lebensjahr ihrer Kinder. Danach trägt der Vater die Sorge für die Kinder. In den Kommentaren zum ZGB wird dies zum einen mit den Bedürfnissen des Kindes begründet, zum anderen wird ausgeführt, dass dies den biologischen Instinkten von Mutter und Vater besser entspräche.[30] Diese Regelung kommt insbesondere im Scheidungsfall zur Anwendung.[31]

2.1.3.3. Das Scheidungsrecht

Der Grundsatz aus dem islamischen Recht, wonach das Recht auf Scheidung das Vorrecht des Mannes ist, wurde im ZGB übernommen. Die Scheidung wurde somit als einseitiges Recht des Ehemannes in Art. 1133 ZGB kodifiziert: Der Mann kann, wann immer er es möchte, seine Frau verstoßen. „Wann immer er möchte" im Sinne des Art. 1133 ZGB bedeutet, dass der Ehemann ohne Angabe von Gründen seine Frau verstoßen konnte. Die Verstoßung wirkte wie eine Kündigung. Sie war lediglich an die Einhaltung von Formalitäten gebunden: sie musste im Beisein zweier Zeugen ausgesprochen und ernst gemeint sein, und sie bedurfte seit 1931 zu ihrer staatlichen Wirksamkeit der Eintragung in den staatlichen Eheschließungs- und Ehescheidungsbüros.

Wollte die Ehefrau sich vom ihren Ehemann trennen, so ergaben sich zwei wichtige Unterschiede: zum einen musste sie das Gericht anrufen, und zum anderen musste sie nachweisen, dass ihr Ehemann seine ehelichen Pflichten verletzt hatte.[32] Erst, wenn dem Gericht einwandfrei diese Verletzungen

---

[27] *Kātūzīān, N.*, Bd. 2, S. 139. *Ṣafā'ī, S.Ḥ., Emāmī, A.*, Ḥoqūq-e ẖānevāde. Bd. 2, S. 119.

[28] *Ṣafā'ī, S.Ḥ., Emāmī, A.*, Moẖtaṣar-e ḥoqūq-e ẖānevāde. Teheran 1999, S. 342.

[29] Art. 1168 ZGB.

[30] *Ṣafā'ī, S.Ḥ., Emāmī, A.*, Ḥoqūq-e ẖānevāde. Bd. 2, S. 124 ff.

[31] *Ṣafā'ī, S.Ḥ., Emāmī, A.*, Moẖtaṣar-e ḥoqūq-e ẖānevāde. S. 330.

[32] Art. 1133 ZGB alte Version gab der Ehefrau vier Gründe für die Scheidung: erstens, die Weigerung des Mannes, Unterhalt zu zahlen, zweitens, wenn der Ehemann die übrigen zwingenden Rechte der Ehefrau missachtete und er zur Beachtung nicht gezwungen werden konnte, drittens, wenn der Ehemann sich seiner Ehefrau gegenüber derart schlecht benahm, dass er das eheliche Zusammenleben für sie unerträglich machte und schließlich

nachgewiesen wurden, konnte der Richter dem Antrag auf Scheidung stattgeben. Während also der Mann weder eine gerichtliche Mitwirkung noch Gründe brauchte, waren dies die conditiones sine qua non für die Ehefrau.[33]

2.1.4. Konsequenzen des Systems

Diese gegenseitigen Rechte und Pflichten bedingen sich. Verletzt also eine Partei ihre Pflichten, so darf die verletzte Partei ihre Pflichten zurückhalten. Kommt etwa der Ehemann seiner Unterhaltspflicht nicht nach, so kann sich die Ehefrau seinem Willen entziehen, ohne dabei ihre eigenen Ansprüche zu verwirken. Bei anhaltender Weigerung des Mannes, seinen Pflichten nachzukommen, ergab sich daraus schließlich ein Recht auf Scheidung für die Frau. Andererseits verwirkt sie ihren Unterhaltsanspruch oder ihre Scheidungsgrundlage, wenn sie ohne triftigen Grund ihre ehelichen Pflichten verletzt.

Auch im Sorgerecht gibt es ähnliche Regelungen: Verletzen Vater oder Mutter ihr Sorgerecht, indem sie das Kind vernachlässigen oder es verwahrlosen lassen, so kann das Sorgerecht auf das andere Elternteil übertragen werden. Gleiches gilt, wenn ein Elternteil ein unmoralisches Verhalten zu Tage legt, das eine Gefahr für die seelische oder körperliche Gesundheit des Kindes birgt.[34]

2.2. Die Phase der Expansion 1941-1979, Moḥammad Reżā Pahlavī

1941 dankt Reżā Šāh ab. Am Ende seiner Herrschaft war das Recht weitgehend in kodifizierter Form vorhanden und die Phase der Rezeption beendet. Der Iran war positivrechtlich mit allen Instrumenten ausgestattet. Sein Sohn und Nachfolger Moḥammad Reżā Šāh setzte den säkularen Trend, den sein Vater Reżā Šāh eingeschlagen hatte, konsequent fort. Auch er verfolgte die Ziele seines Vaters Reżā Šāh, den zentralen Staat zu konsolidieren und eine funktionierende Verwaltung und Gerichtsbarkeit, die seiner Kontrolle unterstanden, zu errichten und den Einfluss der Geistlichen insbesondere aus ihrem ureigenen Gebiet, dem Familienrecht, zurückzudrängen. Die politischen Turbulenzen dieser Zeit mit der Besetzung des Landes durch die Alliierten nach dem zweiten Weltkrieg, dem ersten Aufkeimen politischer Parteien, der Konsolidierung des Parlamentarismuses, der Konfrontation zwischen dem Šāh und dem Premierminister Mosaddeq und der Verstaatlichung der Ölindustrie

---

viertens, wenn durch das Bestehen einer ansteckenden und schwer zu behandelnder Krankheit das Fortsetzen der ehelichen Lebensgemeinschaft für die Ehefrau Gefahren barg.

33 *Yassari, N.*, Überblick über das iranische Scheidungsrecht. In: Zeitschrift für das gesamte Familienrecht, FamRZ 16/2002, S. 1088-1094.

34 Art. 1173 ZGB.

machten Moḥammad Reżā Šāh politisch und gesellschaftlich unnachgiebiger und despotischer. Während in der Folge die Zensur verstärkt und der iranische Geheimdienst ausgebaut wurden, setzte sich der säkulare Trend im rechtlichen Bereich ungehindert fort.

1963 wurde das allgemeine Wahlrecht für Frauen eingeführt. 1967 folgte eine sehr wichtige Kodifikation; das erste Gesetz zum Schutze der Familie (FSG 1967). Das FSG 1967 brachte viele wichtige Änderungen im Familienrecht, insbesondere im Scheidungsrecht. Das FSG 1967 ordnete an, dass jeder Eintragung einer Scheidung bei den staatlichen Scheidungsbüros eine gerichtliche Bescheinung über die Unmöglichkeit der Versöhnung des Paares vorausgehen musste.[35] Diese Bescheinigung konnte ausschließlich gerichtlich erwirkt werden, und ihr ging eine Anhörung der Parteien voraus. Damit erreichte man, dass die Ehefrauen von der bevorstehenden Scheidung Kenntnis erlangten und auch die Möglichkeit hatten, dazu Stellung zu nehmen. Die außergerichtlichen Scheidungen seitens des Mannes waren somit durch das erste FSG beseitigt worden. Außerdem erweiterte das FSG 1967 die Scheidungsgründe der Ehefrauen.[36]

1975 wurde das erste FSG novelliert und ein zweites FSG verabschiedet. Das FSG 1975[37] erweiterte wiederum den Scheidungskatalog des FSG 1967 auf insgesamt zwanzig Gründe[38] und ordnete an, dass von nun an auch der Ehemann Scheidungsgründe bzw. die Verletzung ehelicher Pflichten seitens seiner Ehefrau angeben musste, um eine Bescheinigung über die Unmöglichkeit der Versöhnung zu erlangen und eine Scheidung zu erwirken.

Auch im Bereich des Kindschaftsrechts brachte das FSG 1975 eine wichtige Neuerung: Wie oben erwähnt, konnten allein der Vater, der Großvater väterlicherseits oder eine vom Gericht bestimmte Person, niemals jedoch die Mutter (Art. 1194 ZGB), *valī* ihres Kindes sein. Art. 15 FSG 1975 räumte nun die Möglichkeit ein, dass auch die Mutter die Rolle des *valī* ausüben konnte. Im Unterhaltsrecht führte das FSG 1975 einen nachehelichen Unterhaltsanspruch für die bedürftigere Partei ein.[39]

Ob sich diese gesetzlichen Änderungen tatsächlich auf die Gesellschaft und die Rechtsanwendung ausgewirkt haben, ist schwer zu sagen, denn die neue Rechtslage dauerte nur vier Jahre, und zwar bis 1979, als im Zuge der Revolution die Monarchie abgeschafft und die islamische Republik ausgerufen

---

35 Art. 8 und 19 FSG 1967.

36 Siehe *Mehrpūr, Ḥ.*, Ḥoqūq-e zan. Teheran 2000, S. 148.

37 Rūznāme-ye rasmī Nr. 8785 vom 3. März 1975.

38 Art. 12 FSG 1975.

39 Art. 11 FSG 1975.

wurde, und somit die Gültigkeit der vor-revolutionären Gesetze in Frage gestellt wurden.

2.3. Die Republik

2.3.1. Weitergeltung vor-revolutionärer Gesetze

In den ersten Jahren nach der Revolution herrschte große Rechtsunsicherheit insbesondere in Bezug auf die Weitergeltung der vor-revolutionären Gesetze. Die neue Verfassung von 1979 postulierte eine islamische Republik, und Grundsatz 4 der Verfassung ordnete an, dass alle Gesetze und Verordnungen in allen Rechtsbereichen mit den Grundsätzen des Islams vereinbar sein müssen. Einige Gesetze oder Gesetzesteile wurden einer Normenkontrolle unterworfen, einzelne Vorschriften und Artikel außer Kraft gesetzt.[40] Im Übrigen wurden die Richter angewiesen, keine „unislamischen" Gesetze anzuwenden. Für zukünftige Gesetze sollte die Islamkonformität von Anfang an mit der Schaffung eines Wächterrates sichergestellt werden.

2.3.2. Die Gesetzgebung in der Islamischen Republik Iran

Gemäß Grundsatz 71 der iranischen Verfassung ist das Parlament (*mağles-e šūrā-ye eslāmī*) das Gesetzgebungsorgan im Rahmen der ihm von der Verfassung verliehenen Kompetenzen. Diese Kompetenzen sind durch Grundsatz 91 der Verfassung durch ein Kontrollorgan eingeschränkt, den sogenannten Wächterrat (*šūrā-ye negahbān*).[41] Der Wächterrat fungiert als eine Art religiöses Verfassungsgremium, welches die Vereinbarkeit der vom Parlament verabschiedeten Gesetze mit dem islamischen Recht und dem Verfassungsrecht überprüft. Der Wächterrat kann mit seinem Vetorecht alle Gesetze, die seiner Meinung nach mit dem islamischen Recht nicht in Einklang stehen, ablehnen, und an das Parlament zur Überprüfung zurückweisen.

Das Parlament seinerseits kann den Gesetzesentwurf entweder überarbeitet wieder einreichen oder auf der ursprünglicher Form bestehen. Bleibt der Wächterrat bei seiner ablehnenden Entscheidung, so ist, um aus dieser Pattsituation herauszukommen, gemäß Grundsatz 112 der Verfassung, ein weiteres Organ vorgesehen: der sogenannten Rat zur Feststellung des nationalen Interesses (*mağma^{c}-e tašẖīs-e maṣlaḥat-e nezām-e kešvar*), im weiteren Feststellungsrat. Können sich Parlament und Wächterrat nicht einigen, so ist der

---

[40] So etwa Art. 15 FSG 1975; Rūznāme-ye rasmī Nr. 10094 vom 16 Mai 1979. Die übrigen Artikel des FSG sind nicht explizit außer Kraft gesetzt worden.

[41] Das Gremium setzt sich aus 12 Mitgliedern zusammen: sechs schiitischer Klerikern, ernannt durch den Revolutionsführer und weiteren sechs Rechtsgelehrten, die das Parlament auf Vorschlag des Justizministeriums ernennt.

Gesetzesentwurf dem Feststellungsrat vorzulegen, der als letzte Instanz über das Schicksal des Gesetzes entscheidet.
Dabei überprüft der Feststellungsrat nicht wie der Wächterrat die Kompatibilität mit dem islamischen Recht, sondern muss eine Abwägung vornehmen und sich daran orientieren, ob besagte Regelung dem Gemeinwohl der Gesellschaft von Nutzen ist. Diese Vorgangsweise beruht ebenfalls auf einem Grundsatz des islamischen Rechts: *al-maṣlaḥa*, dem Grundsatz der Förderung des Wohles der Gemeinschaft der Muslime.[42]

2.3.3. Hat sich das Familienrecht in der islamischen Republik Iran verändert?

2.3.3.1. Kleidervorschrift
Als direkte Wirkung der Bestrebungen, die Gesellschaft zu islamisieren kommt es zu einer Umkehr der Kleidervorschriften: Seit 1980 wurden Frauen zum Tragen des *ḥeǧābs* ermutigt, 1983 wird *ḥeǧāb* Pflicht.[43] Auch Männer dürfen keine kurzen Hosen oder kurzärmelige Hemden tragen; die Krawatte wird als Zeichen der Verwestlichung verpönt und muss aus allen staatlichen Behörden und Unternehmen verschwinden.

2.3.3.2. Gesetz über die Zivilen Sondergerichte
Auch im Bereich des Familienrechts kommt es zu gravierenden Änderungen. Das 1980 erlassene Gesetz über die Zivilen Sondergerichte[44] (GZSG) bestätigt zwar die Ausschließlichkeit der gerichtlichen Scheidung, es beseitigt jedoch den Scheidungskatalog des Art. 12 FSG 1975, indem es bezüglich möglicher Scheidungsgründe ausschließlich auf die des ZGBs und des religiösen Rechts verweist. Damit wurden die Errungenschaften des FSG im Bereich des Scheidungsrechts implizit außer Kraft gesetzt, und die Rechtslage aus den 30er Jahren wiederhergestellt.

2.3.3.3. Gesetz zur Novellierung der Scheidungsgesetze
Erst zwölf Jahre später fruchten die Bemühungen der Reformer, die harschen Regelungen im Scheidungsrecht durch das Gesetz zur Novellierung der

---

42 *Nagel, T.*, Das islamische Recht: eine Einführung. Dransfeld 2001, S. 128.

43 Art. 102 Teil 4 des iranischen Strafgesetzbuches vom 9. August 1983 bestimmt: Eine Frau, die ohne islamischen *ḥeǧāb* in der Öffentlichkeit erscheint, ist mit einer Strafe von bis zu 74 Peitschenhieben zu bestrafen. Rūznāme-ye rasmī Nr. 11278 vom 14. November 1983.

44 Rūznāme-ye rasmī Nr. 10088 vom 11. Oktober 1979.

Scheidungsgesetze vom 19. November 1992[45] (Scheidungsgesetz) etwas abzumildern.
Bemerkenswert im novellierten Scheidungsrecht ist die Einführung eines „Abfindungsanspruches" *oğrat ol-mes̱l* für die Ehefrau für Hausarbeiten und sonstige Dienstleistungen, die sie während der Ehe erbracht hat, zu denen sie jedoch aus religiöser Hinsicht nicht verpflichtet war. Dieser Anspruch besteht nur, wenn der Ehemann die Scheidung beantragt, die Ehefrau keine ihrer ehelichen Pflichten verletzt hat und auf der Fortsetzung der Ehe besteht.[46]
Ebenfalls bemerkenswert ist der religiöse Diskurs, den die Reformer führten, um den Anspruch auf *oğrat ol-mes̱l* zu rechtfertigen. Dabei wurde argumentiert, dass die Ehefrau religiös weder zur Haushaltsführung noch zur Kinderaufsicht verpflichtet sei: Der Ehemann habe nicht einmal einen Anspruch darauf, dass seine Ehefrau die gemeinsamen Kinder stillt[47] oder sie über das gesetzliche Alter hinaus erzieht oder sich um sie kümmert.[48] Übernimmt die Ehefrau nun diese Arbeiten, so muss er sie für diese Dienstleistungen bei einer von ihm allein angestrebten Scheidung entschädigen.[49] Dahinter steht auch der Gedanke, dass der Ehemann, der durch die Unterstützung seiner Ehefrau beruflich und finanziell vieles erreicht hat, diese Erfolge mit ihr teilen soll, und sie nicht durch eine willkürliche Scheidung ausschließen soll. Die Argumente, die letztlich zu der Verwirklichung dieser Novelle geführt haben, sind religiöser Natur. Eine entsprechende Regelung in anderen islamischen Ländern ist nicht bekannt.

2.3.3.4. Heiratsalter

Mit der Konstituierung des sechsten *mağles* in 2000 war das Parlament vorwiegend mit reformorientierten Abgeordneten besetzt. Seither sind einige wichtige familienrechtliche Gesetzesentwürfe verabschiedet worden, darunter das langjährige Anliegen des parlamentarischen Ausschusses für Familienangelegenheiten, das Heiratsalter zu heben.
Vor der Revolution lag das Heiratsalter bei Mädchen bei Vollendung des fünfzehnten Lebensjahres und bei Jungen bei Vollendung des achtzehnten Lebensjahres.[50] In Ausnahmefällen war es möglich, vor Erreichen dieser Altersstufen gerichtlich eine Heiratserlaubnis zu beantragen, sofern das

---

45 Rūznāme-ye rasmī Nr. 13914 vom 10. Dezember 1992.

46 Siehe dazu *Ansari-Pour, M.A.*, Remuneration for Work Done by the Wife under Islamic and Iranian Law. In: Yearbook of Islamic and Middle Eastern Law, Bd. 8, 2002-2003, Den Haag, S. 109-121.

47 Art. 1176 ZGB: Die Mutter ist nicht verpflichtet, ihr Kind zu stillen, es sei denn, die Ernährung in anderer Weise als durch Muttermilch ist nicht möglich.

48 *Mehrpūr, H.*, S. 44-45.

49 Art. 1 Anmerkung 6 Ziffer A und B Scheidungsgesetz.

50 *Ṣafā'ī, S.Ḥ., Emāmī, A.*, Ḥoqūq-e ẖānevāde. Bd. 1, S. 70.

Mädchen mindestens dreizehn und der Junge mindestens fünfzehn Jahre alt waren.
1982 wurde Art. 1041 ZGB, der das Heiratsalter festlegt, novelliert und lautete nunmehr: Eine Eheschließung vor Erreichen des Alters der Pubertät ist verboten. Anmerkung: Eine Eheschließung vor Erreichen des Alters der Pubertät ist nur mit Einwilligung des Vormunds und unter Berücksichtigung des Wohles des Mündels erlaubt.[51]
Art. 1210 Anmerkung 1 ZGB bestimmt das Alter der Pubertät: es liegt bei Jungen bei Vollendung des fünfzehnten Lebensjahres und bei Mädchen bei Vollendung des neunten Lebensjahres.[52] Diese Altersstufen wurden von vielen als zu niedrig angesehen. Im Dezember 2000 brachte das Parlament einen Gesetzesentwurf zur Änderung von Art. 1041 ZGB ein. Laut Entwurf sollte das Heiratsalter für Mädchen von neun auf fünfzehn und bei Jungen von fünfzehn auf achtzehn angehoben werden. Damit wäre das vor-revolutionäre Heiratsalter de jure wiederhergestellt.[53] Als der Gesetzesentwurf dem Wächterrat vorgelegt wurde, wies dieser den Entwurf zurück. Er fand, dass die Anhebung des Heiratsalters den Grundsätzen des islamischen Rechts widerspräche. Das Parlament überarbeitete den Entwurf und reduzierte die Alterstufen respektive auf vierzehn und siebzehn. Doch der Wächterrat lehnte abermals ab. Der daraufhin einschreitende Feststellungsrat bewilligte schließlich im Juni 2002 eine wiederum seinerseits geänderte Version, so dass Art. 1041 ZGB am 17. Juli 2002 mit folgendem Inhalt in Kraft trat:[54]
Art. 1041 ZGB: Die Eheschließung eines Mädchens vor Vollendung ihres dreizehnten Lebensjahres nach dem Sonnenkalender und eines Jungen vor Vollendung seines fünfzehnten Lebensjahres nach dem Sonnenkalender ist nur mit Bewilligung des Vormunds und nach Anhörung und Entscheidung des (zuständigen) Gerichts möglich.
Die nicht erfolgte Anhebung des Heiratsalters für Jungen stellt nach wie vor ein großes Probleme dar, denn eine Person, die das achtzehnte Lebensjahr nicht erreicht hat, kann weder einer (legalen) Vollerwerbestätigkeit nachgehen, noch ein Bankkonto eröffnen und ist auch bis zur Vollendung des achtzehnten Lebensjahres nicht voll geschäftsfähig.[55] Mit der Eheschließung obliegen dem

---

51 Gesetzesnovelle vom 29. Dezember 1983, nochmals bestätigt am 5. November 1995.

52 Dabei handelt es sich um die Vollendung des neunten Lebensjahres nach dem Mondkalender, das entspricht acht Jahren und neun Monaten nach dem Sonnenkalender.

53 See *Moġāvezī, P.*, Marriage age for girls in Iran goes up. In: Enteḫāb (Tageszeitung) vom 18. Oktober 2000.

54 Rūznāme-ye rasmī Nr. 16713 vom 17. Juli 2002.

55 Einziger Artikel des Gesetzes über die Reife der Parteien vom 4. September 1934, Qānūn-e rāše[c] be rošd-e motaʿāmelīn; aus der staatlichen Gesetzessammlung von 1934, S. 47.

fünfzehnjährigen Ehemann jedoch die gesamten Unterhaltspflichten, denen er schwerlich nachkommen können wird.
Mädchen sind nach der neuen Regelung also mit Vollendung des dreizehnten Lebensjahres heiratsfähig. Es soll hierzu auf folgende Statistik hingewiesen sein: Das allgemeine Heiratsalter für Mädchen lag 1966, 1986 und 1996 respektive bei 18, 20 und 22.[56] Wenn man in Betracht zieht, dass im ersten Halbjahr 2003 in den Städten das Heiratsalter für Mädchen bei etwa 28 Jahren lag, so deutet dies darauf hin, dass in ländlichen Gebieten das tatsächliche Alter weit unter 22 gelegen haben muss und die Anhebung durchaus eine wichtige Rolle spielt.

2.3.4. Gesetzesentwürfe

Einige Gesetzesentwürfe befinden sich noch in den Mühlen der iranischen Gesetzgebung: so etwa die Formulierung des Abfindungsanspruch *oğrat ol meṣl*, als erbrechtlicher Anspruch der Witwe gegenüber dem Nachlass.[57] Auch Art. 1133 ZGB, der das Scheidungsprivileg des Ehemannes formuliert, soll laut Gesetzesentwurf vom 25. August 2002 novelliert werden. Bisher lautete Art. 1133 ZGB: Der Mann kann, wann immer er es möchte, seine Frau verstoßen. Laut Gesetzesentwurf soll er lauten: Der Mann kann, wann immer er es möchte, seine Frau verstoßen und die Frau kann, in den gesetzlich erwähnten Fällen, ebenfalls die Scheidung begehren.[58]
Der Zusatz zu Art. 1133 ZGB erscheint zunächst wie eine Wiederholung der bestehenden Rechtslage, denn die Frauen können bereits unter bestimmten Voraussetzungen ein Scheidungsverfahren initiieren. Der Wächterrat lehnte deswegen den Zusatz ab und erklärte, der Zusatz brächte keine Änderung der bestehenden Rechtslage.[59] Es ist richtig, dass das ZGB grundsätzlich Scheidungsanträge von Ehefrauen zulässt, der Zusatz zu Art. 1133 ZGB könnte jedoch unter Umständen ein eigenständiges Scheidungsrecht für Ehefrauen statuieren. Die momentane Rechtslage gibt den Ehefrauen ein Antragsrecht, ein Verfahren zu initiieren, bei dessen positivem Ende wiederum der Mann dazu verpflichtet wird, die Scheidung auszusprechen, oder wenn er sich weigert, kann das Gericht als sein Stellvertreter die Scheidung aussprechen. Der Zusatz zu Art. 1133 ZGB könnte so verstanden werden, dass Frauen ein eigenständiges Recht zur Scheidung haben, das nicht nur die Ausnahme zur Regel ist.
Nachdem der Wächterrat die Ratifizierung abgelehnt hat, liegt derzeit der Entwurf wieder beim Parlament. Besteht das Parlament auf den Zusatz und lehnt

---

[56] Enteḫāb (Tageszeitung) vom 18. Oktober 2000.
[57] Im Juli 2002 legte das Parlament dazu einen Gesetzesentwurf vor. Siehe: Zanān oğrat ol-meṣl mīgīrand. In: Abrār (Tageszeitung) vom 21. Juli 2002.
[58] Ḥoqūq-e zanān (juristische Monatsschrift), Nr. 23/Februar 2003, S. 30.
[59] Hamšahrī (Tageszeitung), vom 29. September 2002.

der Wächterrat abermals ab, so wird die Sache an den Feststellungsrat zu verweisen sein, der als letzte Instanz darüber entscheidet. Wie diese Verfahren letztlich ausgehen werden, bleibt abzuwarten.
Laut Zeitungsberichten hat der Feststellungsrat bisher bei familierechtlichen Gesetzesentwürfen, bei denen sich Wächterrat und Parlament nicht einigen konnten, in einem Verhältnis von 30 zu 70 zu Gunsten der Gesetzesentwürfe des Parlaments entschieden.[60] Im ersten Halbjahr 2002 habe der Feststellungsrat alle sieben zur Entscheidung vorgelegten Fälle zu Gunsten des Parlaments entschieden, sagte der General-Sekretär des Feststellungsrates Mohsen Reżā'ī. Auch die Rechtsberaterin im parlamentarischen Ausschuss für Frauen-, Jugend- und Familienangelegenheiten, Ašraf Gerāmīzādegān, bestätigte in einem persönlichen Gespräch, dass der Feststellungsrat in Angelegenheiten des Familienrechts die Gesetzesentwürfe des Parlaments tendenziell billigen würde oder zumindest in modifizierter Form zugelassen habe. Diese Angelegenheiten hätten keine politische Brisanz und machten gute Stimmung im Wahlvolk.

3. Das Teheraner Familiengericht

Ich hatte die Gelegenheit, im Juli 2000 und Juli/August 2002 einige Wochen am Familiengericht in Teheran Verhandlungen beizuwohnen und somit einen Einblick in die Rechtspraxis zu bekommen.[61] Meine Erfahrungen beschränken sich allerdings auf das Teheraner Gericht, das nicht unbedingt beispielhaft für alle iranischen Gerichte ist. In Yazd, so sagte man mir, sei die Scheidungsrate sehr niedrig. Das liege zum einen daran, wurde mir versichert, dass die Yazdis friedfertiger seien als die anderen Iraner, und außerdem gäbe es in Yazd nicht so viele Zugewanderte. Tatsächlich ist Teheran das größte urbane Ballungsgebiet mit einer großen Migration aus dem Umland und den ländlichen Gebieten.
Die Familiengerichtsbarkeit ist im Laufe der letzten 30 Jahre mehrmals novelliert worden. Die Gesetze zum Schutze der Familie führten zunächst die sachliche Zuständigkeit von Familiengerichten ein, die ausschließlich mit Angelegenheiten des Familienrechts befasst waren. Das Gesetz über die Zivilen Sondergerichte 1980 sowie das Scheidungsgesetz bestätigten dies. Bis zum Sommer 2003 gab es für ganz Teheran nur ein Familiengericht, das bedeutete ein Familiengericht für etwa 12 Millionen Einwohner. Im Herbst 2003 ist ein zweites Familiengericht für Teheran eingerichtet worden.
Zum Richteramt kommt man im Iran auf zwei Wegen: zum einen durch ein Hochschulstudium der Rechtswissenschaften, zum anderen durch eine

---

60 Teheran Times (Tageszeitung), vom 4. August 2002.

61 Siehe für einen Bericht über Familiengerichte im Iran in den 90er Jahren *Mir-Hosseini, Z.*, Marriage on Trial, a Study of Islamic Family Law in Iran and Morocco. 1993.

Ausbildung im islamischen Recht an einem theologischen Seminar. Alle Richteramtsanwärter müssen sich einer Prüfung unterziehen. Bislang war die ratio 50 zu 50. Heute beobachtet man allerdings einen Rückgang der Theologen, der zum Teil auf die Verschärfung des prozessualen Teils der Eintrittsklausur zurückgeführt wird.[62]

Das Familiengericht 1 besteht aus 60 Abteilungen, denen jeweils ein männlicher Richter vorsitzt. Seit 1992 können bei den Familiengerichten auch weibliche Beisitzerinnen herangezogen werden[63], sodass heute etwa 30 % der Richter eine weibliche Beisitzerin haben. Diese tragen nicht den Namen Richterin, *qāżī*, sondern weibliche Beraterin, *mošāver-e zan*. Sie sind nicht zeichnungsbefugt, verrichten jedoch inhaltlich die gleiche Arbeit wie der männliche Vorsitzende. Man sollte vielleicht erwähnen, dass Frauen erst in den späten 70er Jahren zum Richteramt zugelassen worden sind. Als die Revolution ausbrach, gab es im ganzen Iran etwa 60 Richterinnen, darunter die spätere Nobelpreisträgerin Šīrīn ᶜEbādī.

Jede Abteilung hat bis zu 400 Fälle im Monat. Der Parteienverkehr ist täglich außer Freitag von 8:00 Uhr bis 14:00 Uhr. Der Richter vergibt durchschnittlich neun Termine am Tag. Daneben kann er mit Parteien befasst werden, die ohne Terminvereinbarung erscheinen dürfen, wie etwa bei einer einvernehmlichen Scheidung oder bei allgemeiner Rechtsberatung. Der Gerichtsraum ist gleichzeitig das Arbeitszimmer des Richters. Insgesamt halten sich gleichzeitig folgende Personen im Gerichtssaal auf: Der Richter, wenn vorhanden die Beisitzerin, die Sekretärin, die die Akten bearbeitet, die Parteien, ihre, sie begleitenden Verwandten, zum Teil Vollzugsbeamte und Zuschauer.

Der erste Eindruck, den man am Gericht bekommt, ist daher oft der eines heillosen Durcheinanders. Das Gebäude hat vier Stockwerke, auf allen Korridoren findet man Menschenmengen; keine Partei kommt ohne weitere Familienmitglieder. Auch im Gerichtssaal bleibt zunächst dieser Eindruck bestehen. Da in familienrechtlichen Angelegenheiten kein Anwaltszwang herrscht, muss der Richter jede Verhandlung leiten und die Parteien belehren. Er erklärt ihnen die Anträge, erläutert die Konsequenzen, beruhigt die Parteien, bringt sie zum Schweigen, oder ermutigt sie zum Reden, verweist laute Verwandten des Raumes oder veranlasst sie zur Aufklärung des Sachverhalts zum Reden. Schließlich protokolliert der Richter alles selbst, alle Akten bis auf einige Formularvordrucke sind handschriftlich, er schreibt das Urteil und

[62] Interview mit Hasan Hamīdīān, dem Präsidenten des Teheraner Familiengerichts 1 im Juli 2003.

[63] Art. 1 Anmerkung 5 Scheidungsgesetz. Siehe *Ansari-Pour, M.A.*, Country Survey Iran. In: Yearbook of Islamic and Middle Eastern Law, Bd. 2 1995, S. 247 für den Unterschied zwischen Vor- und Beisitzer.

verkündet es. Der Eindruck des Chaos wird durch das permanente Hinreichen von Papieren und Dokumenten und das dem Richter mündliche Vortragen der Sach-, Rechts-, aber auch der emotionellen Lage, in der sich eine Partei zu finden glaubt, verstärkt. Wundersamerweise löst sich aber das Durcheinander meist wieder auf, alle Papiere werden behandelt, abgezeichnet, beratschlagt und zurückgegeben.
Im Erdgeschoss des Gerichtsgebäudes ist eine kostenlose Beratungszentrale eingerichtet worden, an die sich die Hilfesuchenden, meist sind es Frauen, mit ihren Fragen wenden können. Diese Einrichtung spielt eine sehr wichtige Rolle und ist ein Schritt in die richtige Richtung, denn der Informationsfluss und die Kenntnis der Rechtslage bleiben für viele (Männer wie Frauen) ein Buch mit sieben Siegeln. Die Strasse, die zum Gerichtsgebäude führt, ist von Personen gesäumt, die offizielles Gerichtspapier sowie Formulare für verschiedene Anträge vor Gericht in der Hand halten und bewaffnet mit einer alten Schreibmaschine ihre Dienste als Antragsschreiber oder Rechtskenner feilbieten. Zum Teil stehen diese Schreiber neben kleinen Gemüse- und Obstverkäufern, so dass im Wirrwarr des Autolärms und der notorischen Bauarbeiten vor dem Gerichtsgebäude neben frischen Datteln und dicken Bohnen auch schnelle Scheidungen und lukrative Unterhaltsvereinbarungen käuflich erworben werden können. Tatsächlich wenden sich in erster Linie unerfahrene und des Schreibens und Lesens unkundige Personen an diese Schreiber, die ihnen nur zum Teil weiterhelfen können.

3.1. Fälle vor Gericht

3.1.1. Die einvernehmliche Scheidung

Viele Scheidungsanträge sind einvernehmliche Scheidungen. Bei dieser Art von Scheidung sind sich beide Parteien einig und haben für alle regelungsbedürftigen Fragen bereits eine Lösung gefunden: die Brautgabe, bei Vorhandensein von Kindern die Sorgerechtsregelung, das Besuchsrecht und die Unterhaltszahlungen, die Zuweisung der ehelichen Wohnung und des Hausrats. Der Richter liest die Vereinbarung laut vor und befragt jeden zu den einzelnen Punkten, um sicher zu gehen, dass keine Seite von der anderen gezwungen wurde, und auch um sicher zu gehen, dass die Ehe nicht zu retten ist. Haben sich die scheidungswilligen Ehegatten in allen Punkten gütlich geeinigt, und ist der Richter mit den getroffenen Entscheidungen einverstanden, so stellt er die Bescheinigung über die Unmöglichkeit der Versöhnung aus. Damit können die Ehegatten die Scheidung eintragen lassen.
Unter den Antragstellern auf einvernehmliche Scheidung sind viele junge und/oder kinderlose Paare, die sehr früh geheiratet haben. Meist handelt es sich dabei um 18-21 Jährige, die, um ihre Beziehung frei leben zu können, geheiratet

haben und, nach kurzer Zeit der „Ehe auf Probe“ die Scheidung beantragen. Statistischen Angaben zufolge findet die Mehrheit aller Scheidungen im Iran in den ersten zwei Ehejahren statt. Einvernehmlich lassen sich außerdem Paare scheiden, die kinderlos geblieben sind, weil das Prozedere hier nicht so langwierig ist. Oft ist der Ehemann eine zweite Ehe eingegangen, so dass seine erste Frau eine „leicht-beweisbare“ Scheidungsgrundlage hat. Paare, die Kinder haben, wählen die einvernehmliche Scheidung, wenn sie sich in Bezug auf das Sorgerecht ihrer Kinder geeinigt haben und eine schnelle Scheidung wollen. In diesen Fällen ist die Rolle des Richters nicht sehr groß, und er greift nur ein, wenn die Scheidungsvereinbarung gegen das Gesetz oder die guten Sitten verstoßen, wenn zum Beispiel ein Teil völlig übervorteilt wird.

3.1.2. Erstrittene Scheidungen

Der Antrag der Ehefrau auf Scheidung kann sich auf die gesetzlichen Gründe des ZGB stützen oder auf die vertraglichen Scheidungsgründe aus dem Ehevertrag. Das Problem in den meisten Fällen liegt für die Ehefrau darin, ihre missliche Lage, die Misshandlungen durch den Ehemann oder seine sonstigen Verfehlungen gerichtlich nachzuweisen. Dabei gibt der Richter den Parteien auf, unbeteiligte Dritte, also keine Verwandten, als Zeugen zu benennen. Nachdem die Verletzung einer ehelichen Pflicht dem Verletzten das Recht gibt, sich seiner Pflicht zu enthalten, laufen die Streitigkeiten vor Gericht meist darauf hinaus zu beweisen, wer zuerst die Verletzung begangen hat.

Hasan Hamīdīān, der Präsident des Teheraner Familiengerichts 1, erläuterte, dass 80 % aller Scheidungsanträge von den Ehefrauen gestellt würden. Dies wird zum Teil auf die Verschärfung der vermögensrechtlichen Konsequenzen der Scheidung durch den Mann zurückgeführt. Die Änderungen im Scheidungsrecht und die Einführung des Abfindungsanspruchs *oǧrat ol meṣl* haben dazu geführt, dass die Ehemänner hohe finanzielle Einbussen erwarten müssen, wenn sie die Scheidung beantragen. Daher ziehen sie es in vielen Fällen vor, die Scheidung nicht zu beantragen, und überlassen es der Ehefrau, vor Gericht zu ziehen, selbst wenn sie die Ehe nicht mehr aufrecht erhalten wollen. Sie warten ab, bis ihr Verhalten die Ehefrau derart verletzt, dass sie den Antrag stellt und somit ihren Anspruch verwirkt.

Auch die Brautgabe, die zur finanziellen Unterstützung und Unabhängigkeit der Ehefrau gedacht ist, kann Spielball der Interessen der Parteien werden, so etwa als Tausch für das Sorgerecht der Kinder, die das gesetzliche Alter der Sorge überschritten haben oder als "Loskauf" von der Ehe.

4. Schlussbemerkungen

Die Beschäftigung mit dem iranischen Familienrecht bleibt vor allem eine Beschäftigung mit den Rechten der Frauen. Die meisten rechtlichen Reformvorhaben berührten die Rechte der Frauen: das Recht auf Scheidung, auf Abfindung, auf das Sorgerecht für die Kinder, auf die Brautgabe usw. Die Familienstrukturen sowie die gegenwärtigen gesellschaftlichen Gegebenheiten des Irans machen Reformen unabdingbar. 75 % der Bevölkerung sind unter 35 Jahre alt. 52 % aller Universitätsabsolventen sind Frauen. Die wirtschaftliche Situation des Landes zwingt bisweilen auch Frauen, die eine traditionelle Rolle einnehmen wollen, auf den Arbeitsmarkt. Und es sind wiederum diese Frauen, die als Ingenieure, Anwältinnen und Ärztinnen ihrem Land dienen, die das überkommene System in Frage stellen. Und sehr oft bedienen sie sich islamischer Argumente, um sich Gehör zu verschaffen.

Eines der größten Probleme der Reformer bleibt das mangelnde Wissen, die Ahnungslosigkeit der Bevölkerung über ihr Rechtssystem und die Vermischung der überkommenen Traditionen der iranischen Gesellschaft mit den Prinzipien des islamisch-schiitischen Familienrechts. In einem Interview mit der Tageszeitung Nourūz im Februar 2002 betonte ᶜEbādī daher die Wichtigkeit der frühen rechtlichen Aufklärung der Kinder und Jugendlichen und plädierte für die Einführung eines Schulfaches, in dem das aktuelle Recht dargestellt wird.[64]

Tatsächlich ist der Informationsstand über die Rechtslage im iranischen Familien- und Erbrecht sehr niedrig. Die meisten Iraner und Iranerinnen spekulieren über den Inhalt ihrer Gesetze; die aktuelle Rechtslage wird oft unvollständig wiedergegeben, und gefährliche Halbwahrheiten kursieren. Der Bevölkerung fehlt das Vertrauen in das Rechtssystem, und der Gang zum Gericht ist für viele keine Option. Trotz der bemerkenswerten Reformen und Änderungen bleibt es also weiterhin sehr wichtig, die Menschen, Frauen wie Männer, anzusprechen und aufzuklären, denn obwohl die Reformen mehrheitlich von Frauengruppen vorangetrieben werden, sind es immer noch die Männer, die das Recht anwenden.

---

64 *Bīǧanī, P.*, Cabinet approves Iran's Joining the global Convention on Discrimination against Women. In: Nourūz (Tageszeitung), vom 13. Februar 2002.

NICHTMUSLIMISCHE MINDERHEITEN IM IRANISCHEN ERBRECHT

Heiko Thoms[1], Berlin

1. Einführung

Der Iran bezeichnet sich seit der Revolution von 1979 als Islamische Republik. Seine Bürger gehören jedoch einer Vielzahl verschiedener Religionsgemeinschaften an. Zahlenmäßig dominieren schiitische Muslime der zwölferschiitischen Richtung, die allein einen Anteil von etwa 90 Prozent an der Gesamtbevölkerung haben.[2] Die zweitgrößte Gruppe stellen sunnitische Muslime. Nichtmuslimische Minderheiten – vor allem Christen, Juden und Zoroastrier – machen nur rund ein Prozent der Bevölkerung aus. In offiziellen Zählungen nicht erfasst werden Angehörige nicht anerkannter Minderheiten. An erster Stelle zu nennen sind hier die Baha'i, deren Zahl auf etwa 300 000 geschätzt wird, und deren Religion von offizieller Seite als Häresie begriffen wird.[3]

Trotz des geringen Anteils nichtmuslimischer Iraner an der Gesamtbevölkerung sind die deutschen Gerichte in zahlreichen Fällen mit familien- und erbrechtlichen Fragen befasst, die diese Minderheiten betreffen. Dies wird belegt durch die Vielzahl entsprechender Gerichtsentscheidungen und Rechtsgutachten, die in den vergangenen Jahren veröffentlicht wurden. Die Vermutung liegt nahe, dass der Prozentsatz der Nichtmuslime in der Diaspora deutlich höher liegt, da sie nach der Revolution in stärkerem Maße ausgewandert sein dürften. Zwar liegen keine nach Religionszugehörigkeit aufgeschlüsselten Zahlen vor; doch dürften in Deutschland – bei einer Gesamtzahl von 88.700 Iranern[4] – mehrere Tausend nichtmuslimische Iraner leben.[5]

Die Informationen zum Recht der Minderheiten, die dem deutschen Rechtspraktiker zur Verfügung stehen, sind jedoch außerordentlich dürftig und zum größten Teil veraltet. So überrascht es nicht, dass die Mehrzahl der

---

1 Der Verfasser war von Mai 2001 bis Juli 2003 als Rechts- und Konsularreferent an der deutschen Botschaft Teheran tätig. Der Beitrag gibt jedoch an keiner Stelle die Haltung des Auswärtigen Amts, sondern ausschließlich seine persönlichen Ansichten wieder.

2 *Sanasarian, E.*, Religious Minorities in Iran.Cambridge 2000, S. 9.

3 *Pistor-Hatam, A.*, Iran als Vielvölkerstaat. Ethnische Minderheiten und staatliche Politik. In: Zeitschrift für Türkeistudien, Essen 6 (1993) 2, S. 242.

4 Statistisches Jahrbuch 2003 für die Bundesrepublik Deutschland, Wiesbaden 2003.

5 Die Zahl der – statistisch nicht erfassten – deutsch-iranischen Doppelstaatler dürfte ein Vielfaches davon betragen.

veröffentlichten Entscheidungen und Gutachten nicht die tatsächliche Rechtslage im Iran widerspiegeln. Dies gilt umso mehr, als es in den letzen Jahren zahlreiche bedeutende Änderungen gegeben hat, bis hin zur Inkraftsetzung vollständig neuer Regelwerke einzelner religiöser Minderheiten. Im Folgenden soll deshalb der Versuch unternommen werden, in einem für die Praxis besonders wichtigen Bereich, dem Erbrecht, die aktuelle rechtliche Situation der nichtmuslimischen Minderheiten im Iran[6] darzustellen und daraus Rückschlüsse auf die Minderheitenpolitik der Islamischen Republik zu ziehen. Die Darstellung beschränkt sich auf die offiziell anerkannten nichtmuslimischen Gemeinschaften. Ausgeklammert bleiben die nicht anerkannten religiösen Gruppen, deren familien- und erbrechtliche Regeln von staatlicher iranischer Seite ignoriert werden und somit auch für den deutschen Richter typischerweise nicht relevant werden.

Die oben erwähnte Bevölkerungsverteilung nach Religionszugehörigkeit spiegelt sich wider in der Verfassung von 1979[7], die unter den verschiedenen religiösen Gruppen eine hierarchische Abstufung vornimmt. Gemäß Art. 12 des Grundgesetzes der Islamischen Republik ist der Islam die offizielle Religion des Irans, und zwar ausdrücklich in seiner zwölferschiitischen Ausprägung. Die vier sunnitischen und die zaiditische Rechtsschule werden jedoch ohne Einschränkungen anerkannt. Sie genießen volle Kultusfreiheit und haben ihr eigenes Personalstatut.

Art. 13 trifft eine Regelung zur rechtlichen Stellung nichtmuslimischer Iraner: „Die zoroastrischen, jüdischen und christlichen Iraner sind die einzigen anerkannten religiösen Minderheiten, die, in den Grenzen des Gesetzes, frei sind, ihre religiösen Bräuche auszuüben und in Angelegenheiten des Personalstatuts und der religiösen Ausbildung gemäß ihren eigenen Statuten zu verfahren.“[8]

Die iranische Privatrechtsordnung ist also in Personalstatutssachen interreligiös gespalten. Dies wirft zunächst die Frage auf, was nach iranischem Verständnis unter den Begriff "Personalstatut" (*aḥvāl-e šahsīye*) zu fassen ist. Die Rechtssprache ist hier uneinheitlich. In einigen Gesetzestexten findet sich die

---

6 Die sich aus dem komplexen Verhältnis von schiitischem und sunnitischem Recht ergebenden, hochinteressanten international-privatrechtlichen Fragestellungen sind für den Iran bisher kaum untersucht worden. Für Pakistan s. *Carroll, L.*, Application of the Islamic Law of Succession: Was the Propositus a Sunnī or a Shīʿī ? In: Islamic Law and Society, Leiden 2 (1995) 1, S. 24ff.

7 Grundgesetz der islamischen Republik Iran vom 1.11.1358 (21.1.1980) in der Fassung vom 6.6.1368 (28.8.1989).

8 Übersetzungen von persischen Gesetzestexten erfolgten durch den Verfasser.

Wendung „Personalstatut *und* Erbrecht".[9] Der Begriff Personalstatut wird hier in einem engen Sinne verstanden, also unter Ausschluss des Erbrechts. In einer zu Art. 8 des deutsch-iranischen Niederlassungsabkommen vom 17.2.1929[10] abgegebenen Erklärung, die nach dem Schlussprotokoll[11] Teil des Abkommens ist, findet sich eine detaillierte Legaldefinition des Begriffs: "Die vertragschließenden Staaten sind sich darüber einig, daß das Personen-, Familien- und Erbrecht, das heißt das Personalstatut, die folgenden Angelegenheiten umfaßt: ..., testamentarische und gesetzliche Erbfolge, Nachlassabwicklungen und Erbauseinandersetzungen, ..." Nach Art. 12 der – unzweifelhaft vorrangigen – Verfassung umfasst das Personalstatut "Ehe, Scheidung, gesetzliches und testamentarisches Erbrecht." Das Erbrecht ist also unstrittig Teil der "*aḥvāl-e šahsīye*", und auch dort, wo das Erbrecht nicht unter das Personalstatut subsumiert wird, wird von einem identischen Anwendungsbereich für beides ausgegangen. Es steht somit außer Zweifel, dass die interreligiöse Rechtsspaltung auch für den Bereich des Erbrechts gilt.

2. Iranisches Interreligiöses Kollisionsrecht in Erbsachen

2.1. Das "Gesetz über die Zulässigkeit der Berücksichtigung des Personalstatuts nichtschiitischer Iraner in den Gerichten"

Die von Art. 13 vorgegebene Rechtsspaltung in Personalstatutsangelegenheiten wird auf einfachgesetzlicher Ebene konkretisiert durch das "Gesetz über die Zulässigkeit der Berücksichtigung des Personalstatuts nichtschiitischer Iraner in den Gerichten" vom 10.5.1312 (1.8.1933). Nach dieser Vorschrift sind die Gerichte verpflichtet, in bestimmten Fällen andere als die allgemeinen, auf zwölferschiitischen Vorstellungen beruhenden Personalstatutsregeln anzuwenden. Voraussetzung ist zunächst, dass der Sachverhalt Nichtschiiten betrifft. Zum zweiten muss deren Konfession offiziell anerkannt sein. Es muss sich also entweder um andere Muslime oder aber um Zoroastrier, Juden oder Christen handeln. Die Anwendung eigener Regeln, etwa für Baha'is oder Mandäer, scheidet somit aus. Schließlich darf die Anwendung der nichtschiitischen Regeln nicht im Widerspruch zur öffentlichen Ordnung stehen, worauf unten näher einzugehen sein wird.

---

9 So etwa das "Gesetz über die Zulässigkeit der Berücksichtigung des Personalstatuts nichtschiitischer Iraner in den Gerichten" vom 10.5.1312 (1.8.1933): "*aḥvāl-e šaḫṣīye va ḥoqūq-e erṯīye*".

10 Reichsgesetzblatt 1930 II, S.1006. Die Fortgeltung des Abkommens wurde mit Wirkung vom 4.11.1954 bestätigt (Bekanntmachung vom 15.8.1955, Bundesgesetzblatt II, S. 829).

11 Reichsgesetzblatt 1930 II, S. 1012.

Sind diese Voraussetzungen erfüllt, ordnet das Gesetz die Anwendung der in der betreffenden Religionsgemeinschaft "unzweifelhaft angewandten Regeln und Gebräuche" an. In Fragen der gesetzlichen oder testamentarischen Erbfolge ist Anknüpfungspunkt die Konfession des Erblassers. Ist der Verstorbene also etwa armenisch-gregorianischer Christ, treffen die Gerichte ihre Entscheidung auf Grundlage des armenisch-gregorianischen Erbrechts.

Die Fortgeltung des Gesetzes von 1933 – und somit die Anwendbarkeit der Personalstatutsregeln religiöser Minderheiten – war nach der Revolution jedoch trotz der unzweideutigen Regelung des Artikels 13 der Verfassung lange Zeit umstritten. Zahlreiche Gerichte lehnten es ab, andere als die für die schiitische Mehrheit geltenden Vorschriften anzuwenden. Große praktische Relevanz besitzt diese Frage etwa bei der testamentarischen Erbfolge: Während das Erbrecht der meisten nichtmuslimischen Konfessionen weitgehende Testierfreiheit gewährt, darf der Erblasser gemäß Art. 843 des iranischen Zivilgesetzbuchs (ZGB) nur über ein Drittel seines Vermögens testamentarisch verfügen. Sofern die Fortgeltung des Gesetzes von 1933 in den betreffenden Entscheidungen überhaupt problematisiert wurde, beriefen sich die Richter schlicht auf die Tatsache, dass der Erblasser in der Islamischen Republik Iran seinen gewöhnlichen Aufenthalt gehabt habe und daher die allgemeinen – schiitisch geprägten – Vorschriften anzuwenden seien.[12] Andere Richter hingegen wandten wie schon vor der Revolution nach Maßgabe des Gesetzes von 1933 die Personalstatutsregeln der nichtmuslimischen Konfessionen an.[13]

Der Oberste Gerichtshof versuchte, diesen Zustand der Rechtsunsicherheit durch einen einstimmigen Beschluss der Plenarversammlung vom 10.12.1984 zu beenden.[14] Der Gerichtshof bestätigte unter Berufung auf die Verfassung die Gültigkeit des Gesetzes von 1933 und rief die Gerichte auf, das Personalstatut der anerkannten religiösen Minderheiten weiterhin anzuwenden. Beschlüsse der Plenarversammlung haben Gesetzeskraft und können nur durch ein formelles Gesetz oder einen späteren Beschluss desselben Gremiums geändert werden.[15]

Anders als zu erwarten gewesen wäre, war die Debatte um die Fortgeltung des Gesetzes von 1933 damit jedoch nicht beendet. Einige Richter lehnten seine Anwendung weiterhin ab – ein in der Islamischen Republik bis dahin einmaliger

[12] So das Zivile Sondergericht Teheran in einer Entscheidung vom 27.4.1362 (18.7.1983), *Parvin, F.*, Conflits internes et conflits internationaux en matière de statut personnel. Unveröffentlichte Dissertation, Université de Paris XI, 15.2.1996, S. 58.

[13] So das Zivile Sondergericht Teheran in einer Entscheidung vom 30.3.1362 (20.6.1983), *ebd.*, S. 59.

[14] Beschluss Nr. 37 vom 19.9.1363 (10.12.1984), Gesetzblatt Nr. 11637 vom 5.11.1363 (25.1.1985).

[15] Gesetzblatt Nr. 7203 vom 20.5.1328 (11.8.1949) und Nr. 3951 vom 17.6.1337 (8.9.1958).

Vorgang.[16] Auch der Wächterrat ging auf Konfrontationskurs: Im März 1990 veröffentlichte er ein Rechtsgutachten, in welchem er den Beschluss des Obersten Gerichtshofs für unvereinbar mit islamischen Grundsätzen erklärte[17], obwohl eine Überprüfung von Beschlüssen der Plenarversammlung gesetzlich gar nicht vorgesehen ist. Die Rechtsunsicherheit bestand somit fort; einzelne Richter beriefen sich in ihren Entscheidungen nunmehr explizit auf die Ansicht des Wächterrats und wandten konsequent auf Personalstatutsangelegenheiten der religiösen Minderheiten das iranische Zivilgesetzbuch an. Andere blieben bei der vorrevolutionären Praxis.
Beendet wurde die Debatte erst weitere drei Jahre später durch den Schlichtungsrat, welcher den Beschluss des Obersten Gerichtshofs wörtlich übernahm und als Gesetz verabschiedete.[18] Die Anwendbarkeit des "Gesetzes über die Zulässigkeit der Berücksichtigung des Personalstatuts nichtschiitischer Iraner in den Gerichten" ist seitdem weitgehend unumstritten. Nur in wenigen Einzelfällen berichten Betroffene, dass radikale Richter noch Ende der Neunzigerjahre auf Erbsachen iranischer Nichtmuslime die Bestimmungen des Zivilgesetzbuchs angewandt haben. Die Fälle konnten aber offenbar entweder informell unter den Beteiligten oder spätestens in der zweiten Instanz gelöst werden. Hinzuzufügen ist, dass über die Berücksichtigung des Rechts der muslimischen Minderheiten, welche sich ebenfalls aus dem Gesetz über das Personalstatut von 1933 ergibt, zu keinem Zeitpunkt Zweifel bestanden.

2.2. Die Regelung des Art. 881 a ZGB

Die Grundregel, dass sich bei einem interreligiösen Konflikt das anzuwendende Erbrecht nach der Religionszugehörigkeit allein des Erblassers bestimmt, gilt jedoch nicht uneingeschränkt. In bestimmten Konstellationen kann auch die Religionszugehörigkeit der Erben maßgeblich sein. Im November 1991, inmitten der eben beschriebenen Auseinandersetzung zwischen Oberstem Gerichtshof und Wächterrat, ergänzte das Parlament das ZGB um den umstrittenen Artikel 881 a. Dieser lautet:
"Ein Ungläubiger erbt nicht von einem Muslim. Befindet sich unter den Erben eines ungläubigen Erblassers ein Muslim, sind die ungläubigen Erben selbst dann von der Erbfolge ausgeschlossen, wenn sie nach Ordnung und Verwandtschaftsgrad dem Erblasser näher stehen."[19]

---

[16] *Parvin*, a.a.O.
[17] *Parvin*, a.a.O., S.59f.
[18] Gesetzblatt Nr. 11637 vom 1.7.1372 (23.9.1993).
[19] Gesetz zur Änderung des Zivilgesetzbuchs vom 14.8.1370 (5.11.1991).

Als Ungläubiger – *kāfir* – im Sinne der Vorschrift ist nach herrschender Ansicht, die sich auf ein Wort Khomeinis beruft, jeder Nichtmuslim zu verstehen. Angehörige der Buchreligionen fallen ebenfalls darunter.
Ein entfernter muslimischer Cousin eines zum Beispiel christlichen oder jüdischen Erblassers schließt also dessen Kinder von der Erbfolge aus.
Man kann sich unschwer vorstellen, welche Konsequenzen diese Regelung in der Praxis hat. Immer wieder wird von Fällen berichtet, in denen es gerade bei bedeutenden Vermögen zur Konversion einzelner Verwandter gekommen ist und der Verdacht nahe lag, dass bei der Entscheidung zum Übertritt zum Islam finanzielle Motive im Vordergrund standen. Erleichtert werden derartige Vorkommnisse noch dadurch, dass nach herrschender Meinung auch ein nach dem Tod des Erblassers erfolgter Übertritt zum Islam zu berücksichtigen ist, sofern das Erbe noch nicht aufgeteilt wurde.[20] Unbeachtlich ist die Konversion nur dann, wenn offensichtlich ist, dass sie durch den Wunsch motiviert ist, andere von der Erbfolge auszuschließen. Hierüber kann durchaus auch Beweis erhoben werden.[21]
Ein Sonderproblem stellt sich, wenn sich unter den Erben eines Nichtmuslims ein sunnitischer Muslim befindet. Nach dem Wortlaut des Art. 881 a ZGB müsste dieser anderen, nichtmuslimischen Erben ebenso vorgehen wie ein Schiit. Anders als im zwölferschiitischen Recht wirkt das Erbhindernis der Religionsverschiedenheit nach übereinstimmender Ansicht der vier sunnitischen Rechtsschulen jedoch in beide Richtungen: Weder kann ein Christ einen Muslim beerben, noch umgekehrt. Nach dem Gesetz über das Personalstatut von 1933 ist diese Regel bei sunnitischen Muslims zu beachten. Es stellt sich also die Frage, welche Regel vorgeht: Art. 881 a ZGB, nach welchem der muslimische Erbe Alleinerbe ist, oder der Grundsatz des sunnitischen Rechts, dass der Muslim vom Nichtmuslim nicht erbt. Die iranischen Gerichte haben sich zu diesem Konflikt bisher offenbar noch nicht geäußert.[22] Sofern iranische Rechtswissenschaftler zu dieser Frage überhaupt Stellung nehmen, gehen sie davon

---

[20] *Parvin, F.*, Conflit interpersonnel de droit iranien en matière de statut personnel. In: Caparros, E. u. L.-L. Christians (Hrsg.), Religion in Comparative Law at the Dawn of the 21st Century, S. 336f.

[21] Dem Verfasser wurde u.a. von folgendem Fall berichtet: Ein katholischer Christ war nach dem Tod seines ebenfalls katholischen Onkels, aber vor Aufteilung des Erbes, zum Islam übergetreten und erhob nun Anspruch auf den gesamten Nachlass. Das Gericht hatte offenbar Zweifel an der Ernsthaftigkeit der Konversion und befragte den Priester der Gemeinde als Zeugen. Nachdem dieser zu berichten wusste, dass die betreffende Person noch nach dem Datum des angeblichen Übertritts zum Islam aus voller Kehle im Kirchenchor gesungen habe, entschied das Gericht für eine Anwendung des katholischen Erbrechts.

[22] *Parvin, F.*, ebd., S. 337.

aus, dass ein Sunnit nichtmuslimische Erben nicht von der Erbfolge ausschließt.[23]
Festzuhalten bleibt, dass bei der Suche nach dem anzuwendenden Erbrecht nicht allein auf die Religionszugehörigkeit des Erblassers, sondern auch auf die der Erben abzustellen ist. Dabei ist es als Frage des internen ordre public anzusehen, dass ein Muslim nicht den Regeln einer nichtmuslimischen Minderheit unterworfen sein darf, was jedoch nur bei schiitischen Muslims möglich sein kann, da diese nach schiitischem Recht durchaus als Erben in Betracht kommen. Kann ein Muslim nach seinem eigenen Personalstatut ohnehin nicht erben, wie es bei den Sunniten der Fall ist, wird dies vom iranischen Recht wohl respektiert.

3. Materielles Erbrecht der religiösen Minderheiten

Trotz der Regelung des Art. 881 a ZGB kommt es doch in der ganz überwiegenden Zahl der Erbfälle, die nichtmuslimische Erblasser betreffen, zur Anwendung der Personalstatutsregeln der jeweiligen Minderheit. Der Zusammenhalt innerhalb der einzelnen Gruppen ist stark, und Ehen mit Andersgläubigen sind stigmatisiert.
Der geringe Anteil von Nichtmuslimen an der Gesamtbevölkerung steht im Kontrast zu der Vielfalt nichtmuslimischer Gruppierungen im Iran. Während Zoroastrier und Juden eine einheitliche Organisationsstruktur haben, findet sich im Land eine Vielzahl christlicher Konfessionen.[24] Bereits seit vorislamischer Zeit auf iranischem Territorium ansässig sind die nestorianischen Christen, also die Angehörigen der Assyrischen Kirche des Ostens. Die größte Gruppe stellen heute jedoch die armenisch-gregorianischen Christen dar, die seit dem 16. Jahrhundert in den Iran kamen. Unter beiden Konfessionen – und immer wieder auch unter Muslimen – haben sowohl Katholiken als auch Protestanten über lange Zeit missioniert, was zu einer Reihe von Abspaltungen geführt hat. So gibt es heute sowohl römisch-katholische als auch mit Rom unierte chaldäische und armenisch-katholische Christen, assyrische, armenische und persischsprachige Presbyterianer und Anglikaner. Hinzu kommen Pfingstler und Adventisten des

---

23 So Sayyed Mostafa Mohaghegh Damad auf einer vom Max-Planck-Institut für ausländisches und internationales Privatrecht am 5.7.2003 in Hamburg veranstalteten Tagung mit dem Titel "The Iranian Family and Succession Laws and their Application in German Courts."

24 Zu diesen s. *Lyko, D.*, Gründung, Wachstum und Leben der evangelischen christlichen Kirchen in Iran. Leiden/Köln 1964, S. 1 ff.

siebten Tages sowie griechisch-orthodoxen und russisch-orthodoxen Christen[25], die vor allem in der ersten Hälfte des 20. Jahrhunderts im Iran heimisch wurden. Allerdings haben nicht alle diese Gruppen eine eigene Personalstatuts-Kodifikation. Einige, wie etwa die lateinischen, chaldäischen und armenischen Katholiken, haben sich ein gemeinsames Regelwerk gegeben. Andere, zum Beispiel die Griechisch-Orthodoxen, sind bisher allen Aufforderungen, ihre Regeln zu kodifizieren, nicht nachgekommen. Solche Aufforderungen werden von der jeweiligen iranischen Regierung seit Erlass des Gesetzes über das Personalstatut von 1933 im Abstand von einigen Jahren regelmäßig wiederholt. Als erste haben daraufhin die gregorianischen Armenier im Jahre 1938 eine Kodifikation vorgelegt. Kurze Zeit später folgten Zoroastrier und Juden. Erst 1953 reichten die presbyterianischen Kirchen einen gemeinsamen Entwurf ein, dessen erbrechtlicher Teil jedoch von der Regierung zurückgewiesen wurde, da er zu unklar gefasst sei. Dennoch betrachten die iranischen Presbyterianer dieses Regelwerk bis heute auch im Erbrecht als maßgeblich. Auch die iranischen Anglikaner wenden die dort niedergelegten Regeln an, jedoch mit Ausnahme der Bestimmungen über die Scheidung. Spätestens in den Fünfzigerjahren hat auch die russisch-orthodoxe Gemeinde einen eigenen Text vorgelegt; das genaue Datum ist heute aber weder dem iranischen Justizministerium noch der Gemeinde selbst bekannt.

Eine Besonderheit stellt das katholische Personalstatut dar. Das kanonische Recht äußert sich zu erbrechtlichen Fragen grundsätzlich nicht, sondern überlässt diesen Rechtsbereich den weltlichen Institutionen. Der iranische Staat beschreitet jedoch, wie oben dargelegt, den umgekehrten Weg, geht also von der Regelungszuständigkeit der Religionsgemeinschaften aus, so dass sich eine Lücke ergibt. Die Verantwortlichen in der katholischen Kirche haben die Alternativen nun offenbar als so unbefriedigend empfunden, dass in ihrer Kodifikation von 1958 auch ein erbrechtlicher Teil enthalten ist. Es handelt sich hier also um den seltenen Fall eines katholischen Erbrechts, welches auch vom Vatikan gebilligt wurde.

Bis heute keine Kodifizierung vorgenommen haben Nestorianer und griechisch-orthodoxe Christen. Die nestorianische Gemeinde sieht das traditionelle ostsyrische Kirchenrecht als maßgeblich an, welches den iranischen Behörden nur in aramäischer Sprache übermittelt wurde. In der griechischen Gemeinde schließlich werden Entscheidungen in Personalstatutssachen auf der Grundlage des modernen griechischen ZGB getroffen.

Insgesamt existieren im Iran somit acht anerkannte nichtmuslimische Personalstatutsregime: ein zoroastrisches, ein jüdisches, ein armenisch-

[25] Zu diesen s. *Igumen Aleksandr (Sarkeschew)*, Russkaja prawoslawnaja zerkow' w persii – irane (1597-2001), St. Petersburg 2002.

gregorianisches, ein nestorianisches, ein protestantisches, ein katholisches sowie ein russisch- und ein griechisch-orthodoxes.
Angesichts der Tatsache, dass die meisten Regelwerke bereits vor mehr als einem halben Jahrhundert verfasst wurden, verwundert es nicht, dass in vielen Gemeinden bereits seit Jahren ein großes Reformbedürfnis gesehen wird. Vieles erscheint heute nicht mehr zeitgemäß. Als erste haben im Jahr 2002 wiederum die armenischen Gregorianer eine umfassend überarbeitete Kodifikation ihrer Personalstatutsregeln vorgelegt. Darin wurde beispielsweise die Position des Ehemanns im Erbrecht, der zuvor am Nachlass seiner Ehefrau kaum beteiligt war, deutlich gestärkt.
Zoroastrier, Protestanten und Katholiken arbeiten bereits seit Jahren an einer Neufassung. Die Arbeit der Kommissionen ist Gegenstand heftiger Debatten innerhalb der Gemeinden. So steht etwa die Vereinigung der zoroastrischen Priester den Reformen größtenteils negativ gegenüber, da sie die beabsichtigte Verbesserung der Stellung der Frau im Ehe- und im Erbrecht für unvereinbar mit ihren Glaubensgrundsätzen halten. Vielfach wird auch die Befürchtung geäußert, dass staatliche Stellen bei einer Neuvorlage den Versuch unternehmen könnten, inhaltlich Einfluss zu nehmen. In dieser Befürchtung ist wohl auch der Grund dafür zu sehen, dass einige Gruppierungen bisher überhaupt keine Kodifikation vorgelegt haben und andere ihre Texte nur sehr zögerlich aus der Hand geben.

4. Einführung des Erbrechts der Minderheiten in das Verfahren

Die Einbringung des materiellen Erbrechts der religiösen Minderheiten in das gerichtliche Verfahren weist einige Eigentümlichkeiten auf. Keineswegs ist es nämlich so, dass der staatliche Richter über die einschlägigen Texte verfügen und auf ihrer Grundlage selbständig eine Entscheidung treffen würde. Die Rechtsfindung liegt in der Praxis vielmehr weitestgehend in der Hand der jeweiligen Gemeinde.
Gehört in einem Erbfall der Erblasser zu einer anerkannten Minderheit, werden die zuständigen Gremien der Gemeinde entweder vom Gericht oder – gerade wenn es um die Beantragung eines Erbscheins geht – direkt von den Erben um Erteilung eines Rechtsgutachtens gebeten. Bei der Erteilung der Auskünfte verfahren die Gemeinschaften jedoch in sehr unterschiedlicher Weise. Einige präsentieren eine komplette, urteilsähnliche Lösung des konkreten Einzelfalles unter Nennung der einschlägigen Regeln ihrer Personalstatutskodifikation. Andere – wohl die Mehrzahl – beschränken sich darauf, die Erbanteile auszurechnen und das Ergebnis dem Gericht mitzuteilen. Sie verzichten bewusst auf die Nennung der angewandten Bestimmungen, wohl um dem Gericht keinen Spielraum zu einer Überprüfung des Ergebnisses zu geben.

Den umgekehrten Weg hingegen beschreitet die römisch-katholische Kirche, welche lediglich die anzuwendenden Vorschriften übermittelt, ohne den konkreten Fall zu würdigen. Dies ist wohl Reflex der oben erwähnten Grundhaltung der katholischen Kirche, erbrechtliche Fragen letztlich dem Staat zu überlassen. Die mit Rom unierten Chaldäer und Armenier sind allerdings weniger zurückhaltend und erteilen Auskünfte unter Nennung der einschlägigen Bestimmungen.
In Gesprächen mit Repräsentanten der verschiedenen religiösen Gruppen wird übereinstimmend berichtet, dass die Rechtsauskünfte von den staatlichen Gerichten uneingeschränkt akzeptiert werden. Zwar äußern die Richter vereinzelt Erstaunen über für sie befremdliche Regeln, etwa die erbrechtliche Gleichstellung von Söhnen und Töchtern. Dies hindert sie jedoch nicht daran, die Vorgaben der Rechtsgutachten umzusetzen.

5. Fazit und Ausblick

Die sehr weitgehende Autonomie, welche die anerkannten religiösen Minderheiten im Bereich des Personalstatuts im Iran genießen, überrascht zunächst. Sie haben nicht nur das Recht, eigene, auf ihren Glaubensvorstellungen beruhende Normen in Kraft zu setzen. Sie kontrollieren in der Praxis auch die Anwendung dieser Normen durch die staatlichen Gerichte, von denen sie vollstreckbare Entscheidungen erhalten. Dies geht weit über das hinaus, was in den meisten anderen islamisch geprägten Staaten zu verzeichnen ist: Fast überall sind im Bereich des Erbrechts noch bestehende Sonderregime im 20. Jahrhundert abgeschafft worden; die gesamte Bevölkerung ist denselben, meist auf islamischem Rechtsverständnis beruhenden Regeln unterworfen. Es hat den Anschein, als bestehe hier ein Widerspruch zu den zahlreichen repressiven Regeln, denen iranische Nichtmuslime unterworfen sind. Um nur zwei Beispiele zu nennen: Der Zugang zu den wichtigsten öffentlichen Ämtern ist ihnen versperrt; bei Körperverletzung oder Tötung sind sie schadensersatzrechtlich deutlich schlechter gestellt als Muslime.
Dieser scheinbare Widerspruch ist jedoch systembedingt: Sowohl die Autonomie der Minderheiten in Personalstatutsangelegenheiten, als auch die diskriminierenden Regeln haben ihre Wurzeln in schiitischen Rechtsvorstellungen, denen nach der Revolution in umfassender Weise zur Geltung verholfen wurde. Wie die oben dargestellte Debatte um die Frage der Anwendbarkeit der nichtmuslimischen Personalstatutsregeln zeigt, wurden zwar – gerade in den ersten Jahren nach der Revolution – auch von der schiitischen Geistlichkeit vielfach extreme Positionen vertreten. Inzwischen haben sich in der innerschiitischen Diskussion zumeist traditionalistische Interpretationen durchgesetzt. Dennoch ist das System in der Gesamtschau letztlich auf eine

Islamisierung der Gesellschaft angelegt. Bestes Beispiel ist der erwähnte Artikel 881 a ZGB, der starke Anreize für einen Übertritt zum Islam bietet und den Zusammenhalt der nichtmuslimischen Gemeinden auf die Probe stellt.
Dies trägt – neben vielen anderen Faktoren – dazu bei, den Auswanderungsdruck auf Nichtmuslime zu erhöhen. Zoroastrier, Juden und ostsyrische Christen, die schon seit vorislamischer Zeit auf iranischem Territorium beheimatet sind, aber auch Gregorianer, Katholiken und evangelische Christen, stehen – auch im eigenen Verständnis – für einen wichtigen Teil iranischer Geschichte und Kultur. Seit den Achtzigerjahren jedoch sind die meisten Gemeinden durch die Emigration ihrer Mitglieder um mehr als die Hälfte geschrumpft. Setzt sich der Exodus fort, – und nichts deutet darauf hin, dass es in Kürze zu einer Trendumkehr kommen wird –, wird der Iran in einigen Jahren vollständig islamisiert sein und seine Jahrtausende alte nichtmuslimische Kultur verloren haben.

PRAXISFRAGEN DER VERTRAGSGESTALTUNG IM DEUTSCH-IRANISCHEN WIRTSCHAFTSVERKEHR

RA Dr. Kilian Bälz, LL.M., Frankfurt am Main

Der Iran ist traditionell einer der wichtigsten deutschen Handelspartner im Nahen und Mittleren Osten. Mit Blick auf die wirtschaftlichen Entwicklungen der letzten Jahre ist der Iran zudem ein interessanter Zukunftsmarkt mit ganz erheblichem Potential. Wer sich als Rechtsanwalt mit den Staaten des Nahen und Mittleren Ostens auseinandersetzt, ist so immer wieder mit deutsch-iranischen Transaktionen befasst. Zu einem großen Teil geht es dabei um Liefergeschäfte, bei denen deutsche Unternehmen Anlagen und andere Wirtschaftsgüter für Industrie- und Infrastrukturprojekte an iranische Abnehmer liefern. Manche deutsche Unternehmen, etwa der Automobilbranche, produzieren auch im Iran. Des Weiteren wird bei privatfinanzierten Infrastrukturprojekten zunehmend verlangt, dass sich ausländische Lieferanten neben der Zulieferung auch dauerhaft an dem Betrieb des Vorhabens beteiligen.

Die Fragen, die sich dem beratenden Anwalt bei der Gestaltung solcher deutsch-iranischen Verträge stellen, stehen im Mittelpunkt meines heutigen Vortrages.[1] Was folgt ist also keine autoritative Darstellung des iranischen internationalen Vertrags- und Zivilverfahrensrechts. Einen solchen Anspruch erhebt der Vortrag nicht. Vielmehr geht es darum, wie die typischerweise im deutsch-iranischen Rechtsverkehr auftretenden Probleme vertraglich abgebildet werden. Das erfordert auch, sich mit den einschlägigen Bestimmungen des iranischen Rechts auseinander zu setzen, allerdings aus einer etwas anderen Perspektive.

Internationale Vertragsgestaltung beruht auf globalisierten Marktpraktiken. Im Mittelpunkt steht der Vertrag, nicht das staatliche Recht, sowie im Wirtschaftsverkehr entwickelte typische Klauseln und standardisierte Verfahrensweisen. Die Vertragsgestaltung wirft daher in solchen Rechtsordnungen besondere Probleme auf, wo diese Praktiken entweder den Marktteilnehmern nicht (hinreichend) bekannt sind oder das staatliche Recht sie nicht anerkennt. Zwar gibt es heute auch im Iran Anwaltskanzleien, die die globalen Standards kennen und Service auf internationalem Niveau anbieten (wenn auch nicht viele). Es kann aber nicht bei allen iranischen Vertragspartnern - gerade der öffentlichen Hand - Erfahrung mit der Gestaltung von internationalen Verträgen vorausgesetzt werden; der Grund hierfür ist, dass der

---

[1] Die Vortragsform wurde beibehalten. Der Text ist lediglich um einige weiterführende Anmerkungen ergänzt.

Iran nach der Revolution von 1979 für zwei Jahrzehnte vom internationalen Rechtsverkehr mehr oder weniger abgeschnitten war. Noch problematischer ist der zweite Aspekt: das iranische Recht weist einige Eigenheiten auf, die von der internationalen Norm abweichen und bei internationalen Verträgen erhebliche Schwierigkeiten bereiten können. Im Folgenden möchte ich mich aus der Perspektive des beratenden Anwaltes der iranischen Rechtsordnung nähern, einige dieser Probleme näher beschreiben und Lösungsstrategien diskutieren. Im Mittelpunkt stehen Beschränkungen bei der Vereinbarung von Schiedsklauseln und der Rechtswahl. Des Weiteren werde ich kurz auf die Immunität von Staatsunternehmen und die extraterritorialen Anwendung des US-Außenwirtschaftsrechts eingehen. Damit sind einige der wichtigen, wenn auch natürlich bei weitem nicht alle Fragen angeschnitten, die sich bei der Gestaltung deutsch-iranischer Wirtschaftsverträge stellen.

Vereinbarung einer Schiedsklausel

Die Regelung von Streitbeilegung und Rechtswahl findet sich üblicherweise ganz am Ende des Vertrages, meist wenige Absätze oberhalb der Unterschriftenzeile, eingeklemmt zwischen salvatorischer Klausel und anderen „sonstigen Bestimmungen.“ Vor diesem Hintergrund bedarf es der Erläuterung, wenn ich Überlegungen zu gerade dieser Klausel ganz an den Anfang meines Vortrages stelle. Aus anwaltlicher Perspektive steht jedoch die Vereinbarung über die Streitbeilegung bei einem internationalen Vertrag nicht am Ende, sondern am Anfang einer jeden Überlegung. Auch Verträge haben einen Empfängerhorizont, und entscheidend für das Verständnis eines Vertrages ist es, wer den Vertrag am Ende autoritativ auslegen wird: Ein staatliches Gericht wird einen internationalen Anlagenbauvertrag, dem die FIDIC-Bedingungen zugrunde liegen, anders verstehen als ein internationales Schiedsgericht. Ein deutsches Landgericht wird nur mit Mühe ermitteln können, ob es eine mit § 313 BGB vergleichbare Regelung über die Störung der Geschäftsgrundlage auch im iranischen Recht gibt und falls ja, ob deren Voraussetzungen vorliegen. Nicht jedes iranische Gericht wiederum wird ohne weiteres auf neuere Literatur und Rechtsprechung zum CISG zurückgreifen können. Folglich determiniert das Verfahren der Streitbeilegung die Gestaltung des Vertrages - oder sollte das zumindest, um im Ernstfall böse Überraschungen zu vermeiden.

In internationalen Wirtschaftsverträgen wird meistens eine Schiedsklausel vereinbart. Staatliche Gerichtsstände sind, sieht man einmal von manchen

Finanzierungsgeschäften ab, nicht sonderlich populär.[2] Eine solche Schiedsklausel hat eine doppelte Funktion. Positiv erlaubt sie, einen möglichen Streit durch ein Gremium entscheiden zu lassen, auf dessen Zusammensetzung und Verfahrensweise die Parteien einen größeren Einfluss haben als auf ein staatliches Gericht. Idealerweise sind Zusammensetzung und Verfahrensordnung des Schiedsgerichtes angepasst an den Gegenstand, das Volumen und auch das Recht des Vertrages.[3] Negativ ist die Schiedsklausel zugleich ein Instrument, einen unliebsamen staatlichen Gerichtsstand auszuschließen.[4] Denn in Verhandlungen ist es oft nicht möglich, sich auf die staatlichen Gerichte eines bestimmten Staates zu einigen. So empfiehlt sich als Kompromiss die Vereinbarung eines Schiedsgerichts. Zu den zentralen Fragen bei der Gestaltung eines internationalen Vertrages gehört daher, ob die Schiedsklausel in allen beteiligten Rechtsordnungen anerkannt wird und so den Rechtsweg zu den ordentlichen Gerichten effektiv ausschließt.

Der Iran ist Mitglied der *New York Convention* von 1958 (NYC), dem wichtigsten internationalen Abkommen auf dem Gebiet der Schiedsgerichtsbarkeit. Nach Art. II (1) der NYC erkennt

„*jeder Vertragsstaat ... eine schriftliche Vereinbarung an, durch die sich die Parteien verpflichten, alle oder einzelne Streitigkeiten, die zwischen ihnen aus einem bestimmten Rechtsverhältnis, sei es vertraglicher oder nicht vertraglicher Art bereits entstanden sind oder künftig entstehen, einem schiedsrichterlichen Verfahren zu unterwerfen.*“

Auch Deutschland ist Mitgliedstaat der NYC. Hieraus folgt, dass Schiedsklauseln im deutsch-iranischen Wirtschaftsverkehr grundsätzlich anerkannt werden und einen staatlichen Gerichtsstand ausschließen. Mit wichtigen Einschränkungen allerdings: nach Art. II (1) der NYC setzt die Anerkennung von Schiedsklauseln nämlich voraus, dass „*der Gegenstand des*

---

2 Ein staatlicher Gerichtsstand kann dann vorteilhaft sein, wenn die Feststellung und Vollstreckung von Zahlungsverpflichtungen im Vordergrund stehen. Das ist der Grund, weshalb in Kreditverträgen, auch in internationalen, häufig die Streitbeilegung durch ein staatliches Gericht vorgesehen ist.

3 Kriterien sind dabei etwa: die Höhe des (erwarteten) Streitgegenstandes und die daraus resultierenden Kosten eines Schiedsverfahrens, die verfahrensrechtlichen Vorschriften i.e.S. (*Discovery* und Kreuzverhör nach US-amerikanischem Vorbild?); das Erfordernis spezialisierter juristischer (etwa: IP) oder technischer Expertise (etwa: Anlagenbau).

4 Aus diesem Grund ist es auch konsequent, ausländische Urteile, die im Widerspruch zu einer Schiedsklausel ergangen sind, nach § 328 ZPO nicht anzuerkennen (dazu *Bälz u. Marienfeld*, RIW 2003, 51 ff.).

Streites auf schiedsrichterlichem Wege geregelt werden kann." Die Schiedsfähigkeit einer Streitigkeit regelt die Konvention nicht, sie überlässt diese vielmehr dem nationalen Recht.[5] Hier sind im Verhältnis zum Iran einige Besonderheiten zu beachten, gerade, wenn der Staat oder ein öffentliches Unternehmen die Vertragspartner sind.

Zwar eröffnet Art. 455 der iranischen ZPO (2000) ausdrücklich die Möglichkeit, ein Schiedsgericht zu vereinbaren. Zudem besteht im Iran seit 1997 ein neues Schiedsgesetz, das auf dem UNCITRAL Modell-Gesetz beruht und so - jedenfalls im Wesentlichen - dem internationalen Standard entspricht. Für Verträge mit der öffentlichen Hand besteht aber eine weitreichende Einschränkung, die aus der iranischen Verfassung folgt. Art. 139 der Verfassung ordnet an:

„*Die Beilegung von Streitigkeiten über öffentliches oder Staatseigentum oder deren Unterwerfung unter die Schiedsgerichtsbarkeit bedarf in einem jeden Fall der Zustimmung des Ministerrates und das Parlament ist davon in Kenntnis zu setzen. Sofern eine der streitenden Parteien ausländisch ist, ebenso wie in wichtigen nationalen Fällen, muss die Zustimmung des Parlaments eingeholt werden. Die wichtigen Fälle werden durch Gesetz bestimmt.*"[6]

Diese Bestimmung der iranischen Verfassung stellt die Praxis vor erhebliche Probleme.

So ist zunächst die Auslegung der Verfassungsbestimmung unklar. Aus dem Wortlaut von Art. 139 der Verfassung folgt, dass die Bestimmung auf Schiedsverfahren über „Staatseigentum und öffentliches Eigentum" anwendbar ist. Weniger eindeutig ist hingegen, ob hiervon auch Verfahren gegen öffentliche Unternehmen erfasst sind, die in einer privatrechtlichen Unternehmensform verfasst sind und die privatrechtliche Verträge abschließen. Soweit ersichtlich, ist diese Frage im Iran gerichtlich nicht entschieden. Die Vertragspraxis geht daher davon aus, dass der Vorbehalt in Artikel 139 der Verfassung auch auf Verträge mit Staatsunternehmen in Privatrechtsform

---

5 Zu dieser Problematik *Bälz u. Marienfeld* (Anm. 4), 52 mit weiteren Nachweisen in Anm. 1.

6 Wiederholt wird diese Regelung in Art. 457 der iranischen ZPO: „*Streitigkeiten über öffentliches oder Staatseigentum dürfen nur dann einem Schiedsgericht unterbreitet werden, wenn der Ministerrat dem zugestimmt und das Parlament davon in Kenntnis gesetzt hat. Wenn die Gegenseite des Schiedsverfahrens ausländisch ist oder der Streitgegenstand nach den anwendbaren gesetzlichen Vorschriften von besonderer Bedeutung ist, ist zusätzlich die Zustimmung des Parlaments erforderlich.*"

Anwendung findet. Unklar ist zudem, ob die nach Art. 139 der Verfassung erforderliche Zustimmung vorab erteilt werden kann und ob diese möglicherweise durch die Ratifizierung der NYC oder durch die gesetzliche Privilegierung bestimmter Branchen (insbesondere Öl und Gas) vom Parlament implizit erteilt wurde. Das vertreten etwa Teile der ausländischen Business Community im Iran. Ob diese Auffassung im Ernstfall einer gerichtlichen Überprüfung standhält, ist fraglich. So kann bestritten werden, dass die Zustimmung überhaupt vorab und generell erteilt werden kann. Des Weiteren überlässt die NYC die Frage der Schiedsfähigkeit eines Streites - wie oben dargelegt - dem nationalen Recht. Folglich lässt sich aus der Ratifizierung der NYC auch keine (einschränkende) Auslegung von Art. 139 der Verfassung herleiten, selbst wenn die Ratifizierung ohne entsprechenden Vorbehalt erfolgt ist. So bleibt es dabei, dass bis auf Weiteres davon auszugehen ist, dass sämtliche Schiedsklauseln in Verträgen mit dem iranischen Staat oder iranischen Staatsunternehmen dem Vorbehalt des Art. 139 der Verfassung unterliegen.[7] Nach iranischer Vorstellung ist ein Schiedsverfahren somit nur zulässig, wenn das Parlament nach Entstehen der Streitigkeit dem Schiedsverfahren zustimmt.

Fraglich ist weiter, wie die in Artikel 139 der Verfassung beinhaltete Einschränkung im internationalen Schiedsverfahrensrecht zu qualifizieren ist. Kann etwa ein Schiedsverfahren an einem Schiedsort außerhalb des Irans eingeleitet werden, wenn die von der Verfassung vorgesehene Zustimmung des Parlaments nicht vorliegt? Führt die Versagung der Zustimmung dazu, dass insgesamt keine wirksame Schiedsklausel vorliegt oder handelt es sich lediglich um eine Bestimmung des iranischen öffentlichen Rechts, die außerhalb des Irans keine Wirkung entfaltet? Auch diese Frage ist, soweit ersichtlich, nicht geklärt. Zwar sprechen Anhaltspunkte dafür, dass ein Schiedsgericht außerhalb des Irans seine Zuständigkeit bejahen würde, auch wenn die Zustimmung des iranischen Parlaments fehlt, weil die Anwendung öffentlichen Rechts im Grundsatz territorial beschränkt ist. So lässt sich vertreten, dass die iranische Verfassungsbestimmung keine Wirksamkeit entfaltet, wenn ein Schiedsort im Ausland vereinbart ist. Aus Sicht des Schiedsgerichts läge dann eine wirksame Schiedsklausel vor und das Verfahren kann unabhängig von der Zustimmung des Parlaments durchgeführt werden. Doch ist es fraglich, ob der deutschen Partei mit einem solchen Schiedsspruch geholfen ist. Denn im Iran wird ein

---

7 Möglicherweise wird hier jedoch Art. 11 des am 17. August 2002 zwischen Deutschland und dem Iran unterzeichneten Abkommens über die gegenseitige Förderung und den gegenseitigen Schutz von Kapitalanlagen Abhilfe schaffen. Dort sind Schiedsverfahren zwischen einem deutschen Investor und dem iranischen Staat vorgesehen. Das Abkommen ist aber bislang (Stand 1.1.2004) nicht ratifiziert. Auch bleibt die Handhabung dieser Bestimmung in der Praxis abzuwarten.

solcher Schiedsspruch nicht vollstreckbar sein, weil ihm nach iranischer Vorstellung keine wirksame Schiedsklausel zugrunde liegt. In einem solchen Fall ist sowohl nach den Bestimmungen der NYC wie auch nach Artt. 35 (1), 33 (1) a) des iranischen Schiedsgesetzes die Anerkennung des Schiedsspruches ausgeschlossen.

Schwierig einzuschätzen sind zudem die Folgen, wenn das Parlament die Zustimmung zur Einleitung eines Schiedsverfahrens versagt. Sind in einem solchen Fall die iranischen Gerichte subsidiär zuständig? Besteht dann wenigstens die Möglichkeit, ein ordentliches Gericht im Iran anzurufen oder wird dieses die Klage unter Hinweis auf den Einwand der Schiedsklausel als unzulässig abweisen (obgleich ein Schiedsverfahren - in Ermangelung der Zustimmung des Parlamentes - nicht durchgeführt werden kann)? Richtigerweise wird hier davon auszugehen sein, dass eine Partei, die sich auf die Unwirksamkeit der Schiedsklausel im Schiedsverfahren beruft, nicht zugleich im Verfahren vor den staatlichen Gerichten die Einrede der Schiedsgerichtsbarkeit erheben kann. Nach einem allgemeinen Grundsatz darf ein solches Verhalten nicht dazu führen, dass der Kläger insgesamt rechtlos gestellt ist,[8] und zwar ganz unabhängig davon, wie man das dogmatisch begründet (implizite Kündigung der Schiedsklausel, Rechtsmissbrauch, Verwirkung etc.). Auch wenn sich hier Argumente finden lassen, die wohl die meisten Gerichte davon überzeugen werden, eine Klage trotz bestehender Schiedsklausel zuzulassen, hat dies in einem jedem Fall zur Folge, dass sich das Verfahren erheblich verzögert. Es bleibt so dabei, dass das Schiedsverfahren bei der Beteiligung von öffentlichen Parteien im Iran mit erheblichen Unsicherheiten verbunden ist; ein Schiedsort außerhalb des Iran kann dabei von Vorteil sein.

Wahl des auf den Vertrag anwendbaren Rechts

Neben der Wahl des Streitbeilegungsverfahrens ist die Bestimmung des auf den Vertrag anwendbaren Rechts ein wichtiges Gestaltungsmittel der internationalen Vertragspraxis. Auch hier ist die Wahl des anwendbaren Rechts auf den Mechanismus der Streitbeilegung abzustimmen. Nationale Gerichte tun sich mitunter schwer bei der Ermittlung ausländischen Rechts; internationale Konventionen sind nicht überall gleichermaßen verbreitet und akzeptiert; Schiedsgerichte sind oft mit Richtern unterschiedlicher Nationalitäten besetzt, was bei der Festlegung auf eine bestimmte nationale Rechtsordnung zu bedenken ist.

---

8 Aus der deutschen Rechtsprechung grundlegend BGHZ 50, 191, 195 ff. sowie aus letzter Zeit OLG Frankfurt, IPRax 1999, 247 ff. (mit Anm. *Hau*).

International ist der Grundsatz der Parteiautonomie weitestgehend anerkannt. Man könnte fast von einem transnationalen Rechtsprinzip sprechen, wonach ein internationaler Vertrag der von den Parteien gewählten Rechtsordnung unterliegt (so die Parteien eine solche Wahl getroffen haben).[9] Allerdings: Keine Regel ohne Ausnahme. Denn dieser Grundsatz erfährt in einigen Rechtsordnungen interessante Einschränkungen, so zum Beispiel im Verhältnis zum Iran. Zwar bestimmt Artikel 27 des Schiedsgesetzes:

„Das Schiedsgericht soll den Schiedsspruch nach den materiell-rechtlichen Bestimmungen erlassen, die die Parteien für die Streitentscheidung festgelegt haben. Die Wahl der Gesetze oder des Rechts eines bestimmten Landes, wie immer diese zum Ausdruck kommt, soll soviel bedeuten wie ein Verweis auf das materielle (interne) Recht dieses Landes."

Diese Bestimmung, die sich am UNCITRAL Modellgesetz orientiert, beinhaltet eine Rechtswahlmöglichkeit nach internationalem Zuschnitt. Anders aber Artikel 1307 des ZGB, der bestimmt:

„Verpflichtungen aus Verträgen unterliegen den Gesetzen am Abschlussort, außer in Fällen, in denen beide Parteien Ausländer sind und ausdrücklich oder stillschweigend den Vertrag einer anderen Rechtsordnung unterworfen haben."

Nach einer in der iranischen Praxis verbreiteten Auffassung soll diese Vorschrift auch bei der Vereinbarung eines Schiedsgerichtes Anwendung finden (ohne Ansehung dessen, dass die Rechtswahl auch - und eigenständig - im Schiedsgesetz geregelt ist). Mit Blick darauf, dass bislang international (noch) keine Einigkeit darüber besteht, welche IPR-Regeln ein Schiedsgericht anzuwenden hat[10] kann nicht ausgeschlossen werden, dass auch ein internationales Schiedsgericht die Bestimmung des iranischen ZGB heranzieht, und sei dies ergänzend oder kumulierend zu anderen Vorschriften.

Der Inhalt des Art. 1307 ZGB (und erst recht der Sinn der Vorschrift) erschließt sich dem Leser nicht ohne Weiteres. Die Anknüpfung des Vertragsstatuts an Abschlussort und Staatsangehörigkeit ist archaisch; die iranische Rechtspraxis

---

9 Überblick bei *Schröder u. Wenner*, Internationales Vertragsrecht, 2. Aufl. 1998, 9 ff.

10 Hierzu *Craig u. Park u. Paulsson*, International Chamber of Commerce Arbitration (1998) 323 ff. Weiterhin verbreitet ist die Auffassung, in Zweifelsfällen *kumulativ* das IPR sämtlicher (möglicherweise) beteiligter Rechtsordnungen anzuwenden. Mit Blick auf einen deutsch-iranischen Vertrag kann das zur Folge haben, dass Schiedsrichter auch dann die Bestimmungen des iranischen internationalen Vertragsrechts berücksichtigen, wenn der Schiedsort außerhalb des Iran liegt.

versucht zudem, die Bestimmung des ZGB „rechtswahlfreundlich" auszulegen. Hier werden die folgende Fallgruppen unterschieden:

(1) Ein *im Iran* abgeschlossener Vertrag zwischen *zwei iranischen Staatsbürgern* unterliegt iranischem Recht. Eine Rechtswahlmöglichkeit besteht auf Grund von Art. 1307 ZGB nicht. Das leuchtet bei einem reinen Inlandsfall ohne Auslandsbezug ein (wenn es auch weniger zweckmäßig sein mag, dies an der Staatsangehörigkeit festzumachen).

(2) Ein *im Iran* abgeschlossener Vertrag *zwischen einem iranischen und einem ausländischen Staatsbürger* unterliegt ebenfalls zwingend iranischem Recht. Auch dieser Fall ist von Art. 1307 ZGB umfasst. Soweit der Fall einen Auslandsbezug aufweist, der über die ausländische Nationalität des Vertragspartners hinausgeht, kann hier eine Rechtswahl wünschenswert sein.

(3) Ein *im Iran* abgeschlossener Vertrag zwischen *zwei ausländischen Staatsbürgern* unterliegt im Grundsatz iranischem Recht. Die Parteien haben jedoch die Möglichkeit, eine andere Rechtsordnung als die iranische zu bestimmen. In diesem Fall greift also die Auflockerung, die Art. 1307 ZGB vorsieht. Eine Rechtswahl kann dabei ausdrücklich oder stillschweigend erfolgen und im Vertrag selbst oder einem anderen Dokument enthalten sein. Eine solche Fallkonstellation ist jedoch wohl eher selten.

(4) Ein Vertrag, der *außerhalb des Irans* zwischen *zwei iranischen Staatsbürgern* oder einem *Iraner und einem ausländischen Staatsbürger* abgeschlossen wird, unterliegt dem Recht am Abschlussort oder einem anderen von den Parteien gewählten Recht, sofern das IPR des Abschlussortes eine Rechtswahl zulässt. Art. 1307 ZGB ist nach dieser Ansicht also keine Sachnormverweisung (wie das bei einer entsprechenden Kollisionsnorm zu erwarten wäre), sondern verweist auch auf die kollisionsrechtlichen Bestimmungen am Abschlussort. Für einen in Deutschland unterzeichneten Vertrag folgt hieraus, dass eine Rechtswahl zulässig und wirksam ist, weil Art. 27 (1) EGBGB und § 1051 (1) ZPO dies gestatten.

Im Ergebnis ist eine Rechtswahl in einem deutsch-iranischen Vertrag dann (und nur dann) möglich, wenn der Vertrag außerhalb des Irans abgeschlossen wird (und das IPR am Abschlussort eine Rechtswahl zulässt). Aus diesem Grund versuchen die Parteien häufig, den Abschlussort nach Deutschland (oder sonst ins Ausland) zu verlagern, um von der Möglichkeit einer Rechtswahl Gebrauch zu machen. Das muss im Streitfall allerdings auch zweifelsfrei nachgewiesen werden können. Mitunter wird deshalb ein an sich nicht beurkundungspflichtiger

Vertrag zu Beweiszwecken beurkundet. Alternativ dazu ist es möglich, die Unterschriften der Unterzeichner notariell beglaubigen zu lassen, was sehr viel kostengünstiger ist. Soweit ersichtlich fehlt es jedoch an gerichtlichen Präzedenzfällen, die diese Praxis bestätigen. So bleibt auch in diesem Fall die Unsicherheit, ob der Abschlussort im Ausland zur Überzeugung des (iranischen) Gerichtes oder Schiedsgerichtes bewiesen werden kann.

Geht man davon aus, es bestehe eine Rechtswahlmöglichkeit, stellt sich als nächste Frage, welchem Recht der Vertrag zweckmäßigerweise zu unterstellen ist. Dabei sind verschiedene Gesichtspunkte zu berücksichtigen.[11] Zunächst wird eine iranische Partei wenig Bereitschaft zeigen, den Vertrag der ihr unbekannten deutschen Rechtsordnung zu unterstellen. Das ist gerade bei öffentlichen Unternehmen der Fall, die sich in der Praxis nicht (oder nur sehr ungern) auf eine Wahl ausländischen Rechts einlassen. Gleiches gilt für ein beteiligtes deutsches Unternehmen, das ebenfalls vor dem juristischen „Sprung ins Dunkle" zurückschrecken wird. Mit Blick darauf, dass die iranische Rechtsordnung für viele der Verträge des modernen Wirtschaftsverkehrs bislang keine entsprechenden Regeln entwickelt hat, die Veröffentlichungspraxis der Gerichte zurückhaltend ist und iranische juristische Literatur schwer zugänglich ist, sprechen zudem weitere Argumente gegen die Wahl iranischen Rechts. Als Alternative bleiben die Wahl eines neutralen Rechts - beliebt ist hier das der Schweiz oder das Österreichs - oder eine Verweisung auf das CISG (das, bei einer Wahl deutschen Rechts, ohne anderweitige Vereinbarung bereits als Teil des internen Rechts anzuwenden ist). Ideal ist keine dieser Möglichkeiten. Das CISG ist keine komplette Rechtsordnung und öffnet verschiedene Einfallstore für nationale Bestimmungen. Auch die Nachbarrechtsordnungen der Schweiz und Österreichs können in - entscheidenden - Einzelfragen vom deutschen Recht abweichen. Es empfiehlt sich daher, bei einer solchen Rechtswahl das Vertragwerk auch durch einen in der betreffenden Jurisdiktion qualifizierten Juristen prüfen zu lassen, was allerdings die Transaktionskosten erhöht.

Kann die Frage der Rechtswahl nicht zur Zufriedenheit aller Beteiligten gelöst werden, bleibt die Möglichkeit, im Wege einer vertraglichen Komplettregelung die Bedeutung des Vertragsstatutes so weit als möglich zu Gunsten vertraglicher Regelungen zurückzudrängen. Das ist bei Verträgen größeren Volumens weit verbreitet, so dass in einem solchen Fall die Bedeutung der Vertragsstatutes beschränkt ist auf die zwingenden Bestimmungen des anwendbaren Rechts. Problematisch kann jedoch sein, dass die ausführlichen Verträge anglo-

---

11 Zu den bei der Rechtswahl zu berücksichtigenden Gesichtspunkten (allgemein, ohne Beschränkung auf den Iran) *Mankowski* RIW 2003, 2 ff.

amerikanischen Musters, mit seitenlangen Definitionskatalogen am Anfang, detaillierten Regelungen von Gewährleistungen und Stichtagen, ausführlichen Vereinbarungen über Maß, Zeit und andere Selbstverständlichkeiten, ergänzt durch eine Vielzahl von Vertragsanlagen, nicht der iranischen Geschäftspraxis entsprechen. Gerade Verhandlungspartner der öffentlichen Hand legen meist Wert auf konzise, klar strukturierte und einfach formulierte Verträge. Ein Overkill an Dokumentation kann Verhandlungen leicht vorzeitig beenden. Um diese Situation zu vermeiden kann es daher empfehlenswert sein, zunächst in einem *Letter of Intent* die wirtschaftlichen Eckpunkte des Geschäfts zu fixieren und erst dann einen ausführlichen Vertrag zu verhandeln. Auch sollte man die iranische Seite dazu ermuntern, sich bei der Verhandlung des Vertrages entsprechend anwaltlich vertreten zu lassen.

Unbeschadet einer wirksamen Rechtswahl sind auf einen deutsch-iranischen Vertrag zugleich die international zwingenden Bestimmungen der iranischen Rechtsordnung anwendbar, also diejenigen Regeln, die unabhängig vom Vertragsstatut Geltung beanspruchen.[12] Zum einen geht es hier um Bestimmungen des iranischen öffentlichen Wirtschaftsrechts. Ungeachtet der Liberalisierungsbestrebungen aus jüngerer Zeit ist die wirtschaftliche Tätigkeit im Iran weiterhin stark staatlich reguliert. Gerade Staatsunternehmen sind einer Vielzahl zwingender Bestimmungen unterworfen, die auch auf Verträge einwirken können. Des Weiteren tun sich Probleme auf, die den Kennern des islamischen Rechts zur Genüge bekannt sind: das Verbot der Zinsen und das der Forderungsabtretung, die - nach iranischer Vorstellung - wohl beide international zwingend sind. Entsprechende Klauseln sind regelmäßiger Bestandteil internationaler Lieferverträge. Diese Probleme der iranischen Rechtsordnung lassen sich jedoch im Wege der Vertragsgestaltung vergleichsweise einfach in den Griff bekommen. Statt Verzugszinsen wird eine „Vertragsstrafe“ oder eine „Gebühr“ vereinbart, die sich durchaus an internationalen Zinsreferenzsätzen wie dem LIBOR orientieren darf; iranische Gerichte, so jedenfalls die (beschränkte) bekannte Praxis, akzeptieren solche Vereinbarungen, auch wenn sie wirtschaftlich der Vereinbarung von Verzugszinsen entsprechen. Anstelle einer Forderungsabtretung kann eine Einzugsermächtigung vorgesehen werden, nach der der „Neugläubiger“ zur Einziehung der Forderung ermächtigt wird. Alternativ dazu ist auch eine Übertragung der Forderung möglich, wenn die Zustimmung des Schuldners eingeholt wird. Eine solche Struktur kann aus insolvenzrechtlichen Gründen vorteilhaft sein (auch wenn die Einzelheiten bislang nicht geklärt sind).

---

12 *Craig u. Park u. Paulsson* (Anm. 10) 338 ff.

In solchen Fällen bleibt natürlich ein gewisses Risiko, gerade für den Fall, dass nicht-iranische Schiedsrichter über den Vertrag entscheiden und die einschlägigen islamischen Verbote möglicherweise strenger handhaben als die iranische Rechtsprechung, die sich mit diesen Beschränkungen in pragmatischer Weise arrangiert hat. Gerade bei der Wahl von Gutachtern, die für Fragen des iranischen Rechts eingeschaltet werden, sollte man darauf achten, dass diese nicht nur das klassische schiitische Recht, sondern auch die heutige iranische Praxis kennen. Die unreflektierte Anwendung von historischen Scharia-Prinzipien, möglicherweise unterstützt durch den Verweis auf Bestimmungen der iranischen Verfassung, ist in einem Schiedsverfahren meist kontraproduktiv. Ausgangspunkt sollte vielmehr stets die *Praxis der iranischen Gerichte* sein. Wo eine solche nicht bekannt ist, sollten die Schiedsrichter zunächst den Vertrag auslegen, anstatt vorschnell Bestimmungen des islamischen Rechts anzuwenden.

Immunität von Staatsunternehmen

Wie bereits erwähnt, sind im Iran-Geschäft Verträge mit öffentlichen Auftraggebern von zentraler Bedeutung. Neben den vorgenannten Aspekten stellt sich hier die Frage, inwieweit sich der iranische Staat oder ein iranisches Staatsunternehmen im Falle einer Verurteilung durch ein Gericht oder Schiedsgericht auf den Grundsatz der staatlichen Immunität berufen kann (bzw. dies bereits der Einleitung eines Gerichts- oder Schiedsgerichtsverfahrens im Wege steht). International setzt sich bei Verträgen mit der öffentlichen Hand dabei die Tendenz durch, wonach sich der Staat bei privatwirtschaftlicher Betätigung nicht auf staatliche Immunität berufen darf, also eine Unterscheidung getroffen wird zwischen der *hoheitlichen* und der *wirtschaftlichen* Tätigkeit des Staates.[13] Diese Unterscheidung vollzieht im Grundsatz auch das iranische Recht, allerdings mit gewissen Vorbehalten, gerade was die Vollstreckung von Entscheidungen angeht.

Die Vollstreckung eines Titels gegen den iranischen Staat ist nur auf Grund und unter den engen Voraussetzungen eines Spezialgesetzes möglich, des *Gesetzes über das Verfahren der Erfüllung von Urteilen gegen den Staat und Beschränkungen der Vollstreckung in Staatseigentum*. Danach sind Vermögensgegenstände der öffentlichen Hand i.w.S. vom normalen Zwangsvollstreckungsverfahren ausgenommen. Das Gesetz soll nach einer verbreiteten Auffassung auch auf die Vollstreckung gegen Staatunternehmen in privater Rechtsform Anwendung finden. Jedenfalls kann nicht ausgeschlossen werden, dass sich ein Staatsunternehmen im Vollstreckungsverfahren auf dieses

13 *Craig u. Park u. Paulsson* (Anm. 10) 670 ff.

Gesetz berufen wird, auch wenn es vom Wortlaut her auf den Fiskus zugeschnitten ist und auf Staatsunternehmen in Privatrechtsform jedenfalls nicht unmittelbar anwendbar ist. So sind die Beschränkungen dieses Gesetzes auch dann zu beachten, wenn der Vertragspartner ein Staatsunternehmen und nicht der Staat selbst ist.

Eine Vollstreckung gegen die öffentliche Hand setzt nach den einschlägigen Vorschriften einen entsprechenden Haushaltstitel voraus. Besteht ein solcher nicht, muss ein weiteres Verfahren eingeleitet werden, damit im kommenden Haushaltsjahr ein entsprechender Betrag im Haushalt ausgewiesen wird, aus dem die titulierte Forderung erfüllt werden kann. Im Ergebnis ist eine Vollstreckung gegen die öffentliche Hand oder Staatsunternehmen im Iran langwierig und - mit Blick auf die verschiedenen rechtlichen Hürden - wenig erfolgversprechend. Die Zahlungsmoral der öffentlichen Auftraggeber war in der Vergangenheit jedoch in aller Regel gut, weitaus besser jedenfalls als die in anderen Schwellenländern. Folglich war die praktische Bedeutung der vorstehend geschilderten, vollstreckungsrechtlichen Probleme weniger signifikant. Zudem kann der Versuch unternommen werden, diese Probleme im Wege der Vertragstechnik einzufangen. So kommt in Frage, einen ausdrücklichen Verzicht auf den Einwand der staatlichen Immunität in den Vertrag aufzunehmen. Ein solcher Verzicht ist bei manchen Vertragstypen, etwa bei Staatsanleihen oder in Konzessionsverträgen, weit verbreitet und üblich. Bei einem Liefervertrag mit einem iranischem Staatsunternehmen hilft eine entsprechende Vertragsklausel im Ernstfall aber kaum weiter. Denn wird am Ende doch im Iran vollstreckt, ist nicht zu erwarten, dass ein iranisches Gericht eine solche Vereinbarung anerkennt. Vielmehr ist davon auszugehen, dass die betreffende Klausel mit Blick auf die zwingenden, den iranischen Staat schützenden Vorschriften über die Vollstreckung gegen die öffentlich Hand nicht wirksam ist. In vielen Fällen besteht aber die Möglichkeit, durch die Vereinbarung von Abschlagszahlungen und die Stellung von Garantien eine gesicherte Position zu erlangen, die eine Vollstreckung im Iran nicht erforderlich macht. Einer solchen Struktur ist in einem jeden Fall der Vorzug zu geben.

Extraterritoriale Anwendung des US-Außenwirtschaftsrechts

Bei den meisten Irangeschäften taucht zudem die Frage nach der extraterritorialen Anwendung des US-Außenwirtschaftsrechts auf. Auf in den USA tätige Unternehmen findet bekanntlich der *Iran Libya Sanction Act* (1996)

Anwendung.[14] Auch deutsche Unternehmen, die in den USA präsent sind, befürchten häufig, Sanktionen (oder zumindest Sanktionsdrohungen) nach diesen Vorschriften ausgesetzt zu sein. Der *Iran-Libya Sanction Act* gehört gewiss zu den weniger erfreulichen Aspekten des internationalen Rechtsverkehrs. Seine rechtlichen Implikationen für europäische Unternehmen werden allerdings oft überschätzt. In diesem Zusammenhang sind zwei Fragen voneinander zu unterscheiden:

So stellt sich zunächst die Frage, ob ein bestimmtes Geschäft überhaupt von der amerikanischen Sanktionsgesetzgebung erfasst ist. Der *Iran Libya Sanction Act* ist komplex formuliert, arbeitet mit verschiedenen Schwellenwerten und sieht unter bestimmten Voraussetzungen auch Befreiungsmöglichkeiten vor. Folglich unterliegt nicht jedes Irangeschäft von vornherein den Bestimmungen des *Iran Libya Sanction Act*. Es kann sich im Einzelfall daher durchaus lohnen, die Frage der Anwendbarkeit des Gesetzes ebenso wie die einzelnen Befreiungsmöglichkeiten zu prüfen. Die Folge kann sein, dass ein bestimmtes Geschäft so strukturiert werden kann, dass es überhaupt keine Sanktionsmöglichkeiten nach dem *Iran Libya Sanction Act* auslöst.

Die zweite Frage ist die nach der extraterritorialen Anwendung der amerikanischen Sanktionsbestimmungen. Zwar ist anerkannt, dass im öffentlichen Interesse erlassene Boykott- und Sanktionsbestimmungen unter bestimmen Voraussetzungen auch extraterritoriale Wirkung entfalten können.[15] Für den *Iran Libya Sanction Act* gilt dies aber gerade nicht. Vielmehr bestehen europäische Vorschriften, die es einem deutschen Unternehmen untersagen, den Bestimmungen des *Iran Libya Sanction Act* Folge zu leisten. Dazu hat die Europäische Union die *Verordnung (EG) Nr. 2271/96 zum Schutze vor den Auswirkungen der extraterritorialen Anwendungen von einem Drittland erlassener Rechtsakte sowie von darauf beruhenden oder sich daraus ergebenden Maßnahmen* erlassen.[16] Die Verordnung sieht eine Reihe von „Abwehrmaßnahmen" gegen US-amerikanische Sanktionen vor. Art. 5 der Verordnung *verbietet* es insbesondere europäischen Unternehmen, dem *Iran Libya Sanction Act* Folge zu leisten. Des Weiteren stellt die Verordnung in Art. 4 klar, dass amerikanische Maßnahmen auf Grundlage des *Act* nicht anerkennungsfähig sind. Das US-amerikanische Gesetz ist daher keine

---

[14] Die Geltungsdauer des Gesetzes wurde bei Ablauf seiner ursprünglichen Geltungsdauer im Jahr 2001 um weitere fünf Jahre verlängert; der *Iran Libya Sanction Act* ist daher weiterhin in Kraft.

[15] Grundlegend: BGHZ 34, 169 (177) - „Borax"; BGHZ 59, 82 (851) - „nigerianische Masken";

[16] Informativ hierzu *Meng*, EuZW 1997, 423 (425 ff.).

Eingriffsnorm, die in einem Verfahren von einem europäischen Gericht oder Schiedsgericht zu beachten wäre und hat keinen Einfluss auf die Wirksamkeit von Verträgen, deren Inhalt oder Zweck gegen die amerikanische Sanktionsgesetzgebung verstoßen. Im Ergebnis sind europäische Unternehmen vor US-Sanktionsmaßnahmen *rechtlich* weitgehend geschützt, auch wenn der *politische* Druck weiter beachtlich sein kann.

Diese Bestimmungen werden auch von amerikanischen Unternehmen mitunter dazu genutzt, über ihre in Europa ansässigen Konzernunternehmen Irangeschäfte zu tätigen. Von Seiten der USA aus wird diese Praxis anscheinend weitgehend geduldet. Ebenso sind die USA sehr zurückhaltend, Verstöße europäischer Unternehmen gegen den *Iran Libya Sanction Act* auch tatsächlich zu sanktionieren (selbst wenn dies in der Vergangenheit wiederholt angedroht wurde). Zweifelhaft mag allerdings erscheinen, ob dies auch für Strukturen gilt, bei denen ein US-Unternehmen lediglich ein „Vehikel" in Europa für das Irangeschäft gründet, das „zwischengeschaltet" wird, um in den Genuss der europäischen Abwehrgesetzgebung zu kommen. Dann liegt eine Umgehung der US-amerikanischen Außenwirtschaftsbestimmungen nahe. Fraglich ist, inwieweit dies dem Ziel zuträglich ist, Sanktionen nach dem *Iran-Libya Sanction Act* zu vermeiden.

Aus rechtlicher Perspektive steht der *Iran Libya Sanction Act* daher den Irangeschäften deutscher Unternehmen nicht im Wege. Hingewiesen sei gleichwohl darauf, dass Exportgeschäfte in den Iran meist den Bestimmungen des *deutschen* Außenwirtschaftsgesetzes (AWG) unterliegen werden. Auch aus dem AWG können sich Beschränkungen ergeben, gerade soweit *Dual Use* Güter betroffen sind, also zivile Güter, die möglicherweise auch zu militärischen Zwecken verwandt werden können. So ist es empfehlenswert, stets auch die Fragen der Exportkontrolle zu prüfen. In Zweifelsfällen kann es ratsam sein, eine aufschiebende Bedingung in den Vertrag aufzunehmen, wonach dieser erst wirksam werden soll, wenn die betreffende Lieferung nach den Bestimmungen des AWG freigegeben ist.

Zusammenfassung und Ausblick

Die Vertragsgestaltung im deutsch-iranischen Wirtschaftsverkehr weist einige Besonderheiten auf. Anders als man vielleicht erwarten würde, haben diese Besonderheiten mit dem islamischen Recht in aller Regel nichts zu tun. Ihren Ursprung haben die betreffenden iranischen Bestimmungen vielmehr im französischen Recht, das im Iran rezipiert und dann nur noch sehr unvollkommen an die Rechtsentwicklung in Frankreich angepasst wurde. Das

Ergebnis ist eine Regelung von Rechtswahl und Schiedsfähigkeit, die nicht dem internationalen Standard entspricht und der Praxis erheblich Probleme bereitet. Die weitgehende internationale Isolation der iranischen Rechtsordnung während der beiden letzten Jahrzehnte hat weiter dazu beigetragen, dass sich diese Bestimmungen haben unverändert halten können.

Seit einigen Jahren ist der Iran bestrebt, verstärkt um ausländische Privatinvestoren zu werben und auch die iranische Rechtsordnung entsprechend anzupassen. So bestehen inzwischen verschiedene Gesetze, die die Staatsquote verringern und ausländische Privatinvestoren anziehen sollen. Hinzu kommen der Beitritt zur NYC und das neue Schiedsgesetz von 1997, von denen eine Signalwirkung für den internationalen Rechtsverkehr ausgehen. Um diese Entwicklung weiter voranzutreiben und abzuschließen, wird es erforderlich sein, auch das internationale Vertragsrecht an internationale Standards anzupassen.

ISLAMIC SHARIA[1] AND CYBERSPACE[2]: REFLECTIONS ON THE INTERACTIONS OF SHARIA AND IRANIAN SOCIETY IN CYBERSPACE

Dr. Hassan Rezaei, Freiburg

1. Introduction

From the moment the Ottoman Empire, the last Muslim Empire, adopted the ***Mecelle-i Ahkam-i Adliye***[3] under the influence of the Code Napoleon of 1807

---

1 Islamic Sharia herein means what Muslim societies, specifically Iran in our present discussion, made and make of Islamic texts in the Koran and Sound Sunna. Unlike abstract, subjective definitions of Sharia as Allah's injunctions or intentions, this concept of Sharia is an objective matter which is not only related to the established texts, but which can also be easily traced throughout the history of Muslim societies in the form of authoritative *fatwas* (scholarly judgments) and institutions established in accordance with them.

2 By cyberspace I mean a non-physical terrain created by computer systems where electronic entities interact. Online networks, for example, create an electronic space within which people can communicate with one another via e-mail, conference, do research, or simply window shop. Like physical space, cyberspace contains *objects* (files, mail messages, graphics, etc.) and different modes of transmitting and interaction. Unlike real-world space, however, exploring cyberspace does not require any physical movement other than pressing keys on a keyboard or moving a mouse. Some programs, particularly computer games, are designed to create a special cyberspace, one that resembles physical reality in some ways but defies it in others. In its extreme form, called *virtual reality* (http://sbc.webopedia.com/TERM/C/virtual_reality.htm), users are presented with visual, auditory, and even tactile feedback that makes cyberspace feel real. For more details on cyberspace definition see *Balsano, A.M.*, An International Legal Instrument for Cyberspace? A Comparative Analysis with the Law of Outer Space, in: The International Dimensions of Cyberspace Law (UNESCO Publishing: Ashgate UK, 2000), pp. 128-130.

3 The *Mecelle* in Turkish or *Al-Majallah* in Arabic, compiled from 1868 to 1876, was the first codification of Islamic Sharia in modern history. Based on the Hanafi school of Sharia, it codified the Sharia decrees on property in addition to some general principles of Sharia, in particular a number of general rules related to ownership and transaction. It was published in 1868 under the name of "Compilation of Juridical Provisions". The Ottoman Penal Code, also called the *Mecelle*, was adopted 11 years later. The *Majallah*, which was a product of the first systematic reform movement among Muslims, had been implemented in the large territory of the Ottoman Empire before its destruction, including present-day Turkey, Palestine, Egypt, Saudi, Iraq, Syria, Jordan, Lebanon, Cyprus, Albania, Bosnia and Herzegovina. Some provisions of *Mecelle* are still in effect in Arabic countries. See *Onar, S.S.*, The Majalla. in: M. Khadduri (ed.), Law in the Middle East, Vol. 1. New York: AMS Press, 1984. pp. 292-308.

until now, Islamic Sharia has addressed principles, concepts and institutions of modern law, particularly human rights, without any open, inclusive or trustful reconciliation. A history of conflicting legal dualism among Muslim countries starts with the *Majallah*, which are on the one hand attached to traditional perceptions of Sharia and on the other forced to adopt modern model of codes of law. Despite a long period of encounter with the law of the modern world, considering the actual dilemmas of Sharia in most Muslim countries, one can still firmly claim that Sharia, particularly its criminal and family justice rulings, may be regarded as the harshest system of law facing modernity in comparison with other traditional legal systems throughout the world.

While the world community is deeply concerned about Islamic Sharia, especially after the events of 11 September disclosed its acute crisis, it seems that progressive Muslims within the Muslim world who witness the actual problems of established Sharia in their own communities are also losing their patience for Sharia to be transformed into a modern system of law based on human rights in the near future. What makes this transition more urgent is not the aftermath of New York events, but instead the last decade of the twentieth century and the aftermath of merging information in post-industrial societies with their postmodern philosophies and literature. The more the modern world enters the age of information and communication, the more Muslim societies find that the timely transition from the current Sharia is inevitable. Owing to rapid developments in information and communication technologies (ICT) and their prevalence across the world, many Muslim societies have access to these technologies, especially the World Wide Web. Along with this increase in the access of many Muslims to the internet, calls have arisen for instant resolution of the dilemma of Sharia and modernity. Currently, many strong online voices from all over the world (including most of the western strategic studies centers) are calling for emergency, short-run transformation in Islamic Sharia.

As ICT technologies expand within the Muslim societies and the internet in particular gains increasingly more validity among middle-class Muslims, we can see more reflection on the how the kernel of these societies (*i.e.*, Islamic Sharia) is represented in cyberspace, and about the impacts of the information society and its main component, the internet, on the development of Sharia in the future. By considering the existing features of online Sharia with a Shia reading of it in the Iranian context, this article seeks to show that with the expansion of cyberspace among the masses, people become conscious about the historicity of Sharia rulings, and that one can expect a revolution in Shia Islam through this public consciousness. Without depicting any utopian, emancipatory account of the information revolution, I want to argue that the "open" networks that are increasing rapidly among Iranians, when added to the historical discourses of rationalism and justice in Shia and the very young and well-educated majority of the Iranian population (40 millions under 30 years old), will create an historical openness in the closed space of existing understandings of Sharia.

Two main assumptions ground this argument. First, a peaceful transition of Iranian society to an open, democratic one is only possible through a paradigm shift in Sharia. In other words, a sustainable, authentic democracy is not foreseeable in Iran without the advent of a rights-based legal system evoked from Sharia traditions. In order to avoid being labeled as a foreign or alien plan, this goal must be pursued by means of a serious criticism from inside Muslim society. As Iran's century-long experience shows, modernist or secular discourses that see no role for Sharia discourse in the public sphere of Muslim societies cannot further the institutionalization of democracy and tolerance in societies with such strong roots in tradition. Secondly, there is currently an understanding of Islamic Sharia developed by various social, non-violent members of Iranian society, in particular women and youth, which can pave the way for the peaceful advent of a right-based legal system which is compatible with the emerging postmodern information society.

2. The Enthusiasm of Iranian Society for IT technologies

Although Iranian society is located among the developing countries with regard to industrial economic infrastructures, it has made substantial progress in communication infrastructures as a result of impressive investment in the communication system since 1994, particularly the completion and implementation of the 30,000 km project of fiber-optic cable. As the Middle East leading IT observer, Madar Research Group, reports, Iran is set on exploiting information and telecommunication technology as part of a drive to boost and reform the economy.[4] According to this progressive investing, the levels of penetration of IT technologies are growing quickly in the society, even in rural areas. Many villages will be brought into the net by the installation of thousands of digital communication switches.[5]

By March of 2004, an estimated four and half to five million people were the users of the internet.[6] Considering the country-wide success of the impressive

---

4 According to the latest report of Madar Research Journal on Iran eLandscape, available at http://www.madarresearch.com/main/mpage.aspx.

5 According to general information in *The CIA World Factbook 2003* available at http://www.cia.gov/cia/publications/factbook/geos/ir.html.

6 According to the statements of the director general of the Iranian data communication company, Reza Rashidi, see http://itna.ir/archives/news/024607.php.

fiber-optic cable project and subsequent reduction in the costs of broad band connections (ADSL), and according to the high level of willingness of bazaar to invest in e-business projects, it is estimated the current number of users will increase explosively to 15 million by the end of 2005.[7] This figure will be realistic for Iranian society if we bear in mind that the highest rate of internet usage is among young people. Furthermore, there has been a drastic increase in the number of personal computers (PCs) in the past two years. In February 2002, an Iranian computer store employee working in the computer bazaar in Tehran said, "...there is a sort of fever here in Iran. All the families who can afford it have a computer. All of the children are taking classes, and we sell a lot of educational software."[8] After Israel, Iran is currently the second country in the Middle East and North Africa with respect to the growth and expansion of internet access.[9] It is interesting to note that by 2001, Tehran alone boasted 1,500 internet cafes, making Iran one of the leading countries in the Middle East in terms of the number of internet cafes per major metropolitan area.[10]

In a country that two-thirds of the population is under 30[11], it is clear that the majority of people in designing their lives have little in common with a strict religious legal system imposed by elderly unelected clerics. Appetite for the new media is partly an accidental product of the Islamization policy. Since 1979, clerics who opposed the modern arts and entertainments as symbols of decadent West encouraged people, especially women, to go to schools and education centers. As a result, literacy levels have dramatically increased, rising from 47.5% in 1977 to 79.4% in 2003.

---

7 According to the statement of the director general of telecommunications of Iran to the World Telecommunication Development Conference in Istanbul, 2002 at http://www.itu.int/newsarchive/wtdc2002/iran.html.

8 *Hammersley, B.*, "Iran nets another revolt," The Guardian, February 21, 2002. Available online at http://www.guardian.co.uk/online/story/0,3605,653282,00.html.

9 See *Rahimi, B.*, "Cyberdissent; The Internet in revolutionary Iran", Middle East Review of International Affairs (MERIA Journal), Volume 7, No. 3, September 2003; also *Rubin, M.*, "What are Iran's Domestic Priorities?", MERIA Journal, Vol. 6, No. 2, June 2002. Both are avilable online at http://meria.idc.ac.il.

10 For more details see *Rahimi* 2003, ibid.

11 By 2002, the median age in Iran was in total 22.9 years: 22.7 years for males and 23.2 for females. See http://www.cia.gov/cia/publications/factbook/geos/ir.html.

Figure 1:

Year	Male Literacy Rate (%)	Female Literacy Rate (%)
1980	60.9	38.2
1985	65.8	45.9
1990	72.2	54.0
1995	78.0	61.9
2000	83.0	68.9
2005	87.0	74.9
2010	89.8	79.3
2015	91.9	82.6

Source: UNESCO Institute for Statistics, July 2002

Universities are constantly generating an unprecedented number of graduates. The rapidly growing demand for information and communication technology can be a manifestation of deep-seated changes in Iranian society. [12]

Thanks to the unprecedented development of universities and higher education centers throughout the country, the influence of the internet and information technologies is extending beyond major urban areas like Tehran. As former university students return to their homes from urban universities, they strive to remain connected to this new medium and, in the process, introduce their rural families and friends to the internet's possibilities. Because of this, rural areas in Iran have become exposed to the outside world to a degree that previously would have been difficult to conceive. It is this phenomenon in particular that has made the internet revolution in Iran reach far wider and deeper than might otherwise be expected from abroad.[13]

Besides dozens of growing critical and informative Websites belonging to the press inside Iran, there are currently numerous eJournals, news and political-cultural websites founded by Iranian's ca. 3.5 Million population living in the

12 The statistics are from the Iran Statistical Yearbook, 1381 (March 2003) published by the Statistical Centre of Iran. According to this Center, Iran presently has 17,196,588 students at schools and 1,673,757 students at universities and higher education centers, of which 45,621 are doctoral candidates.
See http://www.sci.or.ir/persia/index.htm.

13 *Rahimi* 2003, ibid.

west. They publish mainly dissent voices about the established Sharia. They aggregate important headlines, reports and essays from the inland press with lively opinion and commentary from people inside and outside the country. [14] In fact, their role is building bridges between Iranians inside and the rest of the world.

Since about 2002, one of the world-known Iranian contents of the internet called Weblogs[15] or Blogs, have suddenly appeared. These Weblogs are mainly online notebooks where cyber-diarists communicate with one another about the latest news in their personal lives, religion, politics, literature, cinema, music or sports. In a closed real socio-political system, these Weblogs enable young Iranians to build a fiercely individualistic community to share their experiences of the Islamized world they live in. "Ladysun", for example, is an English teacher in Tehran who has a Weblog in both English and Persian. She writes about this special space in Iran by referring to the deaths of the Iranian conjoined twins Ladan and Laleh Bijani: "I see a big irony comparing the sad death of these most-ever-loved-in-Iran twins with current events of Iran. Some people are ready to die for having their individuality back; some people are ready to kill, to take others' individuality away."[16]

Considering present Persian Weblogs on the internet that rapidly became a phenomenon around the cyberspace, it is now true to speak about an "Iranian Internet or Cyberspace". The internet statistics networks estimate that currently more than 60,000 Persian Weblogs are on the Web. It seems about 60% of them might be active. As indicated below, Farsi is the third language in the world of Weblogs. This fact shows clearly the importance of Weblogs between Iranians. More than 75% of Farsi content in the internet refers to Persianblog. It also uses the biggest Persian advertisement system in the internet.[17]

---

14 Some top sites of this kind are gooyanews, iran emrooz, achbar rooz, BBC Persian, radio farda, VOA Persian, Peiknet, peikeiran, shahrvand, sobhaneh and roushangari.

15 Rebecca Blood, author of the first reference book on Weblog culture, in her definition of Weblog says: " A Weblog is a coffeehouse conversation in text, with references as required" For more information on Weblog see *Blood, R.*, The Weblog Handbook, Perseus Publishing, 2002.

16 From the Lady Sun weblog at: http://www.ladysun.blogspot.com/2003_06_01_ladysun_archive.html.

17 Language identification is done using TextCat, a program that looks at the statistical distribution of three-letter clusters. See the NITLE Weblog Census at http://www.blogcensus.net.

Figure 2: Language Distribution of Weblogs

Language	**Count**	
English	1114392	
Portuguese	76894	
Persian (Farsi)	63058	
French	51125	
Polish	42574	
German	24030	

If we consider the issue of sexual freedom as one of the most unsolved problematics of traditional Sharia facing the modern world, then we can understand how much the established Sharia jurists dislike the openness of cyberspace. Control over the sexual organs and relationships are fundamental to existing Sharia discourse in Iran. The Islamization discourse around this issue is extremely closed, so that no open public discourse is possible. It seems, for instance, that for the Islamic government the protection of headscarfs on the heads of Iranian women has priority over the complicated problems of Iran's economy. The internet, however, offers a new public space for Iranians to express themselves freely and anonymously on various aspects of sex and love. Probing the freedom provided by this space, internet users, especially young girls and boys, are finding in Weblogs an alternative medium for expression that is denied to them in real public spaces.

The internet in Iran gives users access to a forbidden world. The famous case of a former prostitute's Weblog, detailing the underworld life of Iranian society in which sex and romance outside marriage is otherwise taboo, demonstrates how Iranians are defying the strict Sharia penal codes imposed by the Islamic government.[18] Such unabashed online diaries offer rare insight into the frustrated lives of the post-revolution generations who have grown up under strict governmental Sharia limitations. Interestingly, a number of these sexual-critical Weblogs use the language of *fiqh* and Muslim Sufis in their writings.[19]

---

18 Reuters' report from Tehran, June 16 2003 Available online at: http://reuters.com/newsArticle.jhtml?type=internetNews&storyID=2943120. Although her Weblog (http://www.faheshe.persianblog.com) has been recently disabled by the Islamic government, like many similar Weblogs that were banned and then opened in another domain, she now bloggs at http://faheshe.blogsky.com. For a top list of such sites see http://www.topsitelists.com/bestsites/hotpersianlinks/topsites.html.

19 A good example of this is the Weblog at http://www.shurideh.com.

Remarkably, the internet in Iran remains largely unregulated, although the government, without having any clear policy on the matter,[20] has occasionally tried to filter, censor and even hack pornographic sites and sites it deems anti-Islamic or anti-clergy.[21] But until now, because of new anti filtering software and technologies, the regime has not been able to prevent free flow of information on the internet as it wishes. Recently, because the Iranian government has understood that the establishment of an impenetrable firewall in cyberspace is impossible, it has resorted to various judicial surveillances and procedures to force the critical inland Websites to censor themselves.

In a new development emerged during recent parliamentary election the cyber dissents send text messaging (SMS) on mobile phones of ayatollahs to protest against Sharia establishment.[22]

Since April 2000 more than 85 liberal, critical and reformist newspapers have been banned; however, a new critical journalism is being produced on the internet, mainly by young writers and journalists who worked in those banned papers. They are using the internet as an alternative arena for their critical, political publications, and also publish their previously censored works on these sites.[23]

3. Different Online Voices on Sharia

It should be mentioned here that this enthusiasm is not only limited to youth in Iran. Since the internet was introduced to Muslim societies, many Shia authoritarian clerics and institutions were among the first groups to go online.[24] Now, opening an advanced, multimedia website for possible imitators is a sign of being nominated as a grand ayatollah. Currently, in the city of Qom alone, there are more than 150 religious research centers which use the Internet and IT technologies. There are also about 30 professional computer centers, mainly in the Qom seminary, that are continuously working on the digitalization of as much Shia literature as possible. Up to now, they have produced tens of CDs on various Islamic issues. Since 1996 there has been an important project at the

---

20 It is reported that some Internet Service Providers (ISPs) are blocked according to the Act of Prohibition of Use of Satellite Receivers of 1994. See BBC Report at http://www.bbc.co.uk/persian/science/030510_h-banned-sites.shtml.

21 *McLaughlin, E.*, "Iran keeps an eye on the bloggers," report of CNN, July 18, 2003.

22 Report of Sharq Daily. Available at http://www.sharghnewspaper.com/archive.htm.

23 Such as http://www.behnoudonline.com/ or Ebrahim Nabavi's column at: http://news.gooya.com/nabavi/.

24 According to the statistics of Shia Search, the greatest Shia directory, there are currently about 1315 (Register979 and Free Domain336) Shia websites in 26 language on the internet. See http://www.shiasearch.net/?newlang=eng.

software research center of the Qom Seminary called "Building a knowledge-base and expert system for Islamic Sharia", under which the all fatwa processes and resources will be mediated by computer intelligence.[25] Another important product of this center is the Encyclopedia of Shia Jurisprudence *(Al-Mojam Program)*, which helps Sharia researchers to search easily in the more than 500 authoritative textbooks of Shia and analyze and compare different juristic views throughout the history of the Shia school of Sharia, instead of wasting time searching for and collecting data sources.[26] It seems realistic that by the production of this software, one no longer needs to spend 30 to 40 years of his life in religious seminary to become a grand ayatollah; rather, this goal can be reached in less than one third of that time.

In addition to the websites of advocates of the Islamic state and the theory of Ayatollah Khomeini, there are other critical sites belonging to critical ayatollahs or religious intellectuals who reject this theory. The active website of the first Iranian president of the Republic, *Abolhassan Banisadr*,[27] who has lived in exile since 1981, can be considered one of the competing readings of Sharia. In addition to maintaining his personal website, together with his colleagues he publishes a biweekly e-journal called "Islamic Revolution in Exile," in which he regularly writes very critical essays about the established Sharia system in Iran. While he was always censored, he could attract a significant audience for his different paradigm of Islamic discourse among the reformist movements that have religious motivations within Iran by using the internet and email. Among the critical clerics are the multi-language websites of Ayatollah *Montazeri*,[28] Ayatollah *Y. Saanei*[29] and Ayatollah *M. Shirazi*.[30] In December 2000, Ayatollah *H. Montazeri*, who was supposed to be the successor of Ayatollah *Khomeini* but turned into a dissenter of him, published his 786-page memoir[31] against the practices of the regime online. An enlightening chapter in the interaction of Shia clerics and the internet ensued. These memoirs, which provide a unique insight into the history of the Islamic revolution, have been banned in Iran. The online publication of this book has caused many sharp criticisms against the Islamity of the regime. Recently, Ayatollah *Montazeri* and two prominent members of his fatwa office, Hojjatol-Islams *M. Kadivar* and *H. Qabel*, have published online

---

25 For more information about these ambitious projects, see http://noorsoft.org.

26 For an online version of the encyclopedia, look at: http://www.almarkaz.net/almojamlist.asp.

27 He has published all his books online at http://www.banisadr.com.fr/.

28 See http://www.montazeri.ws/.

29 See http://www.saanei.org/.

30 See http://www.shirazi.org.uk/.

31 See http://www.iranvision.com/pdf/khaterat.pdf.

fatwas on the question of *hijab*, arguing that *hijab* is, firstly, a "right" of Muslim women and secondly, that its "form" is not considered to be an essential of Sharia.[32] *Kadivar* also points out that Sharia prescribes only a minimum standard for *hijab*, which is less than conventional dressing, and *Qabel,* in the form of an analytic *fatwa,* expresses that covering the hair is not mandatory for women in Sharia. Namely, a woman can be called Muslim without having *hijab* or a head scarf.[33] It is only by virtue of the internet that the public issuing of these *fatwas* became possible in Iran.

Beside the Websites of critical-religious scholars like *Abdelkarim Soroush,*[34] *Ali Shariati*[35] and *Melli-Mazhabiha,*[36] there is a group of Websites belonging to post-revolutionary intellectuals who have good knowledge of the content of Islamic Sharia, like *Mohsen Kadivar, Akbar Ganji,*[37] *Emad Baqi,*[38] *Mehdi Khalaji*[39] and *Hanaei Kashani.*[40] Apparently, they oppose Sharia rulings and their application in Iran. However, it seems that during the last decade a new movement of other-thinking has been created among young students of Shia seminaries. It is in relation to this fact that the expansion of internetized or informationized Sharia has the potential to open up an express way for them to transcend the traditional, totalitarian networks of Shia's ayatollahs. Although their presence on the internet is still unimpressive, if they begin to build online alliances to challenge the established Sharia, by their communicative strength they should be regarded as one of the most effective catalysts of Shia Protestantism in our era.

And finally, If finding or publishing a critical or pagan publication concerning Sharia or the Islamic ideology of power was among the hardest tasks in Iran a decade ago, today one can easily find thousands pages of these kinds presently

---

32 This surprising fatwa of Ayatollah Montazeri is available at http://www.nashrieh-nameh.com/article.php?articleID=109.

33 The texts of new fatwas are available at: http://www.womeniniran.org/archives/FN/000236.php and http://www.kadivar.com/Htm/Farsi/Speeches/F-List-82.HTM.

34 http://www.drsoroush.com/Persian.htm

35 http://alishariati.com/

36 *Melli-Mazhabiha* is a broad group of liberal, nationalist and religious reformists. For more information see their website at http://www.mellimazhabi.org/.

37 http://www.akbar-ganji.homepage.com/

38 http://www.emadbaghi.com/

39 At the Malakut group Weblog that contains 38 Bloggs. See http://ketaabcheh.malakut.org/.

40 http://fallosafah.org/

with the electronic movement on the Web.[41] Secularist websites publish the most forbidden books in Iran because their sharp critiques of Sharia rules are absolutely censored. The most deconstructive works of *Ahmad Kasravi* on Shia, Sufism and Islam are now online at his website,[42] and the works of significant Iranian seculars such as *Sadeq Hedayat*,[43] *Manouchehr Jamali*,[44] *Ali Mirfetroos*[45] and *Mohammad Reza Nikfar*[46] are now online as well. Also, there are some Persian websites that define themselves as Iranian atheist, agnostic, skeptic, humanist and hedonist.[47]

4. Dialectics of Sharia and Being of Iranians on the Web

Sharia has traditionally been in struggle with the main Greek and Persian inputs to Islam (i.e., philosophy and mysticism). During the twentieth century and as a result of decades of practical secularization in terms of relative structural differentiations in culture, education, economy and politics, it has been forced to come face to face with new questions such as women's consciousness, the expansion of capitalist economy, modern arts, literature and public demand for active participation in politics. Now again, without resolving any questions of the last century, it should fall out with the multiple questions of cyberspace and the information era. With the spread of the internet which is regarded as the fastest spread of technology in recorded human history, the hidden dimensions of the battlefield of Sharia and modernity are becoming highly visible for the Iranian public.

Historically, the greatest effort of Muslim jurisprudents has been devoted to ignoring the spatio-temporal dimensions of Sharia. The ignorance of space and time, something like virtual reality, has proceeded in the history of Sharia because it was needed to show that Sharia rulings are universal and non-accidental. This ahistorical understanding has made a virtual reality from the living Sharia of the early Muslim communities of Arabia. The main argument of

---

41 Some significant titles of forbidden literature are online at: http://alefbe.com/buecher.htm.

42 Ahmad Kasravi was assassinated for his radical critique of Shiism in 1946 in Tehran by a Muslim Shia fundamentalist group called Fedaaeian Islam. For more details see http://www.kasravi.info/.

43 His works are available at this Website: http://www.sadeghhedayat.com/.

44 See his personal Website at http://www.jamali-online.com/.

45 See his personal Website at http://www.mirfetros.com/.

46 His main articles are available at http://www.nilgoon.org/.

47 For example, these two constantly updated websites: http://www.kaafar.com/ and http://farhangshahr.com/.

the Islamic State introduced by Ayatollah Khomeini in Iran was also based on this understanding. He insisted that because Sharia rulings are valid for all space and time, the government should proceed according to those unchangeable norms, islamicized. As this Sharia was being separated from the reality of Muslim society, the Islamic State in Iran was forced to use coercion and violence to apply its contents. The increasingly violent events in the post-revolutionary period, the total application of Sharia falsified by coercive power, the particularly dysfunctional mechanism of legislation as a result of a permanent struggle between the Guardian Council as the guardian of that visionary ahistorical-infinite Sharia and the changing exigencies of space and time as recognized by representatives of Parliament, have shown that no social order can be maintained by enforcement of the traditional Sharia. Ayatollah Khomeini might have understood this problem, but just when he started to announce his new perspective on the matter, it was too late. He died less than seven months after his famous message to the Shia clerics, in which he asked them to pay attention to the important role of space and time in their contemporary *Ijtihads* (=innovative interpretations). Owing to his special influence on the clerics and society and to the real power he held, it was very possible that he might have transformed the existing Sharia paradigm. After his death, traditional Shia seminaries continued with their conventional paradigm and failed to address this issue as society required. Present radical changes in family, social, cultural, economic and political life in Iran are clear manifestations of the rule of a reactionary, subjective and figurative Sharia rather than an active, living and existential one. Real socio-political life shows that there is no longer a meaningful relationship between the real, uncovered world of Iranians and their legal system, which is forcefully covered by traditional Sharia. Ironically, Sharia guardians have succeeded in accomplishing one thing; that is, by establishing their religious absolutism, they deleted the elements of time and space from Sharia rulings in the reality of Iranian society.

The points of departure between Sharia rule and the real Being of the majority of Iranians are everywhere in sight; they can be clearly seen in the Islamized laws related to property, the media, women, youth, non-Muslims, international affairs and other thinkers-other beings. When we compare these laws with the present Being of the media, women and etc. in Iranian society, we realize how much dissonance is felt between them, as if the real Being of Iranians is in deep conflict with their legal status. Today, while the women, youth and other thinkers' Being herald a society without deep discriminatory laws, the Islamized legal system prescribes a wide rang of discriminations. It is in such a state that many Iranians are unable to "understand" why they should respect the rule of these laws. It seems it is beyond their grasp. Really, for most young Iranians today these laws, like the Islamic Penal Code of 1991 (IPC), are foreign and strange. Strangeness and foreignness are signs of the allegorical existence of these laws.

It is here worth mentioning that the IPC alone contains more than 100 specific articles on sexual relations, as if Iran is the center of sexual deviance. While the minimum marriage age in Sharia is nine for girls and thirteen for boys,[48] the average age at marriage in females has risen constantly from 19.8 in 1986 to 22.4 in 1996 and 25 in 2004; for males in urban areas during the same period it rose from 23.6 to 25.6 and more recently to 27.5.[49] This increase means that the time period between sexual maturity and marriage is more than 15 years. Cultural and socio-economic changes, the growth of literacy and educational attainment have played an important role in the postponement of marriage, especially among females.

Now, consider these social facts from the perspective of the Islamized legal system. Articles 63-107 and 637-638 of the IPC, for example, stipulate that any form of association or friendship between the sexes outside marriage is severely punishable by flogging, imprisonment, forced marriage, execution and even stoning, depending on the different circumstances in sexual relationships. The conflict of Iranians' law and their contemporary Being in the cases of *qisas*, or retaliation, and *diya*, or blood money, are even more telling. The IPC defines blood money compensation for a man as one of the following: 100 camels, 200 cows, 1,000 sheep, 200 silk dresses, 1,000 gold coins and 10,000 silver coins. As these subjects are not absolutely applicable in Iran, the courts have opted for cash equivalents instead. A woman's blood money is worth half that of a man's.[50]

Historically, Sharia punishments like stoning, amputation, crucifixion or whipping that are meaningless today might have been meaningful for early Arabic-tribal societies. That is, they were able to understand their sense and necessity. For instance, *qisas*, or the law of retaliation, was an understandable symbol of penalty in the event of murder among Arabs tribes who were always in blood feud situations. But these penalties are now, in the view of modern

48 The legal age of marriage was eighteen years before the revolution. Recently, the Expediency Council have approved a law to raise the age at which girls can get married to thirteen; fifteen for boys.
See http://www.unescobkk.org/ips/arh-web/demographics/iran2.cfm.

49 According to the studies of the known Iranian economist M. H. Adib, that are accessible at http://www.tehraneconomist.com/archive.aspx.

50 See articles 297-300 of the IPC. For a critical discussion, see *Gholami, H.*, "The islamisation of criminal justice and its developments in Iran", Tilburg Foreign Law Review , vol. 7 (1999), no. 3, pp. 213-220.

Muslim societies, symbols of cruelty, violence and inhumanity. Thus, the question is not whether these Sharia penalties are symbolic or not; rather, it is about their meaning for the public reason of contemporary Iranians. The imposition of these penalties on modern Muslim societies is a clear expression of the lack of a communicative dimension in the Islamization discourse. The amputation of a theft's hand was justifiable at that time because human knowledge about the theft was focused on the relationship of the physical act of the thief's hand, while today, human reason has explored the various complicated relationships in theft. We know that there is a significant relationship between the act of theft and proprietorship, the economic system, the physio-psychological characteristics of thief and cultural and social patterns, and that we can not reduce theft into the simplified definitions of classic Sharia rulings.

At another level, for example, while the language and viewpoint of society demands public participation in lawmaking, human dignity and rights, the Sharia establishment is continuously speaking about the mandatory guardianship of Muslim jurisprudence over people, the duties of mankind's servitude before the sacred legislature and absolute obedience to early Arabic-Islamic models of behavior. At present, when the authentic discourse is a discourse of rights, the coercive repetition of the duties of servitude is really something figurative and false. This anachronism shows the climax of Sharia subjectivism and, at the same time, reveals why power-seeking clergy in Iran need so much to mystify Sharia rulings. In fact, the current system of Sharia rulings, which are the product of the monolog mind of Muslim jurists, are the basis of the discourse of power in Iran.

The manner in which the Islamic government tries to enforce this virtual Sharia is itself an interesting phenomenon. The government officially introduces these rulings as expressions of authentic Persian-Islamic traditions and values. With these permanent references to the utopian past, they want to stress the necessity of applying these falsified percepts of Sharia to the protection of Muslim society from the cultural invasion of the west. But as the present Being of Iranians is very clear and self-expressive, the Islamic-revolutionary lawmaker has created a vague, ambiguous legal language. In fact, ambiguities are shields for the falsified percepts called Islamic codes. The everyday realities of Iranian society are obscured by these ambiguities in legal discourse. However, as the people – especially women and youth – become self-conscious, this language become weaker.

If the constant disassociation of Sharia from the real world of Iranians is not accompanied by the critical self-reflection of Sharia guardians, it amounts to the expansion of hate, distrust and finally the prescription of violence towards the real world. Perhaps this is the real reason that the judiciary in Iran from time to time uses naked coercion to implement Sharia rulings.

The principal reason for the disassociation of contemporary Iranian Being from the post-revolutionary Islamized legal system is that the relationship of Sharia, as the main source of legislation, and the free flow of information and knowledge is disconnected. When the flow of knowledge dried up in Sharia discourse, it became irrelevant to real life of majority of Iranians. The Muslim jurists, looking for their utopia in the past, see modernity as a danger for Sharia and, because of this devastating fear, have closed the door on new experiments and evaluations. Therefore, Sharia discourse is radically departing from today's Iranian discourse. There is no other way to treat this acute syndrome but the attempt to open the way for the free flow of information and knowledge in Sharia discourse. In the words of contemporary Norwegian thinker *Jan Kjaerstad*,[51] when reality becomes unreal, the mission of unrealities (i.e. metaphors, figurations and symbols) will paradoxically be to return those unrealities to the real world. Hence, the presence of Sharia on the open-information highways of cyberspace can effectively contribute to the restoration of Sharia discourse. In cyberspace, there is an exceptional possibility for the participation of public reason. The internet is one of the most accessible tools that modern mankind has for breaking down the subjective walls of Sharia interpreters and thereby returning them to the real world. Undoubtedly, this is not an easy transition for Sharia. Through the constant critical rethinking of its assumptions and preconceptions, Sharia, being available online regardless of time and space, now faces real deconstruction.[52]

---

51 *Kjaerstad, J.*, "Eine Metapher für unsere Zeit,“ Schreibheft, Nr.56, Mai 2001, S. 21.

52 By "deconstruction" I mean a method of deep criticism that sees Islamic Sharia as a complex ontological, philological, theological, historical, cultural and political process. The starting point in this method is the critical rethinking of the assumptions and pre-understandings of Sharia rulings or, in deconstructive terms, to place it "under erasure". Notably, if anything is destroyed in a deconstructive reading of Sharia, it is not the sacred texts of Islam, but the monolog interpretations and claims to the unequivocal domination of one mode of Sharia discourse over another. Therefore, a deconstructive reading of Sharia is a reading which analyses the specificity of Sharia rulings' critical difference from themselves." For detailed discussion on the term of deconstruction see *Cuddon, J.A.*, A Dictionary of Literary Terms and Literary Theory, third ed., London: Blackwell, 1991.

5. Perspectives of Hope

If modernity is understood as the emergence of the notions of public sphere, independent reason and the essentiality of human rights, then developments in present-day Iran suggest that we are living through an era of profound modern, plural Islam within cyberspace for the majority of Iranians. The emergence of an Islamic-Iranian cyberspace is an encouraging phenomenon in a time when Islamic fundamentalism is penetrating the world. A combination of mass education and mass communication is transforming the Iranian world. Since the penetration of the internet and new IT technologies such as satellite broadcasting channels, DVDs, mobile phones and digital radios which render ineffective the traditional violent censorships, the debate on Sharia rulings is no longer a closed technical discourse within religious seminaries. Actually, internet chat rooms, online libraries, data banks, blog sites, link directories, and news gathering organizations are integral parts of civil society in Iran today, albeit a surrogate element. The collective strength of access to online data bases, social internetworking groups, blogging, instant messaging and email across thousands of actors must be considered signs of a paradigm shift in the Islamization discourse in Iran from the bottom up, i.e., with grassroots participation. If the symbols of power-based Sharia were swearing and the Qoranic verses of Jihad, the net and highways of information are going to be symbols of a new paradigm of Sharia.

As Iranian society undergoes a complex ideological and cultural transformation as a result of the radical disassociation from power-based Islam and in an atmosphere where the conventional press is repressed, the internet and other IT technologies are functioning as catalysts for this revolutionary space. Currently, on the internet, Iranians participate in an open, boldly discourse on Sharia perceptions on a mass scale, particularly on sensitive issues such as women rights, religious freedoms, sexual relations and Islamic criminal sanctions. Unprecedented access to sources of information and knowledge about human rights, religion and many forbidden aspects of social life has made it difficult for the hierarchical guardians of Sharia to any longer control what the people to know and what they think. For example, thousands of copies of banned or forbidden publications on existing Sharia have been printed through the internet.[53]

---

[53] At the same time, however, one should be cautious that an expanding public sphere does not necessarily indicate the prompt advent of a humane, rights-based Sharia.

If Iran's 1979 Islamic Revolution was clearly one of the major turning points of twentieth century history in shattering the myths of modernization, then the growing penetration of the internet, launching of open networks and subsequent emergence of an Iranian information society in which public debate over Sharia takes place, has the potential to contribute to the deconstruction of the current power-based discourse of Sharia at the dawn of the twenty-first century. Cyberspace can increasingly demystify Sharia discourse. It could stimulate a new paradigm of *Ijtihad* (innovative-independent interpretation) in Sharia; a cyber, communicative and participatory *Ijtihad* which will allow anonymous contributions from every Muslim, regardless of his or her place and world view. This soft revolution can transform Sharia from the bottom up by promoting individual involvement in the formation of Sharia discourse.

It can be so depicted that when all Sharia judgments become available online, then the free flow of information and knowledge will electronically deconstruct existing Sharia-subjectivism whether the autocratic, hard-line clerics like it or not. The mechanism for this deconstructive process, for which Iranians made three revolutions during the last century, is the emergence of a cyber, democratic public sphere in which a paradigm shift in assumptions and preconceptions of classical power-based Sharia will take place. This time the internet revolution will be matched by a revolution in Islamic Sharia because a soft, open and transparent cyberspace will break the hegemony of Sharia institutions and their hard rules over individuals. The new Sharia that will show itself primarily in cyberspace and which feeds from it will be a system of rights, including the rights of both human beings and nature; its discourse is not power, but freedom.

The Iranian internet, through alliance building and community networking,[54] not only develops ways to foster individual enlightenment, but only facilitates ways to develop a higher social awareness. In the young Iranian cyberspace we can easily hear the voices of future, the aspirations of a new generation born after the revolution to live in an open, free and happy society and to enjoy their God-given rights. Interestingly, these voices are largely stressing nonviolence. The more Iranian cyberspace grows, the more Sharia discourse becomes public and intersubjective and reaches out to the broader world. The emergent Iranian right-based readings of Sharia in cyberspace contain new promises and aspirations, not only for the Iranian people, but also for the entire Muslim world and even for the world community.

---

54 Particularly by considering the phenomenon of the Weblogs that are probably the most advanced examples of *Social Software* today.

To give a schema of this paradigm shift in Sharia discourse, in the annexed (figure 3) under I have compared some significant preconceptions of the two paradigms as they relate to criminal justice.

Figure 3: A comparison of two different paradigms of Sharia

Concept	Power-based Sharia	Right-based Sharia
Justice	1) Exclusive, monologic, perceived as the consequence and effect of *fiqh* norms 2) Permitting a broad range of discriminations in law	1) Inclusive, dialogic, perceived as the cause and scale of legal norms 2) Negating any from of discrimination in law
Jihad	Using violence against enemies (Others who are opposed to us)	Striving for peace and justice universally, responding to injustice
Crime	1) To perpetrate a *harām* act 2) defined as violation of the authority of the Islamic ruler and his rulings which create guilt before both Allah and the Ruler, deserving pain in both this world & another world (Double jeopardy) 3) Offence understood in Arabian-shaped, religious morality terms 4) Stigma of crime unremovable, specially in corporal punishments	1) Violation of codified rights with criminal sanctions 2) defined as violation of right-based relationships 3) Offence understood in its whole context - moral, social, cultural, economic, political and global (both social /individual harms and needs) 4) Stigma of crime removable through restorative practices
Responsibility	Paradoxically focus on establishing blame, on guilt, on pain, on past wrongdoings (did he/she do it?) and taking punishment, on one hand, and stressing on minority of the most people except with authoritarian fuqaha.	Focus on problem solving, on future, on mutual liabilities and obligations of all members of community to repair relationships and making thinks as right as possible (who has been hurt, what are their needs & whose responsibilities are these?)

Life	1) Dependent on the certainty/speculation of the Faqih 2) Prevalence of retaliation and execution 3) No consideration of moral damages 4) Sectarian and ideological definition of life 5) Priority of religious beliefs over life (e.g. execution of apostates), reason (e.g. execution on third repetition of drinking alcohol), offspring (stoning and execution of sexual offenders), and property (execution on third repetition of theft)	1) Abolishment or tight restriction of execution (only for serious murder such as genocide.) 2) Definition of life includes physical and moral aspects, humans and other beings. 3) Life as the ultimate goal of the legislator.
Sexual Relations	Maximal involvement of the criminal law by stoning, whipping, and execution	Involvement of the criminal law as last resort only to protect rights

In conclusion, the absence of power, in a Foucaultian sense, is necessary for a new paradigm of Sharia to *be*. In other words, the context of the Being of the new Sharia is an interactive, dialogic and intersubjective one which evolves constantly. It is freed from any discourse of power. Hence, it is inevitably through the discourse of freedom that Sharia justice will be legitimated, renewed, universalized and, of course, resonated to the only Self there is in the entire universe. It will do this by transcending the letter of the canonical scriptures and the ego of fundamentalists. This Sharia is secular (not secularist) because it is rooted in Being that does not suffer a dualism of matter and spirit.[55] It is revealed. It is always present and open towards the future because it crosses

[55] Traditional and power-based Sharia readings suffer from an infinite dualism that is essential; between the Creature and the Created, between matter and spirit, between man and woman, between the world and the hereafter, between Self and Other , between Imam/ Vali (ruler) and people, between Muslim and Non-Muslim, between expert and layperson, etc. A short look at the post-revolutionary legislations which are basically discriminatory reveals the broad consequence of this worldview.

in time and space. It is in our nearness and comprehensibility because it is in dialogue with us; here, hierarchy has no place. It discloses itself constantly. We do not need to make it. It is simply *in-the-world-with-us*. It is our Existential. It discloses itself in our Sites and we are all in the Site of its disclosedness.

DIE WIEDEREINFÜHRUNG DES *ḪUL'* UND DIE STÄRKUNG DER FRAUENRECHTE

EINE STUDIE ZUR REFORM DES PERSONALSTATUSRECHTS IM ISLAMISCHEN RECHTSKREIS AM BEISPIEL DES ÄGYPTISCHEN GESETZES NR. 1 VON 2000[1]

Hendrik Denker, MA, Dortmund

Überblick:

---

[1] Der vorliegende Aufsatz basiert auf einer Magisterarbeit, die der Autor im Wintersemester 2002/2003 an der Ruprecht-Karls-Universität Heidelberg im Fach Islamwissenschaft anfertigte. Ein besonderer Dank sei den beiden Gutachtern dieser Arbeit, Prof. Dr. Raif G. Khoury und Prof. Dr. Omaia Elwan, für die hervorragende Betreuung während der Zeit des Forschens und Verfassens und die instruktiven Hinweise bei der Überarbeitung für diesen Beitrag.

A. EINLEITUNG

Als im Januar 2000 das ägyptische Parlament über das Gesetz Nr.1 debattierte, stritten die Abgeordneten nicht nur über Sinn und Unsinn einer neuen Ordnung für das Personalstatusrecht. Die Auseinandersetzung drehte sich darüber hinaus um die Frage nach dem richtigen Platz für das islamische Recht in ihrer Gesellschaft. Während einige das neue Gesetz zur Ordnung der gerichtlichen Verhältnisse und der Verfahren in Fragen des Personalstatus – meist kurz, wenn auch inhaltlich nicht ganz zutreffend, als „Personalstatusgesetz" benannt – als einen Abschied vom islamischen Recht sahen, begrüßten es andere als die Wiederherstellung der ursprünglich von Gott erdachten Gerechtigkeit in der Familie. Kern des Streits war die Einführung eines Scheidungsrechts auch für die Ehefrau, für das man an das in der islamischen Rechtswissenschaft altbekannte Rechtsinstitut *ḫulᶜ* anknüpfte.

Das Familienrecht einschließlich des Scheidungsrechts stellt einen der Kernbereiche des islamischen Rechts dar. Noch heute sind in Ländern mit muslimischer Bevölkerungsmehrheit die geltenden Gesetze maßgeblich von den gleichen Normen geprägt, die der Prophet Muḥammad vor fast 1400 Jahren verkündete. Dabei ist diese Rechtsmaterie aber niemals eine bloß statische gewesen, sondern ist von Anfang an Dynamiken unterlegen.

Muḥammad hinterließ bei seinem Tod nur einen kleinen Bestand von Rechtsregeln, die im Koran niedergelegt waren, oder die er mündlich an seine Gefährten weitergegeben hatte oder die diese bzw. ihre Nachfahren später aus der Erinnerung an die prophetische Lebenspraxis herleiteten und schriftlich niederlegten (*ḥadīṯ*). Aus der Notwendigkeit, das expandierende islamische Gemeinwesen führen zu können, entwickelte sich ein Rechtssystem, in dem bis zum dritten islamischen Jahrhundert eine verbindliche Rechtsquellenlehre gefunden war. Neben dem Koran standen die Prophetenüberlieferung (*sunna*) als Primärquelle sowie der Gelehrtenkonsens (*iğmāᶜ*) und der Analogieschluss (*qiyās*) als Mittel zur Verfügung, mit denen für bisher ungelöste Rechtsfragen neue Antworten gefunden werden konnten. Im Rahmen der beiden letztgenannten Mittel konnten die Rechtsgelehrten den *iğtihād*, das eigene Bemühen um die Rechtsfindung, ausüben. Auf diese Weise stellte sich das islamische Recht als eine anpassungsfähige Rechtsmaterie dar, die sich im Diskurs der Gelehrten an den Erfordernissen der Praxis weiterentwickelte. Zu Beginn des 10. Jahrhunderts hat sich dieser Zustand geändert. Im Zuge sich immer fester fixierender Rechtsschulen, deren Gründer in den verschiedenen Gegenden der islamischen Welt den Grundstein für sich ausdifferenzierende Lehrmeinungen und Traditionen gelegt hatten, geriet das Rechtsfindungsprinzip des *iğtihād* in den Hintergrund und wurde durch das Prinzip der Nachahmung (*taqlīd*) ersetzt. Rechtsgelehrte stellten sich nun mehr und mehr in eine

bestimmte Tradition und erforschten zur Beantwortung einer neuen Rechtsfrage zuvorderst die Antworten ihrer Rechtsschulkapazitäten auf die Fragen aus deren Zeit. Diese Phase, die in der Wissenschaft im Nachhinein als die Zeit des „sich schließenden Tores des *iǧtihād* " bezeichnet wurde, läutete eine rechtliche und geistesgeschichtliche Orientierung auf die Tradition ein, die tiefgreifende Veränderungen in der islamischen Welt im folgenden Jahrtausend erschwerte.[2]
Für die Reform des Rechts in der Neuzeit ist die Frage nach dem Verhältnis von *taqlīd* und *iǧtihād* neu gestellt und beantwortet worden. Der *taqlīd*, wie er in den vier heute erhaltenen Rechtsschulen des sunnitischen Islams, der im Mittelpunkt dieser Untersuchung steht, praktiziert wurde, wurde als Hemmnis für Innovation ausgemacht und – teilweise – durch eine Erinnerung an die Zeit vor der Fixierung auf die Rechtsschulen überwunden.
Inwieweit sich durch diese Neuorientierung die Chancen für eine Rechtsreform eröffnet haben, die sowohl den Erfordernissen der Gegenwart als auch den Anforderungen der Offenbarung gerecht wird, ist Gegenstand dieser Untersuchung. In ihrem Mittelpunkt steht die Analyse des Gesetzes Nr.1/2000. Es wird gezeigt, dass das Zustandekommen dieses Regelungswerkes einen vorläufigen Höhepunkt der Rechtsentwicklung darstellt. Es wird herausgearbeitet, in welcher Weise der moderne ägyptische Gesetzgeber die Rechtstradition, wie sie in Primär- und Sekundärquellen niedergelegt ist, aufgreift und im Sinne eines neuen *iǧtihād* innovativ auslegt.
In einem ersten Teil wird nach einem Überblick über die Grundzüge des islamischen Scheidungsrechts die Quellenlage zum Rechtsinstitut *ḫulʿ* dargestellt. Dabei erfolgt eine Konzentration auf die Fragen, in denen der moderne nationalstaatliche Gesetzgeber von den in den sunnitischen Rechtsschulen vertretenen Lehren abweicht. Es wird aufgezeigt, inwieweit die Quellen eine solche Abweichung rechtfertigen.
Der zweite Hauptteil stellt die Frage nach der Methodik des Reformprojekts im 20. Jahrhundert. Anhand der Reformlehre der *salafīya*–Bewegung werden wichtige Impulse für die praktischen Rechtsreformen vorgestellt und anhand der ihr vorausgehenden und folgenden Reformschritte in arabischen Ländern erläutert. Dem schließt sich eine Zusammenfassung der Reformgesetzgebung im ägyptischen Familien- und Scheidungsrecht bis zum Jahr 2000 an, deren Reformschritte in den zuvor hergestellten theoretischen Rahmen der allgemeinen Reformdiskussion eingeordnet wird.

---

2 Siehe zu diesem Komplex und der "Schließungsthese" insbes. die Beiträge von *Hallaq, W.*, Was the Gate of Ijtihad Closed? In: IJMES, 225 (1993), S. 587 – 605, und *ders.*, On the Origins of the Controversy about the Existence of Mujtahids and the Gate of Ijtihad. In: Studia Islamica 63 (1986), S. 129–141 sowie *Peters, R.*, Idjtihād and Taqlīd in 18th and 19th century Islam. In: WI 20 (1980), S. 131–145.

Im dritten Hauptteil wendet sich die Untersuchung dem Gesetz Nr. 1/2000 zu und stellt die wichtigsten Argumente der Gesetzesdebatte dar. Die weitreichendste Neuerung stellt dabei die *ḫulʿ*-Regelung des Art. 20 dar, der danach anhand der einzelnen Tatbestandsvoraussetzungen ausführlich analysiert wird. Dabei wird neben neuesten arabischen Fachpublikationen auf Zeitungstexte von Anfang des Jahres 2000 und Interviews mit ägyptischen Experten zurückgegriffen, die der Autor bei einer Forschungsreise nach Ägypten im Oktober 2002 sammeln bzw. führen konnte. In die Erläuterung des Gesetzestextes ist eine Stellungnahme zu den wichtigsten Streitpunkten eingearbeitet.

Im Schlussteil wird der Frage nachgegangen, welche Bedeutung das Gesetz Nr. 1/2000 für die Reformdiskussion hat. Als Fazit wird aufgezeigt, in welcher Art sich der Gesetzgeber bisher in Ägypten unbekannter Methoden bedient hat und in welcher Weise dieses Gesetz für Ägypten ein Novum geworden ist.

B. DAS ISLAMISCHE SYSTEM DER SCHEIDUNG: *ṬALĀQ* UND *ḪULʿ* IM KLASSISCHEN RECHT

I. Scheidungsgründe im islamischen Recht

Es ist von muslimischen Autoren oft betont worden, dass der Islam als Religion die Stellung der Frau verbessert hat. War sie vor der Verkündigung des Propheten in der Gesellschaft auf der arabischen Halbinsel wenig mehr als ein bloßes Objekt in den Händen des sie beherrschenden Mannes, so wird sie durch die islamische Botschaft zu einem vor Gott gleichen Subjekt, dem Gottes Anspruch und Regeln genauso gelten wie den männlichen Mitmenschen.[3]

Gleichzeitig verfestigt sich für das gesellschaftliche Zusammenleben von Mann und Frau eine Ordnung, die beiden Geschlechtern unterschiedliche Rollen zuteilt. Aufgrund biologischer Unterschiede wird eine Lehre entwickelt, in welcher der Mann als dominierendes Wesen in der ehelichen Beziehung vorgesehen ist. In Sure 4, 34 findet dieses Verhältnis seinen Ausdruck: „Männer stehen über den Frauen, weil Gott sie (von Natur aus vor diesen) ausgezeichnet hat und wegen der Ausgaben, die sie von ihrem Vermögen (als Morgengabe für die Frauen) gemacht haben." Dieses Verhältnis spiegelt sich in einer Reihe von koranischen Rechtsvorschriften wieder: Männer z.B. werden beim Erbrecht bevorzugt, ihre Zeugenaussage gilt per se mehr als die einer Frau, und sie haben

---

3 *El-Nimr, R.*, Women in Islamic Law. In: *Yamani, M.*, Feminism and Islam: legal and literary perspectives, Reading 1997, S. 33; vgl. zum Ganzen *Walther, W.*, Die Frau im Islam, Leipzig 1997, S. 33ff.

das Recht, mehrere Frauen zu heiraten, während Frauen auf einen Partner beschränkt sind. Auf der anderen Seite unterliegen Männer auch mehr Pflichten. Insbesondere sind sie dafür zuständig, ihre Ehefrauen ausreichend mit Unterhalt zu versehen. Sie müssen also durch ihre Arbeit genügend erwirtschaften, dass die Familie ernährt werden kann. Die Aufgaben der Ehefrau werden dagegen eher im häuslichen Bereich festgemacht; sie schuldet ihrem Ehemann Gehorsam und hat für sexuelle Kontakte bereit zu stehen.
Die unterschiedliche Rollenzuteilung der Geschlechter spiegelt sich auch im islamischen Scheidungsrecht wider. Dieses ist dadurch gekennzeichnet, dass der Mann recht einfach eine einseitige Scheidung herbeiführen kann, während dies für Frauen nicht zulässig ist. Diesen steht aber eine Reihe von Rechten zu, die sie vor der Willkür des Mannes schützen. Von muslimischen Gelehrten wird immer wieder darauf hingewiesen, dass diese Rechte eine Innovation des Islams gegenüber der vorislamischen *ǧāhilīya* seien. Der Tendenz, die Scheidung durch den Mann zu erschweren, entspricht auch folgende vielzitierte Prophetentradition: „Unter den erlaubten Dingen ist die Scheidung (*ṭalāq*) bei Gott das am meisten gehasste.“[4]
Das Scheidungsrecht nimmt in allen Quellen des islamischen Rechts und bei den Rechtsschulen breiten Raum ein. Die Dogmatik und die Einteilung der verschiedenen Arten der Eheauflösung (*furqa*, *tafrīq*, *taṭlīq*) sind dabei im Einzelnen sehr unterschiedlich. Grundsätzlich wird unterschieden zwischen *ṭalāq* und *fasḫ*. Während mit ersterem die Arten der Eheauflösung gemeint sind, die vom Mann ausgeführt werden, bezieht sich die zweite auf Auflösungen wegen Problemen des Ehevertrags. Hierbei können anfängliche Vertragsmängel und nachträgliche, unvorhergesehene Ereignisse sowie die Nichteinhaltung von vertraglich geschuldeten Leistungen zur Auflösung führen.[5]
Das islamische Recht unterscheidet eine Vielzahl von einzelnen Scheidungsarten, deren konkreter Gehalt verschiedene Ausformungen in den Rechtsschulen gefunden hat. Den breitesten Raum in Theorie wie Praxis nimmt der *ṭalāq* als Verstoßung durch den Ehemann (*taṭlīq al-zauǧ*) ein. Daneben stehen die archaischen aus vorislamischer Zeit stammenden *īlāʾ*, *ẓihār* und *liʿān* als einseitige Beendigungsmittel durch den Mann, die in der heutigen Zeit keine

---

4 „*Abġaḍ al-ḥalāl ʿalā Allāh al-ṭalāq*“, *Abū Dāwūd, S.*, Sunan Abī Dāwūd, Beirut, ohne Datum, Nr. 231; *ḥadīṯ* z.B. zit. in Art. Ḫulʿ. In: *Wizārat al-auqāf wa al-šuʾūn al-islāmīya*, al-mausūʿa al-fiqhīya, 29. Band, Kuwait 1990, S. 234–259 (240); *Jawad, H.*, The Rights of Women in Islam – An Authentic Approach, London 1998, S. 72.

5 Art. Ḫulʿ. In: *Wizārat al-auqāf...*, a.a.O., S. 236; *Naṣṣār, A.*, Asbāb al-taṭlīq fī al-šarīʿa al-islāmīya wa āṯāruhu, Alexandria 2000, S. 5; Art. Faskh (*Chehata, C.*). In: Encyclopedia of Islam (EI), Bd.2, 2. Aufl., Leiden seit 1960, S. 836.

große Rolle mehr spielen.[6] In der Praxis ebenfalls bedeutsam sind die Formen der gerichtlichen Scheidung auf Verlangen der Frau (*taṭlīq/tafrīq al-zauǧa*), mit denen nach Geltendmachung eines Scheidungsgrunds durch Urteil eines Richters die Trennung veranlasst werden kann. Diese Art der Scheidung stellt die praktisch wichtigste Trennung auf Initiative der Frau dar. Mögliche Scheidungsgründe sind die anfängliche Impotenz des Mannes, die fortdauernde Abwesenheit des Ehemanns (*ġaybat al-zauǧ*), das Ausbleiben der angemessen Unterhaltsaufwendungen (*ʿadam ʾinfāq al-zauǧ*), die Option bei Erwachsenwerden einer als Minderjährigen verheirateten Frau (*ḫiyār al-bulūġ*), die Standesungleichheit der Ehepartner sowie die Schädigung während der Ehe (*ḍarar*). Außerdem führt die Apostasie vom Islam (*ridda*) zur automatischen Auflösung der Ehe.[7] Bei der Anerkennung der einzelnen Gründe und bei deren Geltendmachung im Verfahren unterscheiden sich die Rechtsschulen sehr stark. Gemeinsam ist ihnen, dass die Ehefrau die Darlegungs- und Beweislast für die von ihr vorgebrachten Gründe trägt. So entsteht denn auch ein Hauptproblem dieser *taṭlīq*-Scheidungen, wenn die Versuche, sie vor Gericht zu erwirken, wegen mangelnder Beweise scheitern. Die Frauen sind dann gezwungen, weiter bei ihren Männern zu bleiben, obwohl die für eine Ehe nötige Vertrauensbasis normalerweise nicht mehr gegeben sein dürfte. Weil die Gefahr des Scheiterns sehr groß ist, ist der Anreiz für Scheidungsanträge dieser Art begrenzt. Shaham hat in einer Studie über das Ägypten des frühen 20. Jahrhundert, in dem der Großteil der genannten Gründe mittlerweile eingeführt war, ermittelt, dass nur in knapp 50% der Fälle ein solcher Prozess zu dem von der Frau gewünschten Ergebnis führt, obwohl er für diese Zeit annimmt, dass die Richter bei vielen Bestimmungen einer für die Frau günstigeren Auslegung folgten als in den Jahrhunderten davor.[8]

Zu einer weiteren Gruppe von Scheidungsgründen gehören die in Übereinstimmung zwischen den Ehepartnern vereinbarten. Es sind dies die Verstoßung gegen Entgelt (*ṭalāq ʿalā māl*) und der *ḫulʿ*. In beiden Fällen ist die Frau dabei verpflichtet, ihrem Mann eine bestimmte Summe als Gegenleistung dafür zu zahlen, dass er sie ziehen lässt.

---

6 Siehe zum *īlāʾ* Koran Sure 2,226 und die Kommentierung bei *Khoury, A.*, Der Koran: Übersetzung und wissenschaftlicher Kommentar, Gütersloh 1994, Bd. 3, S. 81 und zu *ẓihār* und *liʿān* bei *El Alami, D./Hinchcliffe, D.*, Islamic Marriage and Divorce Laws of the Arab World, London 1996, S. 26f.

7 Auflistung der Gründe in jeweils leicht abweichender Form bei *Naṣṣār, A.*, a.a.O., S. 6f; *El Alami, D./Hinchcliffe, D.*, a.a.O., S. 29ff; *Shaham, R.*, Judicial Divorce at the Wife's Initiative: The Sharīʿa Courts of Egypt, 1920-1955. In: ILS 1 (1994), S. 217-257 (222f).

8 *Shaham, R.*, a.a.O., S. 251.

II. *Ṭalāq* als Normalfall der Ehescheidung

In der Praxis mit Abstand am bedeutendsten ist der *ṭalāq* als einseitige Verstoßung durch den Mann. Dies geschieht bei einer wirksam geschlossenen Ehe durch gesprochene oder geschriebene Worte oder durch Zeichen. Die Anwesenheit der Frau ist dabei ebenso wenig Voraussetzung wie der Zugang der Erklärung des Mannes an die Frau. Es müssen lediglich zwei Zeugen bei der Willensäußerung des Ehemannes zugegen sein, welche die Erklärung als solche mitbekommen haben.[9]

Eine der wichtigsten von Muḥammad eingeführten Innovationen ist die Wartezeit (*ʿidda)* für die Frau, die in Sure 2, 228, 234 genannt wird. Während eines bestimmten Zeitraums soll die Frau warten, bis sie eine neue sexuelle Beziehung in einer Ehe eingeht. Damit soll zum einen eine erneute Schwangerschaft der Frau sicher einem Mann zuordbar sein, so dass die Vaterschaft geklärt ist. Zum anderen soll dem Mann Zeit gegeben werden, seine Verstoßungsentscheidung zu überdenken.[10] Während der *ʿidda* ist – jedenfalls bei der Mehrzahl der *ṭalāq*-Arten – ein Widerruf und eine Wiederaufnahme der ehelichen Beziehung möglich, egal ob dies der Frau recht ist oder nicht.[11] Während der *ʿidda* hat die geschiedene Frau das Recht, in der ehelichen Wohnung zu bleiben und von ihrem Mann Unterhaltszahlungen zu verlangen (*nafaqat al-ʿidda*).

Das klassische Recht hat verschiedene Kategorien zur Wirkung von Scheidungserklärungen entwickelt. Dabei besteht eine wichtige Unterscheidung zwischen der widerrufbaren (*ṭalāq raǧʿī*) und der endgültigen bindenden Scheidung (*ṭalāq bāʾin*). Eine Scheidung bleibt widerrufbar, wenn der Mann eine Erklärung ein- oder zweimal abgegeben hat und die Wartezeit der Frau noch nicht abgelaufen ist. Verstreicht die Wartezeit, ohne dass er widerruft, und fügt er innerhalb der Wartezeit keine dritte Erklärung hinzu, wird aus der widerrufbaren eine unwiderrufliche Scheidung. Die Unwiderruflichkeit hat hier die Wirkung im kleinen Grad (*bāʾin baynūna suġrā*). Im Gegensatz dazu steht die in hohen Grad unwiderrufliche Wirkung (*bāʾin baynūna kubrā*). Diese tritt

---

9 *Naṣṣār, A.*, a.a.O., S. 17; *Nasir, J.*, The Status of Women under Islamic Law and under Modern Islamic Legislation, London 1994, S. 79.

10 Die Länge der *ʿidda* ist je nach körperlichem Zustand der Frau unterschiedlich lang. In der Regel dauert sie drei Menstruationszyklen (*qurūʿ* - Sure 2,228), bei Frauen, welche die Periode nicht mehr oder noch nicht haben, sowie bei Witwen wird die Wartezeit nach Tagen berechnet. Sie dauert drei Monate im ersten Fall (Sure 65,4), bei Witwen beträgt sie vier Monate und 10 Tage (Sure 2,234). Schwangere befinden sich in der Wartezeit bis zur Geburt des Kindes (65,4). Siehe zum Ganzen, Art. ʿidda (*de Bellefonds, Y.*). In: EI, Bd. 3, S. 1010.

11 *El Alami, D./Hinchcliffe, D.*, a.a.O., S. 23.

ein, wenn der Ehemann während der Wartezeit die *ṭalāq*-Erklärung dreimal wiederholt. Der Unterschied zwischen den beiden Scheidungswirkungen zeigt sich bei der Frage der möglichen Wiederheirat der beiden Partner miteinander. Eine solche ist im Falle der Wirkung im kleinen Grad bei gegenseitigem Einverständnis möglich. Bei der Wirkung im hohen Grad ist die nochmalige Heirat dagegen ausgeschlossen, solange die Frau nicht mit einem anderen Mann verheiratet gewesen ist.[12]

Eine weitere Kategorisierung des *ṭalāq* in der hanafitischen Rechtsschule ist die Unterteilung in die ordnungsgemäße Scheidung (*ṭalāq al-sunna*) und die irreguläre Scheidung (*ṭalāq al-bidʿa*). Beide Sorten der Scheidung sind wirksam, jedoch unterscheiden sie sich in ihrer ethischen Bewertung. Eine Form des *ṭalāq al-bidʾa* ist die der dreimaligen Verstoßung in einer einzigen Erklärung. Hierbei gibt der Mann seinem Scheidungswillen in endgültiger Weise Ausdruck und kann während der Wartezeit seine Entscheidung nicht wiederrufen. Somit entfällt die intendierte Prüfungszeit für den Mann. [13]

Aus dieser Darstellung tritt deutlich die existierende Ungleichbehandlung der Partner in der Ehe zutage. Während der Mann die Scheidung jederzeit mit wenigen Beschränkungen vornehmen kann, steht der Frau kein entsprechendes Recht zu. Gerechtfertigt wird diese Differenzierung mit dem Verweis auf die im Koran grundsätzlich vorgesehene Überlegenheit des Mannes. Diese zeige sich insbesondere auch darin, dass Männer von ihrer Veranlagung her weniger emotional agierten als Frauen und darum bei der Scheidung besonnener vorgingen. Wäre den Frauen dasselbe Recht verliehen worden, so wären Scheidungszahlen unverantwortlich in die Höhe gestiegen. Eine andere Begründung besteht in dem Verweis auf die finanziellen Pflichten des Mannes. So fallen bei Beendigung der Ehe auf ihn die weitere Unterhaltszahlung während der *ʿidda*-Periode sowie möglicherweise die Auszahlung des zu Beginn der Ehe gestundeten Brautgeldes (*mahr/ṣadāq*) oder einer Entschädigung

---

12 Grund dafür ist, dass entsprechend Sure 2,230 nach dreimaliger Verstoßung die Frau für den Mann als Ehefrau für verboten (*ḥarām*) gilt. Diese Vorschrift wurde dadurch umgangen, dass die Frau mit einem anderen die Ehe einging und kurz darauf von dem neuen Ehemann wieder geschieden wurde, um für den ersten Mann wieder erlaubt zu sein (*taḥlīl*). Dieses Vorgehen gilt den Rechtsschulen zwar als moralisch verwerflich, da die zweite Ehe nicht nur pro forma geschlossen worden sein dürfe, sondern vollzogen zu sein hat, doch bürgert sich diese Form des *taḥlīl* in den Lehren der Rechtschulen ein und wird von diesen als wirksam eingestuft. Vgl. *Nasir, J.*, a.a.O., S. 82f; *El Alami, D./Hinchcliffe, D.*, a.a.O., S. 23.

13 *El Alami, D./Hinchcliffe, D.*, a.a.O., S. 22f: *Mahmood, T.*, No more Talaq, Talaq, Talaq. In: ICLQ 7 (1987), S. 1-12 (3); *Jawad, H.*, The Rights of Women in Islam – An Authentic Approach, London 1998, S. 79f.

(*mutʿa*).[14] Wegen dieser finanziellen Konsequenzen sei folglich auch der Mann in der weitsichtigeren Position, da ihn eine Scheidung viel einschneidender träfe als die Frau.[15]

III. *Ḫul'* als Sonderform der Scheidung im klassischen Rechtssystem

Eine weitere Scheidungsmöglichkeit stellt in der *šarīʿa* der *ḫul*ʿ[16] dar. Es handelt sich dabei um eine Lösungsmöglichkeit auf Verlangen der Frau, bei der sie gegen Zahlung eines bestimmten Betrags von dem Eheverhältnis loskommt. Meist wird dieses Rechtsinstitut unter den einverständlichen Scheidungen aufgeführt, bei denen beide Partner mit der Trennung einverstanden sein müssen.

1. *Ḫul'* im Koran

Anders als der *ṭalāq*-Begriff findet sich der Ausdruck *ḫul*ʿ nicht im Koran. Trotzdem wird seine Basis in der Offenbarung gesehen und seine Ausgestaltung hieraus abgeleitet. Benutzung finden in der Offenbarung dagegen einige der

---

14 *Naṣṣār, A.*, a.a.O., S. 195f; *Schacht, J.*, An Introduction to Islamic Law, Oxford 1966, S. 137.

15 Dargestellte Argumentation nach *El-Nimr, R.*, Women in Islamic Law. In: *Yamani, M.*, Feminism and Islam: Legal and Literary Perspectives, Reading 1997, S. 87-102 (94).

16 Die Wortbedeutung des Begriffs *ḫul*ʿ leitet sich aus der Wurzel *ḫ-l-*ʿ her. Diese trägt im ersten Stamm (*ḫalaʿa, yaḫlaʿu*) die Bedeutung „entfernen, beseitigen" und wird benutzt im Zusammenhang mit Kleidung als „ausziehen, ablegen". Das Verbalnomen des dritten Stammes *muḫālaʿa* hat die gleiche Bedeutung wie *ḫul*ʿ. Beide bezeichnen das Rechtsinstitut und beziehen sich auf die Entfernung oder das Ablegen des Ehebundes. Das Bild des Kleidungsstück im Zusammenhang mit den Ehegatten ist aus dem Koran (Sure 2,187) bekannt: „Sie sind euch ein Kleid, und ihr seid ihnen ein Kleid." Das Ablegen der Kleidung gleicht dem Beendigen der Ehe (*al-ʿAǧūz, N.*, Daʿwā al-taṭlīq wa al-ḫulʿ, Alexandria 2001, S.15). Synonym zum Begriff *ḫul*ʿ wird *mubāraʾa* benutzt. Es handelt sich hierbei um das Verbalnomen vom dritten Stamm der Wurzel *b-r-ʾ*. Die Bedeutung des ersten Stammes *bariʾa, yabraʾu* lautet „frei sein o. werden". Mit *mubāraʾa* ist das Abkommen gemeint, durch das die Frau von ihren ehevertraglichen Pflichten frei wird (*al-Fiqī, U.*, Daʿwā al-taṭlīq wa al-ḫulʿ, Alexandria 2001, S. 38; Nasir, J., a.a.O., S. 85). Ebenfalls in diesem Zusammenhang geläufig sind die Begriffe *ṣulḥ* und *fidya* bzw. *iftadāʾ*. Beide bezeichnen einen bestimmten Aspekt des *ḫul*ʿ und werden von einigen Rechtsgelehrten als Synonyme hierfür verwendet. *Ṣulḥ* bezeichnet ein Übereinkommen nach einem Streit oder die Versöhnung durch einen Kompromiss. In diesem verzichtet der Mann auf seine ehelichen Rechte und erhält zum Ausgleich eine Gegenleistung der Frau. In Sure 4,128 findet der Begriff auch Verwendung für die Trennung von Ehegatten. Ebenfalls koranischen Ursprungs ist der Begriff *fidya*. Er bezeichnet das Lösegeld, das eine Frau für die Auflösung der Ehe aufbringen muss. In Sure 2,229 wird mit *iftadā* der achte Stamm des Verbes *fadā, yafdī* für das Freikaufen der Ehefrau vom Mann benutzt.

Begriffe, die synonym zu *ḫulʿ* benutzt werden. So steht in Sure 2,229: „Und wenn ihr aber fürchtet, dass sie die Gebote Gottes nicht halten können, so begehen beide keine Sünde, wenn sie sich mit etwas loskauft (*iftadat bihi*).“ Damit wird grundsätzlich erlaubt, dass eine Ehefrau dafür bezahlt, dass die Ehe beendet wird. Voraussetzung ist außerdem, dass die Frau fürchtet, bei Fortsetzung der Ehe die Gesetze Gottes zu übertreten. Gemeint ist hier die Übertretung der moralischen Gesetze der Ehe, also die Furcht vor dem Ehebruch, weil die Partner sexuelle Befriedigung in Beziehungen außerhalb der Ehe suchen oder die Sorge, dem Mann nicht mehr die ihm zustehende Ehrfurcht entgegenbringen zu können.[17] Eine weitere relevante Stelle findet sich in Sure 4,128: „Wenn eine Frau von ihrem Ehemann rohe Behandlung oder Gleichgültigkeit befürchtet, begehen sie keine Sünde, wenn sie sich einvernehmlich auseinandersetzen; denn ein friedlicher Kompromiss ist der beste.“

In beiden Koranzitaten wird die Trennung durch eine Einigung der beiden Ehepartner herbeigeführt. Beide benutzten Begriffe des Loskaufs (*iftidāʾ*) und des Kompromiss (*ṣulḥ*) stammen aus Kontexten, die begrifflich die Zustimmung beider Parteien voraussetzen Von dieser Voraussetzung weichen sie auch im Kontext des *ḫulʿ* nicht ab.[18]

Eine weitere Wertung findet sich in Sure 4,19f. Dort heißt es: „Behandelt sie nicht schlecht, um einen Teil von dem, was ihr ihnen gabt, von ihnen zurückzunehmen (...) Und wenn ihr eine Gattin anstelle einer anderen nehmen wollt, so nehmt nichts von ihr fort, selbst wenn ihr der ersteren einen ganzen Schatz gegeben habt.“ Dieser Vers wird in den Kontext des möglichen Selbstloskaufs der Frau gestellt und gibt den Ehemännern eine wichtige Weisung. Denn diese sollen, wenn sie sich von ihren Frauen trennen wollen, diese nicht dazu drängen, den *ḫulʿ* zu erklären, damit sie selbst den finanziellen Folgen des *ṭalāq* entgehen und sich an den Geschiedenen bereichern. Mit „was ihr ihnen gabt“ ist die Morgengabe gemeint, die bei Eingehen der Ehe in das Eigentum der Frau übergegangen ist.[19]

2. Ḫulʿ in der Sunna

Während der koranische Befund zur *ḫulʿ* relativ spärlich ausfällt, wartet die Sunna mit einigen Überlieferungen aus dem Leben des Propheten zum Thema auf. In den Hauptsammelwerken des *ḥadīṯ* finden sich eigene Kapitel mit der

---

17 Zur Auslegung des Verses siehe z.B. die modernistische Auslegung bei *ʿAbduh, M.*, al-aʿmāl al-kāmila li-l-imām Muḥammad ʿAbduh, Beirut 1972, Bd.4, S. 638.

18 *Arabi, O.*, The Downing of the Third Millenium of Shariʿa, or Women may Divorce at Will. In: ALQ 2001, S. 2-21 (11); *ʿAbduh, M.*, a.a.O., Bd. 1, 637, in seiner Kommentierung zu Sure 2, 229.

19 *ʿAbduh, M.*, a.a.O., Bd.1, S. 639.

Überschrift *al-ḫulʿ* bzw. *al-muḫālaʿa*. Die Anzahl der überlieferten Traditionen ist dabei nicht sonderlich groß. Es werden oft die gleichen Überlieferungen in verschiedenen Variationen erzählt. Im Folgenden zitiere ich Traditionen aus vier kanonischen Sammlungen und versuche eine Interpretation, aus der die wesentlichen Fragen für die Entwicklung des Rechtsinstitutes in den Rechtsschulen und der modernen Entwicklung deutlich werden.
Bei Abū Dāwūd findet sich eine grundsätzliche Wertung über das Verhalten scheidungswilliger Frauen: „Wenn eine Frau ihren Mann nach der Scheidung fragt, ohne dass eine Beeinträchtigung vorliegt, so ist für diese der Geruch des Paradieses verboten."[20] Etwas abgewandelt wird diese Tradition auch unter Weglassung des Satzteils „ohne dass eine Beeinträchtigung vorliegt" wiedergegeben.[21] In der Fachliteratur zum Scheidungsrecht wird an einigen Stellen diese Tradition in den beiden abweichenden Varianten zitiert.

Die Tradition der Frau von Ṯābit ibn Qays in den verschiedenen Fassungen

Es ist eine andere Begebenheit, die - in verschiedener Weise überliefert - zu der Belegstelle schlechthin geworden ist. Sie findet sich in allen sechs kanonischen Sammlungen und gilt als „der erste *ḫulʿ* im Islam"[22]: Das Ereignis von Ḥabība bzw. Ǧamīla bint Sahl, der Frau von Ṯābit ibn Qays, die zum Propheten kommt, weil sie von ihrem Mann loskommen möchte.
Bei al-Buḫārī ist dieser Vorfall folgenderweise niedergelegt: „Die Frau des Ṯābit ibn Qays kam zum Propheten (s.a.) und sagte: „O Prophet, ich tadele Ṯābit ibn Qays weder wegen seiner Moral noch wegen seiner Religion, aber ich hasse den Unglauben am Islam (*ʾakrahu al-kufra fī al-islām*)." Der Prophet sagte: „Gibst du ihm seinen Garten zurück?" Sie: „Ja". Der Prophet (zu Ṯābit ibn Qays): „Nimm den Garten an und verstoße sie mit einer einfachen Scheidungserklärung" (*iqbal al-ḥadīqata wa ṭalliqhā taṭlīqatan*). In einer anderen überlieferten Lesart heißt es: „...sie gab den Garten zurück und er (Muḥammad) befahl ihm (Ṯābit) und er (Ṯ.) trennte sich von ihr (*wa raddat ʿalayhi wa ʾamarahu fa-fāraqahā*)".[23]
In den Fassungen bei Abū Dāwūd verläuft die Tradition etwas anders. In der ersten Fassung kommt eine Frau mit dem Namen Ḥabība bint Sahl im Dunkel der Nacht zum Propheten und stellt sich mit ihrem Begehren vor. Muḥammad sagt nun bezüglich des nicht genauer bezeichneten Brautgelds zu dem Mann:

---

20 „*ʾAyumā imratʾun saʾalat zauǧahā al-ṭalāq fī ġayri mā baʾsin, fa-ḥarām ʿalayhā rāʾiḥat al-ǧannati*"; *Abū Dāwūd, S.*, a.a.O. S. 268, Nr. 2226; parallel überliefert von *Ibn Māǧa, A.*, Sunan, Beirut 1952, S. 662, Nr. 2055.

21 *Al-ʿAǧūz, N.*, a.a.O., S. 48f.

22 Art. Ḫulʿ. In: *al-Zuḥaylī, W.*, Al-fiqh al-islāmī wa adillatuhu, 9. Band, Damaskus 1984, S. 7007-7038 (7009); Art. Ḫulʿ. In: *Wizārat al-auqāf* ..., a.a.O., S. 241, § 9.

23 *Al-Buḫārī, M.*, Sunan al-Buḫārī, Beirut ohne Datum, Bd. 7, S. 60.

„Nimm es von ihr (*ḫuḏ minhā*)". Nachdem Ṯābit dies getan hat, endet die Erzählung ohne Schilderung einer weiteren Scheidungshandlung: „Und sie saß wieder bei ihrer Sippe (*wa ǧalasat fī ahlihā*)."[24] In einer zweiten Fassung kommt Ḥabība zum Propheten weil ihr Mann sie so heftig geschlagen hat, dass er ihr sogar Knochen gebrochen hatte (*kasara baʿaḍhā*). Am Ende ruft der Prophet den Ṯābit zu sich und befiehlt ihm, die Gärten zurückzunehmen und sich von der Frau zu trennen. Diesem Befehl kommt er auch nach.[25] In einer weiteren Überlieferung setzt der Prophet nach vollzogener Trennung die Wartezeit der Frau auf eine Regel fest (*ḥayḍa*).[26]

Auch al-Nisāʾī überliefert zwei Versionen: Die erste entspricht der zweiten von Abū Dāwūd, die zweite ist identisch mit der von al-Buḫārī.[27]

Zwei weitere Fassungen finden sich bei Ibn Māǧa. In der ersten ist überliefert: „Ǧamīla bint Sulūl kam zum Propheten und sprach: „Ich schwöre bei Gott! Ich habe nichts gegen Ṯābit, was die Moral und die Religion betrifft. Aber ich hasse die Sünde gegen den Islam. Ich halte ihn aus Hass nicht mehr aus." Der Prophet: „Gibst du ihm seinen Garten zurück?" Sie: „Ja". Der Prophet befahl ihm (Ṯ.), den Garten von ihr zu nehmen, aber nicht mehr (als diesen) (*fa- ʿamarahu rasūl Allāh (s.a.) ʾan yaʾḫuḏa minhā ḥadiqatahu wa lā yazdād*)."[28]

Die andere Fassung lautet: „Es war aber Ḥabība bint Sahl mit Ṯābit b. Qays b. Šamās verheiratet. Der war ein hässlicher Mann. Sie sprach: ‚Gesandter Gottes. Ich schwöre, so wahr ich Gott fürchte. Wenn er zu mir eingeht, speie ich in sein Gesicht (*ʾiḏā daḫala ʿalayya labaṣaqtu fī waǧhihi*).' Der Prophet: ‚Gibst du ihm seinen Garten zurück? ' Sie sagte: ‚Ja' und gab ihm (Ṯ.) den Garten zurück. Er (Abū Karīm, der Tradent) sprach: ‚Sie gab ihm den Garten zurück' Er (Tradent) sprach: ‚Der Prophet Gottes trennte zwischen den beiden (*fa-farraqa baynahumā rasul Allāh*). '"[29]

Die Unterschiede in den Überlieferungen

Neben mehreren Detailunterschieden differieren die aufgeführten Fassungen an vier Hauptpunkten, die für das Verständnis der Überlieferung als Grundlage des *ḫulʿ* von Bedeutung sind.

Zum einen trägt die Frau des Ibn Qays unterschiedliche Namen. Sie wird z.T. Ḥabība bint Sahl und z.T. Ǧamīla bint Sulūl genannt. Hierbei überwiegt zahlenmäßig zwar die Benennung als Ḥabība, bei der Zitierung des *ḥadīṯ* in der Sekundärliteratur ist aber auffallend oft von der Ǧamīla (so genannt allein bei

---

24 *Abū Dāwūd, S.*, a.a.O., S. 268, Nr. 2227.

25 *Abū Dāwūd, S.*, a.a.O., S. 268, Nr. 2228.

26 *Abū Dāwūd, S.*, a.a.O., S. 268, Nr. 2229 u. 2230.

27 *Al-Nisāʾī, A.*, Sunan: bi šarḥ al-ḥāfiẓ Ǧalāl al-Dīn al-Suyūṭī, Beirut ohne Datum, S. 168f.

28 *Ibn Māǧa, A.*, Sunan, Beirut 1952, Bd. 1, Kitāb al-ṭalāq, Nr. 2056.

29 *Ibn Māǧa, A.*, a.a.O., Nr. 2057.

Ibn Māǧa) die Rede. In jedem Fall kommt dieser unterschiedlichen Benennung keine große Bedeutung zu. Insbesondere handelt es sich nicht um ein Problem von unterschiedlichen sich widersprechenden Traditionen, die sich gegenseitig abrogieren könnten. Denn es ist klar, dass es sich bei beiden Erzählweisen um die selbe Frau, nämlich die des Ṯabit ibn Qays, handelt.[30]
Zum zweiten besteht ein Unterschied bei der Beschreibung des Problems der Ehefrau mit ihrem Mann. Teilweise wird dieser als tadellos beschrieben (wie bei al-Buḫārī, al-Nisāʾī und teilweise bei Ibn Māǧa und Abū Dāwūd), so dass für die Frau als Grund einzig eine Abneigung oder ein Hass gegen diesen besteht. Daneben findet sich bei Ibn Māǧa seine Beschreibung als äußerlich hässlich, was zu einer besonders großen Abscheu der Frau führt, insbesondere wenn es zum Geschlechtsverkehr zwischen den beiden kommen soll. In der modernen Debatte werden noch weitere Varianten der Überlieferung zitiert (allerdings ohne Quellenangabe für das in Bezug genommene *ḥadīṯ*). In diesen Varianten wird das körperliche „Defizit" des Ehemanns genauer beschrieben: Er soll klein gewesen sein und schwarze Hautfarbe gehabt haben, was ihn insgesamt besonders hässlich erscheinen lässt.[31] Eine andere Interpretation dieser Passagen geht in die Richtung, dass der Mann deshalb so stark verabscheut wurde, weil er impotent war.[32] Die dritte Fassung findet sich bei Abū Dāwūd und beschreibt einen Mann, der sich zu seiner Frau grausam verhält, sie schlägt und sogar körperlich verletzt. Es besteht hier die Möglichkeit, zwischen diesen Situationen zu wählen und zu unterschiedlichen Voraussetzungen für den *ḫulʿ* zu gelangen.
Als drittes finden sich unterschiedliche Angaben zu dem von der Ehefrau Zurückgegebenen. Es ist teilweise die Rede von einer Geldsumme, teilweise wird sie aufgefordert, alles vom Mann Erhaltene zurückzugeben. In der Mehrzahl ist der Brautgeldpreis mit einem Garten angegeben. In der Fassung des Ibn Māǧa wird ausdrücklich angeordnet, dass die Frau nicht mehr zurückgibt als den erhaltenen Garten.
Zum vierten steht der jeweils letzte Satz der Überlieferung, dessen Interpretation zu verschiedenen Implikationen für das Wesen des *ḫulʿ* führen kann. In einigen Fassungen wird der Ehemann aufgefordert, die Lösungszahlung anzunehmen. Man kann daraus auf ein Wahlrecht des Mannes schließen, nach dem er die Aufforderung annehmen oder ablehnen kann. Die Aufforderung hat dann lediglich empfehlenden Charakter (*iršādī*). Eine solche Möglichkeit entfällt in

30 So die nach Prof. Muhammad Sirāǧ, Professor am Department for Arabic Language der American University of Cairo, im Interview am 22.10.2002, überwiegende Meinung. Gelegentlich scheinen einige Autoren davon auszugehen, dass es sich um verschiedene Frauen des Ṯābīt handelt, z.B. *Zawīn, Ḥ.*, Daʿwā al-ḫulʿ: ʿilman wa ʿamalan, Kairo 2002, S. 76. der von „Ṯābit und seiner zweiten Frau Ḥabība" spricht.

31 So z.B. ʿAbd al-Fatāḥ Šaiḫ in al-ʿArabī, 28.1.2000.

32 So Prof. Sirāǧ im Interview am 22.10.2002.

der zweiten Lesart. Hier unterliegt er einem Befehl des Propheten, dem er wohl kaum widersprechen kann. Damit kann man die Trennung als verpflichtend (*īǧābī*) nach Leistung der Zahlung ansehen. Die Fassungen von al-Buḫārī, al-Nisāʾī, Abū Dāwūd und die erste von Ibn Māǧa lassen sich auf beide Weisen als empfehlend oder verpflichtend interpretieren. Die zweite Fassung des Ibn Māǧa unterscheidet sich von den anderen in einem Punkt gewaltig: Hier wird der Ehemann gar nicht gefragt. Somit kommt es definitiv nicht auf die Einwilligung des Ehemanns an, sondern der Prophet selber nimmt eine Scheidung vor.

Die vorgestellten Traditionen unterscheiden sich demnach dadurch, dass die eigentliche Trennung der Ehe auf verschiedene Art und Weise zustande kommt. Hier kann man drei verschiedene Formen unterscheiden: Die explizite Frage nach dem Einverständnis, der Befehl des Propheten, die Frau zu verstoßen und die unmittelbare Scheidungshandlung des Propheten. Während bei der ersten Fassung klar ist, dass ohne Einverständnis eine *ḫulʿ*-Trennung nicht möglich ist, so spielt dieses in der dritten gar keine Rolle. Schwierig ist die Einordnung der zweiten Gruppe, die in der Mehrzahl der Traditionen vorkommt, sowie ihre Bedeutung für die Rechtspraxis. Man kann die Autorität des Propheten zu dem Scheidungsbefehl auf unterschiedliche Arten herleiten. Er kann diese qua officium besitzen, wenn man Muḥammad als Richter und Schiedsmann seiner Zeit betrachtet. Man kann sie ihm aber auch qua personam zusprechen, wenn man ihm unabhängig von seiner Stellung als justiziellem oder politischem Führer, ein hohes Maß an persönlicher Autorität zuspricht. Während im ersten Fall ein Widersetzen des Mannes wegen der formellen Stellung des Propheten innerhalb der *umma* undenkbar ist, bleibt dies im zweiten Falle zumindest möglich. Außerdem besteht der Unterschied darin, dass im letzten Fall ein Nachfolger mit derselben persönlichen Autorität nicht mehr vorhanden ist. Im ersten Fall jedoch folgen auf Muḥammad Richter (*qāḍī, quḍāṭ*), die zur Rechtssprechung dienen. Folgt Muḥammads Autorität nun qua officium, so kann die Befolgung einer Anweisung durch den Richter die gleichen Folgen für den Mann haben wie eine des Propheten: Ihr ist unbedingt Folge zu leisten und eine Verweigerung des Einverständnisses spielt keine Rolle. Die *ḫulʿ*-Trennung findet statt, ohne dass die Einwilligung des Mannes hierfür notwendig ist, solange die Frau ihren Teil mit der Rückzahlung der Morgengabe beigetragen hat.

Mit Arabi lässt sich konstatieren, dass die Zustimmung des Ehemanns und damit der Konsens nicht zwingend aus der Quellenlage gefolgert werden kann.[33]

---

33 *Arabi, O.*, a.a.O., S. 18.

3. Die Entwicklung des *ḫul'* in den Rechtsschulen

Bei der Ausgestaltung des Rechtsinstitutes des *ḫulʿ* waren die Rechtsschulen von der beschriebenen Quellenlage ausgegangen. Es entwickelten sich in der Folge sehr verschiedene Antworten auf die in den Quellen nicht oder unterschiedlich beantworteten Fragen.

Die große Mehrzahl der Gelehrten[34] geht aufgrund der Quellenlage davon aus, dass der *ḫulʿ* ein gültiges Rechtsinstitut ist, um die Ehe aufzulösen. Die Ausübung des *ḫulʿ* unterliegt aber moralischen Wertungen, die in einzelnen Fällen auch zu einer Nichtzulässigkeit führen können. So hat sich bei den Hanbaliten eine Kategorisierung in drei Klassen von *ḫulʿ*-Scheidungen durchgesetzt, die sich ähnlich auch bei den anderen finden lässt: Es gibt den erlaubten *ḫulʿ* (*mubāḥ*), wenn der Ehefrau das Bleiben beim Mann verhasst ist und sie Angst vor der Übertretung von Gottes Gesetzen hat. Allerdings besteht insofern eine Einschränkung, als dass die Frau innerhalb der Ehe auch zu Geduld verpflichtet ist. Verlangt der Mann von ihr die Fortführung der Ehe, weil er die Abneigung ihr gegenüber nicht verspürt, so trifft jene die Pflicht, eine Fortführung der Beziehung mit Geduld zu versuchen.[35] Ein *ḫulʿ* ist missbilligt (*makrūh*), wenn eine Frau die Trennung verlangt, ohne die genannten religiösen Gründe zu haben. Sie gilt als unaufrichtig, und sie trifft die Wertung aus der Sunna: Zwar hat ein so vereinbarter *ḫulʿ* Gültigkeit, jedoch kommen auf die Frau jenseitige Strafen zu. Die letzte Kategorie ist die des verbotenen *ḫulʿ* (*muḥarram*): Ein solcher Fall liegt vor, wenn der Mann die Frau durch bewusst schlechte Behandlung dazu verleitet, sich von ihm loszukaufen, indem er sie schlägt oder ihr bestehende Rechte vorenthält. Hier liegt ein Verstoß gegen die koranische Weisung aus Sure 4,19 vor. In einem solchen Fall besteht auf seiner Seite kein Anspruch gegen die Ehefrau auf die Abstandszahlung. Vielmehr gilt der *ḫulʿ* als *ṭalāq raǧʿī*, bei dem den Mann die für die *ṭalāq*-Scheidung üblichen nachehelichen Verpflichtungen treffen.[36]

Als Konsens in den Rechtsschulen können die folgenden Voraussetzungen eines wirksamen *ḫulʿ* gelten, die in den Abhandlungen zum Thema die Struktur der Erörterung vorgeben[37]: Es ist 1) die Zustimmung beider Partner notwendig, 2)

---

34 Als einzige abweichende Meinung wird die des Bakr Ibn ʿAbd Allāh al-Muzanī genannt, der die Ansicht vertritt, dass Koran und Sunna den *ḫulʿ* gerade nicht zulassen. Er meint dabei, dass der Koranvers 4,20 die Stelle 2,228 abrogiert. Die Abrogationshypothese wird allgemein abgelehnt, da keine Situation für eine Abrogation vorliege, weil die beiden Verse nicht zur selben Frage Stellung beziehen. Siehe zu dieser Debatte *al-ʿAǧūz, N.*, a.a.O., S. 48f, *Imām, M.*, Aḥkām al-aḥwāl al-šaḫṣīya li-l-muslimīn: dirāsa tārīḫīya wa tašrīʿīya wa qaḍāʾīya, Bd.2, Alexandria 2001, S.171.

35 *Naṣṣār, A.*, a.a.O., S. 52; Art. Ḫulʿ. In: *Wizārat al-auqāf*..., a.a.O., S. 241, § 10.

36 Art. Ḫulʿ. In: *Wizārat al-auqāf*..., 241, § 10.

37 Folgende Auflistung der Voraussetzungen nach *al-Fiqī*, a.a.O., S. 39f.

müssen sich die Frau und der Mann in einem für den *ḫulʿ* zulässigen Status befinden[38], 3) muss für die Scheidungsformel der Begriff *ḫulʿ* oder eine seiner Ableitungen verwendet werden[39] und 4) muss die Frau eine Ausgleichszahlung leisten. Im Lichte der dargestellten Quellenlage und der modernen Gesetzgebung sind besonders der erste und der vierte Punkt problematisch und werden im Folgenden erörtert.

Die Zustimmung beider Ehegatten

Alle Rechtsschulen gehen davon aus, dass die *ḫulʿ*–Scheidung eine beidseitige Verpflichtung ist, die wie jeder Vertrag durch Angebot (*īǧāb*) und Zustimmung (*qubūl*) zustande kommt. Eine Trennung ohne eine entsprechende Erklärung seitens beider Partner ist nicht möglich. Somit haben sich alle Rechtsschulen dafür entschieden, bei der Interpretation des *ḥadīṯ* die erste der genannten Auslegungsmöglichkeiten zu wählen. Muḥammads Anordnung an Ṯābit wird als bloße Empfehlung angesehen. Ohne Zustimmung des Mannes kann es zu keinem *ḫulʿ* kommen. Seine Zustimmung kann auch nicht durch einen Richterspruch ersetzt werden.[40]

Es spielt keine Rolle, ob zuerst die Frau oder der Mann das Angebot abgeben. Beides ist zulässig, wobei die Initiative für gewöhnlich von der Frau kommt, da dem Mann andere Möglichkeiten zur Beendigung der Ehe zustehen.[41]

Einigkeit besteht bei den Gelehrten, dass der zweite Zweck der *ʿidda*, nämlich die Möglichkeit des Mannes, seine *ṭalāq*-Entscheidung noch einmal zu

---

38 Insbesondere müssen beide Partner rechtsgeschäftsfähig und verpflichtungsbefugt sein (*ṣaḥiḥ al-iltizām*). Siehe zum ganzen: Art. Ḫulʿ.In: *Wizārat al-auqāf...*, S. 244, § 14.

39 Zur Durchführung eines *ḫulʿ* ist die Benutzung der *ḫulʿ*-Formel (*sayġa*) notwendig. Dies geschieht dadurch, dass ein bestimmter Ausdrucks (*lafẓ*), der den *ḫulʿ*-Vorgang beschreibt, in Angebot und Annahme benutzt wird. Zulässige Ausdrücke sind *ḫulʿ* oder ein anderer synonymer Ausdruck wie *fidya*, *ṣulḥ*, oder *mubāraʾa* samt den daraus abgeleiteten Formen (Art. Ḫulʿ . In: *Wizārat al-auqāf...*, a.a.O., S. 257, § 30).

40 *Al-ʿAǧūz, N.*, a.a.O., S. 25; *Arabi, O.*, a.a.O., S. 8 und 15.

41 Unterschiede ergeben sich aber bezüglich der Rechtsnatur der Erklärungen von Mann und Frau. Eingebettet in die Dogmatik der Willenserklärungen werden die Erklärungen der Gatten zumindest bei den Hanafiten verschieden klassifiziert. Die Erklärung des Mannes wird als Schwur (*yamīn*), die der Frau als Erklärung in einem Austauschvertrag (*muʿāwada*) bezeichnet. Der Hauptunterschied hieraus besteht in der Widerrufbarkeit der Erklärung: Während ein *yamīn* den Erklärenden ein für alle Mal bindet, besteht beim *muʿāwaḍa* die Möglichkeit des Widerrufs, sofern dieser vor der Annahme des Gegenübers ergeht. Macht also der Mann den *ḫulʿ*-Antrag, so ist er an diesen gebunden, bis die Frau sich erklärt. Anders verhält es sich in den übrigen Rechtsschulen: Hier gelten beide Erklärungen als *muʿāwaḍa* und sind somit bis zur Annahme durch den anderen widerrufbar. Vgl. Art. Ḫulʿ. In: *al-Zuḥaylī, W.*, a.a.O., S. 7015-7017; Art. Ḫulʿ . In: *Wizārat al-auqāf...*, S. 239, § 8.

überdenken, beim *ḫulʿ* keine Rolle spielt. Auch die Vertreter der hanbalitischen Schule, sehen die Wirkung des *ḫulʿ* gleich der Wirkung einer unwiderruflichen Scheidung (*ṭalāq bāʾin*). Dies ergibt sich aus dem Zweck der *ḫulʿ*, die eheliche Beziehung endgültig zu beenden. Die Frau wie der Mann sollen Rechtssicherheit erlangen, die nicht durch einen Widerruf oder auch durch eine Anfechtung angreifbar wäre.[42]
Für die Durchführung des *ḫulʿ* ist ein Richterspruch wie bei anderen Fällen des *ṭalāq* nicht notwendig. Die Partner können sich in privaten Rahmen unter Hinzuziehung von Zeugen einigen und die Trennung vollziehen. [43]

Leistung einer Ausgleichszahlung durch die Frau

Letztes Charakteristikum für den *ḫulʿ* ist die Leistung einer Abstandssumme (*ʿawwaḍ*) durch die Frau. Erst wenn diese erfüllt ist, treten die Rechtswirkungen des *ḫulʿ* ein. Dabei ist es möglich, diese Zahlung in verschiedenster Form vorzunehmen. Sie kann in einer Geldsumme, einer Schuldübernahme oder der Gewährung eines Gebrauchsvorteils oder eines Dienstes liegen. So ist z.B. das Stillen des Kindes (*riḍāʿ al-ṭifl*) oder das Aufbringen der Mittel zur Erziehung durch die Mutter eine mögliche Ausgleichsleistung. Dies kann auch auf eine bestimmte kürzere Zeit beschränkt sein. Wird die geschuldete Leistung wegen Tod des Kindes unmöglich, so trifft die geschiedene Frau eine Schadensersatzpflicht in Höhe der geschätzten Kosten für ihre Dienste. Während der Verzicht auf den Unterhalt in der Wartezeit (*nafaqat al-ʿidda*) erlaubt ist, weisen die Rechtsschulen den Auszug aus der ehelichen Wohnung (*isqāṭ ḥaqq al-sakan muddat al-ʿidda*) in dieser Zeit als Gegenleistung zurück. Grund hierfür ist die koranische Einsetzung des Wohnungsanspruchs der Ehefrau in Sure 65,1. Die Frau kann als Gegenleitung lediglich vereinbaren, für den Mann die Kosten für die Wohnungsmiete zu übernehmen.[44]
Eine der strittigsten Fragen bei der Einordnung des *ḫulʿ* ist die Frage nach der maximalen Höhe der Ausgleichszahlung. Kann die Summe höher liegen als die Brautgabe oder stellt diese die Obergrenze dar? Während es für die Malikiten und Schafiiten gleich ist, ob die Zahlung höher oder niedriger ausfällt als das ursprünglich Gegebene, solange beide Partner die Summe frei vereinbaren konnten, beschränken es die Hanbaliten auf die Höhe der Brautgeldsumme. Eine Differenzierung nach dem Verursacher der Antipathie, die schließlich zur Trennungsbegehren führt, nehmen die Hanafiten vor: Wenn der Mann diese initiiert hat, gilt die Annahme als missbilligt. Hat er die Frau gar durch schlechte Behandlung dazu getrieben, zum *ḫulʿ* als Ausweg zu flüchten, hat er wegen Sure

---

[42] *Al-Fiqī, U.*, S. 49; Art. Ḫulʿ. In: *Wizārat al-auqāf...*, 237, § 7.
[43] Siehe zum Ganzen Art. Ḫulʿ. In: *Wizārat al-auqāf...*, S. 244, § 14.
[44] Art. Ḫulʿ. In: *al-Zuḥaylī, W.*, a.a.O., S. 7032; Art. Ḫulʿ. In: *Wizārat al-auqāf...*, 254f, § 25.

2, 231f gar kein Recht auf irgendeine Abstandszahlung und er muss eine trotzdem erfolgte Zahlung zurückerstatten. Die von den Partnern als *ḫulʿ* bezeichnete Auflösung der Ehe wird dann als *ṭalāq bāʾin* angesehen.[45] Ist die Frau diejenige, die von sich aus ohne weiteren Grund außer ihrer Abneigung die Trennung begehrt, so kann der Mann zwar mehr als die Brautgeldsumme verlangen, eine negative moralische Bewertung besteht jedoch unter Verweis auf die Ṯābit-Überlieferung auch bei den Hanafiten: In der Fassung des Ibn Māǧa begrenzt der Prophet die Abstandszahlung der Ehefrau auf die Höhe des erhaltenen Brautgelds. Dass diese Stelle nicht bei allen Rechtsschulen zur maßgebenden Norm geworden ist, hängt wohl damit zusammen, dass man den Charakter als vertragliche Vereinbarung im Rahmen der Vertragsfreiheit betont, unter der jeder zu freien Bedingungen einen Vertrag eingehen kann.[46]

C. DIE REFORM DES ISLAMISCHEN RECHTS IM 20. JAHRHUNDERT

I. Ideen und Methoden der Rechtsreform in arabisch-islamischen Ländern

Die Situation des Rechts der arabischen Länder im 19. Jahrhundert zeichnete sich dadurch aus, dass die islamischen Rechtsgelehrten mit den gleichen Techniken der Rechtsfindung arbeiteten wie in den Jahrhunderten zuvor. Zur Lösung einer Rechtsfrage griffen sie zu den Rechtswerken der Autoritäten ihrer Schulen. Jede Lösung war so mit einem umfangreichen Suchprozess verbunden, der viel Zeit in Anspruch nahm, einen umfangreichen Bestand von Literatur voraussetzte und zu unterschiedlichen Ergebnissen führen konnte, je nachdem, auf welche Autorität der einzelne Gelehrte sich stützte.

Dieser Zustand wurde angesichts des wachsenden Kontakts der arabischen Welt mit Europa als unbefriedigend empfunden. Im Gegensatz zu den Rechtsordnungen der ausländischen Mächte erwies sich die Anwendung des islamischen Rechts in Gebieten, die bis dato keine Rolle gespielt hatten, häufig als unbrauchbar. Im Handels- und Wirtschaftskontakt mit den europäischen Mächten wurde daher oft zwangsläufig auf die fremden Rechtsordnungen zurückgegriffen. Die Erneuerung des eigenen Rechts und die mögliche Öffnung für den internationalen Handel wurden als Herausforderung verstanden und angegangen. Seit 1830 kam es zu wichtigen Veränderungen des Rechts, deren Methodik im Folgenden nachgezeichnet wird.

---

45 *Naṣṣār, A.*, a.a.O., S. 54, 56; Art. Ḫulʿ. In: *Wizārat al-auqāf...*, a.a.O., 243, § 11.

46 *Bekhtar, L.*, Encyclopedia of Islamic Law: a Compendium of the Major Schools, Chicago 1996, S. 512.

1. Kodifizierung des islamischen Rechts und Neuordnung des Gerichtswesens

Ein wichtiges Reformmittel zur Vereinheitlichung und Vereinfachung war das der Kodifikation (*taqnīn*). Kodifikationen gewannen an Raum in den Ländern des Mittleren Ostens mit den Kontakten zu Europa. In Verträgen erwirkten einige europäische Staaten, dass auch im Osmanischen Reich für ihre Staatsangehörigen das in der Regel kodifizierte Recht des Heimatlandes mit besonderen Gerichten für diese zu gelten habe. Somit wurde vor Ort nach kodifiziertem Recht geurteilt, wenn zunächst auch ohne Wirkung für die Einheimischen. Es wurde jedoch bei Unklarheiten im eigenen System durch Rückgriff auf die Normen der Ausländer die Lösung gesucht.[47]
Angefangen mit den Tanzimat-Reformen von 1839 bis 1876 wurden im Osmanischen Reich einige Rechtsgebiete in Kodifikationen geregelt, die an vorhandenen europäischen Vorbildern orientiert waren. Dabei standen das Zivil- und Handelsrecht im Vordergrund, aber auch das Strafrecht, das mit den koranischen *ḥudūd*-Strafen einen Kernbereich der *šarīʿa* ausmacht, wurde Gegenstand der Reform. In der Regel wurden die europäischen Vorbilder durch einige islamrechtliche Vorschriften modifiziert.
Kodifikationen von islamischen Rechtssätzen gab es keine, bis 1877 der osmanische Staat mit der Mecelle (arab. *maǧalla*) ein Gesetzbuch über Vertrags- und Obligationenrecht sowie das Prozessrecht einführte. Es basierte auf der hanafitischen Rechtsschule und diente dazu, in den kurz zuvor eingeführten nicht-religiösen Gerichten angewandt zu werden, damit die dortigen Richter leichter das anzuwendende Recht auffinden und umsetzen könnten. Die *maǧalla* hat in großen Teilen der arabisch-islamischen Welt Wirkung entfaltet und wurde in Ländern wie Libanon, Israel und den Palästinensischen Gebieten oder Syrien erst im 20. Jahrhundert durch neue Gesetze abgelöst.[48]
In Ägypten, das formell Teil des Osmanischen Reiches war, aber seit den Tagen des Herrschers Muḥammad ʿAlī (1805-1848) über zunehmende Autonomie gegenüber der Istanbuler Zentralregierung verfügte, verlief diese Entwicklung ähnlich. Ein Teil der osmanischen Reformgesetze, wie das Handels- und das Strafgesetzbuch, wurde übernommen, danach folgten eigene Kodifikationen nach europäischem Vorbild. 1875/76 wurden weltliche „gemischte Gerichte" eingeführt, die für Fälle mit Beteiligung von Ausländern anteilig mit ägyptischen und ausländischen Richtern besetzt waren. Später entwickelten sich hieraus weltliche Gerichte, die in Angelegenheiten, die ausschließlich Ägypter umfasste, nach eigens für die neuen Gerichte erlassenen Gesetzbüchern

---

47 *Dilger, K.*, Das Rechtswesen in Ägypten. In: *Schamp, H.* (Hrsg.), Ägypten: das alte Kulturland am Nil auf dem Weg in die Zukunft, Tübingen 1977, S. 509-539 (511ff).

48 *Schacht, J.*, a.a.O, S. 92; Art. Medjelle, (*Findley, G.*), in: EI, Bd. 6, S. 971; *Nagel, T.*, Das islamische Recht: Eine Einführung, Westhofen 2001, S. 305.

zuständig waren. Die *maǧalla* war in Ägypten nicht übernommen worden. Stattdessen erstellte 1875 eine Kommission unter Leitung des Justizministers Muḥammad Qadrī Pāšā einen eigenen, am hanafitischen Bestand orientierten Zivilrechtsgesetzentwurf, der allerdings ebenso wenig Gesetzeskraft erlangte wie Qadrī Pāšās Versuch, das hanafitische Familien- und Erbrecht in einem Gesetzbuch zusammenzustellen. Dieser mit 647 Artikeln umfassend ausgefallene Entwurf wurde aber von vielen Richtern als Arbeitshilfe benutzt und ist bis heute zur Orientierung über das hanafitische Familienrecht in Umlauf.[49]

Eng verbunden mit der Kodifikation ist das dem Herrscher schon nach klassischen islamrechtlichen Konzeptionen im Rahmen seiner *siyāsa*-Kompetenz zustehende Recht, die Jurisdiktionskompetenz zu ordnen und Verfahrensregeln einzuführen (*taḫṣīṣ al-qaḍā'*). Wie am Beispiel Ägypten im Zusammenhang mit den Kodifikationen erwähnt, hat der Gesetzgeber neue „weltliche" Gerichte geschaffen, in denen bestimmte Rechtsgebiete verhandelt wurden. Zunächst parallel zur überkommenen Struktur der *šarīʿa*-Gerichte existierend verdrängten sie diese nach und nach, indem immer mehr Kompetenzen auf sie verschoben wurden. So wurden in Ägypten 1956 die *šarīʿa*-Gerichte gänzlich abgeschafft, deren Zuständigkeitsbereich schon vorher erheblich beschnitten worden war. Mit den neuen Gerichten zogen neue Verfahrensregeln ein, die insbesondere eine Erweiterung der zulässigen Beweismittel vorsahen. Während sich das klassische Recht generell durch einen Vorrang für mündliche Zeugen auszeichnete, treten in moderneren Kodifikationen andere Beweismittel an seine Seite.[50] Auch wird das Erfordernis von Registrierungen und Beurkundungen eingeführt, um den Zugang zum Gericht zu ermöglichen. So hat der ägyptische Gesetzgeber 1931 zur Eindämmung der stark verbreiteten Kinderheirat eingeführt, dass nur solche auf die Ehe bezogene Klagen entgegen genommen werden, bei denen die Ehe ordnungsgemäß registriert worden ist. Gleichzeitig wurde bestimmt, dass nur Ehen von Partnern im Alter von über 16 (für die Braut) bzw. 18 Jahren (beim Mann) registriert werden können. Auf diese Weise konnte man der zwar islamrechtlich zulässigen, aber gesellschaftspolitisch nicht gewollten Kinderheirat entgegen wirken, ohne sie ausdrücklich verbieten zu müssen. Durch die

---

[49] So hat z.B. die deutsche Sammlung von internationalen privatrechtlichen Gesetzen im Bereich des Familienrecht von *Bergmann, A/Ferid, M.*, Internationales Ehe- und Kindschaftsrecht, Loseblattsammlung, 3. Aufl., Frankfurt seit 1956, S. 32ff, den Entwurf aufgenommen. Vgl. *Elwan, O.*, Gesetzgebung und Rechtssprechung. In: *Steinbach, U./ Robert, R.* (Hrsg.), Der Nahe und Mittlere Osten: Politik, Gesellschaft, Wirtschaft, Geschichte, Kultur, Bd. 1, S. 221-254 (229); *Esposito, J.*, Women in Muslim Law, New York 1982, S. 49f.

[50] *Anderson, N.*, Law Reform in the Muslim World, London 1976, S. 42f.

Erschwerung des Verfahrens wurde die Heirat von Minderjährigen auch tatsächlich eingedämmt.[51]

2. Impulse der salafīya-Bewegung als islamischer Reformbewegung

Die Grundlagen der Salafīya-Bewegung

In der zweiten Hälfte des 19. Jahrhunderts bildete sich als Antwort auf die Herausforderungen der Begegnung mit dem Westen eine islamische Reformbewegung, die als *Salafīya*[52] bezeichnet wird. Geprägt von ihren beiden frühen Protagonisten Muḥammad ʿAbduh und Rašīd Riḍā verbreitete sich ihr Gedankengut von Ägypten aus in die gesamte arabische Welt.[53]
Ausgangspunkt der Bewegung ist die Beobachtung eines inneren Verfalls der muslimischen Gesellschaft und die Notwendigkeit einer Wiederbelebung der Religion von innen. ʿAbduh wie Riḍā betonen, dass Muḥammads Botschaft nicht nur einen Weg für das persönliche Heil der Menschen aufzeigt, sondern gleichzeitig eine politische Dimension besitzt, die das gesellschaftliche Zusammenleben der Menschen bestimmt.[54] In der Konfrontation mit Europa wurde der Islam für eine beobachtbare Rückständigkeit der arabischen Länder in technischen und kulturellen Angelegenheiten verantwortlich gemacht. Hiergegen wehren sich die Vertreter der Salafīya und erklären den Islam als eine besonders vernunftgemäße Religion, die mit den Anforderungen der wachsenden Technisierung der Welt zu verbinden ist – und die, so ʿAbduh in

---

51 *Anderson, N.*, a.a.O., S. 45f.

52 Der Begriff „*Salafīya*" bezieht sich auf die aufrechten Altvorderen oder frommen Vorväter (*al-salaf al-ṣāliḥ)*, die als Vorbilder für einen modernen, mit der Wissenschaft vereinbaren Islam gelten. Sie wirken neben den kanonischen Quellen Koran und Sunna als Garanten für die Authentizität der Reform und dienen als Auslegungsrichtlinie. Die Rückkehr zu den ersten Prinzipien und zu den Ursprüngen ist daher ein Schlüsselbegriff für die Reform. Als Gegenbegriff zu *salaf* wird häufig *ḫalaf* gebraucht, um spätere Generationen zu bezeichnen, die zur Verirrung des Islams beigetragen haben.

53 Hinzuweisen ist darauf, dass der *salafīya*-Begriff heute auch von Vertretern strengster und teilweise gewaltbereiter Gruppen vornehmlich aus dem wahhabitisch-islamistischen Spektrum als Selbstbezeichnung in Anspruch genommen wird. Im Deutschen werden diese Gruppen meist als „Salafisten" bezeichnet (vgl. z.B. *Kepel, G.*, Das Schwarzbuch des Dschihad: Aufstieg und Niedergang des Islamismus, München 2002, S. 175, 236). Es kann hier nicht geklärt werden, ob und inwieweit eine Beziehung zwischen der Erneuerungsbewegung des frühen 20. Jahrhunderts, wie sie hier vorgestellt wird, und diesen „Salafisten" besteht. Es liegt aber auf der Hand, dass die von beiden Strömungen vertretenen Ansätze in Zielen und Mitteln weit voneinander abweichen.

54 *Hourani, A.*, Arabic Thought in the Liberal Age 1798-1939, London 1962, S. 136.

seiner Schrift *Risālat al-tauḥīd*, im übrigen auch der christlichen Religion wegen ihrer Rationalität und den realistischeren ethischen Idealen weit voraus sei.[55]
Um die Vernunftgemäßheit wieder herauszustellen, bedarf es einer Reform (*iṣlāḥ*), die sich dadurch auszeichnet, dass sie zu den ersten Prinzipien der Religion zurückkehrt und sich bei der Bewertung moderner Phänomene und deren Integration in die Gesellschaft an diesen orientiert.
Reform wird dabei als ein in der islamischen Geschichte dauerhaft vorhandenes Unternehmen begriffen. Man beruft sich auf eine Propheten-Überlieferung, nach welcher der Prophet erklärt, die islamische Gemeinschaft (*umma*) brauche regelmäßige Revitalisierung. Riḍā meint, dass jede Generation Erneuerer (*muǧaddidūn*) zur Verteidigung der wahren Sunna und zum Kampf gegen unislamischen Neuerungen (*bidʿa*) besessen hat. Somit stellt er seine Bewegung in eine Reihe mit mittelalterlichen Gelehrten wie Ibn Ḥazm, Ibn Taymīya oder al-Ġazālī.[56] Eine Reform wendet sich demnach gegen die Neuerungen und gegen als Auswüchse der Mystik verstandene Phänomene wie der Heiligenverehrung und will den einzelnen Gläubigen durch bessere Bildung in die Lage versetzen, selber die Quellen der Religion zu durchdringen. Sie nimmt das Aufkommen sozialer Übel wie Spiel und Wette oder Alkohol zum Anlass, durch die Rückführung in ursprüngliche Zustände die überkommenen Trennungen zwischen den Rechtsschulen, aber auch zwischen Sunniten und Schiiten zu überwinden.[57]
Ein solches Reformvorhaben wird aber nicht unter Lossagung jeglicher Tradition vorgeschlagen. Die *Salafīya*-Gelehrten stellen sich gegen die Lehre des *taqlīd* als der Übernahme einer bestimmten Rechtsschultradition. Der *taqlīd* wird ersetzt durch eine andere Autorität: Die der treuen Vorväter *(al-salaf al-ṣāliḥ)*, die man hauptsächlich in den ersten drei Generationen des Islam erblickt und zu denen einige wenige spätere Kapazitäten gezählt werden. Diese Tradition gilt als Anknüpfungspunkt für eine Form des Ur-Islams, von der aus Erneuerung ausgehen kann.

Die Salafīya und ihre Prinzipien der Rechtsreform

Die Forderung nach Rechtsreform stellte von Anfang an einen der wichtigsten Bereiche für das Wirken der *Salafīya* dar, denn vor allem auf dem Feld des geltenden Rechts stellen die Reformer einen starken Widerspruch fest. Auf der einen Seite beobachten sie, wie ab der Mitte des 19. Jahrhunderts die herrschenden Eliten ihrer Länder die *šarīʿa* in wichtigen Gebieten wie dem Zivil-, Handels- und Strafrecht durch Kodifikationen westlicher Prägung

---

55 *Schacht, J.*, a.a.O., S. 420.
56 Art. Iṣlāḥ (*Merad, A.*). In: EI , Bd. 4, S. 141-171 (141).
57 Ebd., 151.

ablösen. Dabei wird an vielen Stellen von überkommenen Prinzipien des islamischen Rechts abgegangen, um den Handel mit westlichen Ländern zu erleichtern. Den Religionsgelehrten fällt es schwer, hierzu handfeste Alternativen vorzuschlagen, die sowohl *šarīʿa*-konform sind als auch den Anforderungen der modernen Zeit entsprechen. ʿAbduh wandte sich gegen diesen Säkularisierungsprozess, denn bei Aussetzung von Teilen der *šarīʿa* gerät für ihn das Gesamtsystem in Gefahr.[58] ʿAbduh formulierte Grundsätze für ein zeitgemäßes Recht, das von den Nachfolgern weiterentwickelt wurde.
Für ʿAbduh ist eines der wichtigsten Ziele jeder Rechtsreform die Vereinheitlichung. Damit soll eine effektive und auch vereinfachte Rechtsanwendung ermöglicht werden. Der Ruf nach der Einheit bedeutet zugleich einen Bruch mit der islamrechtlichen Tradition, in der die Vielfalt von Rechtsmeinungen immer als besonderer Segen gegolten hat.[59] Als Mittel zur Vereinheitlichung bietet sich die Kodifikation an. ʿAbduh fordert dabei, dass diese den bestehenden Landessitten und -gepflogenheiten entsprechen sollen und sieht die Religionsgelehrten in der Pflicht, eine solche umfassende Kodifikation auf Basis der *šarīʿa* zu erstellen. Als Mittel der Rechtsreform plädiert er somit für ein genuin europäisches Verfahren, das in Ägypten wie im Osmanischen Reich längst Praxis geworden ist – nur, dass bei den damals existierenden Beispielen der Schritt der Verifizierung des Ergebnisses durch die *šarīʿa* gänzlich fehlte. Das bestehende Recht rügt er als Einpflanzung von Fremdem, das für Ägypten nicht passe.[60]
Methodisch hält sich die Rechtstheorie der *Salafīya* an das von der Orthodoxie vorgegebene Muster. Als Rechtsquellen (*uṣūl al-fiqh*) werden mit Koran, Sunna, dem Analogieschluss (*qiyās)* und dem Konsens (*iǧmāʿ*) die altbekannten Quellen benutzt. Jedoch zeigen sich bei genauerer Betrachtung einige Verschiebungen in den Details.
Koran und Sunna bekommen in der *Salafīya* als Primärquellen eine besonders herausragende Bedeutung. Der Wortlaut der Offenbarung bildet die Grenze für alle Rechtsregeln. Unterschiedlich wird das Verhältnis zwischen Koran und Sunna gesehen. Während einige von einer Wesensgleichheit der beiden Quellen ausgehen, bauen andere – unter ihnen ʿAbduh – eine deutliche Hierarchie zwischen den beiden schriftlichen Quellen auf, in der die Sunna nachgeordnet

---

58 *Kerr, M.*, Islamic Reform: The Political and Legal Theoriers of Muḥammadʿ Abduh and Rashid Riḍā, Los Angeles 1966, S. 188.

59 *Arabi, O.*, Studies in Modern Islamic Law Jurisprudence, Den Haag 2001, S. 22, hält den Ruf der Salafīyya nach Vereinheitlichung sogar für den eigentlichen „battle cry" der Reformbewegung.

60 *Layish, A.*, The Contribution of the Modernist to the Secularization of Islamic Law. In: MES 1978, S. 264-277 (263); *Hourani, A.*, a.a.O., S. 137.

ist. Überlieferungen dienen als Auslegungsmittel für die koranische Offenbarung.[61]

Unterschiede ergeben sich beim *qiyās*. Dieser wird zurückgeführt auf das Bemühen um die eigene Rechtsfindung (*iǧtihād*). Gezogene Analogieschlüsse der frühislamischen Rechtsgelehrten waren ja letztlich das Produkt des *iǧtihād*. Schon bei einigen der von der Salafīya in Bezug genommenen mittelalterlichen Rechtsgelehrten war es zu Kontroversen darüber gekommen, ob das Ergebnis eines eigenen Bemühens zu einer faktisch der Offenbarung gleichwertigen Rechtsquelle werden kann – Ibn Ḥazm z.B. hatte dies bestritten.[62] Bei der modernen *Salafīya* wird dies durchgehend abgelehnt: Riḍā nennt den *iǧtihād* die „Lebenskraft der Religion" (*ḥayāt al-dīn*)[63]. Das „Tor des *iǧtihād*" sei nicht nur niemals wirksam geschlossen worden, so dass die Möglichkeit zur eigenen Rechtsfindung immer bestanden hat, der *iǧtihād* wird sogar zu einer doppelten Pflicht für die Muslime, die im übrigen niemals so einfach durchführbar war wie im 20. Jahrhundert, in dem rechtliches Wissen durch Bücher und neue Technologien so weit verbreitet ist wie nie zuvor.[64] Zum einen ist es die Pflicht eines jeden einzelnen, sich persönlich mit dem Offenbarungstext auseinander zu setzen und Antworten auf Rechtsfragen zu suchen bzw. sich bei der eigenen Unfähigkeit dazu an Ausgebildete zu wenden. Zum anderen gibt es die legislatorische Dimension des *iǧtihād*, der als Pflicht der Gesamtgesellschaft durch dazu Befähigte ausgeübt werden soll. Der *iǧtihād* wird dadurch zur Aufgabe der politischen Führung. [65]

Die Institutionalisierung dieses gesellschaftlichen *iǧtihād* ist dabei eine der wichtigsten Fragen: Wer soll für die Ausübung verantwortlich sein? Für ʿAbduh waren es generell die qualifizierten Gelehrten (*ūlū al-ʾamr*), die als speziell Ausgebildete zuständig sein sollen. In welchem institutionellen Rahmen dies geschehen soll, erklärt er nicht genauer. Riḍā ist an dieser Stelle spezifischer: Für ihn ist die Kompetenzfrage eng verbunden mit der Frage nach dem richtigen Staatsmodell. Riḍā vertritt die Wiedereinführung des Kalifenamtes, das für ihn zum Wesen eines islamischen Staates unbedingt dazugehört. Bei dem Kalifen liegt als obersten *muǧtahid* die Befugnis, für deren Ausübung er sich von einer - ebenfalls einzuführenden – *šūra* beraten lassen kann.[66] Man hat in diesem Modell Parallelen zu parlamentarischen Systemen gesehen. Der Unterschied besteht aber darin, dass in Riḍās System nur persönlich zum *iǧtihād* qualifizierte

---

61 Art. Iṣlah (*Merad, A.*). In: EI, S. 141. Zu ʿAbduhs *ḥadīṯ*-skeptischer Haltung auch *Brown, D.*, Rethinking Tradition in Modern Islamic Thought, Cambridge 1996, S. 37.

62 *Kerr, M.*, a.a.O., S. 190.

63 *Riḍā, R.*, Tafsīr, zitiert in Art. Iṣlāḥ (*Merad, A.*). In: EI, Bd. 4, S. 153.

64 *Anderson, N.*, a.a.O., S. 59.

65 *Coulson, N.*, A History of Islamic Law, Edinburgh 1964, S. 211.

66 *Layish, A.*, a.a.O., S. 265.

Mitglieder für die Beratung vorgesehen sind. Sobald man auch Nicht-Rechtsgelehrte in diesem Kreis zulässt, gerät das System Riḍās ins Wanken.
Jedoch ist mit Einführung des *iğtihād*-Prinzips nicht einer grenzenlosen Gewissensfreiheit oder kritischer Rationalität Tür und Tor geöffnet. Auch dieses Verständnis von *iğtihād* unterliegt Grenzen der Anwendbarkeit. Dabei wird auf eine Unterscheidung der neo-hanbalitischen Schule zurückgegriffen, die auch für mittelalterliche Gelehrte wie Ibn Taymīya die Grenze war: Es ist dies die Differenzierung zwischen Angelegenheiten des Dogmas und der Liturgie (*ʿibādāt*) auf der einen Seite und solchen des sozialen Zusammenlebens der Menschen (*muʿāmalāt*) untereinander auf der anderen Seite.[67] Während erstere zu einem von Gott ein für allemal gesetzten festen Bestand gehören, kann der Mensch bei letzteren Änderungen vornehmen. Riḍā verfeinert diese Differenzierung noch weiter, indem er auch diejenigen Bereiche innerhalb der *muʿāmalāt* in den unveränderlichen Kernbereich übernimmt, die moralische Prinzipien und Wertungen einführen. Auch diese haben Anspruch auf Gültigkeit. Der Unterschied zwischen *ʿibādāt* und *muʿāmalāt* ist auch für Riḍā insofern maßgebend, als dass in letzteren nur prinzipielle Regeln getroffen werden, bei denen noch ein weiter Ausfüllungsrahmen für die jeweilig lebende Generation besteht.[68]
Jedoch stellt gerade die Differenzierung zwischen den beiden Bereichen und das Herausfinden der grundlegenden Prinzipien des festen Bestands im Einzelfall eine der größten Herausforderungen dar. Einige Kritiker meinen, dass Riḍā bei der Aufstellung dieses Prinzips zwar einen beachtenswerten Programmsatz geschaffen hat, ihn aber nicht mit ausreichenden Kriterien zur Unterscheidung versehen hat. Außerdem sei der Raum für eine wirklich freie Ausübung des *iğtihād* aufgrund der vielen generellen Prinzipien, die Riḍā und seine Schüler aus Koran und Sunna ziehen, sehr eingeschränkt.[69]
Im Zusammenhang mit dem *iğtihād* kommt dem Prinzip des öffentlichen Interesses (*maṣlaḥa*) eine besondere Rolle zu. Dieses Prinzip, das insbesondere in der malikitischen Rechtsschule als *istiṣlāḥ* als ein Instrument zur Korrektur von als mit öffentlichen Interessen unvereinbar gehaltenen Analogieschlüssen verwendet wurde, taucht in der *Salafīya* als das leitende Motiv für die Ausübung des *iğtihād* auf. Damit ist der islamischen Rechtstheorie ein utilitaristisches Prinzip zugefügt, mit dem der Rechtssetzer in den für Veränderung offenen Bereichen Recht an den Erfordernissen der Zeit ausrichten kann. Es tritt damit praktisch an die Stelle des *qiyās*. Wer jetzt den *iğtihād* ausübt, hat als erste

67 *Hourani, A.*, S. 148; Art. Iṣlāḥ (*Merad, A.*). In: EI, a.a.O., S. 154, der von der Unterscheidung zwischen *ʿibādāt* und *ʿādāt* spricht.

68 *Kerr, M.*, S. 189.

69 Art. Iṣlāḥ (*Merad, A.*). In: EI, Bd.4, S. 155.

Referenzgröße das öffentliche Wohl. Das Auffinden einer analogiefähigen Stelle in der Offenbarung wird hierdurch obsolet, sofern keine Grundprinzipien dem Normziel entgegenlaufen.[70]
Für ʿAbduh hat das *maṣlaḥa*-Prinzip sehr weitreichende Folgen. Denn mit Hilfe dieses Instruments kann aus einer ethischen Generalmaxime auf dem Gebiet der *muʿāmalāt* ein spezifisches Gesetz hergeleitet werden. Auf diese Weise können neue Gesetzte „im Geist des Islams" aufgestellt werden. Layish spricht hier von der „Positivation of Religious Law".[71] Dies geht so weit, dass sogar spezielle koranische Weisungen aufgehoben werden können, wenn diese zur Generalmaxime in Widerspruch stehen.[72] Ein Beispiel hierfür ist ʿAbduhs Haltung zur Polygynie, die er aus der Interpretation der Verse in Sure 4,3 und 4,129f herleitet. Während 4,3 die Vielweiberei voraussetzt und unter der Bedingung zulässt, dass der Mann seinen Frauen allen gerecht wird, warnt 4,129 vor der Einschätzung, dass die gerechte Behandlung aller Ehefrauen möglich ist. Während diese Stellen in der Auslegungstradition in der Regel als Zulassung der Polygynie interpretiert und der Gleichbehandlungsgrundsatz als ethischer Auftrag ohne diesseitig-rechtliche Konsequenz an den Ehemann verstanden worden sind[73], schließt ʿAbduh aus der Unerfüllbarkeit der Bedingung in 4,129 ein generelles Verbot. Er begründet dies mit der geänderten Situation von Frauen in frühislamischer und moderner Zeit. Während der Polygynie früher Funktionen wie die Stärkung der Bande zwischen Blutsverwandten und die Versorgung aller Frauen bei einem Überhang des weiblichen Bevölkerungsanteils zugekommen sei, so führe sie heute nur zu Missgunst zwischen den Ehegatten und sei letztlich ein Schaden für die Kinder. Im übrigen seien die Menschen in der Frühzeit des Islams tiefer in der Religion verwurzelt gewesen als die heutigen, so dass den Männern die Gleichbehandlung besser gelungen sei. [74] ʿAbduh setzt hier also das öffentliche Interesse seiner Generation an einer gerechten Behandlung der Frau und ihrer Kinder höher als die spezifische Vorschrift des Korans, die er unter Berücksichtigung der genannten Gründe uminterpretiert.[75]

---

70 *Hourani, A.*, a.a.O., S. 234; *Layish, A.*, a.a.O., S. 266; *Arabi, O.*, Studies…, a.a.O., S. 25.

71 *Layish, A.*, a.a.O., S. 264; ähnlich auch *Arabi, O.*, Studies..., a.a.O., S. 189.

72 *Hourani, A.*, a.a.O., S. 152.

73 Siehe dazu *Khoury, A.*, a.a.O., Bd. 5, S. 36f.

74 *ʿAbduh, M.*, Tafsīr al-qur'ān al-ḥakīm ausgeführt nach Übersetzung bei *Gätje, H.*, Koran und Koranexegese, Zürich 1975, S. 324ff. Siehe auch *Arabi, O.*, Studies..., a.a.O., S. 35ff.

75 Es ist noch hinzuzufügen, dass ʿAbduh die Frage der Zulässigkeit der Polygynie in späteren Jahren auch anders, nämlich bejahend, beantwortet hat Art. Talfīḳ (*Hallaq, W./Layish, A.*). In: EI, Bd.10, S. 161. Auch Riḍā hat die Frage anders beantwortet und die Zulässigkeit der Vielehe für einen unabänderlichen Teil der Offenbarung gehalten (*Layish, A.*, a.a.O., S. 65f; *Hourani, A.*, a.a.O., S. 152f).

Als einen konkreten Schritt zur Ausübung des *iǧtihād* schlägt ʿAbduh die Nutzung des *talfīq* vor. Wörtlich ist hiermit das „Zusammenflicken" von Kleidungsstücken gemeint. Juristisch wird das Schaffen eines neuen Gesetzes unter Rückgriff auf verschiedene Autoritäten des klassischen Rechts verstanden. Es kommt bei dem neuen Gesetz so zu einer Art Mischung der bekannten Autoritäten. ʿAbduh wendet hier das *maṣlaḥa*-Prinzip als leitendes Motiv für die Art der Zusammenstellung der Rechtsmeinungen an. Er schlägt ein systematisches Herangehen an den Bestand des *fiqh* vor, um eine Synthese zu finden. Damit ist auch gewährleistet, dass man sich an bereits bewährten Lösungen der Rechtsschulen orientiert, ohne diese einfach nur zu imitieren.
Als weitere klassische Rechtsquelle zählt der Konsens (*iǧmāʿ*). Auf die schon vorher aktuelle Frage, auf wessen Konsens es ankommt, damit dieser normative Wirkung zeige, gibt Riḍā eine klare Antwort: Anders als bei der Mehrzahl der *fiqh*-Gelehrten hat für ihn nur der *iǧmāʿ* der Prophetengeneration die Stellung einer Rechtsquelle. Ein späterer *iǧmāʿ* – und damit auch der, der zur „Schließung des Tores des *iǧtihād*" geführt haben soll – hat dagegen keinerlei Bindungswirkung für spätere Generationen. Bindend ist daneben lediglich der *iǧmāʿ* der jeweils lebenden Generation, ohne aber eine Stufe von Unfehlbarkeit zu erlangen. Ein solcher *iǧmāʿ* ist jederzeit modifizierbar und aufhebbar. Er ist fehlbar und am jeweils aktuellen öffentlichen Interesse auszurichten.[76] Wie schon bei der Frage nach dem befugten *muǧtahid* wird auch hier wieder Riḍās allgemeine Staatstheorie relevant: Der Ort für die Herstellung des Konsens ist die *šūra*, die als ständige Körperschaft dem Kalifen zugeordnet ist.

3. Kombination der Doktrinen verschiedener Rechtsschulen

Angeregt durch die Lehrer der Salafīya setzt sich im 20. Jahrhundert als weiteres Mittel der Rechtsreform die Vermischung der Regelungen von verschiedenen Rechtsschulen durch. Während der Trend im Jahrhundert zuvor dahin ging, für ein Rechtsgebiet eine bestimmte Rechtsschule als maßgeblich einzusetzen, um das geltendende Recht per Kodifikation zu vereinheitlichen, nimmt sich der Gesetzgeber des 20. Jahrhunderts nun das Recht heraus, bei einzelnen Materien von der vorherrschenden Richtung abzuweichen. Dies geschieht durch Auswahl aus einer Gesamtmaterie von Regeln (*taḫayyur*), die in ein kodifiziertes Gesetz eingefügt werden.[77] Ein zweiter Schritt besteht darin, die möglichen Referenzwerke auch auf solche auszudehnen, die nicht zu den orthodoxen gehören. So wurde auch im sunnitischen Bereich zugelassen, schiitische Elemente zu berücksichtigen oder auf Mindermeinungen, die nur von einzelnen

---

76 Art. Iṣlāḥ (*Merad, A.*). In: EI, Bd. 4, S. 154.

77 *Andersen, N.*, a.a.O., S. 47; *Brown, N.*, Shariʿa and State in the Modern Muslim Middle East. In: IJMES 29 (1997), S. 359-376 (370).

Rechtsgelehrten vertreten wurden, zurückzugreifen. Ein Beispiel hierfür ist die ägyptische Erbrechtsreform von 1946, bei der für die gesetzliche Erbfolge Elemente aus dem schiitischen Recht übernommen wurden.[78]
Dieses Verfahren wird weiterentwickelt zu einer Vermischung der Doktrinen der Rechtsschulen auch innerhalb eines Themenkomplexes (*talfīq*), was dazu führt, dass die einzelnen Versatzstücke der Doktrinen neu miteinander verbunden werden.[79] Ein erstes Beispiel hierfür bietet die *maǧalla*. Von ihrem Selbstanspruch her wollte sie zwar den hanafitischen Korpus der Regeln kodifizieren, jedoch ist darauf hingewiesen worden, dass sie der hanafitischen Schule weit weniger treu gefolgt ist als Qadrī Pāšā in dem ägyptischen Kodifikationsentwurf und stillschweigend nicht-hanafitische Elemente eingeführt hat. Während für die *maǧalla* dieser theoretische Reformansatz nicht offengelegt wurde, gewinnt er im 20. Jahrhundert an Boden und wird insbesondere in der Domäne des *šarīʿa*-abhängigen Familienrechts das am meisten verwendete Reformwerkzeug.[80] Ein Beispiel ist die Einführung einer obligatorischen Abstandssumme, die der Ehemann nach einer von der Frau nicht verschuldeten *ṭalāq*-Scheidung an diese zu zahlen hat. Angeknüpft wurde dabei an das Rechtsinstrument des *mutʿat al-ṭalāq* aus der schafiitischen Rechtsschule. Während die anderen Schulen eine solche Zahlung lediglich als moralische Empfehlung an die Ehemänner kannten, war sie bei den Schafiiten als Rechtspflicht bekannt. Die Gesetzgeber in Syrien, Tunesien und Marokko sowie später in Jordanien griffen nun auf die schafiitische Ausgestaltung zurück und führten in ihre Personalstatusgesetze den nachehelichen *mutʿa*-Anspruch der Frau ein.[81]
Ein weiteres Beispiel für die Anwendung des Reformmittels *talfīq* ist die Regelung des *ḫulʿ* in einigen Familiengesetzen des arabischen Orients. So kombinierte das jordanische Gesetz 61/1976 die hanafitische Lehre mit Elementen anderer Schulen: Die Abstandssumme konnte höher als und sachverschieden zum geleisteten Brautgeld sein (Art. 105). Auch bleiben *ḫulʿ*-Anträge von beiden Partnern widerrufbar, bis sich der andere Gatte äußert. Im hanafitischen Recht war dies wegen des Schwur-Charakters der Erklärung des Manns anders. Ähnlich verhält es sich auch in der syrischen Regelung. Auch

---

78 *Coulson, N.*, a.a.O., S. 193, 203f.

79 *Coulson, N.*, a.a.O., S.184.

80 Art. Medjelle, (*Findley, G.*), in: EI, Bd. 6, S. 971.

81 *Anderson, N.*, a.a.O., S. 60; *Coulson, N.*, a.a.O., S. 209; *El Alami, D.*, Law No. 100 of 1985 Amending certain Provisions of Egypts's Personal Status Law. In: ILS 1 (1994), S. 116-136 (121), Fn. 5; *Kamali, M.*, Divorce and Women's Rights: Some Muslim Interpreations of S. 2:228. In: The Muslim World 74 (1984), S. 85-99 (96).

hier ist der *ḫulʿ* im Personalstatusrecht kodifiziert und enthält Bestandteile aus den verschiedenen Rechtsschulen.[82]

4. (Neo-)*Iǧtihād*

Ein weiteres wirksam gewordenes Reformwerkzeug ist der *iǧtihād*. Anderson und Coulson versehen diesen Begriff mit der Vorsilbe „Neo-", um – der These von der „Schließung" und „Wiedereröffnung" des *iǧtihād*-Tores folgend – zum Ausdruck zu bringen, dass es sich um ein wiederentdecktes Instrument handelt und die Rechtswissenschaft das Zeitalter des bloßen *taqlīd* grundsätzlich überwunden hat.[83] Inhaltlich beschreiben beide Autoren das gleiche wie der dargestellte Ansatz der *Salafīya*-Bewegung: Durch Neuinterpretation der Textquellen können unter Berücksichtigung des Gemeinwohls neue Lösungsmöglichkeiten gefunden werden. Anderson macht Reformschritte dieser Art ab der zweiten Hälfte des 20. Jahrhunderts aus und bemerkt, dass es immer dann benutzt wurde, wenn die genannten Mittel einschließlich des *talfīq* nicht ausreichenden Spielraum boten, um die gesetzgeberischen Ziele zu erreichen.

Als Beispiel führen beide Autoren die Gesetzgebung zur Polygynie an. Diese wurde in Tunesien 1956 unter ausdrücklicher Berufung auf die vorgestellte Lehre von Muḥammad ʿAbduh ausgesetzt.[84] In eine ähnliche Stoßrichtung zielt auch der marokkanische Weg, nach dem eine Zweitheirat des Mannes der Erstfrau als Schädigung (*ḍarar*) gilt, wegen der sie gerichtliche Scheidung verlangen kann. Zum Schutz der Zweitfrau wurde außerdem eingeführt, dass die Zweitheirat generell ungültig ist, wenn die neue Ehefrau von der vorherigen Heirat nicht informiert wurde.[85]

Als eines der ehrgeizigsten Reformprojekte und ein Beispiel für die Ausübung des *iǧtihād* gilt die Neufassung des ägyptischen Zivilgesetzbuchs von 1948, die als Vorbild für die Gesetze in Syrien, Irak und anderen arabischen Staaten gedient hat. Unter der Leitung des Rechtsgelehrten ʿAbd al-Razzāq al-Sanhūrī, einem Schüler Rašīd Riḍās, stellte eine Kommission ein Gesetz zusammen, das

---

82 Art. Ḫulʿ. In: *al-Zuḥaylī, W.*, a.a.O., S. 7026, nennt drei Beispiele.

83 *Coulson, N.*, a.a.O., S. 202, überschreibt sein 14. Kapitel zur Rechtsreform in moderner Zeit mit „Neo-Ijtihād"; *Anderson, N.*, a.a.O., S. 59ff, übernimmt den Begriff.

84 *Coulson, N.*, a.a.O., S. 210, *Kamali, M.*, a.a.O., S. 99.

85 *Anderson, N.*, a.a.O., S. 63. Diese Elemente sind auch in den im Oktober 2003 von König Muḥammad VI. vorgeschlagenen und inzwischen verabschiedeten Gesetzesänderungen enthalten. Diese enthalten neben anderen Vorschriften zur Gleichstellung der Frau auch einen generellen Genehmigungsvorbehalt des Gerichts für jede Zweitheirat. Vgl. „Übersicht über die wichtigsten Änderungen des neuen Familiengesetzbuches im Vergleich mit dem geltenden Text", unveröffentlichte Informationsschrift der marokkanischen Botschaft in Berlin, Herbst 2003. Siehe auch Berichterstattung in Süddeutsche Zeitung vom 13.10.2003.

die Bindungen des Zivilrechts an die *šarīʿa* stärken und gleichzeitig das Recht modernisieren sollte. Dafür wurde als Rechtsquellen auf die eigene ägyptische Rechtstradition und Rechtssprechung, rechtsvergleichende Studien sowie die *šarīʿa* zurückgegriffen. Al-Sanhūrī behauptete dabei, dass es mit den wesentlichen Prinzipien der *šarīʿa* vereinbar sei, ja zur Stärkung dieser diene und von dieser motiviert sei. Der tatsächliche Anteil des islamischen Rechts an dieser Kodifikation wird von vielen für verhältnismäßig klein gehalten; al-Sanhūrī habe sich vor allem der besseren Akzeptanz wegen rhetorisch oft auf dieses berufen, in Wirklichkeit aber eine weitgehende Angleichung an europäische Zivilrechtsmuster betrieben.[86]

5. Rechtsprechung und Reform

Wie in allen Rechtsordnungen stellen auch in arabischen Ländern Gerichtsentscheidungen ein weiteres Mittel der Rechtsreform dar. Durch diese können Richter (i.d.R. die der obersten Gerichte bzw. Verfassungsgerichte) neue Auslegungen für einzelne Rechtsbegriffe im Gesetz einführen oder gar neue Institute aus allgemeineren Prinzipien herleiten. Während ersteres in Rechtssystemen, die dem kontinentalen Zivilrecht nachgebildet sind, vorkommt, ist zweiteres ein Kennzeichen des common law-Systems, das in ehemals britischen Gebieten Einzug gehalten hat. Hier haben Richter weit größere Gestaltungsmöglichkeiten, die z.B. in Pakistan und Indien schon 1967 zur Einführung einer Scheidungsmöglichkeit der Frau ohne Zustimmung ihres Ehemannes unter der Bezeichnung „*ḫulʿ*“ geführt haben.[87] Auch im Falle Algeriens, dessen Rechtssystem allerdings dem französisch-kontinentalen folgt, hat sich die Ausgestaltung des *ḫulʿ* durch die Rechtssprechung des Obersten Gerichtshofs verändert: So darf der Richter nun zumindest die Angabe des Mannes zur Höhe des Lösegeldes festsetzen, wenn dieser die Angabe verweigert.[88]

Speziell für Ägypten ist dieser Weg der Reform aber nicht besonders wichtig geworden. Hier, wo nach französischem Vorbild ein zivilrechtliches System aufgebaut worden ist, kam es dem Gesetzgeber zu, die wesentlichen Reformen

---

86 *Anderson, N.*, a.a.O., S. 83, 96; *Nagel, T.*, a.a.O., S. 308.

87 *Carroll, L.*, Qu'ran 2:229: „A Charter Granted to the Wife“? Judicial Khulʿ in Pakistan, in: ILS 3 (1996), S. 91-126 (96ff); *Anderson, N.*, a.a.O., S. 80.

88 *Dennerlein, B.*, Islamisches Recht und sozialer Wandel in Algerien, Berlin 1998, S. 137ff, macht darauf aufmerksam, dass in Algerien allerdings weiterhin die grundsätzliche Zustimmung des Mannes zum *ḫulʿ* von Nöten bleibt. Diese darf der Richter nach ständiger Rechtssprechung nicht ersetzen, obwohl die Gerichte der ersten und zweiten Instanz gelegentlich auch *ḫulʿ*-Scheidungen gegen den Willen des Mannes vorgenommen haben. Entsprechende Urteile wurden bisher durchgehend durch die höhere Instanz aufgehoben.

auf legislatorischem Weg in Gang zu bringen. Auf die Reformschritte Ägyptens, die auf dem Gebiet des Familienrechts und speziell des Ehescheidungsrechts in Gesetzen ab 1920 eingeschlagen wurden, gehe ich im Folgenden genauer ein.

II: Familienrechtsreform im modernen Ägypten: Die Umsetzung des Reformprogramms und die Erweiterung der Rechte der Frau

Wie dargestellt kam es im 19. Jahrhundert zu keiner Kodifizierung des islamischen Familienrechts in Ägypten. So orientierten sich die für diese Sachen zuständigen *šarīʿa*-Gerichte an den Normen der hanafitischen Rechtsschule. Bewegung kam erst 1920 in die Familienrechtsreform, als nach Beratungen einer Reformkommission ein neues Gesetz verabschiedet wurde.[89]

1. Die Reform von 1920

Das Gesetz Nr. 25/1920 betreffend den Unterhalt und einige Fragen des Personalstatuts vom 12.7.1920 führt neben Regelungen zum Unterhaltsanspruch der Frau während der Wartezeit die Scheidungsgründe wegen Nichtleistung des Unterhalts und der dauernder Abwesenheit des Mannes ein.

Wenn der Ehemann die Leistung von Unterhalt verweigert (*imtināʿ al-zauǧ ʿan al-infāq*) kann die Ehefrau gemäß Art. 6 die gerichtliche Scheidung verlangen. Davor muss die Frau einen vergeblichen Vollstreckungsversuch in das Vermögen des Mannes getätigt haben und der Mann nach Möglichkeit vom Gericht über den Antrag der Frau verständigt und zur Leistung der ausstehenden Zahlung aufgefordert werden. Das gleiche gilt bei einem inhaftierten Ehemann, der die Unterhaltsleistung nicht erbringt. Rechtsfolge der so ausgesprochenen Scheidungen ist die Wirkung eines *ṭalāq raǧʿī*, die für den Mann durch Leistung der ausstehenden Unterhaltsschulden bzw. den Nachweis der Zahlungsfähigkeit innerhalb der Wartezeit zurückgenommen werden kann.

Eine solche Scheidungsmöglichkeit war in der hanafitischen Rechtsschule nicht vorgesehen. Sie bestand aber bei den Malikiten, von woher sie für Ägypten übernommen wurde. Der ägyptische Gesetzgeber hat sich somit des Reformwerkzeugs des *taḫayyur* bedient.[90]

Ein zweiter in der hanafitischen Lehre nicht vorhandener Scheidungsanspruch für die Frau wird in Art. 9 mit der Trennung wegen Krankheit (*tafrīq li-l-ʿayb*) eingeführt. Die Voraussetzungen zur Scheidung liegen vor, wenn der Mann von

---

[89] Die folgenden Gesetze werden zitiert nach der Ausgabe des Verlages *Maktabat Šādī*, Qawānīn al-aḥwāl al-šaḫṣīya, Kairo 1992 (Gesetze von 1920, 1929, 1979, 1985), *al-Ḥassanayn, M.*, Qawānīn al-aḥwāl al-šaḫṣīya ḥattā āḫir al-taʿdīlāt 2002, Kairo 2002 (Gesetz von 2000), sowie der deutschen Übersetzungen in *Bergmann, A./Ferid, M./Henrich, D.*, a.a.O., S. 75ff (bis 1985).

[90] *Saad, W.*, Grundzüge des ägyptischen Ehe- und Kindschaftsrechts. In: StAZ 2001, S. 158.

einer unheilbaren oder unvoraussichtlich lange andauernden Krankheit befallen ist und dadurch der Beischlaf für die Frau gesundheitsgefährdend wird. Zur Feststellung der Erkrankung ist ein medizinisches Sachverständigengutachten erforderlich. In der hanafitischen Schule wird mehrheitlich nur der Scheidungsgrund der sexuellen Impotenz anerkannt. Diese ist hier jedoch nicht beschrieben, kann aber weiter nach altem Recht geltend gemacht werden.[91] Die Erweiterung des Scheidungsrechts auf die gesundheitsgefährdende Krankheit findet sich in den drei anderen Schulen, von wo es der Gesetzgeber im Wege des *taḫayyur* übernommen hat.[92]

2. Die Reform von 1929

Nur neun Jahre später brachte der ägyptische Gesetzgeber mit dem Dekret-Gesetz Nr. 25 von 1929 betreffend einige Fragen des Personalstatusrechts vom 10.3.1929 ein weiteres Reformpaket auf den Weg.

Diesem war die Arbeit einer Reformkommission vorangegangen, die sehr weitgehende Einschränkungen der bis dato zulässigen Polygynie vorschlug. Der dargestellten Auslegung von Muḥammad ʿAbduh teilweise folgend sollte die Zulässigkeit einer Zweitheirat zwar nicht gänzlich untersagt werden, aber von der Genehmigung eines Gerichts abhängig gemacht werden. Diesem sollte die Aufgabe zukommen, zu prüfen, ob der Ehemann zumindest finanziell in der Lage ist, alle Ehefrauen samt Kindern tatsächlich gleichwertig zu unterhalten. Auf diese Weise wäre aus der moralisch-freiwilligen Aufforderung aus Sure 4,129 eine rechtliche Verpflichtung abgeleitet worden und ʿAbduhs *iǧtihād*-Konzept umgesetzt worden. Daneben sollte die Zulässigkeit von ehevertraglichen Abreden entsprechend der hanbalitischen Schule erweitert werden. Danach sollten die Klauseln solange zulässig sein, wie sie nicht grundsätzlichen Prinzipien der Ehe zuwiderlaufen. So wäre z.B. die automatische Scheidung bei Eingehung einer zweiten Ehe ohne Einverständnis der ersten Ehefrau möglich geworden.

Beide Vorschläge wurden zwar vom Kabinett unterstützt, scheiterten jedoch schließlich am Veto von König Fuʾād und wurden nicht in das Gesetz von 1929 aufgenommen.[93] Die Vorschläge sind beide in dieser weitreichenden Form auf der ägyptischen Reformagenda bis heute nicht mehr erschienen. Aber auch ohne diese Elemente ist der Umfang des Gesetzes von 1929 beachtlich.

---

[91] *Saad, W.*, a.a.O., S. 159.
[92] *Shaham, R.*, a.a.O., S. 223.
[93] *Anderson, N.*, a.a.O., S.62; *Esposito, J.*, a.a.O., S. 59f.

Beschränkung des freien Verstoßungsrechts des Mannes

Das erste Kapitel des Gesetzes enthält einige Regelungen zur Form der *ṭalāq*-Erklärung, welche die Wirkung der Erklärung des Mannes einschränken. Anders als in der hanafitischen Tradition sieht Art. 1 die Unwirksamkeit einer Erklärung im Rauschzustand oder unter Zwang vor. Doppelsinnige Ausdrücke entfalten nach Art. 4 nur dann Wirkung, wenn sie mit einer entsprechenden Verstoßungsabsicht abgeben worden sind. Art. 5 bestätigt den bekannten Grundsatz, dass alle *ṭalāq*-Erklärungen widerruflich (*raǧʿī*) sind, sofern die Ehe vollzogen und es sich nicht um die dritte Erklärung handelt oder ausdrücklich im Gesetz die endgültige Scheidungswirkung (*bāʾin*) vorgesehen ist. Von besonderer Bedeutung ist die Regelung des Art. 3. Hiernach wird die dreimalige Erklärung der Scheidung in einer einzigen Erklärung (*ṭalāq bidʿa*) in der Weise eingeschränkt, dass sie nur als einmalige Erklärung gilt.

Hierdurch fand der Gesetzgeber eine Lösung außerhalb der vier Rechtsschulen, die fast ausnahmslos die dreifache Erklärung trotz ihrer moralischen Verwerflichkeit für gültig hielten und ihr sofortige Wirkung zusprachen. Als Ausnahme hiervon gilt die Ansicht von Ibn Taymīya, der neben der moralischen auch die rechtliche Wertung der dreifachen Erklärung negativ ausfallen lässt. Dieser Sicht folgte hier der Gesetzgeber, der somit die *talfīq*-Methode unter Heranziehung einer Minderheitsmeinung anwendet.[94]

Scheidung wegen Schädigung durch den Mann

Auch sieht das Gesetz von 1929 eine Erweiterung der gerichtlichen Scheidungsmöglichkeiten für die Frau vor. So wird im 2. Kapitel der Trennungsgrund der Zwietracht zwischen den Partnern und der Schädigung (*al-šiqāq bayn al-zauǧayn wa al-taṭlīq li-l-ḍarar*) eingeführt. Nach Art. 6 kann die Frau die Scheidung beantragen, wenn sie ihrem Mann Verfehlungen nachweist, die das gemeinsame Leben für Angehörige ihres Standes unmöglich machen. Mit den Schädigungen (*iḍrār*) sind physische und psychische Beeinträchtigungen der Frau gemeint. Damit sind z.B. Beschimpfungen, die Verweigerung von sexuellen Kontakten durch den Mann oder die über das dem Mann zustehende Züchtigungsrecht hinausgehende Gewaltanwendung gemeint.[95] Art. 6 sieht als Rechtsfolge nach einem vergeblichen Schlichtungsversuch durch das Gericht die unwiderrufliche Scheidung (*ṭalāq bāʾin*) vor.

---

[94] *Esposito, J.*, a.a.O., S. 59.

[95] *Naṣṣār, A.*, a.a.O., S. 91, 93; *Saad, W.*, a.a.O., S. 159, besonders Fn. 54 mit Beispielen aus der Rechtssprechung; *Nassar, N.*, Legal Plurality: Reflections on the Status of Women in Egypt. In: *Dupret, B./Berger, M./al-Zwaini, L.* (Hrsg.), Legal Pluralism in the Arab World, Den Haag 1999, S. 190-204 (199f).

Für den Fall, dass der Frau der Nachweis der Schädigung nicht gelingt, kann sie ein zweites Mal Klage erheben und Scheidung wegen eines nicht wiedergutzumachenden Zerwürfnisses (*taṭlīq li-l-šiqāq*) verlangen. In diesem Fall sehen die Art. 7-11 ein Versöhnungsversuchs-Verfahren vor, bei dem aus den Familien der Gatten jeweils ein Schiedsrichter ausgewählt wird. Die beiden Vermittler haben nun sechs Monate Zeit, um den Sachverhalt und die Streitursachen zu klären sowie auf eine Versöhnung hinzuwirken. Gelingt die Versöhnung nicht, haben die Schiedsrichter die Befugnis, die Ehe aufzulösen, wenn sie zu der Ansicht gelangen, dass entweder der Ehemann oder beide Partner gemeinsam für das Zerwürfnis verantwortlich sind. Diese Kompetenz fehlt nur in dem Fall, dass die Frau als Verantwortliche für das Scheitern der Ehe ausgemacht wird. In diesem Fall soll dem Mann das alleinige Verstoßungsrecht gelassen werden. Erst in der Reform von 1979/1985 wurde die Kompetenz der Schiedsrichter zu Auflösung der Ehe auch auf diesen Fall ausgeweitet.[96]

Mit dem *taṭlīq li-l-ḍarar* und *taṭlīq li-l-šiqāq* hat das ägyptische Gesetz ein Prinzip aus der malikitischen Schule übernommen, die als einzige die Schiedsrichter mit einer eigenen Scheidungskompetenz versehen hat. Dabei ist der Gesetzgeber dem in Sure 4,34 niedergelegten Prinzip der Schiedsrichter-Bestimmung zur außergerichtlichen Versöhnung gefolgt. Im Unterschied zur ägyptischen Rechtslage von 1929 können nach der malikitischen Rechtsschuldoktrin die Schiedsrichter auch die Scheidung erklären, wenn sie den Ursprung des Zerwürfnisses bei der Ehefrau sehen. Insofern hat sich der ägyptische Gesetzgeber nicht genau an das malikitische Modell gehalten, sondern dieses durch in den anderen Rechtsschulen vorhandene Einschränkungen ergänzt. Erst 1979 glich er die Rechtslage gänzlich an die malikitische Schule an. Es handelt sich hierbei also um die Anwendung des Reformprinzips der *talfīq*-Methode.[97]

Scheidung wegen Abwesenheit des Ehemannes

In dem Gesetz wird außerdem die Scheidung wegen Abwesenheit des Mannes (*taṭlīq li-ġaybat al-zauǧ*) eingeführt. Nach Art. 12 erhält die Ehefrau das Antragsrecht auf gerichtliche Scheidung, wenn ihr Mann mehr als ein Jahr ungerechtfertigt – also z.B. nicht zu Arbeits- oder Ausbildungszwecken – abwesend gewesen ist, unabhängig davon, ob er der Frau genügend Unterhaltsmittel zur Verfügung gestellt hat. Art. 14 sieht vor, dass auch eine mindestens dreijährige Haftstrafe eine Abwesenheit darstellt. In diesem Fall

---

[96] *Naṣṣār, A.*, a.a.O., S. 116; *Shaham, R.*, a.a.O., 225f.

[97] *Shaham, R.*, a.a.O., S. 226; *Esposito, J.*, a.a.O., S. 57.

kann die Frau ihren Antrag auf Scheidung nach Absitzen von einem Jahr Freiheitsstrafe einreichen.
Der Scheidungsgrund wegen Abwesenheit war in der hanafitischen Schule nur unter merkwürdigen Voraussetzungen möglich. Erst nach dem potentiellen Erreichen des 90. Lebensjahrs durch den Mann war die gerichtliche Scheidung möglich, der so keine praktische Relevanz zukam. Der Gesetzgeber hat mit der beschriebenen Regelung auf den Bestand im malikitischen und hanbalitischen Recht zurückgegriffen, die kürzere Fristen vorsehen. Die Festlegung auf ein Jahr ist dabei insofern bemerkenswert, als sie höher ausfällt als die hanbalitische Regelung von einem halben Jahr. Aus der hanbalitischen Richtung kommen auch die Rechtfertigungsgründe für den Ehemann. Wie auch bei der – so in den Rechtsschulen nicht vorhandenen – Regelung der mindestens dreijährigen Freiheitsstrafe verfährt der Gesetzgeber hier bei der Auswahl aus dem Bestand der anderen Rechtsschulen nach Allgemeinwohlüberlegungen (*talfīq*).[98]
Die ägyptischen Gerichte begannen bald mit der Umsetzung der Gesetze, die den Frauen nun bessere Chancen eröffneten, von ihren gescheiterten Ehen loszukommen. Shaham hat in seiner Studie über die Umsetzung der Gesetze zur richterlichen Scheidung den Zeitraum bis zur Absetzung der ursprünglich zuständigen *šarīʿa*-Gerichte im Jahre 1956 untersucht. Anhand der ihm zugänglichen Entscheidungen der oberinstanzlichen Gerichte kommt er zu dem Ergebnis, dass tatsächlich viele Frauen die Möglichkeit der Klageerhebung nutzen. Dabei sind es in der Mehrzahl Klagen auf Scheidung wegen Schädigung (*taṭlīq li-l-ḍarar*), die eingereicht werden. Außerdem konstatiert Shaham, dass der Interpretationsspielraum der Gerichte bei der genauen Definition von Rechtsbegriffen wie dem der Schädigung recht weit war, so dass ein durchaus weitreichender Kreis von Misshandlungen umfasst war. Allerdings hatten nur ca. 50% der eingereichten Klagen auch den gewünschten Erfolg und führten zur Auflösung der Ehe.[99]

3. Die Reform von 1979: „Lex Ǧihān"

Nach der verhältnismäßig umfassenden Reform von 1929 kam es für fünf Jahrzehnte zu keiner ausgedehnteren Reform des Personalstatusrechtes von Ägypten. Zwar wurden mehrere Reformkommissionen eingesetzt, denen aber keine greifbaren Reformen gelangen. Erst in den 1970er-Jahren wurde unter der Sozialministerin ʿĀʾiša Rātib ein erneuter Reformversuch unternommen. Der von ihr geleitete Ausschuss erhob 1971 weitreichende Forderungen, die die

---

[98] *Saad, W.*, a.a.O., S. 159; *Shaham, R.*, a.a.O., S. 225.
[99] *Shaham, R.*, a.a.O., S. 251; ähnlich auch die Bilanz von *Nassar, N.*, a.a.O., S. 200, für die heutige Zeit. Der Beweis insbesondere für eine psychische Störung gelinge nur sehr selten.

Anhebung des Heiratsalters, die richterliche Genehmigung einer Zweitehe, die Gültigkeit einer *ṭalāq*-Erklärung nur im Gerichtssaal sowie die Ausweitung der Personensorge der Mutter (*ḥaḍāna*) vorsahen.[100] Aus diesem Gesetzesentwurf, dessen Werdegang sich insbesondere Ǧīhān al-Sādāt, die Ehefrau des damaligen Staatspräsidenten, angenommen hatte, entwickelte sich der Gesetzesentwurf, der schließlich als Gesetz Nr. 44 in 1979 zur Änderung einiger Vorschriften des Personenstandswesen Rechtskraft erlangte, und dessen Inhalt in die Texte der Gesetze von 1920 und 1929 eingearbeitet wurde. Aufgrund des maßgeblichen Engagements der Präsidentengattin wurde es auch „Lex Ǧīhān" genannt. Wegen des Widerstandes im Parlament gegen seinen Inhalt wählte Präsident Sādāt den Weg an den Abgeordneten vorbei und erließ das Gesetz als Präsidialdekret.[101] Schon kurz darauf wurde es dem Verfassungsgericht zur Überprüfung vorgelegt, das es schließlich 1985 für verfassungswidrig erklärte, weil sein Zustandekommen dem formellen Verfassungsrecht widersprach. Die in Art. 147 der Verfassung vorgesehenen Präsidialdekrete könnten nur bei einer – in diesem Fall nicht vorliegenden – besonderen Eilbedürftigkeit erlassen werden.[102] Auf materielle Aspekte der Verfassungsmäßigkeit geht das Urteil dagegen nicht ein.

Zwar basierte die Gerichtsentscheidung letztlich auf formellen Gründen, doch war auch der materielle Inhalt des Gesetzes in der ägyptischen Diskussion stark umstritten. Nach Verwerfung des Gesetzes durch das Verfassungsgericht verabschiedete der Gesetzgeber 1985 – dieses Mal auf normalem parlamentarischem Weg – ein Nachfolgegesetz, das inhaltlich größtenteils der Regelung von 1979 entsprach.[103]

Im Mittelpunkt der Kritik stand die in Art. 6a vorgesehene Erweiterung der *ḍarar*-Scheidung um den Grund der Zweitheirat des Mannes. Das Gesetz enthält eine Schädigungsvermutung, nach der die Heirat ihres Mannes mit einer anderen Frau für die Erstfrau automatisch als Schädigung gewertet wird und dieser das Scheidungsrecht zusteht. Daneben sah das Gesetz vor, dass der Mann seine *ṭalāq*-Erklärung der Frau persönlich mitteilen musste, damit diese Wirkungen entfalten kann. Außerdem hat der Mann nach Art. 4a Abs. 1 während der

---

100 *Esposito, J.*, a.a.O., S. 60; *El Alami, D.*, Law No. 100..., a.a.O., S. 116.

101 *Flores, A.*, Die Stellung des Islams und des islamischen Rechts in ausgewählten Staaten: Ägypten. In: *Ende, W./Steinbach, U.*, Der Islam in der Gegenwart, 4. Aufl. München 1996, S. 474-486 (478).

102 Entscheidung des Verfassungsgerichtshofs vom 4.5.1985, S. 7f, 11 (Entscheidungen des Verfassungsgerichts, soweit nicht anders angegeben zitiert nach der amtlichen Sammlung); vgl. auch *Forstner, M.*, Änderungen im ägyptischen Eherecht. In: StAZ 1986, S. 130-134 (130); *El Alami, D.*, Law No. 100..., a.a.O., S. 117.

103 Die Erörterung der im Gesetz von 1985 unverändert gebliebenen Regelungen erfolgt im entsprechenden Abschnitt.

Wartezeit (*ʿidda*) die gemeinsame Wohnung für die stillende Geschiedene und die Kinder zu räumen und sich eine andere Unterkunft zu suchen.[104]
Die Gegner des Gesetzes hielten es für paradox, dass eine im Koran vorgesehene göttliche Ordnung wie die Polygynie per se als Schädigung der Erstfrau anzusehen sei. Damit würde postuliert, dass der göttliche Wille fehlerhaft sei.[105] Außerdem bedeute der Auszug des Mannes eine ungerechte Benachteiligung, die dem klassischen Recht zuwider laufe. Danach stehe dem Mann das Wahlrecht zu, wie die Geschiedene unterzubringen ist. Für Ägypten müsse aber weiter der geoffenbarte Wille des göttlichen Gesetzgebers maßgeblich bleiben. Darum stehe die Regelung nicht nur im Widerspruch zur *šarīʿa*, sondern sei auch verfassungswidrig.[106]

4. Exkurs: Die Verfassungsrechtsänderung von 1980 und ihre Entwicklung durch die Rechtssprechung des Verfassungsgerichtshofs: Ein Schritt zur „Reislamisierung"?

Die Kritik an dieser Regelung wird verständlich im Lichte der Verfassungsreform von 1980, die in Art. 2 der Verfassung den Islam zur Staatsreligion und die Prinzipien der *šarīʿa* von nur *einer* unter mehreren zu *der* Hauptquelle der Gesetzgebung macht.[107] Präsident Sādāt wollte mit Einführung dieser im Referendum von der Bevölkerung akzeptierten Regelung den islamistischen Kräften in seinem Land entgegenkommen und seine eigene Macht durch die Berufung auf traditionelle Werte legitimieren.[108] Mit Erlass dieser neuen Formulierung – in der Verfassung von 1971 war die *šarīʿa* nur *eine* der Quellen der Gesetzgebung – entbrannte auch die Debatte über die richtige Auslegung der Norm. So waren die Fragen nach der Rückwirkung der Verfassungsänderung – also z.B. die Bedeutung für das im Jahr zuvor erlassene Präsidialdekret – und die nach dem Begriff der *al-šarīʿa al-islāmīya* offen geblieben: Wer hat die Vollmacht, über die authentische *šarīʿa* zu entscheiden und wie ist diese zu bestimmen? Besteht etwa die grundsätzliche Bindung an die hanafitische Lehre und damit das *taqlīd*-Prinzip weiter oder kann ein neuer und freier *iǧtihād* vorgenommen werden?
Das ägyptische Verfassungsgericht hat sich diesen Fragen in verschiedenen Fällen seit 1985 angenommen und entwickelte allmählich eine erläuternde Rechtsprechung. In einer Entscheidung aus 1985 entschied es, dass Art. 2 keine Rückwirkung zukommt, sondern erst für Gesetze gilt, die nach der

---

104 *Naṣṣār, A.*, a.a.O., S. 125f.
105 Aufgeführt bei *Forstner, M.*, a.a.O., S. 131.
106 *Forstner, M.*, a.a.O., S. 133.
107 „*mabādiʾ al-šarīʿa al-islāmīya al-maṣdar al-raʾīsī li-l-tašrīʿ*".
108 *Bälz, K.*, Islamisches Recht, staatliche Rechtsetzung und verfassungsgerichtliche Kontrolle, ZaöRV 57 (1997), S. 228-240(232); *Flores, A.*, a.a.O., S. 477.

Verfassungsänderung beschlossen werden. Daher hat der neue Art. 2 nicht zur Folge, dass 150 Jahre ägyptische Normgebungsgeschichte durch richterliche Überprüfung für *šarīʿa*-konform erklärt und u.U. verworfen werden müssen. Vielmehr enthält der Artikel einen auf die Zukunft gerichteten Gesetzgebungsauftrag.[109]

In der Entscheidung aus 1994 führt das Gericht eine äußerst wichtige Unterscheidung zur Feststellung des *šarīʿa*-Begriffes ein. Es ist dies die Unterscheidung zwischen zwingenden (*qaṭʿī fī l-dalāla*) und nicht zwingenden Normen (*aḥkām ẓannīya*) der *šarīʿa*. Während erstere als nicht modifizierbare Regeln der Interpretation (*taʾwīl*) und der Modifikation (*tabdīl*) entzogen sind, sind letztere offen für den *iǧtihād*.[110] In seiner Entscheidung vom 5.7.1997 erkennt das Gericht an, dass auch zwingende Normen einen Interpretationsspielraum bieten können, wie schon die unterschiedlichen Ansichten in den Rechtsschulen zu Einzelfragen zeigen, deren generelles Prinzip zwar vorgegeben ist, deren Details aber durch Auslegung festgestellt werden müssen.[111]

Mit dieser Differenzierung hat das Gericht auf eine alte schafiitische Lehre von der Unterscheidung zwischen textueller und angedeuteter Regelung in der Offenbarung zurückgegriffen. Wenn eine eindeutig im Text vorgegebene Regelung besteht, so beansprucht sie Gültigkeit, anderenfalls besteht der Interpretationsspielraum.[112] Diese Unterscheidung spielt auch in der Rechtslehre der *Salafīya* eine entscheidende Rolle. Sie setzt außerdem auf die Ausübung eines unabhängigen *iǧtihād* und lehnt den bloßen *taqlīd* ab.

Aus den Entscheidungen des Verfassungsgerichts geht weiterhin hervor, wer für die zeitangepasste Auslegung der *šarīʿa* zuständig ist. Es wird nicht ein religiöses Gremium zur Überwachung der Gesetzgebungstätigkeit eingesetzt. Stattdessen obliegt es dem Parlament festzustellen, welche Normen auf welche Weise zu verändern sind. Über die Einhaltung der Normen wacht das Verfassungsgericht selber. Anders also als in der Vorstellung Riḍās ist hier keine Versammlung von islamischen Rechtsgelehrten (*muǧtahidūn*) verantwortlich, sondern der Staat mit weltlichen Institutionen und Akteuren

---

109 Entscheidung vom 4.5.1985, zit. bei *Bernhard-Maugiron,N.*, La Haute Cour Constitutionnelle Egyptienne et la Shariʿa Islamique, in : Awrāq 19 (1998), S. 103-141 (107); siehe auch *Murray, J./El-Molla, M.*, Islamic Shariʿa and Constitutional Interpretation in Egypt. In: *Cotran, E./Sherif, A.*, Democracy, the Rule of Law and Islam, Den Haag 1999, S. 507-524 (511); *Arabi, O.*, Studies…, a.a.O., S. 197.

110 *Bernhard-Maugiron, N.*, a.a.O., S. 112.

111 Entscheidung vom 26.3.1994, französische Übersetzung bei *Dupret, B.*, A propos de la Constitutionnalité de la Sharīʿa: Présentation et traduction de l'arret du 26 mars 1994 de la Haute Cour Constitutionnelle égyptienne. In : ILS 4 (1997), S. 91-113.

112 *Arabi, O.*, Studies…, a.a.O., S. 199.

gestaltet sich sozusagen selbst „seine *šarīʿa*“.[113] N. Brown deutet dieses Vorgehen als ein Wiedererstarken eines Bestandteils des überkommenen Systems in einer Art „neuen *šarīʿa*“: Während ein angemessener *šarīʿa*-Begriff im klassischen Verständnis nicht nur einen Korpus von positiven Normen umschließt, sondern auch ein System der Verantwortlichkeit und Zuständigkeit zur Pflege der Normen beinhaltet, ist der neue *šarīʿa*-Begriff auf den Normenkorpus beschränkt und greift gerade nicht auf das überkommene Prozedere zurück. Insofern stellt die neue Verantwortlichkeit von Parlament und Verfassungsgericht das eigentliche Charakteristikum des neuen Verhältnisses von Staat und *šarīʿa* dar.[114]

5. Das Reformgesetz von 1985

In der infolge des Verfassungsgerichtsurteils umgeänderten Gesetzesfassung von 1985 (Gesetz Nr. 100/1985 zur Änderung einiger Regeln der Personalstatusgesetze) wurden einige der kritischen Stellen des Gesetzes von 1979 entschärft, ohne dass jedoch die generelle Zielrichtung der Regelung verloren gegangen wäre.[115]

Art. 11a Abs. 1 des durch das Gesetz 100/1985 geänderten Gesetzes 25/1929 sieht vor, dass der Ehemann bei einer Zweitheirat im Ehevertrag seinen Ehestand angeben muss. Gibt der Mann fälschlicherweise an, dass er ledig ist, so kann die Zweitfrau nach Art. 11a Abs. 4 von ihm die Scheidung verlangen. Der beurkundende Notar informiert die erste Frau über die erfolgte Zweitheirat. Dieser steht nach der Neuregelung kein automatisches Scheidungsrecht mehr zu. Sie kann aber innerhalb eines Jahres nach Abschluss der Zweitheirat die gerichtliche Scheidung verlangen. Dafür muss sie nachweisen, dass ihr tatsächlich materieller oder immaterieller Schaden entstanden ist. Die gesetzliche Vermutung des Schädigungsfalles, die 1979 die Kontroverse ausgelöst hatte, ist somit entfallen. Die Position der scheidungswilligen Erstfrau hat sich deutlich verschlechtert, denn ein Schadensnachweis ist erfahrungsgemäß schwierig. Insbesondere hat das Parlament den Begriff des immateriellen Schadens nicht genau definiert, aber angedeutet, dass das bloße Gefühl der Eifersucht nicht als solcher anzusehen ist. Außerdem hat der Gesetzgeber auch für den Fall der Zweitheirat einen obligatorischen Versöhnungsversuch vorgeschrieben.[116]

---

[113] Vgl. *Bälz, K.*, a.a.O., S. 462.
[114] *Brown, N.*, a.a.O., S. 371f.
[115] *El Alami, D.*, Law No. 100..., a.a.O., S. 117.
[116] *Naṣṣār, A.*, a.a.O., 128f; *El Alami, D.*, a.a.O., S. 119, Fn. 3; *Forstner, M.*, a.a.O., S. 131; *Nassar, N.*, a.a.O., S. 200.

Art. 11b beinhaltet eine neue Regelung zum Unterhaltswegfall wegen Ungehorsam (*imtināʿ ʿan ṭāʿat al-zauǧ*) der Frau. Als solcher Fall gilt der grundlose Auszug aus der ehelichen Wohnung. Der Mann ist berechtigt, ab dem Datum des Ungehorsams die Unterhaltszahlungen einzustellen, wenn er sie über das Gericht zum Zurückkommen aufgefordert hat. Der Frau kommt in Art. 11b Abs. 2 eine 30-tägige Einspruchsfrist gegen diese Aufforderung zu, in der sie den Grund ihres Auszugs darlegen muss. Im Gegensatz zum Gesetz von 1979 ist die Einspruchsfrist um 20 Tage verlängert worden, was ihre Rechtsposition stärkt. Abgeschwächt wurden die Voraussetzungen für die *ṭalāq*-Erklärung des Ehemanns. Nach Art. 5a muss er nicht mehr persönlich der Frau Mitteilung von der Erklärung machen. Vielmehr kann dies der beurkundende Beamte für ihn tun. Durch diese „Anonymisierung der Scheidung" wird sie für den Ehemann möglicherweise psychologisch leichter durchführbar.[117] Verschweigt der Ehemann die Verstoßung, entfaltet sie erst volle Wirkung bezüglich aller finanziellen Rechte, wenn die Frau Kenntnis erlangt. Der Gesetzgeber folgt mit dem Erfordernis der Benachrichtigung der Ehefrau für die volle Wirkung einer Mindermeinung in den Rechtsschulen, die von Ibn Ḥazm vertreten wurde.[118]
Weggefallen im Vergleich zur Fassung von 1929 ist in Art. 11 die Regelung, dass die eingesetzten Schiedsrichter die Ehe nicht auflösen dürfen, wenn sie das Verschulden für das Scheitern der Ehe der Frau zuweisen. Dies ist nach der neuen Regelung jetzt auch für den genannten Fall möglich.[119]
Verändert wurde in Art. 18c auch die Regelung des Wohnrechts während der Wartezeit. Nach der neuen gesetzlichen Regel besitzt jetzt der Mann wieder ein Wahlrecht, ob er der Frau die gemeinsame Wohnung überlässt oder für diese und die Kinder eine Ersatzwohnung beschafft. Nur wenn er es unterlässt, die Ersatzwohnung zu beschaffen, entsteht das Recht für die Frau, den Mann aus der alten Wohnung zu drängen.
In Art. 18a findet sich eine Regelung zur *mutʿa*-Zahlungspflicht des Mannes, der seine Ehefrau grundlos verstößt. Sie beträgt die Summe von mindestens zwei Jahressätzen der monatlichen Unterhaltspflicht während der *ʿidda*. Die Summe wird vom Gericht festgelegt, das bei der Festsetzung die finanziellen Verhältnisse des Mannes ebenso in Betracht ziehen soll wie die Dauer der Ehe. Der ägyptische Gesetzgeber folgt damit dem Beispiel der schafiitischen Schule, das in der gleichen Form schon in anderen arabischen Ländern Eingang in die Kodifikationen gefunden hat.[120]

---

[117] *Forstner, M.*, a.a.O., S. 132.
[118] *El Alami, D.*, Law No. 100..., a.a.O., S. 118, Fn.2.
[119] *Shaham, R.*, a.a.O., S. 225.
[120] Zur *mutʿa*-Zahlung in Ägypten *Naṣṣār, A.*, a.a.O., S. 195ff; *al-ʿAǧūz, N.*, a.a.O., S. 385.

Insbesondere Art. 18a wurde Gegenstand einer Verfassungsklage, über die das Gericht im Jahr 1993 entschied. Das Gericht bejahte die Verfassungsmäßigkeit des Gesetzes und somit auch die Vereinbarkeit mit der *šarīʿa* und sah hierin ein Beispiel für die Interpretationsoffenheit von zwingenden Normen der Offenbarung. Die Koranverse 2,236 und 241 enthalten lediglich den Aufruf, nach Billigkeit Unterhaltsleistungen nach der Scheidung zu zahlen. Das Gericht hielt diese Regelung für eine zwar zwingende, aber auch interpretationsbedürftige Regelung, was schon der höchst differenzierte Meinungsstand in den Rechtsschulen zeige. Das Ergebnis der richterlichen Überlegungen war die Zulässigkeit der Festlegung durch den Gesetzgeber für eine der vorgeschlagenen Lösungen nach dem Maßstab des Allgemeinwohls.[121]

6. Zusammenfassung

Insgesamt bedient sich der Gesetzgeber bei den Ehe- und Scheidungsrechtsreformen seit 1920 hauptsächlich der Reformmittel des *taḫayyur* und des *talfīq*. Dabei greift er besonders auf Elemente der malikitischen Schule zurück, die der Ehefrau die meisten Scheidungsgründe zubilligte, und übernimmt Elemente der schafiitischen Schule. Von einer gänzlich neuen Interpretation der Quellen jenseits der bewährten Doktrinen der Rechtsschulen macht er dagegen keinen Gebrauch. Eine einzige Ausnahme stellt die weitgehende Regelung zur Schädigungsscheidung (*ḍarar*) von 1979 dar, die weit über die Regelung bei den Malikiten hinausgeht, deren Gesetzeskraft wegen des Verfassungsgerichtsurteils von 1985 jedoch nur von kurzer Dauer war.[122]

Was die Verbesserung der Rechtsstellung der Frau angeht, bleibt festzuhalten, dass der ägyptische Gesetzgeber insbesondere bei den Reformen von 1920 und 1929 zu sehr weitgehenden Regelungen bereit war. Aufgrund des königlichen Vetos ließ sich nur ein Teil dieser Normen durchsetzen. Trotzdem war Ägypten zu dieser Zeit ein arabischer Staat mit einem der progressivsten Personalstatusrechten. In den folgenden Jahrzehnten ist auf diesem Gebiet allerdings eine Stagnation festzustellen. Während in einigen anderen Ländern vor allem in den Fünfziger- und Sechzigerjahren umfangreiche Änderungen im Bereich Scheidungsrecht der Frau und Schutz vor der einseitigen Verstoßung durch den Ehemann vorgenommen wurde, kam es erst 1979 zu einer weiteren Reform in Ägypten. Insbesondere die in diesem Gesetz vorgesehene Erweiterung des Scheidungsrechts wegen Schädigung stellte – auch in der Neuregelung von 1985 – eine signifikante Verbesserung dar, wenn sich auch mit

---

[121] *Bernhard-Maugiron, N.*, a.a.O., S. 116.
[122] *El Alami, D.*, Law No. 100..., a.a.O., S. 130.

dem Wegfall der Schädigungsvermutung bei Zweitheirat des Mannes eine der frauenrechtlichen Hauptforderungen nicht erfüllte.

D. DIE REFORM DES JAHRES 2000: DAS GESETZ NR. 1 / 2000

I. Rechtsreform durch Prozessrecht

1. Das Gesetz Nr. 1/2000: Neuordnung des Prozessrechts in Personenstandsangelegenheiten

Mit dem Gesetz Nr. 1 / 2000 zur Regelung der Gerichtsverfahren in Fragen des Personenstandswesens (*qānūn raqm (1) li-sanat 2000 bi-tanẓīm baʿḍ ʾauḍāʿ wa ʾiǧrāʾāt al-taqāḍī fī masāʾil al-aḥwāl al-šaḫṣīya*)[123] gab der ägyptische Gesetzgeber einen Korpus prozessrechtlicher Normen heraus, der das bis dahin in verschiedenen Gesetzen verteilte Verfahrensrecht in Personenstandssachen vereinheitlichen sollte. Für ein sich mit Verfahrensfragen beschäftigendes Gesetz eher ungewöhnlich entfachte es eine rege gesellschaftliche Debatte, die in den Tageszeitungen des Landes auf sehr unterschiedlichem Niveau ausgetragen wurde. Der Grund liegt darin, dass einige der Regelungen nicht nur bloßer prozessrechtlicher Natur waren, sondern tief in das materielle Personalstatusrecht des Landes eingreifen. So entfachte sich die Debatte an eben diesen materiellen Fragen, die in vier Artikeln des aus 79 Artikeln bestehenden Gesetzes niedergelegt sind. Zwar wurden in der Mehrzahl auch in diesen Artikeln vor allem verfahrensrechtliche Fragen zur Zulässigkeit von Rechtsstreiten vor Gericht geregelt, jedoch können diese islamrechtlich unter die Kompetenz des *taḫṣīṣ al-quḍāʾ* fallenden Regelungen auch substantielle materielle Änderungen implizieren. Im Mittelpunkt der Kritik steht das erstmalig in einer ägyptischen Kodifikation geregelte Prozedere des *ḫulʿ*, für den der Weg zum Gericht eröffnet ist und der nun auch durch ein gerichtliches Urteil herbeigeführt werden kann.

Art. 20 des Gesetzes, der sog. „*ḫulʿ*-Artikel" (*māddat al-ḫulʿ*) sowie die ursprünglich im Gesetzesentwurf vorgesehene Erleichterung für Ehefrauen bei der Durchführung von Auslandsreisen ohne die Erlaubnis des Mannes (*ǧawāz*

---

[123] Exakter müsste eine Übersetzung lauten: „Gesetz zur Regelung einiger Gegenstände und der Gerichtsverfahren in Fragen des Personenstandswesens". Es ist unklar, was der Gesetzgeber mit „*baʿḍ auḍāʿ*" meint: Möglicherweise impliziert schon dieser Begriff, dass neben prozessrechtlichen auch materielle Regeln eingeführt werden sollen. Offenbar können auch einige Stimmen der Fachliteratur mit dieser Begrifflichkeit nicht viel anfangen. So fehlt in der Gesetzesausgabe bei *al-Dināṣūrī, I./ʿUkkāz, Ḥ.*, al-Taʿlīq ʿalā al-qānūn raqm (1) li-sanat 2000 bi-tanẓīm iǧrāʾāt al-taqāḍī fī masāʾil al-ʾaḥwāl al-šaḫṣīya, Kairo 2000, dieser Teil des Gesetzesnamens im Buchtitel und in den Kapitelüberschriften.

safar al-zauǧa), wurden in der Debatte mit dem Vorwurf konfrontiert, dass diese beiden Instrumente den Bestand der ägyptischen Familie und damit langfristig auch der nationalen Gesamtgesellschaft gefährden würden. Dahinter verbirgt sich die Erwartung, dass sich durch ein weiteres und in mancherlei Hinsicht einfacheres Mittel zur gerichtlichen Scheidung auch die Scheidungsraten drastisch erhöhen würden.[124]
So ist es kein Wunder, dass in der Debatte der offizielle Name des Gesetzes selten auftaucht. Es ist zumeist die Rede vom „neuen Personalstatusgesetz“[125] oder gar vom „*ḫulʿ*-Gesetz“[126]. Dahinter verschwindet der restliche Inhalt des Gesetzes zumeist: Es ist ein Verfahrensgesetz, das Gerichtszuständigkeiten und Fragen der ordentlichen Klageerhebung, der Prozessdurchführung und der Urteilsvollstreckung zum Thema hat.
Dem eigentlichen Gesetzgebungsprozess, der im Januar 2000 innerhalb weniger Tage durch das Parlament mit dem – hier zuständigen – Konsultationsrat (*maǧlis al-šūrā*) und dem Abgeordnetenhaus (*maǧlis al-šaʿb*) vonstatten ging, lag eine langjährige Ausschussarbeit zugrunde. Seit 1991 hatten sich Vertreter des Justizministeriums mit Experten aus verschiedensten Gruppen des öffentlichen Lebens zur Erörterung der anliegenden Fragen getroffen. Die Öffentlichkeit wurde allerdings über die Fortschritte dieser Gespräche nicht unterrichtet, so dass sich viele Stimmen zu Wort meldeten, die ein Übergehen der Öffentlichkeit und ein überhastetes Vorgehen rügten.[127] Präsident Mubārak stellte das Gesetzesvorhaben seiner Regierung in einer Erklärung im 13. Dezember 1999 vor. Danach folgten Erklärungen von Muḥammad Ṭantawī, dem *Šayḫ al-Azhar*, sowie der ebenfalls größtenteils aus Gelehrten der Azhar-Universität bestehenden Akademie für islamische Studien (*maǧmaʿ al-buḥūṯ al-islāmīya*), die den Regierungsentwurf billigten und ihn z.T. als besonders islamkonform lobten.[128] Am 27.1.2000 beschließt schließlich das Parlament nach zwar zeitlich nicht sonderlich langen, aber inhaltlich sehr kontroverser

124 So z.B. *al-ʿAǧūz,N.*, a.a.O., S. 61.

125 So z.B. *Naṣṣār, A.*, der das Gesetz 1/2000 schon im Untertitel seines Buches als neues Personalstatusgesetz bezeichnet (*qānūn al-aḥwāl al-šaḫṣīya al-ǧadīd*); in der Presse wird das Gesetz ganz überwiegend so bezeichnet. Z.B. al-Ahrām, 27.1.2000, am Tag nach dem Gesetzesbeschluss im Parlament.

126 *Al-Ǧindī, M.*, Qirāʾa fī qānūn iǧrāʾāt al-taqāḍī fī masāʾil al-aḥwāl al-šaḫṣīya raqm (1) li-sanat 2000, Kairo 2001/2002, S. 267; in der Zeitungsdebatte siehe z.B. al-ʿArabī, 23.1.2000.

127 So z.B. al-Ǧumhūrīya, 17.1.2000 u. 20.1.2000.

128 Al-Ahrām, 14.1.2000 und 20.1.2000; dagegen berichtet Kamāl Ḥabīb in al-Šaʿb vom 22.2.2000 von einem äußerst knappen und wegen einer Reihe von Verfahrensmängeln umstrittenen Votum der Akademie für islamische Studien und sieht darin das Werk einer demagogischen Regierung, die sich die Zustimmung der Gelehrten erschlichen hätte.

Debatte – noch am Tag der Abstimmung wurde über 80 Änderungsanträge zum Gesetzesentwurf abgestimmt[129] – das Gesetz, das nach Ausfertigung durch den Präsidenten und Verkündung im Gesetzblatt am 29.1.2000 gemäß Art. 6 des Einführungsgesetzes zu Gesetz 1/2000 (*qānūn raqm (1) li-sanat 2000 bi-iṣdār qānūn tanẓīm baʿḍ ʾauḍāʿ wa ʾiǧrāʾāt al-taqāḍī fī masāʾil al-aḥwāl al-šaḫṣīya*) zum 1.3.2000 in Kraft trat.[130]

Zu den wichtigsten Neuerungen zählt zunächst die Aufhebung vorheriger Normen in Art. 4 Einführungsgesetz. Dadurch wird das Prozessrecht von über 600 Paragraphen auf 79 gekürzt.[131] So wird u.a. mit dem vierten Buch des Zivil- und Handelsprozessgesetzes (*qānūn al-murāfaʿāt al-madanīya wa al-tiǧārīya*) das bisher geltende Grundgerüst für den Verfahrensablauf in Personenstandssachen abgeschafft. Ebenso abgeschafft wird das Gesetz Nr. 78/1931 betreffend der Organisation der *šarīʿa*-Gerichte, in dem weite Teile des geltenden Rechts für die Muslime Ägyptens geregelt waren, auch nachdem die Gerichte als solche 1956 abgeschafft worden sind.[132] Hierin war auch geregelt, dass die Rechtsansichten der hanafitischen Rechtsschule für die Fälle maßgebend sind, in denen das kodifizierte Recht keine spezielle Regelung bereithält. Die dadurch entstandene Lücke füllt Art. 3 Abs. 1 Einführungsgesetz, der wieder die hanafitische Richtung als Auffangrecht vorsieht. Hierzu wird angemerkt, dass im ursprünglichen Gesetzesentwurf der Regierung der Rückgriff auf alle vier Rechtsschulen vorgesehen war und erst innerhalb des Gesetzgebungsverfahrens wieder die Beschränkung auf die bewährte Richtung nach Abū Ḥanīfa eingeführt wurde.[133]

---

129 Al-Ahrām, 27.1.2000.

130 *Al-Dināṣūrī, I./ʿUkkāz, Ḥ.*, a.a.O., S. 15.

131 So die Auskunft von Naǧuib Fatḥī in al-ʿArabī, 23.1.2000.

132 *Al-ʿAǧūz, N.*, a.a.O., S. 176.

133 *Al-Dināṣūrī, I./ʿUkkāz, Ḥ.*, a.a.O., S. 10. Weitere wichtige prozessuale Neuerungen bestehen in der Auflockerung des sonst obligatorischen Anwaltszwangs vor ägyptischen Gerichten und der Art der Fristenberechnung. Nach Art. 3 Abs. 1 kann bei den Eingangsgerichten für Bagatellsachen (*maḥkama ǧuzʾīya*) die Klage auch ohne Rechtsanwalt erhoben werden. Gegebenenfalls sorgt dann das Gericht für eine Prozessvertretung des mittellosen Klägers (*al-ʿAǧūz, N.*, a.a.O., S. 161f; *Rohe, M.*, Das neue ägyptische Familienrecht: Auf dem Weg zu einem zeitgemäßen islamischen Recht, StAZ 2001, S. 193-207 (203). Zur Fristenberechnung bei Personenstandsprozessen wird neuerdings der westliche Sonnenkalender (*taqwīm mīlādī*) statt des Mondkalenders (*taqwīm hiǧrī*) angelegt (*al-Dināṣūrī, I./ʿUkkāz, Ḥ.*, a.a.O., S. 16). Daneben finden sich Regelungen zu Mitwirkungsrechten und –pflichten der Staatsanwaltschaft bei Personenstandsstreitigkeiten (z.B. Art. 23), die Vermögenssorge für beschränkt Geschäftsfähige (Art. 26-51) sowie die erforderliche Form von Beschlüssen und Urteilen und der dagegen möglichen Rechtsmittel (Art. 52-64) und schließlich zur Vollstreckung von Urteilen (Art. 65-79).

2. Materiellrechtliche Neuerungen im Rahmen der Prozessrechtsreform

In das materielle Recht hineinwirkenden Verfahrensregeln finden sich im dritten Abschnitt des Gesetzes unter der Überschrift „die Erhebung der Klage und ihre Prüfung" (Art. 16 ff). So sieht das Gesetz in Art. 17 Abs. 1 als Mittel gegen die Heirat Minderjähriger vor, dass Ansprüche nur geltend gemacht werden können, wenn beide Partner bei Klageerhebung das Mindestalter von 16 bzw. 18 Jahren erreicht haben, was der alten Rechtslage entspricht.[134] Neu ist Art. 17 Abs. 2, in dem erstmals auch Scheidungs-Klagen (*taṭlīq-* und *fasḫ*-Klagen) aus einem Ehevertrag zugelassen werden, der ohne die erforderliche notarielle Beurkundung zustande gekommen ist. Es ist dies eine Maßnahme gegen die sog. „Traditionsehe" (*al-zawāǧ al-ʿurfī*), bei der Eheverhältnisse ohne die erforderliche Beurkundung eingegangen werden. Dabei stehen den Ehepartnern nicht dieselben gesetzlichen Rechte zu wie nach ordentlichem Prozedere Verheirateten. Solche nichtbeurkundete Ehen sind in Ägypten verbreitet und werden oft mit Zweitfrauen geschlossen, deren Rechtstellung gegenüber mit beurkundetem Vertrag verheirateten Frauen schlechter ist. Zwar kann die ohne Beurkundung verheiratete Ehefrau auch nach der Neuregelung nicht sämtliche Ansprüche wie Unterhalt geltend machen, zumindest kann sie nun aber Scheidungsklage erheben, um die eheliche Beziehung zu beenden.[135]

Weitere Regelungen mit materiellen Folgen für das Eherecht finden sich in Art. 21 und 22. Art. 21 schützt die Ehefrau bei der Ausübung des einseitigen *ṭalāq*-Rechts durch den Mann. Nach klassischer Lehre und nach bisher geltendem ägyptischem Recht braucht die Ehefrau nicht bei der Aussprache der Verstoßungsformel zugegen sein. Trotzdem treten die Wirkungen der Scheidung ein. Nun wird in Art. 21 vorgeschrieben, dass im Falle des Bestreitens der Erklärung durch die Frau eine Scheidungserklärung nur dann Wirkung entfaltet, wenn der Mann zum Beweis eine notariell beurkundete Erklärung vorlegen kann. Diese ist nach Abs. 3 im Beisein der Partner oder ihrer Stellvertreter auszustellen. Der die Erklärung aufnehmende Notar ist verpflichtet, die Ehepartner über die Gefahren der Scheidung aufzuklären und mit Hilfe zweier Schiedsrichter zwischen den Partnern zu schlichten. Auf das Schlichtungsverfahren kann er verzichten, wenn die Partner auf der Wirksamkeit des bereits erfolgten *ṭalāq* bestehen oder einvernehmlich angeben, dass er während der Sitzung stattfinden soll oder wenn der Mann darauf besteht, die Verstoßung bereits ausgesprochen zu haben. In den beiden letzten Fällen beginnt die Wartezeit (*ʿidda*) der Ehefrau mit dem Sitzungstag zu laufen.[136]

---

134 *Al-ʿAǧūz, N.*, a.a.O., S. 158.

135 *Al-ʿAǧūz, N.*, a.a.O. S. 163f; *al-Dināṣūrī, I./ʿUkkāz, Ḥ.*, a.a.O., S. 65.

136 Zum ganzen Absatz: *al-Dināṣūrī, I./ʿUkkāz, Ḥ.*, a.a.O., S. 83f; *Muhsin, A./Abu al-Qumṣān, N.*, al-Ḫulʿ, Kairo 2000, S. 40ff.

Auf ähnliche Weise schützt Art. 22 die Frau vor ihr unbekannten Rücknahmeerklärungen bei widerrufbaren Verstoßungen (*ṭalāq raǧʿī*). Dies schützt sie in dem Fall, dass sie z.B. nach Ablauf der von ihr angenommenen Wartezeit erneut heiratet und ihr alter Ehemann seine Verstoßung widerruft, indem er einen späteren Zeitpunkt für seine erste Verstoßungserklärung angibt. In diesem Fall muss er mit Hilfe einer beglaubigten Urkunde beweisen, dass er den Widerruf rechtzeitig vorgenommen hat und dieser der Frau mitgeteilt wurde. Das Gesetz unterscheidet bei den Wirkungen zwischen Fällen von Ehefrauen mit und ohne Regel. Bei ersteren ist der Widerruf rechtzeitig, wenn er innerhalb von 60 Tagen ab der ersten Regel nach der Verstoßungserklärung abgegeben wird, bei letzteren beträgt die Frist 90 Tage ab der Verstoßung. Al-Dināṣūrī/ʿUkkāz sehen bei dieser erst im Gesetzgebungsverfahren eingefügten Differenzierung für die Praxis den Streit voraus, dass sich die Frau auf die kürzere Frist für Menstruierende beruft, während der Mann auf Anwendung der nach Monaten zu berechnenden Frist beruft. Dieser Streit sei durch eidliche Aussage der Frau zu lösen.[137]
Der Streit um die Erlaubnis des freien Auslandsreiserechts für die Frau, der in Art. 26 des Gesetzesentwurf vorgesehen war, wurde durch Streichung der Norm gelöst.[138] So galt zunächst die Verordnung des Innenministers weiter, nach der Frauen auf Antrag ihrer Ehemänner auf eine Personenliste gesetzt werden konnten, für die keine Reisepapiere von Behörden ausgestellt werden durften. Damit ist dann eine Auslandsreise für die betroffene Frau unmöglich. Diese Verordnung hat das Verfassungsgericht in der Entscheidung vom 4.11.2000 mit der Begründung aufgehoben, dass sie dem Recht der persönlichen Freiheit widerspricht. Nach dem Urteil besteht die Verpflichtung der Behörden, die Papiere auszustellen. Jedoch ist damit noch nicht die volle Reisefreiheit der Frau gewährleistet, denn die Männer können jetzt ein gerichtliches Reiseverbot für ihre Frauen erwirken.[139]

III. Art. 20 und die Neuordnung des *ḫulʿ*

1. Der Normtext

Art. 20 des Gesetzes Nr. 1/2000 lautet in Übersetzung folgendermaßen:

> (1) Die Ehepartner können sich über eine *ḫulʿ*-Trennung zwischen ihnen einigen. Falls sie sich nicht einigen konnten und die Ehefrau Klage auf ihr (Trennungs-)Begehren erhebt und sich selbst loskauft (*iftadat nafsahā*) und sich von ihrem Mann trennt (*ḫālaʿat zauǧahā*), indem sie

[137] *Al-Dināṣūrī, I./ʿUkkāz, Ḥ.*, a.a.O., S. 86.
[138] *Muhsin, A./Abu al-Qumṣān, N.*, a.a.O., S.25 - 27.
[139] Entscheidung des Verfassungsgerichtshofs vom 4.11.2000, 3648, 3652; siehe auch Frankfurter Allgemeine Zeitung vom 11.11.2000 „Mehr Freiheit für die Ägypterinnen".

auf alle ihre gesetzlichen finanziellen Ansprüche verzichtet (*bi-l-tanāzul ʿan ǧamīʿ ḥuqūqihā al-mālīya al-šarʿīya*) und ihrem Mann das Brautgeld (*al-ṣadāq*) zurückerstattet, das dieser ihr ausgehändigt hat, so spricht das Gericht ihre Scheidung von ihm aus.
(2) Das Gericht entscheidet über die *ḫulʿ*-Scheidung nur, wenn ein Versöhnungsversuch (*muḥāwalat al-ṣulḥ*)[140] zwischen den Partnern stattgefunden hat, bei dem zwei Schiedsrichter (*ḥakamān*) entsprechend Art. 18 Abs. 2 sowie Art. 19 Abs. 1 u. 2 in einer Frist von höchstens drei Monaten mit der Schlichtung betraut wurden, und nachdem die Ehefrau ausdrücklich erklärt hat (*tuqarriru al-zauǧa ṣarāḥatan*), dass ihr das Leben mit dem Partner zuwider ist (*tabġaḍu al-ḥayāt maʿ zauǧihā*) und es keinen Weg zur Fortsetzung des ehelichen Lebens gibt (*lā sabīl li-istimrār al-ḥayāt al-zauǧīya*), und dass sie befürchtet, die Gebote Gottes aus diesem Grund nicht einhalten zu können (*taḫšā allā tuqīma ḥudūd Allāh bi-sabab haḏā al-baġḍ*).
(3) Es ist nicht erlaubt, dass das Entgelt für die *ḫulʿ*-Scheidung in dem Verzicht auf die Personensorge (*ḥaḍāna*) oder dem Unterhalt von Minderjährigen (*nafaqathum*) oder eines sonstigen diesen zustehenden Rechtes besteht.
(4) Die *ḫulʿ*-Scheidung hat die Wirkungen der unwiderruflichen Scheidung (*ṭalāq bāʾin*).
(5) Das Urteil ist in keinem Fall Gegenstand von Rechtsmitteln (*ṭaʿn*) gleich welcher Art.

In Art. 20 Abs. 2 wird auf folgende Normen Bezug genommen:

Art. 18 Abs.2: In Scheidungsklagen entscheidet das Gericht erst, wenn es sich um einen Versöhnungsversuch zwischen den Partnern bemüht hat und dabei gescheitert ist. Falls die Partner Kinder haben, ist das Gericht mindestens zweimal zu einem Versöhnungsversuch verpflichtet. Zwischen den Versuchen muss eine Frist von mindestens 30 und höchstens 60 Tagen liegen.

Art. 19: (1) Bei Scheidungsklagen, in denen das Gesetz die Ernennung zweier Schiedsrichter vorsieht, muss das Gericht beide Partner bis spätestens zur darauffolgenden Gerichtssitzung zur Benennung jeweils eines Schiedsrichters nach Möglichkeit aus der eigenen Familie verpflichten. Falls einer der Partner keinen Schiedsrichter benennt oder

---

[140] In der Gesetzesausgabe von *al-Ḥasanayn, M.*, a.a.O., S. 27, ist der Normtext abweichend mit „*muḥāwalat al-iṣlāḥ*" angegeben.

zur folgenden Sitzung nicht erscheint, bestimmt das Gericht einen Schiedsrichter an seiner statt.
(2) Die beiden Schiedsrichter müssen in der auf ihre Benennung folgenden Sitzung vor Gericht erscheinen, um zu erklären, zu welchen Ergebnis sie gemeinsam gekommen sind. Falls sie sich widersprechen oder einer von ihnen nicht erscheint, hört das Gericht nach ihrer Vereidigung ihre Aussagen oder die Aussage des Anwesenden an.
(3) Das Gericht kann beschließen, zu was die Schiedsrichter gemeinsam gelangt sind oder was einer von ihnen gesagt hat oder davon abweichend nach Lage der Verhandlungsakten entscheiden.

2. Die Tatbestandsvoraussetzungen des Art. 20

Das Gesetz nennt somit eine Reihe von Tatbestandsvoraussetzungen, bei deren Vorliegen das Gericht auf eine *ḫulʿ*-Scheidung der Ehe zu erkennen hat.
Vorrangig ist dabei die einvernehmliche Trennung zwischen den Partnern (Abs.1 S.1). In diesem Fall kommt es zu keiner gerichtlichen Verhandlung. Es wird lediglich die Auflösung der Ehe, die durch einen *ṭalāq* erklärt wird, beurkundet und in den Ehebüchern registriert.[141] Es handelt sich dabei um die Form des *ḫulʿ* wie er in der klassischen Lehre vorhanden war. Dort war der Konsens der Partner eine der Säulen des Rechtsinstitutes. Für den Fall der Nichtverständigung der Eheleute fehlt diese Säule. Der unmittelbare Bezug zwischen S. 1 und S. 2 des ersten Absatzes macht deutlich, dass der Ursprung des *ḫulʿ*-Instituts in der Einvernehmlichkeit liegt, und dass das Folgende eine Weiterentwicklung des ursprünglichen Konzeptes ist.[142]
Diese Weiterentwicklung besteht in dem Anspruch auf richterliche Scheidung unter folgenden Voraussetzungen:

1) Die Frau erhebt Klage mit dem Begehren einer gerichtlichen *ḫulʿ*-Scheidung.
2) Die Ehefrau gibt dem Partner das von ihm als *ṣadāq* erhaltene zurück und verzichtet auf alle ihr zustehenden nachehelichen Ansprüche.
3) Das Gericht führt ein zweiphasiges Schlichtungsverfahren unter Beteiligung von Schiedsrichtern aus den Familien der Partner erfolglos durch.
4) Die Ehefrau gibt vor Gericht eine eindeutige Erklärung ab, dass auch nach durchgeführten Versöhnungsverfahren die Fortsetzung der Ehe für sie undenkbar ist.

Als Rechtsfolgen gibt der Artikel an, dass

1) der *ḫulʿ* die unwiderrufliche Wirkung des *ṭalāq bāʾin* entfaltet und dass

---

141 *Naṣṣār, A.*, a.a.O., S. 73, 75.
142 *Imām, M.*, a.a.O., S. 176; *al-Dināṣūrī, I./ʿUkkāz, Ḥ.*, a.a.O., S. 72.

2) der normalerweise vorgesehene Rechtsweg durch Berufung oder Revision bei *ḫulʿ*-Urteilen verschlossen ist.

3. Die Einführung eines Scheidungsgrundes für die Frau ohne Verschuldensnachweis – Argumente aus der rechtspolitischen Debatte in Ägypten

Mit Art. 20 und der Erweiterung des *ḫulʿ*-Institutes auf Fälle des Nichteinvernehmens des Ehemanns erwächst eine neue Kompetenz für den ägyptischen Richter. Die Gründe, wegen denen eine Ehefrau einen *taṭlīq*-Antrag stellen kann, werden um den *ḫulʿ* erweitert. In der Verlagerung des *ḫulʿ* von der freien Vereinbarung zwischen den Gatten auf den Richter wird der entscheidende Unterschied zum klassischen Recht ausgemacht. Imām bezeichnet diesen Wandel als den „eigentlichen *iǧtihād*" des Gesetzes, neben den die anderen Veränderungen zweitrangig erscheinen.[143] Wegen dieses Umstandes haben einige besonders während des Gesetzgebungsverfahrens das Gesetz als gegen die *šarīʿa* und damit auch gegen die Verfassung verstoßend kritisiert. Die Befürworter der Regelung sahen die parlamentarische Entscheidung dagegen in vollem Einklang mit dem islamischen Recht.

Am Ende des 20. Jahrhunderts waren in Ägypten circa 2,5 Millionen Fälle in Familiensachen vor den Gerichten anhängig. Bei knapp einer Million davon handelte es sich um Scheidungssachen, zumeist Begehren der Frauen auf *taṭlīq li-l-ḍarar*. Diese Prozesse dauern oft jahrelang und gestalten sich für die Frauen als sehr kostspielig. Dabei bleibt das Ende ungewiss.[144] Schon aus dieser – in der Zeitungsdebatte vorgetragenen, aber möglicherweise ungenauen – Zahlenangabe zeigen sich zwei Probleme: Zum einen sind zerfallene Ehen und Familien eine gesellschaftliche Realität. Zum anderen besteht ein verstärktes Bedürfnis nach Beschleunigung der großen Zahl von Fällen. So sind auch die Hauptziele, die der Gesetzgeber mit seiner Initiative zur Einführung des *ḫulʿ* als zusätzlichen Scheidungsgrund erreichen möchte: Er möchte mit der Beschleunigung des Verfahrens einen Ausweg für Frauen schaffen und dadurch letztlich zur Festigung der Familie beitragen.[145]

Die Kritik an dieser Regelung war scharf: Der Neuregelung wird als „Zeitbombe, die die Häuser einzustürzen droht"[146] und als „Imitation des Westens"[147] gebrandmarkt, die Kritiker malen den „Zerfall der Familie und der gesamten Gesellschaft" an die Wand. Es wird befürchtet, dass von den 1,5 Millionen scheidungswilligen Frauen über eine Millionen auf die *ḫulʿ*-Klage

---

143 *Imām, M.*, a.a.O., S. 177.

144 Al-Ahrām, 30.1.2000, geht davon aus, dass Frauen für ihre *taṭlīq*-Klage durchschnittlich 30.000 Pfund für Prozessgebühren und Anwaltskosten aufwenden müssen.

145 So Nazālī al-Šurbīnī in al-Ahrām, 30.1.2000.

146 Überschrift in al-Ahrām, 28.1.2000.

147 Muḥammad Barra in al-Ǧumhūrīya, 17.1.2000.

umspringen und innerhalb kürzester Zeit ihre Männer und ihre Familien verlassen würden. In den düstersten Szenarien wird der Faden von den getrennten Familien weiter zu Heeren von verwahrlosten Kindern und einem entsprechenden Anstieg der Kriminalität gesponnen.[148]
Die Befürworter, angeführt von der Regierung und der regimetreuen Presse, sprechen von einer notwendigen Anpassung der Gesetzeslage an die sich ändernden Zeiten mit ihren Anforderungen. So sei die Frau heutzutage immer mehr in den Arbeitsmarkt integriert und dadurch mehr und mehr selbständig, andererseits verbleibe sie aber in der undankbaren Lage, trotz einer unglücklichen Ehe mit alltäglichem Streit in dieser Beziehung bleiben zu müssen. Sie sei ihrem Mann wehrlos ausgeliefert und als Ehefrau gleichzeitig zu Gehorsam verpflichtet. Die Auswirkungen solcher gescheiterten, aber fortgesetzten Beziehungen auf die Familien und Kinder sei bei weiten negativer als die von sauber getrennten Ehen.[149] Auffallend ist, dass die Debatte durch keinen anderen Aspekt so sehr geprägt ist wie durch die religiöse Dimension. Während die Gegner die Regelung des *ḫulʿ* als nicht *šarīʿa*-gemäß rügen, legitimieren die Befürworter das Gesetz ebenfalls durch den Rückgriff auf die *šarīʿa*. Kaum ein Kommentator kommt ohne mehr oder weniger ausführliche Stellungnahme zu den Grundlagen in Koran und Sunna aus.[150] Wichtiges Argument für die Befürworter ist, dass durch die Ermöglichung des *ḫulʿ* die Frau wieder in die ihr ursprünglich vom göttlichen Normgeber zugedachte Position des Gleichgewichts zum Mann versetzt wird, in der sie frei entscheiden kann, mit welchem Mann sie zusammenlebt. So wie der Mann im *ṭalāq*-Recht die Freiheit hat zu entscheiden, mit wem er die einmal eingegangene eheliche Beziehung fortsetzen will, so kann auch die Frau per *ḫulʿ* ihre Konsequenz ziehen, wenn die bei der Eheschließung abgegebene Einwilligung in die Ehe weggefallen ist. Der Freiwilligkeitscharakter der Ehe wird so über das Einverständnis bei der Eheschließung hinaus zu einer fortgesetzten Freiwilligkeit ausgedehnt.[151]

---

148 So *al-ʿAǧūz, N.*, S. 62.

149 *Naṣṣār, A.*, a.a.O., S. 64. So auch Sahīr Kāmil und Nawāl ʿAmr in al-ʿAǧūz, S. 55.

150 Die Dominanz der religiösen Argumentationen sowohl auf Gegner- als auch auf Befürworterseite hat *Tādrus, M.*, Qānūn al-ḫulʿ fī al-ṣaḥāfa al-miṣrīya, in: *al-Ṣāwī, A.*, al-Ḥaṣād, Kairo 2003, S. 83-100, in ihrer Studie über den Pressediskurs herausgearbeitet. Der Befund bestätigt sich in der mir vorliegenden Literatur. In den Presseartikeln wie in den Fachbeiträgen beschäftigt sich die überwiegende Mehrheit mit den genannten Fragen.

151 So z.B. al-Biyūtī, in al-Ahrām, 14.1.2000, oder der ehemalige Religionsminister Maḥmūd Zaqzūq in al-Ahrām, 27.1.2000. Den Aspekt der fortgesetzten Zustimmung beider Partner betont *Nassar, N.*, a.a.O., S. 194, 202. Für die Wiederherstellung des Gleichgewichts wird sich auf Ibn Rušd berufen, *Imām, M.*, a.a.O., S. 170.

Es geht in diesem Streit um die schon bekannte Frage der rechten Interpretation der beiden Quellen Koran und Sunna und deren relevanten Bezüge zum *ḫulʿ*: Hatte die Anweisung des Propheten an Ṯābit ibn Qays zwingenden (*īǧābī*) oder lediglich empfehlenden (*iršādī*) Charakter oder hat gar der Prophet selbst die Scheidung vorgenommen? An der Erörterung in den mir vorliegenden Presseartikeln wie auch in der juristischen Literatur fällt auf, dass zwar an vielen Stellen diese Frage aufgeworfen wird, die Untersuchungen sich aber wenig am Wortlaut des Quellenmaterials orientieren. Statt die verschiedenen Überlieferungsvarianten und Interpretationsmöglichkeiten wahrzunehmen und zu diskutieren, machen sich die Autoren die Antwort leicht, indem gesagt wird, dass entweder die Textquellen „eindeutig" die Erklärung des Ehemanns fordern oder eben umgekehrt, dass es auf diese Erklärung „eindeutig" nicht ankomme.[152] Ebenso wird von den Kritikern angemerkt, dass alle bestehenden Rechtsschulen samt der vertretenen Mindermeinungen die Zustimmung des Mannes zur *ḫulʿ*-Trennung voraussetzten. Hieraus wird selten gefolgert, dass deshalb auch kein modernes Gesetz etwas anderes vorschreiben dürfe – also auf den Fortbestand des *taqlīd*-Prinzips gepocht wird. Häufiger wird daraus abgeleitet, dass eine abweichende Kodifizierung zwar möglich sei, aber nicht zweckmäßig. Insofern gibt es die Forderung nach der strengen Nachahmung der Tradition nur selten. Der Umgang mit der Rechtsschultradition hat sich verändert. Das Erfordernis der Zustimmung des Mannes wird weniger aus der Rechtsschullehre gefolgert, als direkt aus den Quellen Koran und Sunna.[153]

Die Gegner werfen der Regierung vor, mit dem *ḫulʿ*-Artikel einen Einzelfall unzulässigerweise zur Regel zu machen. Obwohl in der Prophetentradition erwähnt, sei es niemals zu einer regelmäßigen Ausübung und damit Etablierung als Rechtsinstitut gekommen.[154] Man wundert sich, dass sich im islamischen Recht Geschulte dieses Argument zu Eigen machen, ist doch gerade durch die Erwähnung in den Rechtsschulen klar, dass der *ḫulʿ* als Rechtsinstitut etabliert ist. Im Übrigen zeigen auch neuere Forschungsergebnisse, dass Scheidungen durch *ḫulʿ* auch in der islamischen Frühzeit bekannt waren. Offenbar waren sie zu dieser Periode gesellschaftlich weit akzeptierter als in späteren Zeiten.[155]

---

[152] Beispiele für das erstgenannte Vorgehen finden sich in der Aussage des Parlamentariers ʿAbd al-Raḥmān al-ʿAdwī, wiedergegeben in al-Ahrām vom 27.1.2000, oder in der bei *al-ʿAǧūz, N.*, a.a.O., S. 58, wiedergegebene Argumentation von Saʿada Ṣāliḥ. Letztgenanntes Vorgehen z.B. al-Biyūmī, al-ʾArabī, 28.1.2000.

[153] Ein Beispiel hierfür ist die Argumentation von ʿAbd al-Fatāḥ al-Šaiḫ, in al-ʿArabī, 28.1.2000.

[154] *Al-ʿAǧūz, N.*, a.a.O., S. 60.

[155] *Khoury, R.*, Chrestomathie de papyrologie arabe: documents relatifs à la vie privée, sociale et administrative dans les premiers siècles islamiques, Leiden 1993, S. 44, führt ein Papyrusdokument aus dem 10. Jahrhundert als Beispiel für einen *ḫulʿ* auf. In dieser

Die Kritik an der *ḫulʿ*-Regelung ist gekennzeichnet von einem Frauenbild, das diese als extrem stimmungsabhängiges und emotional handelndes Subjekt darstellt. Bedrückte Ehefrauen würden aus spontanen Stimmungen heraus gleich bei den ersten Problemen zum neuen Scheidungsinstrument greifen, statt eine Lösung innerhalb der Partnerschaft ernsthaft zu suchen. Damit sei ihnen ein Drohpotential gegen ihren Ehemann gegeben, durch das dieser nach Belieben mit der Drohung, ihn zu verlassen, erpresst werden könne. Hiergegen wird gehalten, dass gerade darin der Vorteil der Regelung liegt. So wie eine Frau weiß, dass sie bei Nichtnachkommen ihrer ehelichen Pflichten mit dem Verstoßungsbegehren des Partners konfrontiert sein könne und sich zur Vermeidung dessen um eine bessere Pflichterfüllung bemühe, so habe jetzt auch der Ehemann eine zusätzliche Motivation, seine Frau gut zu behandeln.[156]
Als Argument für die Befugnis des Gerichts anstelle des Ehemanns wird die Parallele zum im ägyptischen Recht etablierten Verfahren beim *taṭlīq li-l-šiqāq* genommen, für dessen Kodifizierung auf die malikitische Rechtsschule zurückgegriffen wurde. Auch in dieser Scheidungsart kommt es auf die Zustimmung des Mannes überhaupt nicht an, obwohl mitunter von seiner Seite kein verschuldeter Grund für das Scheitern der Ehe vorliegt. Wenn nun schon in diesem Falle zwei Schlichter die Entscheidung auf Beendigung der Ehe treffen könnten, dann sei es ebenso auch beim *ḫulʿ* zulässig, dem Mann die Dispositionsbefugnis zu entziehen und sie beim Richter in die Hände eines Dritten zu legen. Dies finde seine koranische Grundlage in Sure 4,19, die bei gescheiterter Vermittlung die Trennung durch einen Dritten vorsehe.[157] Jedenfalls stimme die gelegentlich geäußerte Behauptung, nur der Mann alleine habe die Macht, über die Scheidung seiner Ehe zu bestimmen, nicht. Stattdessen gebe die *šarīʿa* auch der Frau ein Initiativrecht zur Scheidung, das in erster Linie im *ḫulʿ* liege.
Nach diesem Überblick über in der Diskussion vertretene Argumente für und gegen die Einführung des Art. 20 werden im Folgenden die einzelnen Tatbestandvoraussetzungen analysiert. Dabei wird neben der juristischen Fachliteratur insbesondere auf die Motive des Gesetzgebers eingegangen, die dieser in seinem offiziellen Gesetzesmemorandum (*al-mudakkira al-īḍāḥīya*) angegeben hat.

Urkunde verpflichtet sich die Ehefrau zur Zahlung eines Lösegeldes gegen Auflösung des Ehevertrags. Diese Abrede wird als *ḫulʿ* bezeichnet (Urkunde Nr. 18, Zeile 4).

156 So wird zitiert: Fauzīya ʿAbd al-Sattār in al-Ahrām, 30.1.2000.

157 ʿAbd al-Raḥmān ʿAdwī, al-Ahrām, 27.1.2000.

4. Die Auslegung der Tatbestandsmerkmale und Rechtsfolgen der *ḫulʿ*-Scheidung in der politischen Debatte und der Rechtsliteratur

Die Klageerhebung der Ehefrau

Die Klageerhebung regelt sich nach den allgemeinen Regeln, die auch für andere Klagen in Familiensachen gelten. Art. 16 Gesetz 1/2000 verweist hierfür auf das Zivil- und Handelsprozessgesetz, welches in Art. 62 vorschreibt, dass eine Klageschrift einzureichen ist, die bestimmte Mindestangaben enthalten muss.[158]

Zusätzlich zu diesen Anforderungen soll in der *ḫulʿ*-Klage auch der Grund für das Scheidungsbegehren angegeben werden. Allerdings beschränkt sich dieser auf die in Art. 20 Abs. 2 Gesetz 1/2000 angegebenen Erklärungen der Frau: Sie muss angeben, dass für sie das eheliche Zusammenleben nicht mehr fortsetzbar ist, weil sie das Leben mit ihrem Mann verabscheue und einen Verstoß gegen die göttlichen Gesetze bei Fortsetzung fürchte. Sie muss diese Gründe zwar nennen, aber nicht für ihren Fall besonders belegen. Insbesondere muss sie keine persönlichen Gründe für ihr Begehren offen legen. Dies ist gedacht als Schutzmaßnahme für ihre eigene Privatsphäre wie auch für die Kinder, die nicht in ein Verfahren hineingezogen werden sollen, in denen das Ansehen ihrer Familie und besonders des Vaters geschmälert wird.[159] Eine solche Erklärung soll, muss aber nicht in der Klageschrift enthalten sein; sie muss in jedem Fall in der letzten mündlichen Verhandlung aufgestellt bzw. aufrechterhalten werden.[160]

Im Unterschied zu allen anderen *taṭlīq*-Arten geht es also bei dem Scheidungsanlass nicht um einen in der Verantwortung des Ehemanns liegenden Grund. Nur auf die innere Konstitution der Frau kommt es an. Auch ist der Beweggrund der Frau ein vollkommen individueller. Ihr Zusammenleben mit dem Mann ist nicht etwa durch einen bestimmten Grund gestört, von dem generell angenommen wird, dass das eheliche Leben unmöglich wird und dessen Vorliegen deshalb von den Gerichten geprüft wird.[161]

Die sachliche Zuständigkeit für das *ḫulʿ*-Verfahren liegt gemäß Art. 10 Abs.1 des Gesetzes 1/2000 beim allgemeinen erstinstanzlichen Gericht (*al-maḥkama al-ʾibtidāʾīya*). Örtlich ist gemäß Art. 15 Abs.1 je nach Wahl der klagenden Ehefrau das Gericht am Aufenthaltsort von ihr selbst oder dem des Ehemanns zuständig.[162]

---

158 *Al-Dināṣūrī, I./ʿUkkāz, Ḥ.*, a.a.O., S. 62.
159 *Naṣṣār, A.*, a.a.O., S. 59.
160 *Al-Ağūz, N.*, a.a.O., S. 372.
161 *Al-ʿAğūz, N.*, a.a.O., S. 368.
162 *Al-ʿAğūz, N.*, a.a.O., S. 155f.

Zulässig – und in der Praxis äußerst bedeutsam – ist die Klageänderung von einer der anderen *taṭlīq*-Arten auf den *ḫulʿ*. Dies richtet sich nach der allgemeinen Norm des Art. 124 Abs. 3 des Zivil- und Handelsprozessgesetzes, der alle Klageergänzungen und -änderungen innerhalb eines Verfahrens für zulässig erklärt, solange der Klagegegenstand (*mauḍūʿ al-daʿwā*) derselbe bleibt und nur der Klagegrund (*sabab al-daʿwā*) geändert wird. Dies ist bei der genannten Umstellung der Fall, da der Lebenssachverhalt, auf den die Klage gestützt wird, derselbe bleibt, während sich nur der rechtliche Grund verändert.[163] Eine solche Änderung kommt insbesondere bei schon länger andauernden Scheidungsverfahren in Betracht. Nicht zulässig ist jedoch die Betreibung beider Scheidungsklagen nebeneinander in der Weise, dass der *ḫulʿ* nur hilfsweise begehrt wird.

Die Rückgewähr des Brautgeldes und der Verzicht auf alle finanziellen nachehelichen Ansprüche – zu den finanziellen Folgen des *ḫulʿ*

Mit dem Verzicht der Ehefrau auf ihr Brautgeld und die nachehelichen Ansprüche hat der Gesetzgeber die finanziellen Folgen der gerichtlichen *ḫulʿ*-Scheidung in Art. 20 Abs.1 aufgenommen. Es wird dadurch eine der wichtigsten Säulen der klassischen *ḫulʿ*-Konstruktion der Rechtsschulen in das moderne Gesetz übernommen. In der Diskussion um das neue Recht hat diese Regelung starke Kontroversen ausgelöst.

Begriff des Brautgelds (ṣadāq) *und Umfang des Rückgewähranspruchs*

Mit der Festsetzung der Abstandssumme auf den Betrag des Brautgeldes (*ṣadāq*) ist die im *fiqh* umstrittene Frage nach der zulässigen Summe für den Loskauf beantwortet worden: Während der frühere Konsens die Höhe des Betrags in das Einvernehmen der Gatten stellte und in einigen Rechtsschulen einen höheren Betrag als das Brautgeld zuließ, legt der Gesetzgeber eine Grenze fest und schließt so das durch das bei der *ḫulʿ*-Klage wegen des fehlenden Einvernehmens entstandene Vakuum.

Trotz dieser Begrenzung auf eine Höchstsumme herrscht in der Literatur über die Auslegung des *ṣadāq*–Begriffs einige Meinungsverschiedenheit. Unstreitig ist, dass hierin die bei Abschluss der Ehe geleistete und in dem Vertrag genau bezeichnete Geldsumme oder Naturalienleistung (z.B. in Form eines Grundstücks) enthalten ist, also das sog. „frühe" bzw. „übergebene" Brautgeld (*muʾağğal al-ṣadāq* bzw. *muqaddam al-ṣadāq)* im Gegensatz zum gestundeten „späten" Brautgeld (*muʾaḫḫar al-ṣadāq*), das zwar ebenfalls im Ehevertrag angegeben wird, dessen Fälligkeit aber auf den Zeitpunkt der Auflösung der Ehe verschoben wird.

---

[163] *Al-Dināṣūrī, I./ʿUkkāz, Ḥ*, a.a.O., S. 78.

Es ist in Ägypten wie auch in vielen anderen islamischen Ländern üblich, den anfänglichen Betrag niedrig zu halten und den später fällig werdenden umfangreich zu vereinbaren. Dies soll den Mann in die Lage versetzen, die Ehe mit der Frau seiner Wahl früher eingehen zu können, weil er keine allzu großen Summen schon bei der Schließung der Ehe aufbringen muss. Zum anderen soll er durch die hohe Summe im Falle der Beendigung der Ehe davon abgehalten werden, leichtfertig den *ṭalāq* zu erklären. Insofern kommt dem *muʾaḫḫar al-ṣadāq* auch die Funktion einer Vertragsstrafe zu, die ihn von der Scheidung abhalten soll.[164]
In *ḫulʿ*-Fällen führt diese Praxis dazu, dass die Ehefrau hier ebenfalls nur einen kleinen Betrag zurückleisten muss. Den größeren *muʾaḫḫar al-ṣadāq* muss sie nun nicht in Geld oder Natura leisten, sie hat allerdings ihren Verzicht auf diesen zu erklären.
Ist der *ṣadāq* in Naturalien geleistet worden, ist für die Wertbemessung nicht der Wert z.Z. der Eheschließung, sondern derjenige zum Zeitpunkt der Klageerhebung maßgebend. Dies kann für die Frau große Nachteile bedeuten, wenn sie die Sache schon während der bestehenden Ehe versetzt hat und das erlöste Geld anderweitig verwendet hat.[165]
Ob über den so definierten *ṣadāq* noch andere Kostenposten umfasst sind, ist streitig. So wird geltend gemacht, dass auch eheliche Geschenke (*hadīya*) sowie die gesellschaftlich übliche Goldgabe, die der Mann seiner Braut vor der Eheschließung während der Verlobungszeit übergibt (*šabka*), enthalten sind. In der Praxis hat es offenbar auch Fälle gegeben, in denen auch von der Frau mit eigenen Mitteln während der Ehe angeschaffte Einrichtungsgegenstände (*al-ǧihāz* bzw. *al-manqūlāt al-zauǧīya*) als zum *ṣadāq* gehörig zurückgegeben wurden.[166] Al-Dināṣūrī/ʿUkkāz meinen hierzu, dass der gesetzlich benutzte Begriff eindeutig sei und nur dasjenige umfasst, das im Ehevertrag als *ṣadāq* bezeichnet wird.[167] Darüber hinaus umfasse das Gesetz nichts. Insbesondere seien Geschenke gleich welcher Art gerade nicht gemeint. Dagegen wird eine *ḥadīṯ*-Interpretation gehalten, nach der die Frau des Ibn Qays ebenfalls nicht nur

---

164 *Ebert, H.-G.*, Das Personalstatut arabischer Länder: Problemfelder, Methoden, Perspektiven, Frankfurt 1996, S. 92. Ebert berichtet außerdem von gesetzlichen Regelungen in einigen arabischen Ländern wie Oman, in denen eine Obergrenze für das zu vereinbarende Brautgeld festgesetzt wird oder in denen Ehefonds für preiswerte Kredite für heiratswillige Männer eingerichtet werden (Vereinigte Arabische Emirate). Dadurch soll einer geradezu inflationären Erhöhung der Summen entgegengetreten bzw. die Eheschließungskosten leichter tragbar gemacht werden, damit die Zahl der ledigen Männer nicht weiter steigt.

165 *Al-Dināṣūrī, I./ʿUkkāz, Ḥ.*, a.a.O., S. 73.

166 *Muhsin, A./Abu al-Qumṣān, N.*, a.a.O., S. 18.

167 *Al-Dināṣūrī, I./ʿUkkāz, Ḥ.*, a.a.O., S. 75.

den *mahr* zurückgegeben habe, sondern sämtliche Dinge, die sie von ihrem Mann bekommen hatte. Die Trennung zwischen *mahr* und Geschenken wie der *šabka*–Gabe sei in der Zeit des Propheten nicht bekannt gewesen – darum könne sie auch für spätere Zeiten nicht konstruiert werden.[168] Außerdem wird behauptet, dass ein sinnvolleres Verständnis des *ṣadāq*-Begriffs auch diejenigen Gaben enthalten müsse, die im Zusammenhang mit der Eheschließung aufgewandt worden seien und deren gesellschaftliche Relevanz mit der Brautgabe quasi identisch seien, mit dem einzigen Unterschied, dass sie nicht so bezeichnet werden. Al-Ǧindī meint, dass aus diesem Grund zumindest die *šabka*-Gabe miteinbezogen werden müsse. Zwar werde diese vor Eheschließung geleistet und nicht im Vertrag festgehalten, aber da die Verhandlungen um diese Gabe häufig mit denen um das offizielle Brautgeld verwoben seien und die Höhe des Geschenkes öffentlich genauso bekannt würde wie die des Brautgeldes, müsse sie auch gleich behandelt werden. Faktisch mache der *šabka* daher den größeren Teil des Brautgeldes aus.[169]
In der Tat stimmt al-Ǧindīs Beobachtung der sozialen Wirklichkeit: Die *šabka*-Beträge sind häufig höher als diejenigen des *ṣadāq*. Es ist jedoch beachtlich, dass der Gesetzgeber diese Gaben weder im Gesetz noch in dem Gesetzesmemorandum erwähnt, obwohl ihm die sozialen Realitäten in Ägypten bekannt sein dürften. Hätte er diese mit in die Ausgleichspflicht hineinziehen wollen, so wäre eine Erwähnung dessen ohne Probleme möglich gewesen. Der Begriff des *ṣadāq* ist gesetzlich in Ägypten verhältnismäßig klar umrissen und auf den ehevertraglichen Betrag begrenzt. Dies ist auch obergerichtlich bestätigt worden: Nach der Rechtssprechung des Kassationshofs richtet sich nur der im Ehevertrag versprochene Betrag nach den Normen des Personalstatusrechtes. Voreheliche Geschenke können dagegen bei Auflösung einer Verlobung nur nach allgemein-zivilrechtlichen Normen zurückgefordert werden.[170] Von diesem Begriff wird auch im Falle des *ṭalāq*, bei dem die Frau gegenüber dem Mann anspruchsberechtigt wird, keine Erweiterung hin zu versprochenen Geschenken o.ä. vorgenommen, sondern einzig der Ehevertrag zugrundegelegt. Daher liegt es nahe, denselben Begriff zur Feststellung des *ṣadāq* im *ḫulʿ*-Falle zu benutzen und von diesem nicht zu Lasten der Frau abzuweichen.
Offensichtlich ist es in Ägypten üblich, dass eine geschiedene Ehefrau von sich aus das *šabka*-Geschenk ihrem Mann nach erfolgter Verstoßung zurückgibt. Dazu ist sie gesetzlich nicht verpflichtet, allerdings scheint es eine Art

---

168 Interpretation der Prophetenüberlieferung nach Muṣṭafā Abū Zayd, zit. in: *Zawīn, Ḥ.*, Daʿwā al-ḫulʿ: ʿilman wa ʿamalan, Kairo 2002, S. 75f.

169 *Al-Ǧindī, M.*, a.a.O., S. 271; so auch M. Abū Zayd, zitiert in: *Zawīn, Ḥ.*, S. 76, der meint, dass der *ṣadāq* traditionell aus den beiden Teilen *mahr* und *šabka* besteht, also nicht mit dem *mahr* allein gleichgesetzt werden kann.

170 *Zawīn, Ḥ.*, a.a.O., S. 77f, unter Verweis auf die einschlägige Rechtsprechung.

Ehrenkodex zu geben, nach dem diese Geschenke zurückzugeben sind.[171] Möglicherweise kann sich dieser gesellschaftliche Brauch auch für *ḫulʿ*-Scheidungen durchsetzen, so dass die dargestellte Diskussion nicht von allzu großer praktischer Relevanz sein wird. Allerdings ist zu bemerken, dass die Frau im Fall des *ṭalāq* auch ohne das *šabka*-Geschenk ausreichend versorgt ist, während sie beim *ḫulʿ* mit einer großen finanziellen Anstrengung konfrontiert wird.

Die Falschbeurkundung des ṣadāq *im Ehevertrag*

Ein weiteres Problem ist für Ägypten die weitverbreitete Praxis der fehlenden oder falschen Beurkundung des *ṣadāq* im Ehevertrag. Da die im Vertrag beurkundete Summe maßgeblich für die fällige Notargebühr ist, ist es üblich, diesen Betrag entweder niedriger zu beurkunden als er tatsächlich geleistet worden ist oder gar keinen exakten Betrag anzugeben. Stattdessen setzen die Parteien in den Vertrag nur das „zwischen den Partnern vereinbarten Brautgeld". Für die Gebührenberechnung wird dann von der Mindestsumme von 25 Piastern ausgegangen. So werden die fälligen Gebühren möglichst klein gehalten.[172] Seltener kommt es vor, dass Familien aus Prestigegründen einen höheren Betrag als den tatsächlich geleisteten angeben, um in der Öffentlichkeit als besonders reich oder freigiebig dazustehen.[173] Dies kann im Falle eines *ṭalāq* zu Streitigkeiten über die tatsächliche Höhe des Brautgelds führen, da nicht die beurkundete, sondern die tatsächlich geleistete Summe die maßgebliche für die Rückabwicklung im Scheidungsfall ist.

Der Gesetzgeber hat dieses Problem in Art. 19 Gesetz 25/1929 gelöst. Hier wird der Ehefrau die Beweislast für die von ihr behauptete Summe auferlegt. Kann sie diesen Beweis nicht erbringen, ist die unter Eid abgegebene Erklärung des Mannes maßgeblich. Von dieser wird nur abgewichen, wenn die Summe das für die Frau „standesgemäße Brautgeld" unterschreitet. Dann legt das Gericht die Summe fest, indem sie die bei anderen Frauen ihres Standes übliche Summe zugrunde legt. Maßstab für die Standesgemäßheit sind dabei die nahen weiblichen Verwandten der Frau. Angeknüpft wird an deren Brautgeldsumme und die Vergleichbarkeit zur Geschiedenen in punkto Alter, Schönheit, Benehmen usw.[174]

Fraglich ist, wie bei *ḫulʿ*-Verfahren mit dem falsch oder gar nicht beurkundeten Brautgeld umgegangen werden soll. In dem offiziellen Gesetzesmemorandum

---

171 So jedenfalls die Auskunft der Frauenrechtlerin Āmāl ʿAbd al-Hādī, Rechtsanwältin und Referentin im Kairoer Center for Women's Legal Assistance (CEWLA), im Interview am 4.11.2002.

172 *Al-Dināṣūrī, I./ʿUkkāz, Ḥ.*, a.a.O., S. 73; *Zawīn, Ḥ.*, a.a.O., S. 74.

173 *Zawīn, Ḥ.*, a.a.O., S. 73.

174 *Al-ʿAǧūz, N.*, a.a.O., S. 380.

zu Art. 20 Gesetz 1/2000 wird vorgeschlagen, den Art. 19 Gesetz 25/1929 auch auf *ḫulʿ*-Verfahren anzuwenden. Diesem Vorschlag folgt die Mehrzahl der Kommentatoren kritiklos.[175] Dafür spricht, dass es keine anderen gesetzlichen Anhaltspunkte zur Problemlösung gibt und dass sich auf diese Weise praktikable Lösungen ergeben können. Dabei wird aber nicht angesprochen, dass sich die Interessenlagen bei den Fällen des *ṭalāq* und des *ḫulʿ* deutlich unterscheiden. Im ersten Fall hat die Frau regelmäßig ein Interesse daran, die Summe möglichst hoch zu veranschlagen, da diese ihr im Scheidungsfall zukommt. Es ist hierbei angemessen, ihr auch das Beweisrisiko aufzubürden und beim Verfehlen des Beweises den in der Regel niedrigeren Vorschlag des verstoßenden Mannes zu folgen bzw. auf einen üblichen standesgemäßen Betrag zurückzugreifen. Beim *ḫulʿ* läuft das Interesse der Frau jedoch genau in die Gegenrichtung: Hier hat sie das Interesse, den Betrag möglichst niedrig zu veranschlagen, während der Mann an einem hohen Betrag interessiert ist, der ihm von der Geschiedenen bezahlt werden muss. Es wäre in diesem Fall weitaus interessengerechter, dem Mann die Beweispflicht aufzuerlegen und im Falle des nicht erbrachten Beweises der beeidigten Erklärung der Frau zu folgen. Immerhin ist es der Mann, der bei Beurkundung des Ehevertrags dafür verantwortlich ist, die Summe anzugeben und vor allem die anfallenden Gebühren zu begleichen. Seine Ersparnis bei Vertragsschluss kommt zwar indirekt auch der mit ihm verheirateten Frau zugute, direkt hilft sie allerdings nur seiner finanziellen Lage. Es wäre daher angemessener, dem Mann für diesen Fall seiner Pflichtverletzung bei Angabe des Betrages und seiner dadurch erhaltenen Ersparnis wenigstens das Beweisrisiko aufzuerlegen.

Das neue Gesetz hat in seinem begleitenden Memorandum (*al-muḏakkira al-īḍāḥīya*) der Frau bei der *ṣadāq*-Rückerstattung eine Erleichterung zugebilligt. Ihr steht offen, das erhaltene Brautgeld, statt direkt dem Ehemann zukommen zu lassen, bis zum Urteil bei der Gerichtskasse zu hinterlegen. Ihre Verpflichtung zur Rückzahlung gilt damit als erfüllt. Der Mann erhält das Hinterlegte erst nach Urteilsverkündung.[176] Diese Regelung kommt der Ehefrau insbesondere zugute, wenn der Mann einen höheren *ṣadāq* fordert als in der Eheurkunde angegeben. Das für die *ḫulʿ*-Klage zuständige Gericht verfügt über keine Kompetenz zur Prüfung des tatsächlichen Brautgeldes und macht daher die Rückzahlung des wirklichen Betrages auch nicht zu einer Voraussetzung für sein Urteil. Entscheidend ist allein, dass die Frau die genannte Summe zurückerstattet, indem sie dem Mann das hinterlegte Brautgeld ab dem Urteilstage zugänglich macht. Dem Mann steht allerdings nun offen, in einem separaten Verfahren vor

---

175 *Naṣṣār, A.*, a.a.O., S.68; *al-ʿAǧūz, N.*, a.a.O., S.379; *al-Dināṣūrī, I./ʿUkkāz, Ḥ.*, a.a.O., S.73.

176 *Al-Dināṣūrī, I./ʿUkkāz, Ḥ.*, a.a.O., S.74.

einem anderen Gericht – hierfür ist nach Art. 9 Abs. 1 Nr. 4 Gesetz 1/2000 das Eingangsgericht für Bagatellsachen zuständig – auf die Rückzahlung des tatsächlichen Betrages zu klagen. In diesem Verfahren wird dann der wahre Betrag nach der in Art. 19 Gesetz 25/1929 genannten Methode ermittelt. Letztlich läuft dies darauf hinaus, dass regelmäßig nicht der tatsächlich vereinbarte Betrag, sondern ein vom Gericht als standesgemäß aufgefasster zurückerstattet wird.[177]

Al-Ǧindī sieht in dieser Regelung des offiziellen Gesetzesmemorandums einen offenen Widerspruch zum Normtext des Art. 20. Dort sei die Rede vom *ṣadāq* und damit könne nur der wirklich an die Frau oder deren Stellvertreter gezahlte, nicht aber ein scheinbarer (*ṣadāq ṣūrī*), also falsch beurkundeter gemeint sein. In dieser Weise versteht er auch die Prophetenüberlieferung der Frau von Ṯābit ibn Qays: So wie in diesem Präzedenzfall das wirkliche Brautgeld erstattet worden sei, müsse es auch in einer *šarīʿa*-konformen Kodifikation geschehen. Seines Erachtens könne das Gericht die *ḫulʿ*-Scheidung daher nur aussprechen, nachdem die Frage des tatsächlichen Brautgeldes geklärt worden ist. Auf diese Weise könne der Vorgang der Ehescheidung zwischen den Partnern ein für alle Mal abgeschlossen werden, ohne dass Folgeprozesse die finanziellen Beziehungen der geschiedenen Partner weiter belasten.

Hierzu ist anzumerken, dass die von al-Ǧindī angebotene Alternative das *ṣadāq*–Problem nicht zu lösen vermag. Egal ob der für den *ḫulʿ* zuständige Richter oder ein nachgeordneter im unabhängigen Verfahren die Prüfung durchführt, wird dieser mit dem Problem der sich widersprechenden Angaben der Partner bezüglich des tatsächlichen Umfangs konfrontiert sein. Wenn die Lösung in der sinngemäßen Anwendung von Art. 19 Gesetz 25/1929 liegt, dann werden beide Richter auf dasselbe Ergebnis kommen: Die rückzuzahlende Summe ist nicht die tatsächlich geleistete, sondern eine gerichtlich fingierte. Al-Ǧindīs Vorschlag würde also keine Änderung bringen, sondern lediglich zur Verlängerung des *ḫulʿ*-Prozesses führen. Dies impliziert eine Erweiterung der richterlichen Aufgabe: Im Gesetz wird sie als moderierend beschrieben, nicht aber als mit einer Brautgeld-Festlegung inhaltlich gestaltend. Außerdem widerspricht eine Verlängerung des Verfahrens dem zweiten Gesetzeszweck: der Ehefrau soll ein verhältnismäßig schneller Weg aus der gescheiterten Ehe garantiert werden.

Der Verzicht auf alle gesetzlichen Finanzansprüche der Ehefrau

Neben der Rückzahlung des *ṣadāq* muss die Ehefrau auf sämtliche finanziellen Ansprüche verzichten, die ihr bei anderen Arten der Scheidung von ihrem Mann zustehen würden (*bi-l-tanāzul ʿan ǧamīʿ ḥuqūqihā al-mālīya al-šarʿīya*). Es sind dies neben dem schon erwähnten gestundeten Brautgeld (*muʾāḫḫar al-ṣadāq*)

---

[177] *Al-Ǧindī, M.*, a.a.O., S. 270; *al-ʿAǧūz, N.*, a.a.O. S. 380.

der Unterhaltsanspruch während der Wartezeit (*nafaqat al-ʿidda*) sowie der Entschädigungsanspruch für den Scheidungsfall (*nafaqat al-mutʿa*).[178] Mit dem Wartezeitunterhalt verliert sie gleichzeitig den Anspruch, während der Wartezeit in der ehelichen Wohnung bleiben zu dürfen.

Nicht Gegenstand des Verzichts dürfen dagegen Rechte sein, die der Frau in Bezug auf ihre Kinder zustehen. So darf die Fürsorge für die Kinder (*ḥaḍāna*) oder ein Besuchsrecht bei diesen, wenn dem Vater die Fürsorge zukommt, oder der Unterhalt für die Kinder nicht Gegenstand ihres Verzichts sein. Grund hierfür ist, dass die Frau nicht als die alleinige Inhaberin dieser Rechte gilt, sondern es sich dabei auch um Rechte der Kinder handelt, die außerhalb der Dispositionsbefugnis der Geschiedenen liegen.[179] Ebenfalls darf die Ehefrau nicht auf die Bereitstellung der Wohnung für die von ihr zu versorgenden Kinder verzichten, zu der der Ehemann als Vater verpflichtet ist. Auf diese Weise kann der geschiedenen Mutter wiederum ein Wohnrecht in den Räumen des Mannes zukommen, der ihr so einen Teil des durch das *ḫulʿ*-Begehren verwirkten Rechtes zurückerbringt.[180]

Obwohl die Frau mit Rückgabe des erhaltenen Brautgeldes und dem Verzicht auf ihre finanziellen Rechte häufig ihre gesamte finanzielle Grundlage aufgibt, um von ihrem Mann loszukommen, ist für einige Kritiker dieses Opfer noch nicht groß genug. So fordert eine im wesentlichen aus Azhar-Angehörigen bestehende Gelehrtengruppe der Akademie für islamische Studien in einem Appell an Präsident Mubārak, dass auch die *ḥaḍāna* für gemeinsame Kinder zulässiges Verzichtsobjekt sein müsse, da sonst der Vater unbillig überlastet ist: Er habe u.U. jahrzehntelang für Frau und Kinder gesorgt und verliere jetzt alles. Wenigstens die Kinder sollten ihm bleiben.[181]

Eine noch weiter gehende Position nimmt al-ʿAǧūz ein, die fordert, dass dem verlassenen Ehemann je nach den Umständen neben den schon erhaltenen Leistungen noch eine zusätzliche Entschädigung zukommen müsse. Sie begründet dies mit dem Verweis auf die *šarīʿa*, nach der das ägyptische Gesetz wegen der fehlenden Einverständnis-Voraussetzung durch den Ehemann nicht wirklich als Regelung des *ḫulʿ* gelten könne, sondern eher einem speziellen Fall des *taṭlīq li-l-ḍarar* darstelle. Es handele sich um einen *ḍarar*-Fall unter „umgekehrten Vorzeichen“: Nicht die Frau sei die Geschädigte, sondern der Mann, der nach vielen Jahren einer glücklichen Ehe von seiner Frau kurzfristig gegen seinen Willen geschieden werden könne. Er erleide dadurch einen

---

178 *Al-Dināṣūrī, I./ʿUkkāz, Ḥ.*, a.a.O., S. 73; *Naṣṣār, A.*, a.a.O., S. 69.

179 Siehe zum Ganzen Art. Ḥaḍāna (*de Bellefonds, Y.*). In: EI, Bd. 3, S. 16f.

180 *Al-ʿAǧūz, N.*, a.a.O., S. 377f; *Naṣṣār, A.*, a.a.O. S. 68. *Zawīn, Ḥ.*, a.a.O., S. 86, führt eine Gegenmeinung auf, nach der der Geschiedenen in keinem Fall ein Wohnrecht zusteht. Sie müsste dann getrennt von den Kindern leben.

181 Der Appell ist wiedergegeben in al-Ahrām, 28.1.2000.

beträchtlichen persönlichen Schaden immaterieller Art, da er zum einen mit einem ehrenrührigen Prestigeverlust in der Öffentlichkeit zu leben habe und zum anderen seine Chance, eine neue Frau zu finden, aufgrund seines mitunter fortgeschrittenen Alters sehr gering geworden sei. Da diese Interessenlage in etwa der der – sei es durch *ṭalāq* oder durch *taṭlīq li-l-ḍarar* – verstoßenen Frau entspräche, die ihrerseits mit dem *nafaqat al-mutʿa* einen Entschädigungsanspruch gegen den Ehemann habe, müsse diesem im umgekehrten Fall ein ähnlicher Anspruch zustehen. Al-ʿAǧūz beruft sich dabei auch auf den verfassungsmäßigen Gleichbehandlungsgrundsatz (Art. 40 Verfassung) und sieht als Rechtsgrundlage für diesen Anspruch den allgemeinen Schadensersatzanspruch des Art. 163 des Zivilgesetzbuches (*al-qānūn al-madanī*): „Jedes Fehlverhalten, das bei einem anderen einen Schaden verursacht, verpflichtet den Schädiger zum Ersatz." Da nach der ägyptischen Rechtssprechung hiervon auch immaterieller Schaden umfasst ist, gelte diese Norm auch für den Fall des schuldlos verlassenen Ehemanns. Hier sei die Frau eines Fehlverhaltens schuldig und daher ersatzpflichtig.[182]

In der Tat spricht al-ʿAǧūz hier mit der Ungleichbehandlung der Geschlechter ein echtes Problem an. Das Familien- und Scheidungsrecht ist von dieser Ungleichheit durch und durch geprägt. Die Einführung eines relativ freien Scheidungsrechtes für die Frau ist eine teilweise Durchbrechung dieser Ungleichheit, durch die ein gewisses Gleichgewicht im System gestört wird. Dieses beruhte darauf, dass nur der Mann seine Frau scheiden kann, er dafür aber einen mitunter schmerzhaften Betrag zu leisten hatte. Dies entspricht einem der wichtigsten Grundsätze des islamischen Rechts, dem Gerechtigkeitsgrundsprinzip: „*lā ḍarar wa lā ḍirār*" („keine Schädigung ohne Gegenschädigung"). Nach diesem Grundsatz, der auf dem Talionsprinzip beruht, trifft den Schädiger eine Ausgleichspflicht. Wenn der Mann der Frau einen Schaden durch die Verstoßung zufügt, hat er diesen durch eine Gegenleistung wieder auszugleichen. Umgekehrt gilt das gleiche: Nach der *šarīʿa*-Konzeption hat die Frau für den ihrem Mann durch das Verlassen zugefügten Schaden auf alle ihre finanziellen Rechte zu verzichten. Die Mehrzahl der Kommentatoren, die den Gerechtigkeitsgrundsatz zitieren, sieht diesen Grundsatz durch die Rückgabe und den Verzicht erfüllt. Dafür dass die Frau von ihrem Mann loskommt, wickeln die Partner alle entstandenen finanziellen Ansprüche ab – neue Ansprüche sollen hingegen gerade nicht entstehen. Beim *ṭalāq* ist diese Konstellation anders: Durch die Verstoßung bringt der Mann der Frau neben immateriellen auch materiellen Schaden. Ihre Versorgungslage wird von einem Augenblick zum nächsten ungewiss, da ihre ehelichen Ansprüche beendigt werden. Es sind in erster Linie diese Ansprüche einschließlich der daraus

[182] *Al-ʿAǧūz, N.*, a.a.O., S. 383ff.

folgenden psychischen Situation, die durch die *mutᶜa*-Entschädigung ausgeglichen werden. Es besteht daher m.E. kein Grund von der Lösung der Rechtsschulen abzuweichen: Die von der Frau erbrachten Leistungen reichen aus, um dem Gerechtigkeitsgrundsatz Genüge zu tragen.
Im Übrigen hantiert al-ᶜAǧūz mit den juristisch schwer handhabbaren Kategorien von Verantwortung und Schuld. Menschliche Beziehungen, die scheitern, lassen sich in den seltensten Fällen auf eine einfache Schuldzuweisung reduzieren. Eine alleinige Ursache für das Scheitern ist selten zu finden, denn meist geht dem schädigenden Ereignis ein ebensolches voraus, das es provoziert. So ist eine Ehefrau, die das Leben mit ihrem Mann ohne Schädigung durch diesen leid hat, immer im Zusammenspiel mit dem Partner zu dieser Auffassung gelangt. Das langfristige Auseinanderleben ist mitverursacht durch Kommunikationsblockaden, die auf beiden Seiten verortet werden können. Die Aufgabe, hier Schuld für eheliches Scheitern zu finden, ist daher unsachgemäß und überfordert regelmäßig die Gerichte.[183] Auch daher ist es unbillig, den Frauen zusätzlich zu ihrem Verzicht und der Brautgeldrückerstattung noch eine weitere Entschädigungspflicht aufzulegen.

„Scheidungen nur für reiche Mädchen" – Rechtliche und wirtschaftliche Gleichheit

Ein weiterer Kritikpunkt, der nicht nur al-ᶜAǧūz' Position der zusätzlichen Entschädigung, sondern das gesamte System des finanziellen Ausgleichs beim *ḫulᶜ* in Frage stellt, besteht darin, dass die Regelung des Art. 20 von der Frau während der Ehe erbrachte Leistungen völlig außer acht lässt. Durch Hausarbeit oder die Sorge um die Kindererziehung hat sie Leistungen für die Familie wie für ihren Ehemann erbracht, die bei der Auseinandersetzung nicht berücksichtigt werden. Durch die Widmung ihrer Zeit für die Familie hat sie Erwerbs- und Bildungschancen vorbeiziehen lassen, die sie nun, nach Beendigung der Ehe von einer qualifizierten Berufsausübung abhalten. Gelegentlich – und in der modernen Zeit immer häufiger – sind Ehefrauen auch einer Erwerbstätigkeit nachgegangen, deren Lohn in den Unterhalt der Familie geflossen ist. Diese Gelder werden ebenso wenig berücksichtigt wie etwaige Aufwendungen, die die Frau mit ihrem Privatvermögen, z.B. aus *ṣadāq* oder *šabka*, getätigt hat.[184] Damit hat sie, in den islamrechtlichen Kategorien der Geschlechterdifferenzierung ausgedrückt, Leistungen erbracht, die eigentlich in der Verantwortungssphäre des Mannes liegen. Dieser ist für den Familienunterhalt

---

[183] Auf diesen Zusammenhang macht auch *Nassar, N.*, a.a.O., S. 198f, aufmerksam.

[184] *El Alami, D.*, Remedy of Device? The System of Khulᶜ and Effects of its Incorporation into Egyptian Personal Status Law. In: Yearbook of Islamic and Middle Eastern Law 6 (1999-2000), S. 134-139 (139).

zuständig, den er teilweise von der Gattin hat bestreiten lassen. Nun ist die Frau aber trotzdem verpflichtet, alles von ihm bei Beginn der Ehe Erhaltene zurückzuerstatten, unabhängig davon, ob sie dieses Vermögen überhaupt noch besitzt oder ob sie während der Ehe anderes Vermögen erwirtschaftet hat, aus dem sie das eheliche Leben bestritten und mit dem sie ihrem Mann mitversorgt hat. U.U. hat der Mann somit mehrmals von dem Vermögen der Frau profitiert und lässt sich am Ende noch einmal auf ihre Kosten auszahlen.

Das Gesetz 1/2000 trägt dieser Konstellation keine Rechnung. Eine scheidungswillige Frau hat große finanzielle Opfer zu bringen, die sie häufig an den Rand des finanziellen Ruins führen werden. Zwar kann dies auch bei einem scheidungswilligen Mann passieren, doch kommt ihm in der patriarchalischen Gesellschaft Ägyptens die einfachere Möglichkeit zu wirtschaftlicher Betätigung zur Erfüllung seiner Verpflichtungen zu.

Die Konsequenz hiervon lässt sich auf den Punkt bringen: Das gesetzliche Scheidungsrecht für die Frau ist nur ein solches für die wohlhabende Frau. Nur diejenige, die über genug eigene finanzielle Potenz verfügt oder die Möglichkeit hat, zur eigenen wirtschaftlich ausreichend versorgten Familie zurückzukehren, kann praktisch von dem neu hinzugekommenen Recht profitieren. Frauen ohne diesen Rückhalt werden durch die *ḫulʿ*-Scheidung völlig mittellos. So ist das Gesetz auch in der Öffentlichkeit teilweise als Recht für eine begrenzte Elite von Frauen angesehen worden.[185] Teilweise wird hierin auch wegen der Verletzung des Gleichheitsgebots ein Verfassungsverstoß gesehen, weil die ärmeren Schichten faktisch benachteiligt werden.[186] Dagegen wird eingewandt, dass in den verschiedenen sozialen Schichten auch entsprechende unterschiedliche Beträge als Brautgeld üblich wären und deshalb ärmere Frauen auch nur relativ kleine Beträge zurückgeben müssten. Von einer Ungleichbehandlung könne daher keine Rede sein.[187]

Letzteres Argument scheint mir geeignet, den Vorwurf der rechtlichen Ungleichbehandlung zu entkräften; es gehört zu den Grunderfahrungen menschlichen Lebens, dass wohlhabende Menschen oft mehr Chancen zur Lebensgestaltung haben. Rechtliche Gleichheit kann soziale Ungleichheit nicht völlig ausgleichen. Auf sozialer Ebene aber bleibt der Vorwurf erhalten: Frauen aus den unteren Schichten müssen im Verhältnis erheblich größere Opfer bringen, indem sie ihre eigene Grundversorgung aufs Spiel setzen. Dies sollte dem Gesetzgeber zu denken geben. Möglicherweise soll dies aber auch eine für den Gesetzgeber willkommene Bremse für die Praxis sein: die Scheidungs-

---

185 So z.B. die Überschrift in al-Ǧumhūrīya, 12.1.2000: „*al-ḫulʿ li-banāt al-ḏawāt faqaṭ.*"

186 So ʿAli Fahmī in al-Ǧumhūrīya, 20.1.2000.

187 Fauzīya ʿAbd al-Sattār in al-Ǧumhūrīya, 20.1.2000; so auch ʿĀʾiša Rātib, zit. in: *al-ʿAǧūz, N.*, a.a.O., S. 54.

zahlen wegen *ḫulʿ* bleiben auf diese Weise niedrig – das Leid der betroffenen Frauen jedoch auch entsprechend hoch.

Das Fehlen von Schutzmechanismen gegen den Missbrauch des ḫulʿ *zu Lasten der Frau*

Weder das Gesetz noch das Gesetzesmemorandum erwähnen ein Mittel gegen den möglichen Missbrauch der *ḫulʿ*-Scheidung. Der Ehemann kann, wenn er sich von seiner Frau trennen will, aber die finanziellen Folgen des *ṭalāq* nicht tragen will, die Frau dazu treiben, von sich aus die *ḫulʿ*-Klage zu erheben. Er kann dazu Schädigungshandlungen benutzen, die unterhalb der Schwelle des gesetzlichen *ḍarar* liegen, bei dessen Vorliegen der Frau ein gerichtliches Scheidungsurteil wegen *taṭlīq li-l-ḍarar* zustehen würde.
In den Rechtsschulen wurde dieses Problem erkannt und mit einer negativen moralischen Wertung versehen, für die jenseitige Bestrafung angedroht ist. Der *ḫulʿ* sollte in einem solchen Fall vom Mann nicht benutzt werden. Diese Wertung ist bei den Hanafiten mit der Rechtsfolge verbunden worden, dass der vereinbarte *ḫulʿ* unwirksam wird und die Ehe als weiter gültig gilt. In anderen Schulen gilt die vereinbarte Scheidung weiter als gültig, jedoch wird sie nicht mehr als *ḫulʿ*, sondern als *ṭalāq raǧʿī* angesehen. Die Frau hatte dann einen Anspruch auf Rückzahlung der geleisteten Zahlung, und die Scheidung sollte als normale Verstoßung gelten.
Diese Wertung ist in das neue Gesetz nicht aufgenommen worden. Es ist nicht anzunehmen, dass der Gesetzgeber die Fortgeltung der hanafitischen Rechtsschule gewollt hat, da in Art. 20 ansonsten besonders betont wird, dass der *ḫulʿ* endgültige Wirkungen herbeiführen soll. Somit müsste auch der auf diese Weise missbräuchlich herbeigeführte *ḫulʿ* gültig bleiben, ohne dass die Geschiedene eine Möglichkeit hätte, die Summe zurückzufordern.
Der ägyptische Gesetzgeber hätte diesen Fall regeln können, indem er bei nachträglich festgestellter Schädigung eine Überprüfung des Urteils samt Umstellung der finanziellen Folgen vorgesehen hätte.

Zusammenfassung: Die finanziellen Folgen des ḫulʿ *nach Art. 20*

Zusammengefasst lassen sich bei dem Punkt der finanziellen Verpflichtungen der zur *ḫulʿ*-Scheidung entschlossen Ehefrau einige Mängel im Gesetz konstatieren: Der unzureichend definierte Begriff des *ṣadāq* kann zu Rechtsunsicherheiten bei der praktischen Ausführung führen. Ebenso ist die Regelung bei nicht ausreichend beurkundeten Brautgeldsummen nicht für eine interessengerechte Feststellung der zahlbaren Summe geeignet. Es dominiert die Aussage des Mannes, der von einer höher angesetzten Summe profitiert. Daneben ignoriert das Gesetz völlig die von der Frau während der Ehe erbrachten Leistungen: Weder Dienst- noch Sachleistungen werden in angemessener Weise bei der Festlegung ihrer Verpflichtungen berücksichtigt. Die hohe Belastung für die Frau droht zu einer Reduzierung des neuen Rechts auf reichere Schichten zu führen. Außerdem scheint eine missbräuchliche Ausübung durch den Ehemann, der die für ihn hohen Kosten einer *ṭalāq*-Verstoßung umgehen will, vorprogrammiert.

Aus diesem Grund besteht für den Gesetzgeber Handlungsbedarf, die offenen Punkte in erläuternden Verordnungen näher zu fixieren. Die in sonstigen Rechtsgebieten zur Verfügung stehende Fixierung offener Rechtsbegriffe und -verfahren durch höherrangige Gerichte steht dem System wegen des Rechtswegausschlusses nicht zu. Somit ist der Gesetzgeber bzw. die von diesem dazu ermächtigte Regierung berufen, die Lücken zu füllen. Nur so lassen sich die notwendigen gerechten Lösungen für die beteiligten Frauen erreichen.

Das Schlichtungsverfahren unter Leitung des Gerichts

Art. 20 Gesetz 1/2000 sieht im *ḫulʿ*-Prozess ein vom Gericht beaufsichtigtes Versöhnungsverfahren vor. Durch den Verweis auf Art. 19 und 20 wird das *ḫulʿ*-Prozedere der Schlichtung durch Gericht und private Schiedsrichter anderen familienrechtlichen Verfahren gleichgestellt. Die Schlichtung zwischen den Partnern ist z.B. auch im Beurkundungsverfahren bei der *ṭalāq*-Verstoßung nach Art. 21 und im *taṭlīq li-l-ḍarar*-Verfahren vorgeschrieben. Bei letzterem gelten zusätzlich auch die speziellen Vorschriften der Art. 6 und 11 des Gesetz 25/1929.

Bei dem Schlichtungsverfahren im *ḫulʿ*-Prozess handelt es sich um einen zweiphasigen Vorgang. In der ersten Phase wird gemäß Art. 18 das angerufene Gericht verpflichtet, selber auf die Versöhnung zwischen den Partnern hinzuwirken. Diese sollen zur Fortsetzung der Ehe ermahnt werden und über die negativen Folgen der Scheidung aufgeklärt werden. In der Kommentierung wird oft betont, dass gerade beim *ḫulʿ* die Schlichtungsversuche von besonderer Bedeutung sind, da der Grund hier in der individuellen Einstellung der Frau liegt, die – so wird allgemein angenommen – besonders abhängig von ihrem psychologischen Zustand sei und zur emotionalen Schwankung neige.[188]

In der ersten Phase des Schlichtungsversuchs hat das Gericht „sich um die Versöhnung zu bemühen“ (*tabḏul al-maḥkama ǧuhdan fī muḥāwalat al-ṣulḥ*). Dieses „sich mühen“ ist in der Rechtssprechung des Kassationsgerichtshofs zur Schlichtung in *taṭlīq li-l-ḍarar*-Verfahren genauer definiert worden. Danach reicht es nicht, dass das Gericht die Partner nur „pro forma“ zur Versöhnung auffordert und es bei der bloßen Aufforderung belässt. Vielmehr muss es tatsächlich mit Vorschlägen und einer umfassenden Aufklärung über die Folgen der Scheidung auf die Verständigung der Partner hinwirken. Diese Bemühungen

---

[188] *Naṣṣār, A.*, a.a.O., S. 70.

müssen im Sitzungsprotokoll festgehalten und im Urteil als durchgeführt vermerkt werden.[189]

Art. 18 Abs. 2 sieht eine mindestens einmalige Wiederholung der gerichtlichen Schlichtungsbemühungen vor, wenn aus der Ehe Kinder hervorgegangen sind. Zwischen den Versöhnungsversuchen müssen mindestens 30 und höchstens 60 Tage liegen. Damit bekommen die Beteiligten die Möglichkeit, ihre Position zu überdenken, ohne dass das Verfahren über das notwendige Maß hinaus in die Länge gezogen wird. Aus dieser Bestimmung zeigt sich das leitende Interesse des Gesetzgebers, das dieser auch in dem Gesetzesmemorandum angibt: Ihm geht es um die Erhaltung der bestehenden Familie.[190]

Nach dem Scheitern der gerichtlichen Versuche kommt das Versöhnungsverfahren in seine zweite Phase. In dieser werden gemäß Art. 20 Abs. 2 in Verbindung mit Art. 19 durch das Gericht zwei Schiedsrichter oder Schlichter ernannt, die aus den Familien der beiden Gatten stammen sollen. Finden sich keine geeigneten Schlichter in den Familien, ernennt das Gericht geeignete Personen, die sich aus dem öffentlichen Leben im Umfeld der Ehepartner rekrutieren können, wie z.B. örtliche Verwaltungsbeamte oder den Bürgermeister des Dorfes.[191] Auch die beiden Schiedsrichter haben nun die Aufgabe, auf eine Verständigung zwischen den Gatten hinzuwirken, die auch in der Herstellung der einvernehmlichen Trennung liegen kann. In der ihrer Ernennung folgenden Sitzung haben sie dem Gericht mitzuteilen, ob ihr Versöhnungsversuch von Erfolg gekrönt war oder nicht. Durch die Ernennung von Verwandten als Schlichter sollen Personen für die Schlichtung gewonnen werden, die die Partner gut kennen und mit den Problemen der beiden vertraut sind. Außerdem sollen die Probleme innerhalb des Familienbundes gelöst werden.[192]

Art. 19 enthält in seinen Abs. 3 im Vergleich zum Schlichtungsverfahren bei *ḍarar*-Scheidungen eine gewisse Schwächung der Schlichterposition. Danach kann das Gericht den Vorschlag der Vermittler übernehmen. Es steht ihm aber ebenso frei, den Vorschlag zu verwerfen und nach Lage der Prozessakten in eigenem Ermessen zu entscheiden. Die Stellung der Schlichter im Verfahren des *taṭlīq li-l-ḍarar* nach Art. 6 und 11 des Gesetz 25/1929 ist insoweit weitgehender: Hier ist das Gericht an den Vorschlag der Schlichter gebunden.[193] Allerdings ist zu bemerken, dass Art. 19 Abs. 3 für das *ḫulᶜ*-Verfahren keine Bedeutung hat, da den Schlichtern hier keine Aufgabe über die Herstellung der

---

189 *Al-Dināṣūrī, I./ᶜUkkāz, Ḥ.*, a.a.O., S. 67; *Naṣṣār, A.*, a.a.O., S. 70.

190 Gesetzesmemorandum zitiert in *al-Dināṣūrī, I./ᶜUkkāz, Ḥ.*, a.a.O., S. 68.

191 So die Auskunft des Justizministers während der Parlamentsdebatte, in: *al-Dināṣūrī, I./ᶜUkkāz, Ḥ.*, a.a.O., S. 69.

192 *Al-Fiqī, U.*, a.a.O., S. 63.

193 *Al-Dināṣūrī, I./ᶜUkkāz, Ḥ.*, a.a.O., S. 70.

Versöhnung hinaus zukommt. Insbesondere obliegt es ihnen nicht, irgendwelche Verantwortlichkeiten für das Scheitern der Ehe auszumachen, nach denen dann die finanziellen Folgen der Scheidung zu bemessen sind. Während dies die wichtigste Funktion der Schlichter nach malikitischer Tradition wie nach ägyptischen Gesetz zur *ḍarar*-Scheidung war, fällt die Aufteilung von finanziellen Lasten beim *ḫulʿ* gerade weg, da es hier keine gegenseitigen nachehelichen Verpflichtungen mehr geben soll. Außerdem hat das Gericht bei seiner Entscheidung keinen Spielraum, sondern vergewissert sich nur, dass das Verfahren ordnungsgemäß durchgeführt wurde, um dann mit der Entscheidung auf unwiderrufliche Scheidung gebunden zu sein.

Wird das Versöhnungsverfahren nicht ordnungsgemäß durchgeführt, hat dies der Rechtssprechung des Kassationsgerichtshofs zufolge zumindest bei den Fällen des *taṭlīq li-l-ḍarar* die Nichtigkeit des Urteils zur Folge. Dabei ist in der Rechtslehre umstritten und vom Gericht offen gelassen, ob es sich dabei um eine absolute (*buṭlān muṭlaq*) oder relative Nichtigkeit (*buṭlān nasbī*) handelt. Al-Dināṣūrī/ʿUkkāz schlagen eine Differenzierung vor, je nachdem, ob das Gericht wenigstens einmal den Versuch ausgeführt hat. Hat das Gericht lediglich versäumt, das Verfahren zu wiederholen, sprechen al-Dināṣūrī/ʿUkkāz von relativer Nichtigkeit, die durch spätere Nachholung heilbar ist. Hat überhaupt kein solcher Versuch stattgefunden, ist dagegen von nicht heilbarer absoluter Nichtigkeit auszugehen, da das zu schützende Rechtsgut des Bestands der Familie ein so überragendes Gut darstelle.[194]

Fraglich ist, wie diese Überlegungen bezüglich anderer Scheidungsklagen, bei denen Rechtsmittel gegeben sind, auf *ḫulʿ*-Verfahren übertragbar sind. Es stellt sich beim *ḫulʿ* nämlich das Problem des Rechtswegausschlusses. Es ist keine Instanz ersichtlich, die die Nichtigkeit eines *ḫulʿ*-Urteils feststellen könnte.

Zu dem gesamten Komplex des Schlichtungsversuchs bei der *ḫulʿ*-Klage ist anzumerken, dass es sich um ein langwieriges und für die Gerichte arbeitsaufwendiges Verfahren handelt. Durch die Wiederholung des gerichtlichen Schlichtungsversuchs wie durch die Sitzung mit den benannten Schlichtern kommen auf die Gerichte mindestens drei Termine zu, um eine Ehe zu scheiden. Wenn man bedenkt, dass im Regelfall die Ehen schon vor dem ersten Gerichtstermin als endgültig gescheitert angesehen werden können und die Ehefrau sich nach einem zumeist längeren Denkprozess zur Scheidung entschlossen hat, ist den Schlichtungsversuchen eine relativ kleine Erfolgschance zuzutrauen. Diese geringe Erfolgschance wird im übrigen wohl von der Praxis bestätigt: es sind keine Fälle bekannt, in denen durch die Schlichtung eine Trennung abgewendet werden konnte.[195] Daneben ist die im

---

194 *Al-Dināṣūrī, I./ʿUkkāz, Ḥ.*, a.a.O., S. 68.

195 So jedenfalls die Auskunft von Āmāl ʿAbd al-Hādī, im Interview am 4.11.2002.

Vergleich zum *taṭlīq li-l-ḍarar*-Verfahren beschränkte Funktion der Schiedsrichter zu beachten. Ihnen kommt nicht zu, die Ursprünge und Verantwortlichkeiten des ehelichen Scheiterns zu begutachten und Ausgleichsquoten festzusetzen. Diese Aufgabe der Schiedsrichter erfordert sicherlich mehr Zeit als der bloße Versuch zur Versöhnung. Für diese Klageart ist das aufwendige Verfahren eher angemessen als für die *ḫulʿ*-Scheidung.
Es wurde dem gesamten *ḫulʿ*-Verfahren mit den womöglich häufig folgenden Brautgeldfestlegungsklagen vor einem anderen Gericht und insbesondere dem Schlichtungsverfahren prophezeit, an der Überbelastung der Gerichte zu scheitern.[196] Möglicherweise wurde durch die kurzfristig erweiterte Schlichtungsregelung im Gesetz auch versäumt, die gerichtlichen Voraussetzungen zu deren Durchführung zu schaffen. M.E. ist es daher fragwürdig, den Partnern ein solch langwieriges Verfahren mit derart geringen Erfolgsaussichten zuzumuten. Ein verkürztes Verfahren, in dem das Gericht einmal über die Folgen der Scheidung aufklärt, sollte dagegen ausreichend sein, um den Zweck des Verfahrens zu erreichen.

Die eindeutige Erklärung der Ehefrau zum Scheitern der Ehe
Nach erfolgloser Durchführung der Schlichtung folgt als letzte Voraussetzung für das richterliche Urteil die Erklärung der Ehefrau zum Scheitern der Ehe. Dabei muss ihre Erklärung eindeutig und unmissverständlich abgegeben werden, und sie muss die gesetzlich genannten Gründe angeben, ohne diese allerdings genauer spezifizieren zu müssen. Sie muss also die Punkte noch einmal angeben, die sie schon in der Klageschrift genannt haben kann.[197]
Durch die Wiederholung ihrer Scheidungsgründe nach Durchführung des Versöhnungsverfahrens soll dem Gericht versichert werden, dass sie trotz aller Aufklärung über die Folgen einer Scheidung und trotz aller Versuche der Wiederherstellung des Familienfriedens nicht in der Lage ist, die Ehe fortzuführen.
Die Erklärung der Ehefrau muss gemäß Art. 20 Abs. 2 letzter Halbsatz drei Elemente enthalten: Sie muss eindeutig erklären (*tuqarrir al-zauǧa ṣarāḥatan*), dass ihr das Leben mit dem Partner zuwider ist (*tabġaḍu al-ḥayāt maʿ zauǧihā*) und es keinen Weg zur Fortsetzung des ehelichen Lebens gibt (*lā sabīl li-istimrār al-ḥayāt al-zauǧīya*). Schließlich muss sie angegeben, dass sie befürchtet, die Gebote Gottes aus diesem Grund nicht einhalten zu können (*taḫšā allā tuqīma ḥudūd Allāh bi-sabab hāḏā al-buġḍ*). Wie schon festgestellt handelt es sich um allgemeine Aussagen, die die Frau nicht zu konkretisieren braucht. Insofern interessiert es das Gericht auch nicht näher, welcher Art z.B.

196 ʿAbd al-ʿAzīz Muḥammad zitiert in al-Ahrām, 30.1.2000.
197 *Al-Dināṣūrī, I./ʿUkkāz, Ḥ.*, a.a.O., S. 74

die Gebote sind, gegen die die Frau zu verstoßen vermeiden will oder ob sie überhaupt „religiöse" Gründe für ihr Begehren hat. Mit dem Bezug auf die „Gebote Gottes" hat der Gesetzgeber ein Merkmal eingeführt, das schon Koran Sure 2, 229 enthält, wo die Trennung in diesem Fall für zulässig gehalten wird. Obwohl das Gesetz die eindeutige und unzweideutige Erklärung der Ehefrau erfordert, schließt es eine Stellvertretung bei dieser Aussage nicht aus. Auch der Prozessvertreter oder ein Dritter können die Erklärung an ihrer statt abgeben.[198] Offensichtlich haben einige zuständige Richter dieses Tatbestandsmerkmal insofern spezifischer verstanden, als dass sie das persönliche Erscheinen der Ehefrau vor Gericht zur Abgabe ihrer Erklärung verlangten und das Urteil verweigerten, solange diese nicht erscheint.[199] Diese Auslegung ist nicht abwegig, wenn man den Zweck der Erklärung bedenkt: Das Gericht will sich noch einmal vergewissern, ob die Scheidungsabsicht der Frau trotz des hohen Aufwands für die Versöhnung noch immer besteht. Diese Vergewisserung kann bei persönlichem Erscheinen noch sicherer erfolgen. Allerdings besteht aufgrund des gesetzlichen Wortlautes und des Fehlens ergänzender Bemerkungen im Gesetzesmemorandum kein Anlass zur Abweichung von den üblichen Prinzipien des ägyptischen Verfahrensrechts, das die Zulässigkeit anwaltlicher Prozessvertretung grundsätzlich erlaubt.

Das gerichtliche Urteil und die Wirkung der *ḫul*ʿ-Scheidung

Liegen die beschriebenen Voraussetzungen vor, hat das Gericht das begehrte Urteil zu erlassen und die eheliche Verbindung zwischen den Partnern zu beenden. Es hat bei seiner Entscheidung keinerlei Spielraum und beschränkt sich bei der Abfassung des Urteils auf die Protokollierung der durchgeführten Prozesshandlungen. Es hat insbesondere festzuhalten, ob der finanzielle Verzicht und die Rückgabe des Brautgeldes stattgefunden haben. Dabei ist es offenbar übliche Praxis, keinen Betrag im Urteil aufzunehmen, sondern lediglich zu notieren, dass Verzicht und Rückgabe stattgefunden haben.[200] Auch darf das Urteil nicht unter Bedingungen erlassen werden. So ist ein Urteil unzulässig, nach dem die Partner geschieden werden, sobald die Frau die geschuldeten Leistungen erbracht hat.[201]

---

198 *Naṣṣār, A.*, a.a.O., S. 72.

199 So berichten *Sulaymān, ʿA./Ṣalāḥ, ʿA.*, al-Ḫulʿ qānūnan wa taṭbīqan. In: *al-Ṣāwī, A.*, a.a.O., S. 13-28 (18), für einige Prozesse vor den Gerichten in Kairo.

200 So die Auskunft des Rechtsanwalts Fuʾād Rušdī Mīḫāʾīl im Interview am 18.10.2002. Dagegen sieht der mir vorliegende Formularvorschlag für ein *ḫul*ʿ-Urteil bei *al-Fiqī, U.*, a.a.O., S. 68ff, die Nennung eines konkreten Betrages vor; al-*Fiqī, U.*, S. 65, hält es für die ausdrückliche Pflicht des Gerichts, den Betrag festzusetzen. Von dieser Pflicht ist bei den anderen mir vorliegenden Autoren dagegen keine Rede.

201 *Al-Dināṣūrī, I./ʿUkkāz, Ḥ.*, a.a.O., S. 74.

Die Wirkung des so ergangenen Scheidungsurteils ist die der unwiderruflichen Scheidung (*ṭalāq bāʾin*). Durch den *ḫulʿ* sollen endgültige Verhältnisse geschaffen werden, so dass es sich von selbst versteht, dass der Mann keine Möglichkeit zur Rücknahme der Scheidung hat, um das ehelichen Leben fortzusetzen. Wie bei der regulären Verstoßung tritt bezüglich der Wiederheiratsmöglichkeit der beiden Partner die Unwiderruflichkeit im kleinen Grad (*bāʾin baynūna ṣuġrā*) ein, so dass eine Wiederheirat mit einem neuen Ehevertrag möglich ist. Dies ist nur in dem Fall anders, in welchem dem *ḫulʿ* bereits eine zweifache *ṭalāq*-Erklärung vorangegangen ist. Hier ist die Unwiderruflichkeit im großen Grad (*bāʾin baynūna kubrā*) gegeben, bei der die Partner nur wieder heiraten dürfen, wenn die Frau davor mit einem anderen Mann wirksam verheiratet und geschieden gewesen ist (sog. *taḥlīl*).[202]
Das Gesetz lässt die in den Rechtsschulen unterschiedlich beantwortete Frage nach der rechtlichen Kategorisierung des *ḫulʿ* als Unterfall des *ṭalāq* oder des *fasḫ* genauso offen wie die Frage nach der Länge der Wartezeit. Es haben sich in der Debatte zu beiden Fragen verschiedene Stimmen zu Wort gemeldet, die die abweichenden Positionen der Rechtsschulen aufgriffen.[203] Letztlich ist bei diesen Fragen die Antwort in Art. 3 Einführungsgesetz zu finden, der bei gesetzlich nicht geklärten Fragen auf die hanafitische Rechtsschule verweist. Nach dieser wird der *ḫulʿ* als *ṭalāq*-Fall klassifiziert – hierzu passt im übrigen die im vorherigen Abschnitt erläuterten differenzierten Folgen der Unwiderruflichkeitsgrade – und die Wartezeit mit drei Monaten angegeben. Außerdem spricht hierfür, dass der ägyptischen Gesetzgeber den *ḫulʿ* als *taṭlīq* bezeichnet und behandelt. Damit eingeschlossen ist auch die Wartezeit, die in bei den übrigen Verfahren ebenfalls drei Monate beträgt.[204]

Der Ausschluss des Rechtswegs

In Art. 20 Abs. 5 enthält das neue Gesetz eine Regelung zum Rechtswegausschluss, nach der bei erfolgtem *ḫulʿ*-Urteil jede Überprüfung durch höher-instanzliche Gerichte ausgeschlossen ist (*yakūn al-ḫulʿ – fī ǧamīʿ al-aḥwāl – ġayr qābil li-l-ṭaʿn*). Das ägyptische Rechtssystem kennt als Rechtsmittel gegen ein Urteil die Berufung (*ʾistiʾnāf*), die Revision (*naqd*) sowie das

---

202 *Al-ʿAǧūz, N.*, a.a.O., S. 380f.

203 So z.B. Šauqī al-Sayyid, al-Ahrām vom 20.1.2000, und ʿAṭīya ʿAbd al-Wuǧūb, al-Ǧumhūrīya, 20.1.2000, die für die Klassifizierung als *fasḫ* eintreten.

204 Al-Ǧindī, M., fügt in al-Ǧumhūrīya vom 17.1.2000 außerdem an, dass ein Hauptzweck der Wartezeit, nämlich die Sicherstellung von Kindesabstammungen, nur mit der längeren Wartezeit von drei Monaten garantiert werden kann. Dagegen wird angeführt, dass der zweite Zweck, nämlich die Selbstprüfungsfrist für den verstoßenden Mann gerade nicht relevant sei, da ihm die Möglichkeit der Rücknahme nicht zukommt. Dies spräche für die kürzere Frist von einem Monat, wiedergegeben z.B. im gleichen Artikel vom 17.1.2000.

Wiederaufnahmeverfahren (*iltimās iʿādat al-naẓar*).[205] Alle diese Instrumente werden unter dem Sammelbegriff des *ṭaʿn* zusammengefasst. Der Rechtmittelausschluss stellt für den Bereich des Personalstatusrecht und besonders des Scheidungsrechts ein Novum dar: Alle anderen in diesen Bereichen ergangenen Urteile können gerichtlich angefochten werden.[206]
Im Gesetzesmemorandum heißt es dazu, dass dieser Ausschluss die logische Folge der getroffenen *ḫulʿ*-Regelung darstelle. Nach Durchführung des mehrstufigen Verfahrens mit all seinen Schritten könne man nur dann ein Interesse an einer höherinstanzlichen Überprüfung des Urteils haben, wenn man der Frau zumuten wolle, auf Jahre hin für die Dauer des fortgesetzten Verfahrens weiter an ihren Mann gebunden zu bleiben, ohne von irgendwoher versorgt zu werden. Durch das umfangreiche Verfahren sei hinreichend gesichert, dass die gesetzlichen Gründe vorliegen.[207] Das Gesetzesmemorandum schweigt allerdings über den Fall eines Fehlers in eben diesen Verfahren. Es bleibt unklar, was passiert, wenn z.B. das Schiedsrichterverfahren oder die Zahlung des Brautgeldes unterblieben sind oder fehlerhaft durchgeführt wurden und trotzdem ein Urteil erging.
Abs. 5 wird von einigen restriktiv ausgelegt, indem der Rechtsmittelausschluss nur auf diejenigen Fälle reduziert wird, bei denen die Trennung einvernehmlich vonstatten geht. Dabei spiele es keine Rolle, ob das Einvernehmen von vornherein vorgelegen hat oder ob es nach Klageerhebung, z.B. während des Schlichtungsverfahrens, hergestellt worden ist. Bei diesen Konstellationen sei der Rechtsweg verschlossen, in den übrigen Fällen hätten dagegen die allgemeinen Grundsätze zu gelten, die die gerichtliche Überprüfung zulassen.[208] Hiergegen spricht aber der Wortlaut der Norm, der sich auf gerichtliche Urteile (*al-ḥukm*) bezieht, nicht aber bloße Beurkundungshandlungen, auf die sich die gerichtliche Tätigkeit im Einvernehmensfall normalerweise beschränkt. Folglich wäre in diesem Fall gar kein anfechtbares Urteil vorhanden, wegen dem die höhere Instanz angerufen werden könnte, und die Regelung von Abs. 5 liefe ins Leere. Es bleibt für diese Theorie nur dort Raum, wo trotz Erreichung eines Einvernehmens während des laufenden Verfahrens ein Urteil erlassen wird. Da in diesem Urteil nur dasjenige wiederholt wird, auf das sich die Partner vorher geeinigt haben, dürfte der gesetzliche Rechtswegausschluss kaum praktische

---

[205] *Al-Ǧammāl, M.*, al-Aḥwāl al-šaḫṣīya li-ġayr al-muslimīn, Alexandria 2001, S. 404.
[206] *Al-Ǧindī, M.*, a.a.O., S. 273.
[207] Gesetzesmemorandum wiedergegeben nach *Zawīn, Ḥ.*, a.a.O., S. 81f.
[208] Ḥasan Manṣūr, al-Ahrām, 5.1.2000; zitiert auch in *al-Sakrī, A.*, al-Ṭaʿn fī al-ʾaḥkām wa al-ḫulʿ wa al-taḥkīm wa al-safar li-l-ḫāriǧ wa al-wirāṯa: šarḥ wa ṣayġ ʿalā ḍauʾ al-qānūn 1 li-sanat 2000 (m) wa al-muḏakkira al-ʾīḍāḥīya, Kairo 2000, S. 55.

Bedeutung haben. Die Partner haben hier im Normalfall kein Interesse an der nochmaligen gerichtlichen Überprüfung.[209]

Nach der Gegenmeinung wird der Ausschluss auf sämtliche Fälle des *ḫulʿ* bezogen, gleich ob es sich um einvernehmliche Scheidungen mit oder ohne Urteil oder um nichteinvernehmliche Trennungen handelt. Ihre Verfechter verweisen hierfür auf den Wortlaut und auf die im Gesetzesmemorandum angegebenen Motive: Nur durch die umfassende und nichtanfechtbare Wirkung des Urteils kann die Ehefrau in die angestrebte sichere Lage versetzt werden, für die sie mit Aufgabe ihrer finanziellen Absicherung sehr viel aufgewendet hat.[210]

Eine Mittelposition findet sich insoweit, als dass die Rechtswegverkürzung nur auf die Fälle, in denen ein reguläres Verfahren stattgefunden hat, bezogen wird. Sofern aber eine der notwendigen gesetzlichen Voraussetzungen fehlt, müsse eine Instanz zur Berichtigung gegeben sein.[211] Hierfür spricht zwar eine gewisse Plausibilität, denn ohne Richter kann ein Verfahrensstoß nun einmal nicht festgestellt werden. M.E. fehlt hierfür aber ein Anknüpfungspunkt im Gesetz. Der Wortlaut kennt keine Differenzierungen zwischen den grundlegenden Verfahrensfehlern und Motiven auf Seiten einer der Partner, die ein Urteil anfechten könnten, sondern schließt pauschal alle Urteile vom Rechtsweg aus.

Um den Rechtsmittelausschluss sind scharfe Diskussionen entbrannt. Viele halten ihn für verfassungswidrig. Offensichtlich ist auch eine Klage vor dem Verfassungsgerichtshof anhängig, welche die gesamte Regelung aufgrund der fehlenden Anfechtungsmöglichkeit anficht.[212] Der Vorwurf der Verfassungswidrigkeit wird auf islamrechtliche wie auf verfassungsrechtliche Gründe gestützt. So macht Naṣṣār darauf aufmerksam, dass das islamische Recht die Möglichkeit von Falschurteilen berücksichtige und deren Vermeidung und Korrektur großes Gewicht beimesse. So habe schon der Prophetengenossen ʿUmr ibn Ḫiṭāb in einem Brief an einen Gouverneur geschrieben, dass die Rückkehr zum Recht einen Segen bedeute („*al-ruǧūʿ ʾilā al-ḥaqq ḫayr*").[213] Daher habe die islamische Rechtswissenschaft den Grundsatz entwickelt, dass dem Richter die Möglichkeit zur Berichtigung seines Fehlers möglich sein muss. Im modernen Recht hätten sich daraufhin die Grundsätze des Rechtswegs mit den verschiedenen Instanzen gebildet.

---

209 So wohl *Naṣṣār, A.*, a.a.O., S. 79f.

210 *Al-ʿAǧūz, N.*, a.a.O., S. 382; *al-Dināṣūrī, I./ʿUkkāz, Ḥ.*, a.a.O., S. 77.

211 *Al-Dināṣūrī, I./ʿUkkāz, Ḥ.*, a.a.O., S. 76, nennen diese Ansicht, ohne allerdings zur näheren Begründung Angaben zu machen.

212 So die Auskunft von Rechtsanwalt Fuʾād Rušdī Mīḫāʾīl im Interview am 18.10.2002. Leider war es dem Verfasser nicht möglich, nähere Informationen zu Verlauf und Stand dieses Verfahrens zu beschaffen.

213 *Naṣṣār, A.*, a.a.O., S. 79.

Auch die Befürworter der Regelung beziehen sich in ihrer Argumentation auf die *šarīʿa*. Sie verweisen auf den Präzedenzfall der Frau des Ṯābit ibn Qays, bei dem der Prophet eine endgültige Entscheidung ohne die Möglichkeit der Anfechtung getroffen hätte. Auch hier wird unter Angabe der *ḥadīṯ*-Zitate aus den unterschiedlichen Überlieferungen darüber gestritten, ob Muḥammads Anweisung überhaupt die Scheidung herbeigeführt hat. Wäre auf eine Zustimmung durch den Ehemann abzustellen, so läge eine einvernehmliche Trennung vor, bei der es keinen Grund für ein *ṭaʿn*-Verfahren gibt. Naṣṣār betont auch für die Annahme des Falles eines bindenden Befehls durch den Propheten, dass dieser aufgrund seiner herausragenden Stellung nicht mit dem heutigen Richter gleich zu setzen ist und sich daher nicht als Anknüpfungspunkt eignet.
Daneben sieht Naṣṣār einen Verstoß gegen modernes Recht: Art. 281 des Zivilprozessgesetzes schreibt vor, dass grundsätzlich in allen Verfahren der weitere Rechtsweg für die benachteiligte Partei – nach Naṣṣār ist dies bei *ḫulʿ*-Urteilen der Mann – gegeben ist. Dies wird unterstrichen durch Art. 67 der Verfassung, der eine Rechtsweggarantie als Grundrecht für jeden Bürger vorsieht.[214] Außerdem liege in der bestehenden Regelung ein Verstoß gegen das Gleichbehandlungsgebot des Art. 40 der Verfassung. Es bestehe bei Art. 20 Abs. 5 eine Ungleichbehandlung zwischen solchen Männern, die durch *ḫulʿ* gerichtlich geschieden werden und solchen, die aus anderen Gründen durch das Gericht getrennt werden. Während letzteren die Möglichkeit der Anfechtung der Scheidung im Rechtsweg zukäme, fehle diese für erstere.[215]
Was die Auslegung der verfassungsrechtlichen Rechtsweggarantie angeht, so weisen die Kommentatoren auf eine Entscheidung des Verfassungsgerichtshofs aus dem Jahr 1993 hin. Hierin wird die Verkürzung eines Verfahrens auf eine Stufe gebilligt, sofern der Gesetzgeber diese beschlossen hat. Das Grundrecht sei dagegen erst verletzt, wenn für eine Beschwer überhaupt kein Rechtsweg bestehe, den der Geschädigte einschlagen könne.[216] Da die Beschränkung im Gesetz 1/2000 sich in diesem Rahmen hält und nicht schon die Eingangsinstanz vorenthält, ist hier nach Meinung vieler Kommentatoren die Verfassung nicht verletzt.
Bezüglich der gerügten Ungleichbehandlung ist fraglich, ob mit den genannten geschiedenen Männern überhaupt ein vergleichbares Objektspaar benannt ist, bei dem eine Ungleichbehandlung vorliegen kann. Die beiden Fälle sind nämlich grundlegend unterschiedlich insofern, dass der nach *ḫulʿ* Geschiedene

---

[214] *Naṣṣār, A.*, a.a.O., S. 81, dort auch die anderen im Absatz angegeben Gegenargumente.
[215] *Al-Ǧindī, M.*, a.a.O., S. 274; *Zawīn, Ḥ.*, a.a.O., S. 83.
[216] Entscheidung des Verfassungsgerichtshofs vom 19.6.1993, zitiert in *Zawīn, Ḥ.*, a.a.O., S. 83; unter Bezug auf dieses Urteil hält auch *al-ʿAǧūz, N.*, a.a.O., S. 382, den Ausschluss bei *ḫulʿ*-Urteilen für verfassungsgemäß.

von seiner Frau eine beträchtliche Summe ausgezahlt bekommen hat und von nachehelichen Ansprüchen befreit worden ist. Der auf andere Art Geschiedene muss diese Aufwendungen dagegen noch erbringen und ist damit erheblich belastet. Wegen dieser unterschiedlichen Voraussetzungen ist auch eine Ungleichbehandlung bei der Eröffnung von Rechtsschutzmöglichkeiten gerechtfertigt.[217]
Von den Kommentatoren wird die fehlende Anfechtungsmöglichkeit in der Regel als negative Wirkung für den Mann dargestellt. Selten kommt es hingegen zu einer Kritik aus der Perspektive der Ehefrau. Auch diese kann u.U. ein Interesse an einer Überprüfung der gerichtlichen Entscheidung haben. Dies ist insbesondere bei einer unzutreffenden Festlegung des Brautgeldes der Fall. Wenn ein Gericht z.B. die *šabka*-Gabe entgegen den Wortlaut zum *ṣadāq* gezählt hat, hat die Frau keine Möglichkeit, ihr verlorenes Recht zurückzugewinnen.
Bedeutender als die verfassungsrechtlichen Bedenken wegen des fehlenden Rechtswegs sind m.E. die rechtsmethodischen Konsequenzen. Im ägyptischen Rechtswesen spielen die Gerichte eine starke Rolle bei der Vereinheitlichung der Gesetzesauslegung. Durch die bestehende Gerichtshierarchie ist gesichert, dass alle einem Berufungs- oder Revisionsgericht unterstellten Spruchkörper sich an die Rechtsprechungspraxis der Obergerichte halten. Im Falle des *ḫulʿ* entfällt aber die Möglichkeit der Beschäftigung mit den neuen Normen durch die Obergerichte völlig. Dadurch bleiben die umstrittenen Rechtsfragen ganz in der Entscheidungssphäre der Spruchgerichte. Als Konsequenz hieraus ergibt sich zum einen die Gefahr einer beträchtlichen Rechtsunsicherheit für den Bürger, der nicht abschätzen kann, welchen Standpunkt das für ihn zuständige Gericht zu einer einzelnen Rechtsfrage einnimmt. Zum anderen entsteht eine beträchtliche Diversität zwischen den verschiedenen Gerichten. Auf diesen Sachverhalt weist auch eine erste empirische Studie zur Umsetzung des neuen Gesetzes hin (s.u.).
Die Alternative zur vereinheitlichenden Rechtsprechung liegt in einer konkreteren Gesetzgebung bzw. der Delegierung derselben an die Exekutive. Diese Möglichkeit besteht auch im Falle des Gesetz 1/2000, das in Art. 6 Einführungsgesetz dem Justizminister die Befugnis verleiht, nach eigenem Ermessen Durchführungsverordnungen (*al-qarārāt al-lāzima li-tanfīḏ aḥkām al-qānūn*) zu erlassen. Der Justizminister hat zwar von dieser Ermächtigung Gebrauch gemacht, jedoch finden sich in seiner Verordnung keine Hinweise auf Art. 20.[218] Wie aufgezeigt besteht jedoch an einigen Stellen Klärungsbedarf.

---

217 *Al-Dināṣūrī, I./ʿUkkāz, Ḥ.*, a.a.O., S. 77.
218 *Al-Dināṣūrī, I./ʿUkkāz, Ḥ.*, a.a.O., S. 13, zählen einige Durchführungsverordnungen auf; so auch die Auskunft von Āmāl ʿAbd al-Hādī, im Interview am 4.11.2002.

Zusammenfassung: Stärken und Schwächen des Art. 20

Art. 20 des Gesetzes 1/2000 bietet mit der Ermöglichung einer Klagemöglichkeit für die Ehefrau einen Ausweg für verzweifelte Partnerinnen aus ihrer Ehe in relativ kurzer Zeit. Die Frau kann die eigene Scheidung erwirken, ohne mit der Darlegungs- und Beweislast für ein Verschulden auf Seiten des Ehemannes beschwert zu sein. Auch braucht sie während des Verfahrens keine privaten Geheimnisse preiszugeben, sondern kann die Motive für ihr Begehren weitgehend für sich behalten. Durch diese Regelung ist die Rechtsstellung der Frau zweifellos gestärkt worden.
Sie muss für diese Erweiterung ihrer Rechte allerdings einen hohen Preis zahlen. Durch die Rückgabe ihres Brautgeldes und den Verzicht auf ihre nachehelichen Ansprüche erbringt sie ein großes Opfer, das sie häufig an den Rand ihrer finanziellen Möglichkeiten bringen wird. Für viele in ihrer Ehe leidende Frauen wird der Weg zur *ḫulʿ*-Scheidung aus finanziellen Gründen verschlossen bleiben. Ein „Scheidungsrecht nur für Reiche" kann nicht im Interesse des ägyptischen Gesetzgebers liegen.
Das Gesetz 1/2000 weist Schwächen bei der Regelung der finanziellen Folgen auf: So ist der genaue Umfang wie die Festsetzung des Brautgeldes unzureichend geregelt. Außerdem trägt das Gesetz der aus den Rechtsschulen bekannten Gefahr des Missbrauchs des *ḫulʿ* durch den Ehemann keine Rechnung: Es fehlen rechtliche Mechanismen, die ihn von einer Provokation der Frau zum *ḫulʿ* abhalten. Zudem enthält das Gesetz eine fragwürdige Regelung des Schlichtungsverfahren: Aufgrund ihres zeitlichen wie inhaltlichen Aufwands droht es die Gerichte zu überlasten, ohne den versprochenen Effekt der Rettung von bedrohten Ehen herbeiführen zu können. Des Weiteren hat der Gesetzgeber durch den Ausschluss des Rechtswegs die Möglichkeit zu einer Fixierung des Rechtsinstituts durch höherinstanzliche Gerichte verbaut und hierdurch zu einer Rechtsspaltung im ägyptischen Familienrecht beigetragen.
M.E. überwiegen die positiven Folgen des Gesetzes. Gleichzeitig besteht Nachbesserungsbedarf an den genannten Stellen.

5. Die *ḫulʿ*-Scheidung und die nicht-muslimischen Minderheiten

Anlass zur Diskussion hat die Frage nach der Anwendbarkeit von Art. 20 auf die nichtmuslimischen Minderheiten Ägyptens gegeben. Im Land leben etwa 10% Christen der verschiedensten Konfessionen und eine nur noch wenige tausend Personen ausmachende jüdische Minderheit.[219] Diese religiösen Gruppen unterliegen im Personalstatusrecht anderen Normen als die muslimische Mehrheit. Die traditionell in Ägypten vertretenen und anerkannten Religionsgemeinschaften hatten vor Aufhebung der religiösen Gerichte 1956 ihre eigenen

---

[219] Vgl. *Ebert, H.*, a.a.O., S. 14.

Spruchkörper (*al-maḥākim al-millīya*), für die die Kirchen eigene Gesetze erlassen konnten. Nach der Auflösung wurden die Kirchengesetze als staatliche Gesetze übernommen, die nun vor dem staatlichen Einheitsgericht für die Kirchenmitglieder weiter angewandt wurden.[220] Dies spiegelt sich in Art. 3 Abs. 2 Einführungsgesetz 1/2000 wider, in dem die Gerichte befugt werden, Urteile nach dem Recht der Religionsgemeinschaften zu erlassen, wenn die Betroffenen Angehörige derselben Konfession und desselben Ritus (*miṣrīyūn ġayr muslimīn al-mutaḥḥidī al-ṭāʾifa wa al-milla*) sind, diese Gruppe vor 1956 einen eigenen Rechtsapparat gehabt hat und die Prinzipien dieses Rechts nicht dem ordre public des geltenden ägyptischen Rechts widersprechen.[221]

Art. 17 Abs. 3 des Gesetzes 1/2000 sieht vor, dass Scheidungsklagen von Nichtmuslimen, die derselben Konfession und demselben Ritus angehören, nur zulässig sind, wenn das anzuwendende religiöse Gesetz die Scheidung vorsieht. In den Gesetzen der christlichen Minderheit ist dies nur sehr begrenzt möglich: es besteht in keiner der Kodices ein freies Scheidungsrecht, die Ausnahmen für die Eheauflösung aus wichtigen Gründen sind weit eingegrenzter als bei den Muslimen oder sogar gänzlich unbekannt.[222] Auch eine der *ḫulʿ* vergleichbare richterliche Scheidung ist unbekannt. Gehören die Partner dagegen unterschiedlichen Konfessionen und Riten an, sieht die Lage anders aus: Es ist dann nicht ein spezielles konfessionelles Gesetz anwendbar, sondern es kommt das allgemeine ägyptische Personalstatusrecht, also das muslimische, zur Anwendung.

Da nun in den konfessionellen Ordnungen eine Lösungsmöglichkeit für die gescheiterte Ehe weitgehend fehlt, hat sich als Ausweg herausgestellt, dass einer der Partner die Konfession wechselt und dann das Gericht unter Berufung auf das allgemeine Gesetz für die Scheidung anruft. Zwar darf der Konfessionswechsel eigentlich nicht zur Umgehung des Rechts der eigenen Gruppe stattfinden, doch gelingt es praktisch doch.[223] Dies ist für den *ṭalāq* als einseitige Scheidung des Mannes vom Kassationsgericht anerkannt worden, und die Ehe wurde rechtsgültig geschieden. Für den *ḫulʿ* gilt dies genauso.[224]

Die Konsequenz ist, dass nun christliche Ehepartner entgegen der Normen praktisch aller Konfessionen die Scheidung betreiben können. Für die Kirchen, die mit dieser Konsequenz nicht einverstanden sind, bliebe als Ausweg, ein neues einheitliches Personalstatusrecht zu erarbeiten, unter das alle ägyptischen

---

220 *Dilger, K.*, a.a.O., S. 512f; dazu detaillierter *al-Ǧammāl, M.*, a.a.O., S. 1ff, der die Kodifikationsbewegung Ägyptens als Vereinheitlichungsbewegung für das geltende Recht charakterisiert.

221 *Al-Dināṣūrī, I./ʿUkkāz, Ḥ.*, a.a.O., S. 9f, näher zur Auslegung dieser Voraussetzungen.

222 *Al-Ǧammāl, M.*, a.a.O., S.320ff.

223 *Dilger, K.*, a.a.O., S. 521.

224 *Al-Ǧammāl, M.*, a.a.O., S. 152. Siehe auch ʿAbd al-Muʿaṭī ʾAḥmad, al-Ahrām, 25.1.2002.

Christen fallen. Dann bliebe als Ausweg nur der Übertritt zum Islam, um der konfessionellen Norm zu entkommen.
Einer Erarbeitung des gemeinsamen Gesetzes stehen bisher praktische Probleme entgegen: Die verschiedenen Kirchen, die seit langem die Kodifikation als Ziel angeben, können sich nicht auf eine gemeinsame Linie einigen. Zusätzlich kommt das Problem hinzu, wie ein von den Kirchen beschlossener Gesetzesentwurf auch Gesetzeskraft erhalten kann. Allgemeine Gesetze in Ägypten werden vom Souverän beschlossen, der seinerseits in die Angelegenheiten der Kirchen nicht eingreifen und diese nicht gesetzlich bestimmen darf. Für eine *ḫulʿ*-Scheidung christlicher Ehen ergeben sich Besonderheiten bei der Festsetzung der finanziellen Folgen, weil in fast allen Konfessionen die Zahlung eines Brautgeldes bei Eheschließung nicht vorgesehen ist. Folglich kann dann auch kein Brautgeld zurückerstattet werden.[225]
Laut Auskunft aus der Praxis haben seit Einführung des Gesetzes etliche christliche Ehefrauen von der Möglichkeit des Konfessionswechsels Gebrauch gemacht, um von ihren Männern loszukommen. Die anderen Kirchen nehmen die Betroffenen auf und lassen sich den Übertritt durch Gebühren bezahlen. So berichtete der Rechtsanwalt Fuʿād Rušdī Mīḫāʾīl von einem Übertritt zur griechisch-orthodoxen Kirche, die diese sich mit mehreren tausend Pfund bezahlen ließ.[226]
Dies ist das Ergebnis einer Rechtsspaltung, die für konfessionell pluralistische Rechtssysteme typisch ist. Das Fehlen eines einheitlichen Regelwerks erhöht das Leid der Betroffenen weiter. Kirchen und Staat sind hier aufgerufen, Abhilfe durch neue verbindliche Regelungen zu schaffen.

III. Zur Umsetzung des Art. 20 von Gesetz 1/2000 in der Rechtswirklichkeit

Seit der Einführung des neuen Gesetzes sind knapp vier Jahre vergangen. Die heftig geführte Diskussion während des parlamentarischen Verfahrens ist abgeklungen, und mit der Umsetzung des Gesetzes wurde unter anfänglich intensiver Medienbegleitung[227] begonnen. Leider liegen noch keine umfang-

---

225 *Al-Ǧammāl, M.*, a.a.O., S. 152; zu den finanziellen Verpflichtungen bei der Eheschließung siehe dort S. 293ff.

226 Interview vom 18.10.2002.

227 So z.B. die umfangreichen Reportagen in al-ʿArabī am 31.1. und 1.2.2000 über Wafāʾ Musaʿad, der ersten Frau, welche die Klage erhob. Sie tat dies gerade 48 Stunden, nachdem das Parlament das Gesetz verabschiedet hatte. Zeugnis von der umfangreichen Anteilnahme der Bevölkerung gibt auch der im Herbst 2002 laufende Kinofilm „*Muḥāmī al-ḫulʿ*" („der *ḫulʿ*-Anwalt"), einer Komödie sozusagen rund um das neue Rechtsinstitut, die in mehreren großen Lichtspielhäusern Kairos zu sehen war.

reichen und soliden empirischen Studien zur Implementierung des Gesetzes vor. Die folgenden Ausführungen beruhen auf einer ersten statistischen Studie des Center for Egyptian Women's Legal Assistance (CEWLA), einer Kairoer Frauenrechtsorganisation, die diese im Herbst 2002 auf einer Tagung in Kairo vorgestellt hat.[228]

In dieser Studie wurden in sechs ägyptischen Provinzen Daten zur Häufigkeit von Klageerhebungen auf *ḫulʿ*-Scheidung und entsprechenden Urteilen gesammelt. Das Zahlenmaterial stammt offensichtlich von den Gerichtsverwaltungen in den einzelnen Provinzen und umfasst den Zeitraum vom 1.3.2000 bis zum 31.3.2002. Die ausgewählten Provinzen sind über das gesamte Land verteilt und umschließen sowohl die großen städtischen Zentren Kairo und Alexandria als auch Gebiete in Oberägypten wie Sohag und Qena. Dabei wurden jeweils die Klage- und Urteilszahlen von *ḫulʿ*- und *taṭlīq*-Klage nebeneinander erhoben und verglichen.

Erstes Ergebnis der Studie ist, dass die Zahl der Klageanträge für *ḫulʿ* und andere *taṭlīq*-Arten insgesamt gestiegen ist. Dabei ist die Steigerung im Vergleich zur Zahl für die Nicht-*ḫulʿ*-Anträge von 1999 aber vergleichsweise moderat ausgefallen. Die Anträge auf *taṭlīq*-Scheidungen sind dabei leicht zurückgegangen. Es ist zu vermuten, dass manche der schon vorher anhängigen Klagen auf *taṭlīq li-l-ḍarar* auf *ḫulʿ*-Begehren umgestellt wurden. Dazu gibt die Erhebung allerdings keine genaueren Auskünfte.

Es fällt auf, dass in den sechs Provinzen das Zahlenverhältnis zwischen den Klagearten stark variierte. So liegen in den Großstädten die Zahlen für *ḫulʿ* leicht über den Vergleichzahlen für *taṭlīq*-Begehren. Ganz anders ist die Lage in den ländlichen Gebieten: In diesen erreicht die Zahl der *ḫulʿ*-Begehren nicht einmal die Hälfte der *taṭlīq*-Quote.[229] Daraus kann geschlossen werden, dass in den ländlichen Gebieten größere Hemmungen bestanden, von der neuen Regelung Gebrauch zu machen als in den Städten.

Die durchschnittliche Dauer für ein Verfahren von Einlegung der Klage bis zur Entscheidung wird mit acht Monaten angegeben, wobei die einzelnen Dauern zwischen vier und 17 Monaten variieren. Als eine Erklärung wird in der Studie angegeben, dass die Richter das vorgesehene Versöhnungsverfahren ohne Grund in die Länge ziehen.[230]

---

[228] Die Beiträge wurden später im folgenden Band gesammelt und werden im Folgenden aus diesem zitiert: *al-Ṣāwī, A.* (Hrsg.), al-Ḥaṣād - ʿamān ʿalā al-ḫulʿ. Dirāsa taḥlīya, Kairo 2003.

[229] In Kairo im Jahr 2000 2695 *ḫulʿ*, 2509 *taṭlīq*-Klagen, in 2001 2740 (*ḫ.*) zu 2368 (*t.*); Giza 2000: 1199 (*ḫ.*) -1125 (*t.*); 2001: 1160 – 1117; dagegen al-Fayyūm 2000: 131 (*ḫ.*) – 293 (*t.*), 2001: 80 – 244; Suhāg 2000: 186-352; 2001: 159-490, *Sulaymān, ʿA./Ṣalāḥ, ʿA.*, al-Ḫulʿ qānūnan wa taṭbīqan. In: *al-Ṣāwī, A.*,a.a.O., S.18.

[230] *Sulaymān, ʿA./Ṣalāḥ, ʿA*, a.a.O., S. 35.

Das bemerkenswerteste Ergebnis der Studie bezieht sich auf die Entscheidungsquote: Es wurden in weniger als 5% der erhobenen *ḫulʿ*-Klagen ein Urteil erlassen. Während die Quote in Giza immerhin 6,9% betrug, war sie in Qena auf Null: dort ist kein einziges Urteil ergangen.[231] Die Autorinnen der Studie stützen auf diesen Befund eine wichtige These: Ein beachtlicher Teil der ägyptischen Richterschaft, die ausnahmslos aus Männern besteht, verzögere die Umsetzung des Gesetzes und führe die Verfahren unter Missachtung der den Ehefrauen im Gesetzestext verliehenen Rechte durch.[232]
Dies ist ein wahrhaft spektakulärer Befund! Allerdings muss auf einige Fragwürdigkeiten bezüglich der Verallgemeinbarkeit dieser Aussage hingewiesen werden. Die Studie bezieht für die Frage der Entscheidungsquote lediglich die Fälle des ersten Jahres des Erhebungszeitraums (1.3.2000-31.3.2001) in Betracht. Schon wegen dieser Beobachtung drängen sich auch andere Erklärungen für die geringe Entscheidungshäufigkeit neben der These der „Umsetzungs-Verweigerung durch den männlichen Richter" auf: So ist offensichtlich, dass bei jedem neuen Gesetz die nicht eingearbeiteten Richter einen gewissen Zeitraum brauchen, um sich mit dem neuen Gesetz und dem Verfahren vertraut zu machen. Außerdem wird übersehen, dass schon nach dem gesetzlich vorgeschriebenen Verfahren mit den mehrstufigen Versöhnungsverfahren die Prozedur einige Monate dauern muss. Daraus ergibt sich, dass mindestens alle im letzten Drittel des Untersuchungszeitraums eingebrachten Klagen frühestens im zweiten Jahr entschieden werden können. Insofern sind die Zahlen verzerrt, und der von den Forscherinnen gezogene Schluss ist keinesfalls verallgemeinbar. Weit aussagekräftiger wäre gewesen, die diesbezüglichen Zahlen für das zweite Jahr zu erheben und auszuwerten. Es ist zu vermuten, dass die Entscheidungsquote dann erheblich höher ausfällt.[233]
Obwohl die statistischen Angaben der Studie aus den genannten Gründen nur von begrenzter Aussagekraft sind, enthält die Untersuchung einige bedenkenswerte Kritikpunkte am Gesetz, die teilweise schon bei der Besprechung der einzelnen Tatbestandsvoraussetzungen erwähnt worden sind. Besonders hervorzuheben sind dabei die unterschiedlichen Definitionen des *ṣadāq*-Begriffs, von denen die Richter in den verschiedenen Gerichten ausgegangen sind und die z.T. sogar von der Frau angeschaffte Möbelstücke für die gemeinsame Wohnung miteingeschlossen haben. Dem von den Autorinnen der Studie gezogenem Fazit, dass beim Gesetzgeber noch einiger

---

231 *Sulaymān, ʿA./Ṣalāḥ, ʿA,* a.a.O., S. 33.

232 *Sulaymān, ʿA./Ṣalāḥ, ʿA,* a.a.O., S. 34.

233 Auf meine schriftliche Anfrage, warum die vorliegende Studie keine Angaben zur Entscheidungsquote im zweiten Jahr enthält, bekam ich leider keine Antwort. Die zuständige Mitarbeiterin des Instituts verwies mich auf eine Folgestudie, die im Laufe des Jahres 2004 durchgeführt werden soll.

Klärungsbedarf für weitere Durchführungsverordnungen besteht, ist zuzustimmen.[234]

E. FAZIT: DAS GESETZ NR.1/2000 ALS MEILENSTEIN DER RECHTSREFORM

Der ägyptische Gesetzgeber hat im neuen Gesetz zur Prozessrechtsreform in Personalstatusangelegenheiten mit dem *ḫulʿ* ein Rechtsinstitut kodifiziert, das in dieser Form dem islamischen Recht bisher unbekannt war: Neben einer einvernehmlichen Trennung, als die der *ḫulʿ* in den Lehren der Rechtsschulen konzipiert war, ist nun auch die richterliche Scheidung von diesem Begriff umfasst. Dies ist bemerkenswert als Stärkung der Rechtsstellung der Frau. Es ist ebenso bemerkenswert unter rechtsmethodischen Gesichtspunkten: Ägypten hat sich auf dem Gebiet des Familien- und Scheidungsrechts erstmals des Instruments des *iǧtihād* bedient.

Wie dargestellt wurden in Ägypten seit 1920 in drei Gesetzesnovellen die Rechte der Frau gestärkt. Dies geschah zum einen durch ein Erschweren des traditionell freien Verstoßungsrechts des Ehemanns. Zum anderen bekam auch die Frau weitere Möglichkeiten, um eine für sie nicht mehr auszuhaltende Ehesituation aufzulösen. Insbesondere die Scheidung wegen Schädigung durch den Ehemann (*taṭlīq li-l-ḍarar*) hat der Frau das Tor zum Gericht geöffnet, das nun in der Pflicht steht, ihren Fall zu prüfen und bei Vorliegen der gesetzlichen Voraussetzungen die Scheidung auszusprechen.

Methodisch wandte der Gesetzgeber in den Gesetzen von 1920 und 1929 ausschließlich das Mittel der Vermischung von Rechtsschulenansichten (*taḫayyur* bzw. *talfīq*) an. Während er zumeist die für die Frau weit günstigeren Bestimmungen aus der malikitischen Rechtsschule heranzog, wich er gelegentlich auch auf Ansichten aus, die nur von kleinen Minderheiten innerhalb der Rechtsgelehrsamkeit vertreten wurden. Dagegen machte der Gesetzgeber auf dem Gebiet des Ehe- und Scheidungsrechts – im Gegensatz zu anderen Rechtsgebieten wie dem allgemeinen Zivilrecht – keinen Gebrauch eines freien Bemühens um die Rechtsfindung. Der *iǧtihād*, der von den ideologischen Vordenkern der *Salafīya*-Bewegung als Korrektivmittel durch Rückkehr zu den ursprünglichen Quellen gedacht war, spielte für den ägyptischen Familienrechtsgesetzgeber lange keine Rolle. Erst 1979 wurde mit dem Versuch, die Zweitheirat des Ehemanns mit einem automatischen Scheidungsrecht der Erstfrau zu sanktionieren, ein Element eingeführt, das über die Grenzen der bekannten Rechtsschulansichten hinausging. Diese Neuregelung

---

[234] *Sulaymān, ʿA./Ṣalāḥ, ʿA.*, a.a.O., S. 28.

war allerdings nur von kurzer Gültigkeit. Im Gesetz von 1985 wurde der genannte Scheidungsgrund gestrichen und die Erstfrau wurde wieder mit der Beweislast für einen tatsächlich eingetretenen Schaden auf ihrer Seite durch die neue Heirat konfrontiert.

Einen anderen Weg geht nun der Art. 20 des Gesetzes 1/2000. Mit dem *ḫulʿ* wurde ein altbekanntes Instrument in neuer Form eingesetzt. War in der Rechtsschuldogmatik für eine Scheidung durch *ḫulʿ* immer das Einvernehmen des Mannes vorausgesetzt, so verlangt Art. 20 dieses nicht mehr. Zwar ist nach Abs. 1 weiterhin auch der „einvernehmliche *ḫulʿ* " möglich, er wird jedoch begleitet von einem Klagerecht der Ehefrau, falls dieses Einvernehmen wegen der Zurückweisung des Manns nicht besteht. Diese Veränderung bezeichnet Arabi zurecht als „radikale Diskontinuität mit dem bestehenden islamischen Familienrecht".[235]

Was aber waren für den Gesetzgeber die leitenden Motive bei der Reform? Für Arabi steht im Vordergrund, dass der Gesetzgeber hier dem Quellentext von Koran und Sunna „absolute Priorität" eingeräumt hat.[236] Statt auf die Lehre der Rechtsschulen habe man sich auf die Quellen besonnen und hieraus eruiert, dass zwar der koranische Befund von einer Zustimmung des Ehemannes ausgehe, die Sunna-Versionen jedoch auch die Interpretation des *ḫulʿ* als Scheidungsmittel gegen den Willen des Mannes zuließen. Es sei in keinem Falle eindeutig, dass diese Zustimmung notwendige Voraussetzung ist. Arabi stellt diesen abweichenden – vielleicht sogar widersprüchlichen – textlichen Befund in Koran und Sunna in eine schafiitische Kategorisierung, nach der auch gesetzliche Einsetzungen im *ḥadīṯ*-Text möglich seien, ohne dass sie Erwähnung im Koran fänden. Koran und Sunna stünden so als unabhängige Rechtsquellen nebeneinander. Dies spiegele sich wieder in Art. 20 Abs. 1, der im ersten Satz das koranische Rechtsinstitut und in den darauffolgenden Sätzen das Institut aus der Sunna enthalte.[237]

In der Tat handelt es sich bei Arabis Erklärung um eine schlüssige Deutung. Allerdings verzichtet er bei der Herleitung auf Verweise auf die aktuelle Debatte und die tatsächlichen Motive des Gesetzgebers: Von einer widersprüchlichen Quellenlage in Koran und Sunna, die durch den Vorzug der Prophetentradition gelöst wird, findet sich weder in dem offiziellen Gesetzesmemorandum noch in der mir vorliegenden arabischen Literatur ein Hinweis. Vielmehr wird ein solcher Widerspruch gerade nicht gesehen und die Ausgestaltung des Art. 20 ausdrücklich auch als mit dem Koran übereinstimmend dargestellt. Anders

---

[235] *Arabi, O.*,Downing of the Third Millenium..., a.a.O., S. 4.
[236] *Arabi, O.*, a.a.O., S. 21.
[237] *Arabi, O.*, a.a.O., S. 18f.

sehen es dagegen die Reformgegner, die aber ebenso von einem eindeutigen und einstimmigen Befund gegen die Neuregelung ausgehen.
M.E. sind es andere Gründe, die für den Gesetzgeber ausschlaggebender waren. Wichtiger als der Quellenwortlaut bezüglich des *ḫulʿ* waren für ihn die allgemeinen Prinzipien des islamischen Rechts und die praktischen Bedürfnisse der modernen Gesellschaft. In der Diskussion wird auf das Gemeinwohl (*maṣlaḥa*) verwiesen, das zugunsten der Frau und der leidenden Familie erfordert, eine weitreichendere Beendigungsmöglichkeit von gescheiterten Ehen zu schaffen, sowie auf den Gerechtigkeitsgrundsatz (*lā ḍarar wa lā ḍirār*), nach dem die Trennung durch die Frau geboten ist und diese gleichzeitig verpflichtet ist, ihren Mann durch die Rückgabe des Brautgelds zu entschädigen.
Die Orientierung am Gemeinwohl bedeutet jedoch nicht, dass damit die Bindung des ägyptischen Systems an den Islam und das islamische Recht angegriffen oder gar aufgehoben ist. Ganz im Gegenteil zeigt die Debatte um die Einführung des *ḫulʿ* die Wichtigkeit des religiösen Diskurses. Alle Teilnehmer stützen ihre Argumentation auf die Quellen und beziehen ihre Gründe aus den Grundsätzen der Religion.
In der Debatte um die Rolle des islamischen Rechts für die Reform des staatlichen Rechts haben einige Orientalisten die Auffassung vertreten, dass zwar für die Begründung von Reformvorhaben auf Argumente des religiösen Diskurses zurückgegriffen werde, dass die leitenden Motive aber ganz andere seien. So konstatiert Kerr, dass der islamische Modernismus à la ʿAbduh und Riḍā, die eine gesellschaftliche Erneuerung aus der Religion herleiten wollten, am herrschenden säkularen Nationalismus gescheitert sei.[238] Layish spricht vom „Lippenbekenntnis" der säkularen staatlichen Modernisierer, die sich nur wegen der womöglich höheren Akzeptanz der Massen religiöser Argumente bedienten.[239] Auch Schacht vertritt die Ansicht, dass für die Gesetzgeber weniger die eigene religiöse Tradition die Impulse für die rechtliche Erneuerung gebe, sondern im Wesentlichen westliche Muster nachgeahmt würden.[240]
Es fällt auf, dass diese Autoren sich alle in den Sechzig- und Siebzigerjahren des vergangenen Jahrhunderts geäußert haben. In dieser Zeit erlebten tatsächlich säkulare Ideologien wie der (arabische) Sozialismus eines Ǧamāl ʿAbd al-Nāṣir ihre Hochzeit. Allerdings wurde für die Zeit danach – beginnend mit dem für die arabischen Länder desaströsen Ausgang des Sechstagekrieges von 1967 – ein Wiedererstarken des Islam auch auf gesellschaftlicher Ebene festgestellt. Die

---

238 *Kerr, M.*, a.a.O., S. 221.
239 *Layish, A.*, a.a.O., S. 274.
240 Art. Idjtihād (*Schacht, J.*). In: EI, Bd. 3, 1027.

verstärkte Rolle des Islam in Art. 2 der ägyptischen Verfassung ist ein Beispiel hierfür.[241]

Mit diesem Erstarken – gelegentlich als „Re-Islamisierung“ apostrophiert[242] – ist auch auf der rechtlichen Ebene eine Neujustierung verbunden. So wird in Ägypten mit der Rechtsprechung des Verfassungsgerichts zu Art. 2 der Verfassung von 1980 eine Abkehr vom traditionellen Rechtsverständnis getätigt: Nicht mehr das in Jahrhunderten geformte Recht der Schulen ist der Maßstab für die Rechtsetzung und Rechtssprechung, sondern ein vom modernen Staat neuinterpretiertes. N. Brown beschreibt die eigentliche Erneuerung des islamischen Rechts als Wechsel des Systems weg von den klassischen Instanzen und Personal hin zur Konzentration der *šarīʿa* auf den Inhalt. Statt der klassischen *ʿulamāʾ* sind nun vielseitig geschulte Juristen am Werk.[243] Dadurch bestimmt nun der Staat mit seinem Personal in Parlament und Verfassungsgericht, welcher Teil der *šarīʿa* wie Geltung hat. In diesem Sinn macht sich der Staat gleichsam seine eigene *šarīʿa*.

Allerdings gilt diese Freiheit nicht grenzenlos. Der grundsätzliche Teil des offenbarten Rechts bleibt für den Gesetzgeber unverfügbar. Für die Wiedereinführung des *ḫulʿ* in das Scheidungsrecht bedeutet dies, dass sich seine Ausgestaltung am Wortlaut der Offenbarungstexte hält. Während es dem ägyptischen Gesetzgeber möglich war, mit dem Einvernehmenserfordernis eines der Grundprinzipien des klassischen *ḫulʿ*-Konzepts zu entfernen, so hat er die Verpflichtung zur Zahlung einer Lösegeldsumme beibehalten. Während man auf das erstgenannte Prinzip bei entsprechender Interpretation der Quellen verzichten kann, ist das zweitgenannte in allen Texten vorhanden. Die in den Quellen vorgesehene Ungleichheit zwischen den Geschlechtern wird durch das Gesetz so beibehalten: Zwar kommt der Frau auch ein Recht auf freie Scheidung zu, jedoch nicht, ohne dafür einen hohen Preis zu zahlen. Ein darüber hinausgehendes Recht der freien Scheidung ohne Rückgewähr des Brautgeldes wäre wohl definitiv ein Verstoß gegen den Kernbestand des offenbarten Rechts.

Mit dem Gesetz 1/2000 hat der *iǧtihād* im ägyptischen Familienrecht Einzug gehalten. Anders als bei dem Versuch im Jahre 1979 besteht dieses Mal kaum die Gefahr, dass das Verfassungsgericht das Gesetz annulliert. Zu sehr passt das Gesetz in die Direktive des Gerichts: Die grundlegenden Normen des Islams

---

241 *Flores, A.*, a.a.O., S. 476.

242 So z.B. *Klingmüller, E.*, Betrachtungen zur Reislamisierung im Recht. In: *Baumgärtel, G./Becker, H.*, Festschrift für Heinz Hübner zum 70. Geburtstag, Berlin 1984, S. 85-100(85). Es ist in der Literatur auf die Schwierigkeiten dieses Begriffes hingewiesen worden; es handelt sich nicht wirklich um eine Re-Islamisierung, da der Islam als Religion niemals abwesend gewesen ist, so dass er wieder eingeführt werden müsste. Der Begriff soll das Wiedererstarken der Religion im öffentlichen Leben beschreiben.

243 *Brown, N.*, a.a.O., S. 371.

werden nicht verletzt, sondern ihnen wurde zu einer neuen Bedeutung verholfen. Der Gesetzgeber orientiert sich an Text und Gemeinwohl und verwirklicht so den *iǧtihād,* wie ihn die Reformgelehrten der *Salafīya*-Bewegung im Sinn hatten.
Das moderne islamische Recht hat somit wieder ein ähnliches Entwicklungspotential erreicht wie in den Anfangsjahrhunderten der islamischen Geschichte. Die Phase des *taqlīd* als bloßer Nachahmung der von Vorgenerationen übernommenen Weisheiten scheint jedenfalls überwunden. Im Mittelpunkt der Rechtsfindung steht wieder das eigene Bemühen um das richtige und zeitangepasste Recht. Dies ist der *iǧtihād.*

LEIPZIGER BEITRÄGE ZUR ORIENTFORSCHUNG

Herausgegeben von Hans-Georg Ebert
Begründet von Günter Barthel

Band 1 Lutz Knörnschild: Zur Geschichte der Nilwassernutzung in der ägyptischen Landwirtschaft von den Anfängen bis zur Gegenwart. 1993.

Band 2 Henner Fürtig / Rolf Müller-Syring (Hrsg.): Ursachen gewaltförmiger Konflikte in der Golfregion. Internationale und zwischenstaatliche Faktoren. 1993.

Band 3 Ingelore Goldmann (Hrsg.): Beiträge zur Fachdidaktik Arabisch. Didaktische und methodische Probleme des modernen Arabischunterrrichts. 1993.

Band 4 Roland Kühnel: Die sprachliche Situation an Hochschulen des Maghreb und die offizielle Sprachpolitik – Eine soziolinguistische Untersuchung. 1995.

Band 5 Henk Knaupe / Ulrich G. Wurzel: Aufbruch in der Wüste. Die Neuen Städte in Ägypten. 1995.

Band 6 Wolfgang Reuschel: Aspekt und Tempus in der Sprache des Korans. 1996.

Band 7 Hans-Georg Ebert: Das Personalstatut arabischer Länder. Problemfelder, Methoden, Perspektiven. Ein Beitrag zum Diskurs über Theorie und Praxis des Islamischen Rechts. 1996.

Band 8 Uwe Pfullmann: Politische Strategien Ibn Sa^{c}ūds beim Aufbau des dritten saudischen Staates. Eine historische Studie unter besonderer Berücksichtigung deutschen Archivmaterials. 1996.

Band 9 Hans-Georg Ebert (Hrsg.): Beiträge zum Islamischen Recht. 2000.

Band 10 Anja Wünsch: Innenansichten ökonomischer Restrukturierung. Wirkungen und Wirksamkeit der Strukturanpassung in Jordanien, 1989-1999. 2001.

Band 11 Thoralf Hanstein: Islamisches Recht und Nationales Recht. Teil 1 und 2. Eine Untersuchung zum Einfluß des Islamischen Rechts auf die Entwicklung des modernen Familienrechts am Beispiel Indonesiens. 2002.

Band 12 Hans-Georg Ebert / Thoralf Hanstein (Hrsg.): Beiträge zum Islamischen Recht II. 2003.

Band 13 Hans-Georg Ebert / Thoralf Hanstein (Hrsg.): Beiträge zum Islamischen Recht III. 2003.

Band 14 Hans-Georg Ebert: Das Erbrecht arabischer Länder. 2004.

Band 15 Silvia Tellenbach / Thoralf Hanstein (Hrsg.): Beiträge zum Islamischen Recht IV. 2004.